Public Sector Criminological Research

Russell G. Smith

Public Sector Criminological Research

The Australian Institute of Criminology, 1972–2022

Russell G. Smith
College of Business, Government and Law
Flinders University
Adelaide, SA, Australia

ISBN 978-3-031-28355-0   ISBN 978-3-031-28356-7   (eBook)
https://doi.org/10.1007/978-3-031-28356-7

For D.G.S.

Foreword

The Australian Institute of Criminology @ 50: From a golden age

The idea for an Australian Institute of Criminology (AIC) was nurtured in a golden age of Australian law officers: Nigel Bowen; Tom Hughes; Lionel Murphy and Robert Ellicott. The idea for an Australian Law Reform Commission (ALRC) was conceived by Nigel Bowen; implemented by Lionel Murphy and rescued from elimination by Bob Ellicott. Such a fate could easily have followed the dismissal of the Whitlam Government. It was Bob Ellicott who gave the ALRC its first exciting programmatic references. As this book shows, Bowen liked the idea of a criminology institute. Hughes supported it. Murphy carried it forward and appointed the first Director, an Englishman, Bill Clifford. And Ellicott was supportive of any institution of legal research and reform.

The times were suitable for major reforms back in the 1960s and 1970s. The election in 1972 of the first Labor Government since 1949, with Whitlam as Prime Minister and Murphy as Attorney-General, was instrumental in a huge agenda of reforms. Although Fraser was sometimes portrayed as a stiff, unbending conservative, this was far from the truth. His first Attorney-General, Ellicott, had been dedicated to securing major law reforms as an essential feature in his concept of liberalism. This is the context in which the Australian Institute of Criminology is celebrated in this book. The initial success of these political performers, in shaking up Australia's institutions, led to exciting reforms. It invited refreshing inventiveness.

Of course, the creation did not begin and end with these four ministers. Nor was the momentum provided only by politicians. The proposal for the ALRC had the support of many leading judges and a host of key officials in the Federal Attorney-General's Department and elsewhere. The latter included an unexpected reformer [Sir] Clarrie Harders. But also senior officials like Peter Loof who was also to play such an important role in the early days of the AIC. With such energetic support, the AIC was dedicated to creating a novel and world leading institution. In a sense, the departmental officers became caught up in the enthusiasms of their ministers. The unconventional Murphy, in particular, delighted in shaking up the staid officials, saying that they enjoyed it and deserved it.

I was appointed to the ALRC from 1 January 1975. This was almost two years after Murphy's commission as Federal Attorney-General. Initially, he invited me to serve as a part-time member of the new Commission. Later he persuaded me (unwisely as I initially thought at the time) to step into the challenge as chairman (as the office was then called). So for me this was a heady time.

I knew all of the foregoing members of the AIC, ALRC, officials and participants and many more. They played vital roles in the creation of exciting new legal institutions of the Commonwealth. They strongly supported them. I was still in the ALRC when a very conservative lawyer from Western Australia, Senator Peter Durack, succeeded Bob Ellicott. He was seemingly determined to turn off the lights. In his view, they had gone too far and for too long.

I had not been so appointed when the AIC was created. Still less in the earlier days in the 1960s, when, as explained in these pages, a Victorian judge, Sir John Barry, began to make earnest appeals for an Australian research institute into crime and punishment (Kirby 2007, pp. vii–x). Barry became a 'gadfly' … who, as Professor Geoffrey Sawer said, 'would have set a brilliant non-conformist mind against the powerful but deeply conservative thought of Sir Owen Dixon' if he had been appointed to the High Court of Australia (Simpson 2001, p. 25). Barry wanted an institution that would pursue a radical program: conducting deep and broad research into the causes and consequences of crime; the ways to address the topic empirically; to secure proper scholarly assistance; with the establishment of institutional cooperation among traditional adversaries and competitors including politicians, departmental officers and independent scholars. Barry saw the importance, most unusual for his time, to engage with experts overseas; and to participate in conferences to gather ideas. As I was later to find to my cost, this was a notion that many Australian lawyers found deeply unsettling (*Al-Kateb* v *Godwin* (2004) 219 CLR 562). Yet, Barry came back from encounters with international leaders in criminology energised to question the previously unquestionable and to think the unthinkable.

Apart from ministers and high officials this was a golden age of experts and scholars in criminology: Dr Norval Morris (Melbourne, Adelaide and Chicago); Gordon Hawkins (Sydney and UK Prisons); Duncan Chappell and many others. Many of them were also to join me in the ALRC, including in a project on reform of federal sentencing law and practice (Australian Law Reform Commission 1980).

The appointment of Bill Clifford as the first director of the AIC brought to the fore a person who sometimes seemed perplexed, as many English observers are, by the mysteries, rivalries and economic inefficiencies of federalism. After the establishment of the AIC, without much delay, he and his colleagues were plunged into unsettling and distracting jurisdictional conflicts; institutional jealousies; and 'razor gangs' that perennially assaulted brave new ideas in new institutions and sought to undermine them by hostility thinly disguised as economic efficiency.

The author of this book has been prudent and a little understated in telling of stories of this disruption in the periodic political hostility and economic cutbacks inflicted on the brave spirits who entered the portals of the AIC and ALRC believing that they would be consistently funded; appropriately staffed; and supported by successive governments in building more rational laws and practices in Australia. They hoped and believed that the AIC and the ALRC would respond to crime and punishment in a more effective way than had commonly been the attitude of Australian citizens, reflected consequentially in their hard-nosed politicians and bureaucrats.

When I assumed office in the ALRC in 1975, the AIC was already up and running. The history and challenges faced by the AIC in those foundational days is well told in this book. Working in the ALRC with an institution of more modest size, with no formal links at all to State and Territory governments, my visits to the AIC usually left me jealous. It enjoyed larger resources and intergovernmental links that it had successfully extracted from Federal Government (Kirby 2017). And also from State Governments. The ALRC, on the other hand, was always scrounging for resources and political support. It had no formal links with the States. Being always based in Canberra, the AIC, under successive directors, seemed to have a secret that eluded me. This included securing, from its commencement, strong and effective links to all the governments throughout the nation. The AIC boasted that it was an example of 'cooperative federalism', with an overlapping mandate for the States, and with much contact and momentum.

Eventually, both of these ambitious institutions faced envy and hostility from officials and politicians who succeeded Bowen, Hughes, Murphy and Ellicott. I have analysed the story of this rise and decline as it affected the ALRC in many places (e.g. Kirby 2017). The repeated reductions in funding the ALRC especially was graphic. In the place of Harders, Mahony, Loof and Curtis, the AIC and ALRC, sometimes at the same time, had to engage with official hostility and alienation. Officials emerged who wanted to control research on policy issues; to avoid controversy; and to reduce the 'gadflies', who like Barry, embraced too many 'queer notions'—this was the adjective Sir Owen Dixon attributed to Sir John Barry's ideas (Dixon 1964). Dixon had omitted him (although Barry came close) from the list of those who might have been appointed to the High Court of Australia (see Dixon 1964, p. v). These officials also sought to justify the revival of traditional attitudes by their desire to 'protect their minister' from unwanted questions and the potential political dangers that such institutions might cause. The very nature of the ALRC and of the AIC (also the Family Law Council (FLC) and other independent advisors) was a potential source of hostility. Usually policy and research institutions were not abolished outright. But they were often destined, to be wound back so as to avoid undue controversy (Kirby 2017). In this era, federal officials largely reverted to the former way of doing things. It did not seem to depend on the political party that formed the government.

The author of this book, correctly, for an institutional history, looks, where possible, on the bright side. There have been many changes from the ideas that flourished during the 'golden age'. They were not necessarily changes in the right direction. But the institutions generally remained to fight on another day.

All of this said, it is extremely valuable that the history of the AIC has been written. It records the innovative imperatives of rationality, justice and reform that lay behind the AIC's birth. The author examines the AIC as an unusual institution of intergovernmental cooperation in Australia. He outlines some of the tensions that arose during the 50 years that followed the AIC's establishment. Properly, he examines the recurring dilemmas of funding; and providing services that were constantly measured against the precious federal funds paid to sustain them. The shifts in accommodation that faced the AIC are, like the ALRC, explained. So also are the steps designed to ensure the provision of research, training and the promised initiatives of community, professional and expert education as well. He recounts the admirable engagement with United Nations Institutions that was such a novel brainchild of Justice Barry. He analyses the extent to which the AIC lived up to the expectations of its founders. He suggests conclusions that finish on an optimistic note.

He might have put the record of the AIC more clearly in the context of other federal advisory bodies, including the ALRC, FLC, Australian Research Council to name a few. All of them faced struggles for survival. However, the deficit in that respect on the part of the author (if any), I have attempted to repair in this Foreword. I have done so by reference to my own experience in the ALRC during the 1970s and up to the very different world of today.

Of one conclusion we can be sure. The policy challenges affecting research on crime and punishment have not diminished in the past 50 years. They have increased markedly. They continue to expand, in part because of dangerous weapons, cybercrime, terrorism, child abuse, modern slavery and domestic violence. Alien interference in our electoral integrity; personal, family and school bullying; racial tensions and so forth. Injustice to women, to sexual minorities and above all, to the First Nations peoples. The task of the AIC is not finished. In fact, it has barely begun.

The need for an institution that is constantly researching crime and punishment, has grown enormously in the 50 years of the AIC. This record of those years celebrates many notable achievements. But it leads to this conclusion: We must recapture the inspiring spirit of those who initiated and upheld the creation of the AIC so as to make sure that our national response to crime and punishment, and to other needs for reform, was informed by empirical research; community dialogue, political engagement; and rational debate beyond mere prejudiced intuitions. Only when we fully recapture that golden age will Australians enjoy institutions that constantly examine, with critical minds, important laws and practices. Only then will we be able to point the way to the future of our Commonwealth, without nostalgia for the heady golden times of yore.

The Hon. Michael Kirby AC CMG
Justice of the High Court of Australia (1996–2009);
Chairman of the Australian Law Reform Commission
(1975–84); Australian Human Rights Medal (1991)

Sydney,
Australia

References

Australian Law Reform Commission. 1980. *Sentencing of Federal Offenders*, ALRC 15, Canberra: ALRC.

Dixon, Owen. 1964. Retirement of the Chief Justice. *Commonwealth Law Reports*, 110: v–xi.

Kirby, Michael D. 2017. The Decline and Fall of Australia's Law Reform Institutions – and the Prospects of Revival? *Australian Law Journal* 91(10): 841–852.

Kirby, Michael D. 2007. Foreword, in Mark Finnane, *JV Barry: A Life*, pp. vii–x. Sydney: University of New South Wales Press.

Simpson, Troy. 2001. Appointments that Might Have Been, in Blackshield, Anthony R., Coper, Michael and Williams, George (eds.), *Oxford Companion to the High Court of Australia*, pp. 23–25. South Melbourne: Oxford University Press.

Acknowledgements

Although I remain responsible for the final published content of this work, I have drawn on an extensive range of sources that I am pleased to acknowledge with gratitude. The genesis of the work was raised with Dr. Rick Brown, Deputy Director of the Australian Institute of Criminology, as I approached retirement from the Institute in 2020 after almost a quarter of a century of employment there. He responded with enthusiasm and appreciated the need to mark the Golden Jubilee year as an important milestone in the Institute's history. He sought and obtained the director's approval to allow access to the Institute's archives and to allow Institute staff, particularly those in the JV Barry Library, to help with my many requests for access to volumes, photographs, recordings and documents—which they did both promptly and professionally. The Institute's substantial photographic archive was compiled by Senior Librarian, Pamela Garfoot, shortly prior to her leaving the Institute in 2003. The Institute also agreed to purchase some of the published volumes—that facilitated acceptance of the contract with Palgrave Macmillan. Josephine Taylor, commissioning Editor in Criminology, and the production staff at Palgrave, provided support along the journey, which included arranging for four academic referees to review the Proposal and to provide insightful feedback that, I believe, improved the scope and concept of the work in many ways. The final draft was also read in full by Dr. Rick Brown and Emeritus Professor Peter Grabosky who both provided many insightful suggestions.

The isolation of working during the three years of the Coronavirus pandemic from my rural office in the 'charismatic hamlet' of Kyneton in central Victoria, was interrupted on a few occasions when I travelled, both physically and virtually, to conduct interviews with former Institute staff, colleagues and scholars across Australia. The final list of interviewees is provided below, and I thank them all for their interest, knowledge, time and willingness to spend a few, or more, hours with me raking over the coals of their careers in the public sector. John Myrtle, former Principal Librarian at the JV Barry Library, is deserving of particular thanks for his support during my research for this project, as well as for sharing his extensive knowledge of the development of criminology in Australian history and recounting stories of some of its most illustrious identities. John also provided me with information about the research he undertook with Mark Finnane on the life of JV Barry, funded by the Australian Research Council (2003–5, DP0346803). He alerted me to many issues that I was happy to explore and provided access to his own substantial collection of research materials. A number of the photographs of Sir John Barry included in this book were provided with the kind permission of Susy Barry on behalf of the family. I am also grateful to the many other individuals and organisations who agreed for their photographs to be published.

In addition, I was fortunate in having correspondence with numerous people across Australia and internationally—listed below who, along with those I interviewed, gave feedback on specific sections of the work. Professor Matti Joutsen, former Director of HEUNI, in particular was an invaluable source of information about the United Nations Office on Drugs and Crime and the United Nations Crime Prevention and Criminal Justice Programme Network. The Directors of both UNAFEI in Tokyo, Professor Morinaga and UNICRI in Turin, Ms Antonia Marie De Meo, and their staff, kindly agreed to the publication of photographs of their Institutes, for which I am most appreciative. The United Nations

Photo Library in New York also agreed to the inclusion of the various images of the UN Crime Congress meetings in this publication.

Finally, I pay tribute to my partner, Melinda Mockridge, for sharing her views and offering invaluable advice on many aspects of my project during our regular walks in the countryside, and for tolerating hearing about the various people, incidents and events in the Institute's history that I found so fascinating.

December 2022   Russell G. Smith

Interviewees

Emeritus Professor John Braithwaite (former Researcher) 30 January 2021, Kyneton, Victoria

Dr. Samantha Bricknell (current Research Manager) 21 November 2022 (Virtual, Canberra)

Dr. Rick Brown (current Deputy Director) 10 June 2022 (AIC), 4 November 2022 (Virtual, Canberra)

Dennis Challinger (former Assistant Director, Information and Training) 18 February 2022, Canterbury, Melbourne

Fiona Dowsley (Director, Crime Statistics Agency Victoria) 8 December 2020 (Virtual, Melbourne)

Emeritus Professor Richard Fox AM (former Board Chair) 15 February 2022, Hawthorn, Melbourne

Emeritus Professor Peter Grabosky (former Director of Research and Deputy Director) 2 December 2020, ANU, Canberra

Professor Adam Graycar AM, FAIM, FASSA (former Director) 1 March 2021 (Virtual, Adelaide)

Emeritus Professor Richard Harding (former Director) 18 November 2021 (Virtual, Perth)

Emeritus Professor Toni Makkai AM (former Director) 9 June 2022, AIC, Canberra

Anthony Morgan (current Research Manager) 17 November 2022 (Virtual, Canberra)

John Myrtle (former Head Librarian) 3 December 2020, Mawson, ACT

Michael Phelan APM (former Director) 3 November 2022, ACIC, Melbourne

Dr. John Seymour (former Senior Criminologist—Legal) 14 November 2022, Garran, ACT

Jane Shelling (former Library Manager) 23 March 2021, AIC, Canberra

Dr. Adam Tomison (former Director) 26 October 2022 (Virtual, Perth)

John Walker (former Criminologist) 30 November 2020, AIC, Canberra

Dr. Grant Wardlaw (former Deputy Director) 30 November 2020, AIC, Canberra

Correspondents

Sylvia Blomfield, former Librarian in Charge, J V Barry Memorial Library

Honorary Professor Duncan Chappell, University of Sydney

Professor Mark Finnane, Griffith University, Brisbane

Emeritus Professor Arie Freiberg AM, Monash University, Melbourne

Professor Fiona Haines, University of Melbourne

Emeritus Professor Mike Hough, Birkbeck, University of London, UK

Samantha Jackson, AIC Library and Information Services Manager, Canberra

Professor Matti Joutsen, former Director, HEUNI, Helsinki, Finland

Patricia Mayhew OBE, Former Programme Director, Criminal Justice System Analysis, Home Office, UK

Dr. Jocelynne A. Scutt AO, Law School, University of Buckingham, UK

Paul Wilson, former Deputy Director, Research, AIC

Contents

Note on Referencing

In addition to the references cited in the text, reference is also made to the papers of Sir John Barry at the National Library of Australia and the National Archives of Australia, the AICs Annual Reports, Board/Council Minutes and formal Interviews. These are cited in the text as, for example:

NLA—(NLA 2505/30/39-40)
NAA—(NAA A432, 1974/5957)
AIC, Annual Report, 2022, p. 00
AIC, Board Minutes, 1 December 2021, p. 00
Interviews—(Interviewee's name, Interview, 12 November 2022)

Legislation is cited in the text with year and jurisdiction, but not included in chapter reference lists.

About the Author

Russell G. Smith has qualifications in law, psychology and criminology from the University of Melbourne and a Ph.D. from the Faculty of Law, King's College London. He practised as a lawyer in Melbourne and lectured in criminology at the University of Melbourne prior to working at the Australian Institute of Criminology, most recently as Principal Criminologist. Following his retirement in 2020, he is now an Honorary Fellow at the Institute and also holds an Academic Status position of Full Professor in the College of Business, Government and Law at Flinders University. He is a fellow and former President of the Australian and New Zealand Society of Criminology and has published extensively—including *Cybercrime Risks and Responses* (Palgrave, 2015), and two institutional histories, *Medical Discipline: The Professional Conduct Jurisdiction of the General Medical Council, 1958 to 1990* (Clarendon, 1994) and *In Pursuit of Nursing Excellence: A History of the Royal College of Nursing Australia, 1949 to 1999* (Oxford, 1999) in addition to over 200 other authored or co-authored publications. He has received numerous awards including the John Barry Medal in Criminology and Dwight's Prize for Legal History, both from the University of Melbourne.

Abbreviations

ABARE	Australian Bureau of Agricultural and Resource Economics
ABN	Australian Bibliographic Network
ABS	Australian Bureau of Statistics
ACC	Australian Crime Commission
ACCCE	Australian Centre to Counter Child Exploitation
ACER	Australian Council of Educational Research
ACIC	Australian Criminal Intelligence Commission
ACLEI	Australian Commission for Law Enforcement Integrity
ACPC	Australian Crime Prevention Council (formerly the Australian Crime Prevention, Correction and After-care Council)
ACT	Australian Capital Territory
ACVPA	Australian Crime and Violence Prevention Awards
ADCA	Alcohol and Other Drugs Council of Australia
Advisory Council	Criminology Research Advisory Council
AGD	Attorney-General's Department
AGIS	Australian Government Information Service
AIC	Australian Institute of Criminology
AIFS	Australian Institute of Family Studies

AIHW	Australian Institute of Health and Welfare
AIPM	Australian Institute of Police Management
ALIA	Australian Library and Information Association
ALIES	Australasian Libraries in Emergency and Security
ALP	Australian Labor Party
ALRC	Australian Law Reform Commission
AM	Member of the Order of Australia
AML/CTF	Anti Money Laundering and Counter Terrorism Financing
ANROWS	Australia's National Research Organisation for Women's Safety
ANU	Australian National University
ANZSOC	Australian and New Zealand Society of Criminology
APAIS	Australian Public Affairs Information Service
APCCA	Asian Pacific Conference of Correctional Administrators
APM	Australian Police Medal
APMAB	Australasian Police Multicultural Advisory Bureau
APSC	Australian Public Service Commission
ARC	Australian Research Council
ARPANET	Advanced Research Projects Agency Network
ATM	Automated Teller Machine
AUSINET	Australian Information Network
AUSTRAC	Australian Transaction Reports and Analysis Centre
AUSTROM	Australian Periodical Abstracts on CD-ROM
BASEL Institute	Basel Institute on Governance - International Center for Asset Recovery
BJS	Bureau of Justice Statistics within the United States Department of Justice
BOCSAR	New South Wales Bureau of Crime Statistics and Research
CBCS	Commonwealth Bureau of Census and Statistics
CCLS	College for Criminal Law Science, Beijing Normal University
CEO	Chief Executive Officer
CFO	Chief Financial Officer
CINCH	Computerised Information from National Criminological Holdings
COVID-19	SARS-CoV-2 Virus
CPA	Certified Practising Accountant

CPSU	Commonwealth Public Sector Union
CRAC	Criminology Research Advisory Council
CRC	Criminology Research Council
CRG	Criminology Research Grants
Crime Commission	United Nations Commission on Crime Prevention and Criminal Justice
Crime Congress	United Nations Congress on Crime Prevention and Criminal Justice
CSA	Crime Statistics Agency, Victoria
CSAM	Child Sexual Abuse Material
CSIRO	Commonwealth Scientific and Industrial Research Organisation
DIPB	Department of Immigration and Border Protection
DUMA	Drug Use Monitoring Australia
EU	European Union
FMA Act	*Financial Management and Accountability Act 1997* (Cth)
GDP	Gross Domestic Product
GUI	Graphic User Interfaces
HEUNI	European Institute for Crime Prevention and Control
HORU	Home Office Research and Statistics Unit
HREC	Human Research Ethics Committee
I-ADAM	International Arrestee Drug Abuse Monitoring
ICAC	New South Wales Independent Commission Against Corruption
ICCLR&CJP	International Centre for Criminal Law Reform and Criminal Justice Policy
ICPC	International Center for the Prevention of Crime
ICVS	International Crime Victimisation Survey
IDC	Interdepartmental Committee
ILANUD	Latin American Institute for the Prevention of Crime and the Treatment of Offenders
INOIS	Integrated Numerical Offender Identification System
ISPAC	International Scientific and Professional Advisory Council of the United Nations Crime
ISS	Institute for Security Studies (formerly Institute for Defence Policy)
KIC	Korean Institute of Criminology and Justice
LSE	London School of Economics and Political Science

MoG	Machinery of Government
MOU	Memorandum of Understanding
n.p.	Unpaginated
NAA	National Archives of Australia
NAUSS	Naif Arab University for Security Sciences
NCA	National Crime Authority
NDLERF	National Drug Law Enforcement Research Fund
NHMRC	National Health and Medical Research Council
NIJ	National Institute of Justice
NLA	National Library of Australia
NPEAB	National Police Ethnic Advisory Bureau
NT	Northern Territory
OCSAR	Office of Crime Statistics and Research
OPI	South Australian Office for Public Integrity
OSCA	Office of Strategic Crime Assessments
PIC	New South Wales Police Integrity Commission
PM&C	Prime Minister and Cabinet
PNG	Papua New Guinea
PNI	United Nations Crime Prevention and Criminal Justice Programme Network
Razor Gang	Coalition government's *Review of Commonwealth Functions* 1981
RCNA	Royal College of Nursing, Australia
RegNet	Regulatory Institutions Network (ANU)
RMIT	Royal Melbourne Institute of Technology
RWI	Raoul Wallenberg Institute of Human Rights and Humanitarian Law
SHERLOC	Sharing Electronic Resources and Laws on Crime
SII	The Siracusa International Institute for Criminal Justice and Human Rights
SPSS	Statistical Package for the Social Sciences
STAIRS	Storage and Information Retrieval System
STATA	Statistical Package for the Social Sciences
TIJ	Thailand Institute of Justice
UK	United Kingdom
UN	United Nations
UNAFEI	United Nations and Far East-Asian Institute
UNAFRI	African Regional Institute for the Prevention of Crime and the Treatment of Offenders

UNCJIN	United Nations Criminal Justice Information Network
UNICRI	United Nations Interregional Crime and Justice Research Institute
UNODC	United Nations Office on Drugs and Crime
US	United States
WACSAR	Western Australian Office of Crime Statistics and Research
WCJLN	World Criminal Justice Library Network

List of Figures

List of Plates

List of Tables

1

Introduction

Aims

This book seeks to explore the role and development of criminological research in the public sector during the last half-century, determine what benefits it has provided and assess whether the community has received value for the funds expended. The Australian Institute of Criminology (AIC) is used as a case study to illustrate the challenges and pressures facing those who have sought to carry out crime and justice research in the public sector, and to assess whether or not there remains a need for criminologists to be employed by government and what fifty years of work has achieved. Over the five decades, tensions arose for the AIC, and other research agencies, where the outcomes of research have not always accorded with government policy agendas. As the late Gil Geis, former Professor Emeritus in the School of Social Ecology at the University of California at Irvine, observed in a convincingly-argued case for supporting the AIC following government reviews in 1994 that posed a threat to its existence:

© The Author(s), under exclusive license to Springer Nature
Switzerland AG 2023
R. G. Smith, *Public Sector Criminological Research*,
https://doi.org/10.1007/978-3-031-28356-7_1

> The [AIC] provides a quintessential illustration of a government agency structurally and functionally caught between a rock and a hard place. The AIC is funded by the Commonwealth government and operates under the aegis of the Attorney-General. It is charged with conducting research on the socially and politically sensitive topics and crime and criminal justice. If the results of this research… produce distress and discontent in those who fund its fate, they can either grin and bear it with as much grace as they can muster or they can retaliate. The history of the AIC demonstrates the constant tension that this arrangement has created, and recent developments show how vulnerable the Institute can be unless it toes the government line. (Geis 1994, p. 282)

The AIC was chosen as illustrative as it has been fifty years since its official opening on 16 October 1973. The author, a former Principal Criminologist at the AIC, and a staff member for almost 25 years, proposed to undertake the research with the agreement of the AIC and was able to rely on his personal knowledge of the organisation as well as his network of contacts, some of whom agreed to be interviewed and to share their own experience of working at, or with, the Institute at various times over the five decades. Current AIC staff, particularly the current and former staff of the JV Barry Memorial Library at the Institute, assisted in locating archival material and sharing their knowledge of the information holdings of the Institute.

The Reach of Criminological Research in the Public Sector

In order to understand the reach of criminological research in the public sector, we need to begin by considering its definition and scope. In Australia, Sect. 4 of the *Criminology Research Act 1971* (Cth), the Act that established the AIC, defines 'criminological research' as 'research in connexion with: the causes, correction and prevention of criminal behaviour; and any related matter'. The reference to 'causes' should provide some reassurance to critical criminologists such as Brown (1978, 1994) who have condemned the Institute for promoting conservative agendas and ignoring the causes of criminality. The more recent *Australian Crime Commission Amendment (Criminology Research) Bill 2015* (Cth), that sought to repeal the 1971 Act, revised the definition of criminological research to: 'research in connection with: the causes, *consequences*, correction and prevention of criminal behaviour; and any related matter' (emphasis added noting the addition of consequential effects of crime). This sought to provide a wide ambit for research to be conducted by government-employed criminologists—although the Bill was not passed by the parliament. The question that remains, however, is to what exist did the Institute carry out its statutory remit?

Prior to the establishment of the AIC, individuals with an interest in conducting criminological research found employment in a wide range of government entities (Smith 2017, 2021). This was, in part, due to the interdisciplinary nature of criminology. In Australia, criminology is not a statutorily-regulated profession, meaning that anyone is at liberty to engage in criminological research and to call themselves a criminologist without having to demonstrate prescribed standards of education and ethical conduct. As such, it is possible to find individuals engaging in criminological research in many areas of both the public and private sectors—some with higher levels of expertise than others. Criminology is also an unregulated discipline in other countries, apart from rules governing membership of criminological societies—although the criteria for membership of these are unremarkable, making membership of societies freely available—even to reformed offenders. Having lived experience of offending and the criminal justice system is seen by some as a necessary path to understanding fully the causes and responses to crime in the community.

In the public sector, the principal workplaces for criminologists are dedicated criminological research agencies, such as the AIC, criminal justice entities such as law enforcement, prosecution, judicial and correctional agencies and in departments with specific interests in crime-related issues such as those administering law, finance, revenue, Indigenous policy, welfare policy, gender equality issues, education and youth affairs. Qualified criminologists have also found opportunities working in anti-corruption commissions, law reform commissions, legal aid offices, parliamentary committees, professional regulatory agencies and even in pollution control bodies, fisheries regulation departments and in museums.

In the private sector, criminologists may be found working for charitable organisations, policy 'think tanks', political parties, the media, trade union administration, the legal and accounting professions and, increasingly, in business consultancy and market research organisations that engage in risk assessments, policy reviews, evaluations and survey research.

At the intersection of the public and private sectors lie Universities and other tertiary educational institutions that receive some of their funding from government and the balance from non-government sources such as student fees, research grants and other entrepreneurial activities. Universities provide a base for most criminologists today. Interestingly, the AIC sits at the intersection of these various organisational sectors: it is a government-funded entity; it undertakes administrative data collection for government internal uses, but also provides criminal justice evidence and research findings for the public; it conducts evaluative studies such as those undertaken by private sector consultancies; and it adopts the methods, standards of publication and ethics of academic institutions. These differing roles and functions create some inconvenient tensions for those, such as directors, who try to satisfy many competing interests. One example shall suffice.

At the 30th annual conference of the Australian and New Zealand Society of Criminology (ANZSOC), hosted by the AIC in December 2017, sponsorship was, *inter alia*, provided by the Australian Government Department of Immigration and Border Protection (DIBP). As part of promotion and marketing, DIBP-branded pens were distributed in conference satchels to delegates. This seemingly innocuous gift, and its associated funding, led to severe criticism of the Institute and ANZSOC for partnering with this government entity that had presided over Australia's border and asylum-seeker policies that a number of critical criminologists attending the conference, and others, had publicly denounced (see Ryan 2017). Bridges on both sides had to be mended. This stands as an illustration of the potential conflicts of interest that public sector-funded criminological entities face—a topic to be examined further below.

Research Methods

As with other historical accounts of the development of criminology (Radzinowicz 1965; Rock 1988; Finnane 2008; Walston 2009; Liu 2013; Bruinsma 2015; Smith 2017, 2021), the present work relies on a variety of research methods, data sources and historical approaches. It has brought together information published by the agencies examined and refers to some recent commentaries on the nature of criminological research and the role of government in funding, promoting and commissioning it (see Mayhew 2016 and Tonry 2010 in particular). Various reports on the role and future of the AIC have been examined (Loof 1979; Coad et al. 1994; Tanzer 1994) as well as some commentaries on the history of the AIC and whether or not it should be retained (Carson and O'Malley 1989; Finnane 1998, 2006; Geis 1994; James and Sutton 1994).

In keeping with the author's previous research at the AIC, it blends a mixture of quantitative and qualitative research, while integrating academic commentary and critical analyses of the questions canvassed. In many areas of the public sector, there is a tradition of institutional histories and autobiographies being written by former senior staff members on their retirement which invariably entail a keenly personal perspective on what occurred over the period examined (e.g. Macfarlane Burnet 1971; Wilson 1990; Muirhead 1996; Whitrod 2001; Bevan 2005). As one such biographer, John Robson, former Director of Criminological Studies at Victoria University of Wellington, observed:

> I do not want to present the picture of an elderly fellow raking through the embers of his administrative experience, but there are some things in my experience which may be of interest to those who are trying to find answers to problems they encounter in their day's march. (Robson 1971, p. 195)

Adopting an autobiographical approach can carry with it the risk of compromising the objectivity of the account, focussing on the positive rather than the less attractive aspects of the subject of inquiry, and potentially distorting events to paint them in a favourable light.

Zimring (1984) raised this concern prior to embarking on his review of the research carried out at the Centre for Studies in Criminal Justice at the University of Chicago in 1984:

> Library shelves are already groaning under the weight of volumes of self-congratulation and institutional boosterism that have not left the world of ideas a better place. To organize a volume round the contribution of a single research institution is often parochial and occasionally unseemly. (Zimring 1984, p. ix)

The present work has sought to avoid these criticisms by limiting personal observations as much as possible, refraining from the use of first-person pronouns and relying on accounts given by individuals who worked alongside the author, or prior to his arrival at the AIC, and others with the experience of, or views on the work undertaken by the Institute. Eighteen such individuals were interviewed by the author, either face-to-face, or using video-conferencing technologies (due to dictates of government restrictions of movement during the COVID-19 pandemic). Their recollections were presented along with information gathered from published sources as well as primary-source material held in the AICs archival collection in Canberra that includes a number of audio- and video-recorded interviews. Those selected for interview were chosen because of their knowledge of the Institute's work, or opinions as to its value (or lack thereof), along with others with similar knowledge of other comparable Australian and overseas organisations. It was not difficult to find academics with critical views regarding public sector criminology, and a selection of these were either interviewed or, if they declined due to lack of interest (or antagonism towards the project), their published opinions on the topic referred to. In addition, a number of other individuals, referred to as 'correspondents' were approached for their views on various aspects of the study and their written responses were used to supplement actual interviews.

Despite this, there remains the risk that some of the material presented will include the personal recollections of the author who was present during half of the life of the Institute. Of course, as Gordon Hawkins observed when writing his account of the establishment of the Institute of Criminology at Sydney University, 'memory is always selective and frequently faulty... And contemporary history writing is probably more likely to be contaminated by the author's prejudices and values than writing about periods long past' (Hawkins 1990, p. 9 and see Churchill et al. 2022 on the concept of historical criminology).

The research was supported by the AIC, in that it permitted the author to gain access to its archives, conduct research for the book in the last few months of his employment with the Institute prior to retirement and agreed to purchase a quantity of copies of the publication to present to interviewees and supporters of the project, once completed—that helped dispel any concerns of the publisher regarding marketing of such a boutique work. The vast bulk of the research and writing was carried out at the author's own expense, principally during the lockdowns caused by the Coronavirus pandemic during 2020 and 2021.

A number of benefits of the study were identified that, arguably, justify the enterprise. The AIC was, when it was established, and continues to be, one of a small group of public sector criminological research organisations that many look to as a model for the establishment of other such bodies in the future. When proposals have arisen for setting up such an entity, the AIC has occasionally been consulted on how best to develop a workable and effective model. The establishment of the Korean Institute of Criminology (KIC), in Seoul, is a case in point in which the then current director of the AIC, Professor Duncan Chappell, was visited by the Attorney-General of Korea in the 1980s to provide advice on the idea. The present volume, therefore, provides information and commentary on how to deal with the many theoretical and practical issues that a government may encounter in embarking on such an enterprise.

Secondly, the present work documents the views of those who have conducted criminological research for governments that might otherwise have remained unavailable—particularly information gleaned from the interviews conducted. Thirdly, the current study has provided some evidence of the utility and necessity of governments allocating adequate resources to criminological research, and shows how such research has contributed to managing and responding to criminal justice problems for the benefit of the community. Finally, the chapters in this volume that mention the work of comparable research institutes in Australia and internationally, provide an indication of which institutional models work best, and how governments in the future could design new entities that would be most likely to succeed in fulfilling their objectives.

Ethical Considerations

The research was approved by the AICs Human Research Ethics Committee (Protocol P0298A, approved 27 May 2020). This was required owing to the inclusion of interviews with AIC personnel and former staff members as well as others selected for interview. Interviewees were presented, in advance of their interviews, with information on the topics to be canvassed, and the procedures by which their consent to disclose the interview material in the publication was to be obtained. Consent was assumed by their willingness to participate in the interview or video conference with the author, and their permission was obtained to identify them by name, or position (whichever they preferred), and the information provided to be published on condition that they be able to approve specific quotes attributed to them prior to publication. Consent was also provided to publish photographs of them in the book and to record the interview in order to assist in the writing and publication process but not for further dissemination unless specific consent for this to occur was provided.

Ethical clearance was also required because of the need to ensure that confidential, classified government material was not disclosed publicly without first obtaining consent from the relevant entities. This was particularly necessary given the AICs close relationship with the Australian Criminal Intelligence Commission (ACIC) since 2015.

Theoretical and Thematic Approach

The following chapters are arranged thematically rather than presenting material in a strictly chronological way. Within each chapter, however, the content is dealt with chronologically, where appropriate. As indicated above, the time frame for the study was the preceding half-century since the AIC was officially opened—on 16 October 1973. Some sections deal with developments preceding this date when the proposal for establishing the AIC was being developed, and the final chapters are more forward-looking in predicting future developments.

The specific subject-matter examined is described in the chapter outline below. A number of common themes can, however, be identified that have relevance not only to the circumstances of the AIC, but also to other public sector criminological enterprises in Australia and internationally.

1. The first theme concerns the differences that arose between criminological research conducted in the public sector generally and that carried out by academic criminologists based in higher educational institutions. These differences relate to the crime types examined (be they crimes of the powerful or the oppressed), the human subjects of analysis (be they victims, offenders or criminal justice personnel), and the geographical focus of research (be it local, state, national or international).

2. Related to the first theme is the debate that has occurred, particularly in Australia, over the focus of the AICs research activities and whether they should relate primarily to crime types and criminal justice policy questions that affect the Commonwealth of Australia, national questions more generally or provincial crime concerns that affect the Australian states and territories. The questions arising from this theme, that have arisen because of Australia's federal constitutional system, have been pervasive throughout the Institute's history, often arising due to economic factors, and also apply in other federal systems where public sector criminological research institutes have been created.

3. The third theme deals with the methods of research conducted in the public sector as opposed to those employed in the private sector and in the academy. The focus here is on the extent to which quantitative methods are employed, particularly the creation and use of time-series datasets, rather than qualitative, theoretical, sociological, legal or historical methodologies and approaches. Adherence, or otherwise,

to standards of human research ethics also differs depending on the location of the research activity within, or outside public sector.

4. The fourth theme relates to political considerations and the focus of public sector research that supports and informs the views of serving governments, rather than research and commentary of a critical, left-realist or sociological nature. An example of this, is the extent to which public sector criminological research has shown a willingness and interest in dealing with Southern, as opposed to Northern criminological perspectives (Carrington 2018), and how this has affected the nature of research undertaken by governments and its policy outcomes.

5. A final theme focusses on the financing of criminological research and how the topics, methods, timelines and outputs of public sector criminological research differ from private sector and academic research depending on the source, amounts and sustainability of funding sources. Financial considerations also lay at the heart of most attempts to limit or to restrict the activities of the Institute.

These themes will be raised and discussed throughout the work, rather than being examined in separate sections, and will be considered again in the final discussion and conclusions regarding the impact and effectiveness of the AIC, and comparable bodies internationally, in conducting research activities for the benefit of governments and the community.

Scope of the Study

The present study is focussed on the conduct of criminological research within public sector organisations. It begins by exploring the need for criminological research within government agencies and provides examples from Australia and internationally of how this has been achieved. It explores the social and political needs that must be satisfied and identifies a range of competing interests involved in creating government-funded bodies to fulfil these needs, drawing on the experience of research bodies within governments in Australia, New Zealand, the United Kingdom (UK), the United States (US), Canada and selected European Union

(EU) countries as examples. The reference period is from the early 1970s to the end of 2022, although discussion of earlier historical examples will be raised where necessary to show how governments have relied on criminological research at various times in the past, noting, of course, that criminology had its roots in the work of French and Italian government officials in the late nineteenth and the early twentieth centuries (Martin 1990).

The focus of the book is principally on the history of the AIC as an example of a public sector criminological research agency. The work begins by exploring the social, legal and political context of crime and justice research in Australia and overseas in the 1960s, including international models of other research institutes that existed at the time such as in Europe and North America. It examines the role of Sir John Barry, Justice of the Supreme Court of Victoria, and others in the 1960s, who identified the need for government-funded criminological research, particularly the development of statistical collections, and who promoted the need for the AIC as an institution that could satisfy the competing interests of Commonwealth, state and territory governments and the academic community. Consideration will be given to the role of the AICs Board, the Criminology Research Advisory Council (CRAC) (and its predecessors), directors, government ministers and departmental heads, in ensuring that the Institute was sufficiently resourced to satisfy the various interests involved. Examples will be given of how the AICs staff sought to avoid politicised controversies in crime and justice while maintaining their duty as public officials to provide fearless, independent, high-quality research for governments to use—an aim not always achieved. These sometimes sensitive and controversial questions arose not only for the AIC but also for comparable organisations such as the UK Home Office and the National Institute of Justice (NIJ) in the US, as well as in academic criminological research institutes and private sector 'think tanks' and consultancy practices.

Adequate and ongoing funding lay at the heart of many debates about having such research organisations within the public sector. Different funding models have been adopted over time with controversies arising over fee-for-service versus core-funded program funding, and how the delicate balance between the two was favoured by governments of different political persuasions. An assessment will be made of the return-on-investment achieved by the AICs research activities and whether it satisfied both government and community needs and expectations. Again, comparisons are made with other research organisations locally and internationally.

In Australia, the AIC was given jurisdiction over the allocation of some government funding for external research, usually carried out by university-based scholars. The selection of suitable projects for funding, how much funding should be provided and the monitoring and publication of the funded research, raised difficult administrative and political issues concerning the demonstration of value for money and the scope of topics examined by funding recipients. Controversies were inevitable as funding was sometimes provided for research that produced findings unpalatable to governments of the day, or research that could be seen as benefiting a particular political party's electorate.

Fundamental to the AICs work were its staff and the current book considers how the AIC approached recruitment and retention of staff, questions of diversity and gender balance, whether staff could be located away from the capital city, Canberra, and the challenges of matching staffing resources with research priorities. The dilemmas involved in attracting and retaining qualified academic criminologists to work within a government, security-oriented environment, and the AICs relations with the Commonwealth Public Sector Union (CPSU) are also explored.

Another set of complex questions arose concerning the physical accommodation required for a research institute, who should provide this, where it should be located, geographically and administratively, and the type of office layout best-suited to the research staff—be it in university-style offices, or corporate open-plan desks. The COVID-19 pandemic of the 2020s has also provided a natural experiment on home-based work and remote teleconferencing that has been both beneficial and limiting for social scientific research often conducted in teams and requiring fieldwork.

To carry out the Institute's research activities, and to provide an information resource for government policy-makers and the public alike, the AIC established and maintained an extensive library, the JV Barry Memorial Library. The challenges in funding and managing a large collection such as this are examined in light of the transition from paper-based publication of criminological books and serials, to digital resources.

Dissemination of research is clearly one of the main functions of public sector criminological research organisations, and in the many examples of these entities examined, this provided a principal indicator against which governments were able to measure performance. The AIC has, unlike some other entities, always maintained its own publications function with largely in-house editorial and publishing staff. Throughout the 50 years, the publication of research has changed considerably, particularly as online delivery has become the norm. Other dissemination activities including media work and conference presentations are also examined with an analysis of the research topics addressed, which research was most sought-after by government, industry and the public, which projects failed to endure and the proportion of research that was undertaken for government in-confidence but not publicly-released and how this proportion changed over time—particularly since the AICs relationship with the ACIC developed.

In the AICs foundational legislation, one of the functions specified for the AIC was to conduct training for criminal justice personnel. This was promoted by the founders of the Institute along the lines of other criminological research institutes, such as that in Japan—the United Nations and Far East-Asian Institute (UNAFEI). Such training endeavours were, initially, taken seriously by the AICs Directors with programs conducted, mainly for correctional and law enforcement officers, although not on the scale of those generously funded by the Japanese government at UNAFEI. Provision of training could, potentially, provide an important revenue stream, although the AIC found this difficult to achieve. More recent, targeted training initiatives were largely unsuccessful, apart from regular conferences conducted by the AIC. Although in-person conferences lapsed during the pandemic, the Institute continued to present its research findings through the use of digital technologies, and since 2022, face-to-face events have again been revived, with over 700 attending in 2022 alone. Consideration was also given to the conflicts of interest that existed between government, private sector and academic criminological research groups in the provision of training activities, as the market for such activities expanded widely.

To place the discussion of the AIC in the global context of public sector criminological research, consideration will be given to the AICs enduring relationship with the United Nations Office on Drugs and Crime (UNODC), its affiliated UN status over time and membership of the Institutes of the United Nations Crime Prevention and Criminal Justice Programme Network (PNI) and how the AIC model differs from other PNI Institutes. The extent to which the AIC has been used as an international resource for criminological research expertise and information through its library, and the AICs work with other international research bodies and professional associations is also explored.

Two chapters then seek to bring the discussion into the twenty-first century. In 2015, a proposal was developed by the Australian Government to merge the Institute with the Australian Crime Commission (ACC), now the ACIC. Although only partially successful, and remaining incomplete, the partial merger and associated Machinery of Government (MoG) change tried to blend a social science research institute with a national intelligence and security agency, thus raising many complex theoretical and administrative issues including the navigation of access to classified resources and dissemination of research within a closed security environment. Since 2020, the global Coronavirus pandemic has also created fresh challenges for the AIC, and focussed its research directions and manner of conducting research with both positive and negative outcomes.

The discussion then turns to what the AIC, and other public sector criminological research organisations, have achieved over the half-century in terms of their contribution to criminological knowledge—both in Australia and internationally. What have been the successes and failures in policy development, innovation in research methodologies, contributions to national data collections, provision of library and information services, training of young criminologists, raising funds for criminological research, public dissemination of research, international policy development and education of the community generally about crime and justice and its impact on society? The answers to these, and other, questions provide evidence of whether, and in what ways, such research institutes should continue into the future, taking into account the creation of new crime types, fiscal constraints, new government agendas and new technologies of social science research and publication. In conclusion, a summary of thematic findings from each chapter will be followed by observations on the need for further analysis of public sector criminological research and an assessment of the viability of the AIC, and comparable organisations, into the future.

References

Bevan, Colin Russell. 2005. *As the Walrus Said. The Time Has Come . . .* Canberra: Book Surge.

Brown, David. 1994. Facing the Knife. *Alternative Law Journal* 19 (3): 125–128. http://www6.austlii.edu.au/cgi-bin/viewdoc/au/journals/Alt LawJl/1994/59.html. Accessed 18 September 2020.

Brown, David. 1978. Some Notes on the State of Play in Criminology. *Alternative Criminology Journal* 2 (4) and 3 (1): 67–92 http://www.austlii.edu.au/au/journals/AltCrimJl/1978/14.html. Accessed 18 September 2020.

Bruinsma, Gerben, ed. 2015. *Histories of Transnational Crime.* New York: Springer.

Carrington, Kerry, Russell Hogg, John Scott, and Máximo. Sozzo. 2018. *Southern Criminology.* London: Routledge.

Carson, Kit, and Pat O'Malley. 1989. The Institutional Foundations of Contemporary Australian Criminology. *Australian and New Zealand Journal of Sociology* 25 (3): 333–355.

Churchill, David, Henry Yeomans, and Iain Channing. 2022. *Historical Criminology.* London: Routledge.

Coad, William J., Prudence Ford, Malcolm Hazell, Peter Lamb, Norman Reaburn, and Adrian Whiddett. 1994. *Report of the Review of Commonwealth Law Enforcement Arrangements.* Canberra: Australian Government Publishing Service.

Finnane, Mark. 2008. Promoting the Theory and Practice of Criminology: The Australian and New Zealand Society of Criminology and its Founding Moment. *Australian and New Zealand Journal of Criminology* 41 (2): 199–215.

Finnane, Mark. 2006. The ABC of Criminology: Anita Muhl, JV Barry, Norval Morris and the Making of a Discipline in Australia. *British Journal of Criminology* 46 (3): 399–422.

Finnane, Mark. 1998. Sir John Barry and the Melbourne Department of Criminology: Some Other Foundations of Australian Criminology. *Australian and New Zealand Journal of Criminology* 31 (1): 69–81.

Geis, Gilbert. 1994. 'This Sort of Thing Isn't Helpful:' The Dilemmas of the Australian Institute of Criminology. *Australian and New Zealand Journal of Criminology* 27 (3): 282–298.

Hawkins, Gordon. 1990. Present at the Creation: The Inception and Development of the Institute of Criminology. *Current Issues in Crime and Criminal Justice* 2 (1): 9–17. http://www.austlii.edu.au/au/journals/CICrimJust/1990/15.pdf. Accessed 3 February 2022.

James, Steve, and Adam Sutton. 1994. Criminology and Crime Control in Australia. *Australian and New Zealand Journal of Criminology* 27 (3): 299–308.

Liu, Jianhong, Susyan Jou, and Bill Hebenton, eds. 2013. *Handbook of Asian Criminology*. New York: Springer.

Loof, Peter R. 1979. *Establishment of the Australian Institute of Criminology and the Criminology Research Council: Proposals, Criteria and Negotiations Associated with the Establishment of the Institute and the Council*. Canberra: Attorney-General's Department.

Frank, Macfarlane Burnet. 1971. *Walter and Eliza Hall Institute 1915–1965*. Melbourne: Melbourne University Press.

Martin, Randy, Robert J. Mutchnick, and W. Timothy Austin. 1990. *Criminological Thought: Pioneers Past and Present*. New York: Macmillan.

Mayhew, Patricia. 2016. In Defence of Administrative Criminology. *Crime Science* 5 (7): 1–10.

Muirhead, James Henry. 1996. *A Brief Summing Up*. Northbridge: Access Press.

Radzinowicz, Leon. 1965. *The Need for Criminology and a Proposal for an Institute of Criminology*. London: Heinemann.

Robson, John L. 1971. Penal Policy in New Zealand. *Australian and New Zealand Journal of Criminology* 4 (4): 195–206.

Rock, Paul. 1988. *A History of British Criminology*. Oxford: Clarendon Press.

Ryan, Tess. 2017. Australian Critical Race and Whiteness Studies Statement on Border Force Involvement in the 2017 ANZSOC Conference. 8 December. https://acrawsa.org.au/2017/12/08/australian-critical-race-whiteness-studies-statement-on-border-force-involvement-in-the-2017-anzsoc-conference/. Accessed 15 September 2020.

Smith, Russell G., ed. 2021. *The Changing Face of Criminology in Australia and New Zealand*. London: Sage Publications Ltd.

Smith, Russell G. 2017. Public Sector Criminological Research. In *The Palgrave Handbook of Australian and New Zealand Criminology, Crime and Justice*, ed. Antje Deckert and Rick Sarre, 33–49. London: Palgrave Macmillan.

Tanzer, Noel, Des Hill and Grant Wardlaw. 1994. *Review of the Australian Institute of Criminology: Report*. Canberra: Australian Institute of Criminology.

Tonry, Michael. 2010. 'Public Criminology' and Evidence-based Policy. *Criminology and Public Policy* 9 (4): 783–797.

Walston, Catharine, ed. 2009. *Challenging Crime: A Portrait of the Cambridge Institute of Criminology*. London: Third Millennium Publishing Limited.

Whitrod, Ray. 2001. *Before I Sleep: Memoirs of a Modern Police Commissioner*. St Lucia: University of Queensland Press.

Wilson, Paul. 1990. *A Life of Crime*. Newham: Scribe Publications.

Zimring, Franklin E. 1984. Preface. In *The Pursuit of Criminal Justice: Essays from the Chicago Centre*, ed. Gordan Hawkins and Franklin E. Zimring. Chicago: The University of Chicago Press.

2

Public Sector Criminological Research: Objectives and Approaches

The Foundations of Administrative Criminology

Although criminological research in the public sector became more formalised and visible after the Second World War, its roots lay in work carried out by public servants in the nineteenth century (Smith 2017). This early work occurred from the 1820s when official crime statistics first began to appear in France, providing an opportunity to examine relationships between crime and variables such as age, gender, education, occupation and race (Martin et al. 1990). In 1853, the General Statistical Congress was held in Brussels organised by Adolphe Quetelet that called for crime statistics to be collected to permit research to be undertaken of the relationships between demographic and social variables and offending behaviour—particularly for comparative purposes across countries (see Redo 2012, p. 162). Conducting research of this kind required access to groups of potential subjects who could be studied using these new methods, and those working in government were ideally

R. G. Smith, *Public Sector Criminological Research*,
https://doi.org/10.1007/978-3-031-28356-7_2

placed to study prisoners, soldiers and others under public sector control. Cesare Lombroso (1911), for example, an Italian Army physician in the 1860s, was able to study a large cohort of soldiers leading to the development of his atavistic understanding of criminality (Knepper 2018). More recent so-called administrative criminology—that Mike Hough (2018) Emeritus Professor at Birkbeck College within the University of London, called 'a rather irritating term'—displayed some of the hallmarks of Lombroso's work, but nonetheless, occupied public servants for a century and a half—not, however, without criticism. It seems that the term 'administrative' or 'bureaucratic' criminology was first coined by staff at the Home Office who, according to T. S. Lodge had 'the difficult task of maintaining scientific integrity while acting as a servant of the secretary of state' (quoted in Redo 2012, p. 49). Its use became derogatory in the mid-1980s in the hands of Jock Young (Hough 2014). Charles Goring said of Lombroso's research in 1913: 'it is an organised system of self-evident confusion whose parallel is only to be found in the astrology, alchemy and other credulities of the Middle Ages' (Goring 1913, p. 15). Positivism was also rejected because it fitted well into totalitarian patterns of government and could be used to justify racism and engender inequality based on evolutionary principles (Smith 2017, p. 33).

When the Home Office Research Unit (HORU) was established in the 1950s in Britain, it made use of some of the research tools favoured by the positivists—including a heavy reliance on quantitative methods used to analyse official government statistics, rather than theory-based criminology favoured by academic scholars—although the Home Office did commission research by academics as well as conducting its own internal research on a wide scale (see Hough 2014, p. 217). By 1965, 'Home Office grants for criminological research work in universities were worth more than £50,000 a year' (Rock 2019, p. 17).

One of the early internal projects undertaken by the Home Office was the development of the British Crime Survey that was launched in 1981. This survey sought to provide national data on crime trends across England and Wales which was a laudable and novel project at the time for a government research unit to undertake. In 2012, it was renamed the Crime Survey for England and Wales and moved to the Office of

National Statistics—'to remove the spectre of crime statistics seeming to be too much controlled by the government' (Patricia Mayhew, Personal Communication, 21 November 2022). The idea of a national victimisation survey also created a rift with academics who favoured qualitative research that relied on local data collections rather than national surveys conducted by the government. As Mike Hough said in an interview with Ben Bradford in 2018, 'the British Crime Survey was a major achievement and was the first reference point in crime trends at the time' (Hough 2018). He went on to refer to the:

> needless, non-productive gap between government research which was substantially but not entirely quantitative and academic criminology which was much less engaged in policy and much more qualitative.... When Jock Young transformed himself into a New Realist, the Home Office researchers were in competition with the New Realists in using quantitative criminology particularly crime surveys. This led to a spat between the Home Office national survey and local crime surveys.

As a result, academic criminology in Britain disengaged itself from policy-focussed work and became severely critical of 'administrative criminology'. In the words of Morgan and Hough (2007, p. 54):

> It is widely contended, and not just by radical outsiders, that most Home Office-funded criminological research is: almost entirely atheoretical *fact gathering* ...; is *narrowly focussed* – generally on a recent spending or administrative initiative or piece of legislation; and is designed to be, and in its final product invariably is, *policy-friendly.*

Pat Mayhew (2016, p. 9—Plate 2.1) mounted a robust defence to these charges when she received the Stockholm Prize in Criminology with Professor Ronald V. Clarke in 2015, concluding that 'administrative criminologists working *with* government may have a more effective voice than those who simply choose to shout at the side lines'. Interestingly, another Stockholm Prize winner, Jan van Dyk, who is perhaps the quintessential international administrative criminologist, undertook a study early in his career which found that 'in-house research has more

Plate 2.1 Patricia Mayhew OBE, 18 October 2001 (*Source* AIC Archives)

impact on decision-making in government than research conducted by outsiders' (van Dijk 2004, p. 72).

Pat Mayhew was, formerly, the Deputy Head of the Crime and Criminal Justice Unit at the Home Office, and later the Director of the Crime and Justice Research Centre at the Victoria University of Wellington in New Zealand between 2004 and 2008. Shortly before this, she had spent 18 months at the AIC working as a consultant and advising the AICs research staff on a range of projects—including the application of methodologies used at the Home Office in national crime surveys and the calculation of costs of crime. She described her experience at the AIC working on the costs of crime project as 'a technical nightmare and I am trying to forget the bill' (Mayhew 2004, p. 62). The argument of those such as Mayhew and her colleagues that 'criminology is an applied discipline that needs to be engaged with policy' (Hough 2018) was certainly taken on board by those who offered advice when the AIC was being established and continues to underpin its rationale and operations today.

Interestingly, as Rick Brown recalled in his Interview (10 June 2022) 'the negative connotations that came with being an administrative criminologist, were worse in Australia than in the United Kingdom, at that time'. As a result, AIC staff now prefer calling themselves 'applied criminologists' (Anthony Morgan, Interview, 17 November 2022). Sir Leon Radzinowicz (1973, n.p.) commented in his report to the Australian Government shortly after the AIC was established: 'one of the major objectives of the Australian Institute is to act as a centre for information relating to criminological thought, penal policy, and the working of the administration of criminal justice'. Over time, difficult questions had to be addressed about not only the policy-relevant content of the AICs research, but also the research methods most suitable to achieve it—and the level of funding provided to ensure that it was capable of achieving its objectives. As Radzinowicz observed in his autobiography, *Adventures in Criminology* (1999, p. 406):

> The [AIC] had been set up as an independent entity. It was hoped that it would establish good relations with the academic world as well as with the Federal Ministry of Justice. But in practice the connection with the ministry was becoming dominant... This arrangement did not seem to be working as smoothly as had originally been anticipated and there was concern in several influential quarters.

Public Sector Criminological Research Prior to 1972

Prior to the establishment of the AIC in 1972, criminological research in Australia was still in its infancy with most work being undertaken within University departments whose principal focus was not criminology but the more established disciplines of law, medicine, sociology, psychology, psychiatry, politics and economics, among others. The result was a lack of integrated, cross-disciplinary work and an absence of unified approaches to understanding the causes and extent of crime, how to reduce its incidence and how to minimise the harms arising from offending. In

Australia, the first attempts to establish dedicated University departments devoted to criminological research and teaching took place at the Universities of Melbourne and Sydney in the early 1950s—with both being promoted largely by legal academics but closely aligned with criminal justice practitioners, particularly from the courts and correctional agencies.

At the University of Melbourne, criminological research first appeared with the appointment of Dr Anita Muhl, a Jungian psychotherapist, as a visiting lecturer in criminology in 1938—arguably the first time the term 'criminology' had been used to designate an academic position in Australia (Finnane 2012). During her three years at the University, Dr Muhl delivered lectures to Professor George Paton's jurisprudence students in the Law School as well as to members of the Medico-legal Society of Victoria—thus raising the profile of criminology as a fledgling discipline in Melbourne at the time (Finnane 2012). Paton had discussed the idea of establishing criminology as a discipline at the University of Melbourne with another member of the Medico-legal Society of Victoria, the barrister John Vincent Barry, in the early 1940s—around the same time that a Department of Criminal Science within the Faculty of Law at Cambridge University had been created through the efforts of Cecil Turner and Leon Radzinowicz (Walston 2009, p. 16).

Radzinowicz had studied Law as an undergraduate student at the University of Paris in 1924–1925 and at the University of Geneva in 1925–1927. In 1928, he received a Doctor of Law degree from the Institute of Criminology in Rome following which he received a doctorate from the University of Kraków. After undertaking postdoctoral work in Belgium, he went to Cambridge as Assistant Director of Research in Criminal Science in 1936 and later became inaugural Director of the Cambridge Institute of Criminology—a post which he held from its foundation until his retirement in 1973 (Cottee 2005)—shortly after the AIC was established in Canberra.

Developments in the creation of criminology as a discipline in both Melbourne and Cambridge followed similar paths—with both centres being championed by legal academics but having close connections with medico-legal practitioners and public sector officials within criminal justice departments of government. Finding a suitable home for such a discipline raised many difficult questions as Finnane (1998, p. 71) observed:

> In struggles over the proper academic location of criminology which reverberate down the years at Melbourne, the standing of criminology as a department outside the Law Faculty was a matter of contention.

Similar issues were being debated in Britain in the 1950s where arguments were advanced for criminology to be located either at the London School of Economics and Political Science (LSE), ensuring that London's crime problem could be examined within ear-shot of Whitehall, or at Cambridge where the crime problem was minimal but enthusiasm for the idea among scholars was great. In time, the Home Office agreed for the Institute of Criminology to be based in Cambridge within the Faculty of Law and having Radzinowicz as the Foundation Wolfson Professor of Criminology (Walston 2009, p. 17).

Other institutions undertaking criminological research at the time in Britain included the Institute for the Study and Treatment of Delinquency, set up in 1931, and the HORU founded in 1957. These two centres, along with the departments at the LSE and in Cambridge, all followed what Cottee (2005) described as Radzinowicz's 'socially liberal' approach of 'humanitarian reform of the criminal justice system, underpinned by the empirical findings of social scientific research' (at p. 205). This idea also took hold in Australia at the time, with the supporters of the criminological institutions in Melbourne, Sydney and later in Canberra at the AIC, all following Radzinowicz's approach. The close involvement of lawyers and public officials, however, was not without its critics, although Radzinowicz strenuously defended his position that criminology was not positivist and that the Cambridge model required independence from government (see the account of this debate by Cottee 2005 and Radzinowicz's (1965) own account—Plate 2.2).

In Melbourne, the resolution of the question of the disciplinary location of criminology was side-stepped somewhat by creating a Board of Studies in Criminology at the University of Melbourne in March 1951 (Morris 1952)—rather than by having any one Faculty in control of

Plate 2.2 Professor Leon Radzinowicz addressing the 2nd UN Crime Congress, 8 September 1960 at Church House, Westminster, London (*Source* UN Photo/EA—UN7514693)

the institution. The aim was to enable a number of different disciplines to contribute to teaching and research with the enterprise being managed by a Board and the daily work undertaken by a small academic staff working in conjunction with external staff based in other departments. The composition of the Board was novel with Sir John Barry, Justice of the Supreme Court, as its Chair, Professor of Psychology, Oscar Oesler, as Vice-Chair and members including the Vice-Chancellor, Sir George Paton, Dean of Law, Sir Zelman Cowan, Head of Social Studies, Ruth Hoban, psychiatrist, Donald Buckle and academic lawyer, Norval Morris, as Board Secretary. This multi-disciplinary approach was novel at the time, but was likely to satisfy most of the interested parties. In a recent paper to mark the 50th anniversary of ANZSOC, the late Philip

Cummins (2021) identified the primary suspects involved in establishing the Melbourne discipline as 'the Wig' (Sir John Barry), 'the Gown' (Professor Norval Morris) and 'the Stethoscope' (Dr Allen Bartholomew, Psychiatrist at Pentridge Prison). As Morris (1952, p. 12) observed, the Melbourne Department's aim was 'to combine the knowledge of the lawyer, the psychiatrist, the psychologist, and the sociologist'—thus avoiding the criticism by those such as Carson and O'Malley (1989, p. 334) that criminology (and later the AIC) was a child of the law, demonstrating 'unreflective correctionalism, unexplicated positivism and unswerving conservatism'.

Evidence for the multi-disciplinary nature of criminology at the time can be seen in the occupational composition of the members of ANZSOC that was established in Melbourne in October 1967. By 1970, the membership list of ANZSOC showed that almost one-quarter of its members worked in corrections or the probation service, while almost one-fifth had academic appointments. Lawyers and judges made up a further 16 percent with many of these having a keen interest in the social context of the law and law reform generally. Others came from the private sector and various government departments (Smith 2021, p. 6). Simply because the supporters of criminology worked as legal practitioners or judges did not mean that they were uncritical of the law and the functioning of the criminal justice system. Barry's own academic writing, such as his treatises, *Alexander Maconochie of Norfolk Island* (Barry 1958) and *The Life and Death of John Price* (Barry 1964), are clear examples of a reformist judge at work. Over time, the membership of ANZSOC changed considerably, with the vast majority now being academics or students. In 2022, very few practising lawyers were members of ANZSOC. Indeed, as Gordon Hawkins (1990, p. 12) observed, 'for most members of the legal profession, criminology was, and continues by many, to be regarded as a dilettantish and useless pursuit, rather than a serious subject of study'. The Cambridge legal academic, Cecil Turner, similarly observed: 'criminologists were looked upon with greater suspicion than criminals' (Walston 2009, p. 37), while in China at the time, 'criminology, along with other social sciences, was formally declared as "bourgeois pseudo science" and abolished' by the

Communist Party that believed that social issues should be studied from a Marxist perspective (Hebenton and Jou 2018, p. 380).

Carson and O'Malley's (1989, p. 335) assertion that the Melbourne Department was originally 'tied to the legal profession' fails to acknowledge that the original Board of Studies and its staff had representatives from psychology, social studies, psychiatry, social welfare and sociology as well as the legal profession, courts and police. The early Diploma in Criminology course had subject offerings not only from the Law School, but also from psychology, social welfare and included basic criminological subjects such as research methods, the causes of crime and crime prevention (University of Melbourne 1962). This reflected the approach taken in Cambridge as John Seymour reflected on his time undertaking the Diploma of Criminology in 1966:

> In retrospect, it was an old-fashioned course – a lot of criminological theory, the causes of crime (such as maternal deprivation). What benefited me most was the discussion of the criminal justice system and the opportunity to explore current issues in juvenile justice. The course was also very strong on methodology. A most valuable feature was the organisation of visits to prisons and training schools. An attachment to a probation officer was rewarding. (John Seymour, Interview, 14 November 2022)

In Sydney, the creation of an Institute of Criminology was 'the brain child of Professor Kenneth Shatwell, Dean of the University of Sydney Law School from 1947 to 1973' (Hawkins 1990, p. 9). This Institute began work in the mid-1960s with the appointment of three lecturers including Gordon Hawkins, recruited by Shatwell from the English Prison Service in 1960 (Harding 2004) and Duncan Chappell who was appointed Lecturer in Criminal Law and Criminology in December 1965, and who, two decades later, became Director of the AIC. Of importance was the other appointment made in October 1964 of Paul Ward as Lecturer in Statistics—emphasising the need for quantitative research in the Institute. Although the Sydney Institute was created within the Law School, its Advisory Committee, established in May

1965, included members with close ties to the New South Wales government including the Minister of Justice, the Attorney-General and the Solicitor-General—as well as the Chief Justice and Commissioner of Police and representatives from psychology, psychiatry, social work, sociology and addiction studies. As Hawkins (1990, p. 10), observed: 'the cultivation of this kind of extra-mural support was both politically astute and essential as there was no great interest in, nor sense of a need for criminological studies, either in the Faculty of Law or elsewhere'. Gordon Hawkins (Plate 2.3) adhered to Radzinowicz's approach to criminology arguing that it should be evidence-based rather than demonstrating 'theory tottering on stilts of sparse facts and gratuitous assumptions' (cited by Harding 2004, p. 318). Hawkins died on 29 February 2004 after a lengthy and productive career as a criminologist working within a Faculty of Law (Woods 2004). As in Melbourne, the Sydney Institute's work was clearly inter-disciplinary, with both Institutes providing a state-based, public sector criminological resource.

The Need for National Crime Statistics

Although criminology was emerging as a discipline in Australian Universities in the 1960s, the needs of public sector policy-makers were still far from being satisfied. Exposing a small coterie of graduates from the major universities to the basic principles of criminology was a good start to informing governments of the challenges of addressing crime problems, but much more was needed in terms of expanding the research and evidence base needed for effective policy development. In particular, there remained a pressing need for the collection and analysis of crime statistics at a national level.

In Europe in the nineteenth century, criminology had its foundations in the collection of government administrative statistics, as we have seen, but in federal countries such as Australia, the collection of crime statistics was dispersed across jurisdictions, with policies and procedures for uniform data collection and analysis not yet developed. As Alvazzi del Frate (2012, p. 167) noted in her review of the quest for harmonisation of global crime statistics, 'the international community, almost

Plate 2.3 Gordon Hawkins (1919–2004), Director, Sydney Institute of Criminology (*Source* Woods (2004, p. 1) Photo by Michal Zimring)

two centuries after Quetelet's initial efforts, is still struggling to achieve internationally comparable data on crime'.

The result was that the evidence base for developing theories of crime and policies for addressing criminality was inadequate for both academic scholars and public sector policy-makers. In Australia, simple comparisons between patterns of offending in the various states and territories could not easily be made, trends in boutique crime types unable to be charted and the numbers of individuals dealt with by different criminal justice agencies often unknown. As Graycar and Grabosky (2002,

p. 11) observed, state and territory crime statistics 'were not good indicators of actual levels of crime, as what was included and excluded reflected changing interests and priorities over time, as well as inconsistent recording methods'. At the time, the Australian Bureau of Statistics (ABS) had only limited capabilities to coordinate the administrative datasets collected by criminal justice agencies across the country, and the population surveys conducted by the ABS failed to address crime victimisation except in the most general of ways.

The 1960s was also a time of many social changes, some of which led to concerns over increasing patterns of offending. Police jurisdictions throughout Australia collected data on the number of offences coming to the attention of the police, but only selected offence categories were included, and it was not known how many offences took place that were not reported officially. In addition, it was not always known which matters were solved by police, and the proportion that led to prosecution, conviction and punishment. The need for national crime statistics was clear:

> Crime statistics have been used and abused in the past to suit a variety of interests. Across the country policy decisions have been made, laws have been drafted and immense sums of money have been invested on the basis of information which could only have been fragmentary and has generally lacked perspective. (Clifford 1981, p. v)

By way of example, the official statistics collected by police for the decade prior to the establishment of the AIC, showed that all of the principal offence numbers reported to police increased substantially—we know this due to the efforts of the AIC which published a major statistical compilation of crime statistics in the early 1980s (Mukherjee 1981). Before this, it was a difficult task to understand crime trends across the country as some datasets were incomplete, while analysis was needed to provide an understanding of whether the increase in crime was due to changes in its actual incidence or due to other factors such as changes in population demographics, the economy or social behaviour. When Radzinowicz was asked to visit Australia in 1973, his criminological expertise was sought not only by government policy-makers, but even by the popular media. Described by his former student, John Seymour (Interview 14 November 2022) as 'colourful and a great performer and self-promoter', Radzinowicz was interviewed, shortly before coming to Australia, by the *Australian Women's Weekly* at 'his charming house set in a leafy garden' in Cambridge, on why the crime rate among women and girls was rapidly rising, and if this was due to 'Women's Lib'. Sir Leon's explanation referred to the need for better crime statistics—that the creation of an Australian Institute of Criminology could provide (Boys 1973, pp. 4–5).

The Role of Dedicated Crime Statistics Agencies

In order to address these problems, governments in some countries decided that dedicated public sector-funded agencies needed to be created to improve the standard of research and information available on crime and justice. In Australia, as in many other countries, a national statistical agency had been created to manage the collection and dissemination of statistics on all matters of interest to governments—including some aspects of crime and justice. Prior to Australia's federation, that took place in 1901, each jurisdiction in Australia was responsible for collecting its own statistics, leading to problems of inconsistency and lack of coordination in the data collected. As Graycar and Grabosky (2002, pp. 10–11) noted:

> The first Commonwealth Year Book [in 1908] lamented the fact that Australia's statistical collections were not uniform. It noted that 'without uniformity there is no safety in statistics' and that since 'comparisons are valueless unless the data compared are of the same type, it by no means infrequently happens that aggregates are formed from, or comparisons made with, dissimilar data'. This warning is still made at the start of the twenty-first century, and it has only been since 1993 that Australia has had crime statistics that can in any way be described as uniform.

In response to these problems, the Commonwealth Bureau of Census and Statistics (CBCS) was established by the *Census and Statistics Act 1905* (Cth), although state statistical offices continued in various forms until they were unified in the late 1950s (ABS 2005, p. 3). In 1973, the ABS was created as a statutory authority within the Commonwealth Treasury Portfolio.

The ABS was, and remains, responsible for major data collections such as the national census, and, in addition to the collection of statistics relating to the economy, housing, society and business activities, some crime-related data were compiled—coming mainly from state criminal justice agency collections. In addition, the ABS conducted various surveys relating to specific aspects of crime victimisation as part of its crime and safety survey, including the Women's Safety Survey conducted first in 1996 and the Personal Safety Survey since 2005. In her interview for the current study, Fiona Dowsley, the current AIC Advisory Council Member for Victoria, and former ABS employee, noted that:

> The ABS has really great powers around data collection, but because of that it's very tight on access to data – it's very good at providing stable, consistent, foundational datasets for putting together the national picture but if you're looking to produce some sophisticated analysis of the data it's very difficult. (Fiona Dowsley, Interview, 8 December 2020—Plate 2.4)

These views were reiterated by Peter Grabosky in his interview (3 December 2020):

> The ABS was extremely protective of its respondents. They have ethical considerations that they took very seriously, and would not release data to individual researchers... The logistics of negotiating the bureaucracy in gaining access to unit record data was off the agenda for years–I don't think it ever came back on the agenda. I gave up after a while.

Although the statistics collected by the ABS are made available to governments for policy purposes, analysis and commentary were generally undertaken by academics and consultants—hence the need for access to unit record data. It was not until the 1990s that the ABS undertook a major review of its social statistics (including crime and justice

Plate 2.4 Fiona Dowsley, Chief Statistician, Crime Statistics Agency, Victoria, 2014 (*Source* Fiona Dowsley)

data) leading to the establishment of national centres, including the Melbourne-based National Centre for Crime and Justice Statistics in 1996—where Fiona Dowsley had worked (ABS 2005, p. 134). The National Centre was created through the amalgamation of the National Crime Statistics Unit, the National Criminal Courts Statistics Unit and the National Corrective Services Statistics Unit. Statistics were recorded for victim characteristics, matters heard in the criminal courts and correctional statistics.

Despite this attempt to create a national resource, not everyone was happy with the outcome. Economist, and former AIC researcher, John Walker, in his Interview, for example, observed:

When the ABS took over the collection and publication of correctional statistics, they restricted access of researchers to the raw database, cut the scope of tabulations presented in their reports and took a far longer time to produce the published results. Their product may have been of greater statistical integrity than what the AIC had been producing but even the perfect statistic is useless if it is not timely, and they cut many tabulations such as number of prisoners by age, sex and Aboriginality that have immense policy implications. Until the ABSs head, Denis Trewin, made ABS publications free of charge, they also charged for the data. (John Walker, Interview, 30 November 2020)

In the 1960s, however, states and territories found that their statistical needs were not being satisfied and so dedicated state crime statistics agencies were created, beginning with the New South Wales Bureau of Crime Statistics and Research (BOCSAR) established in Sydney in 1969 by Dr Tony Vinson. Vinson, who died in 2017, set up the Bureau to identify factors that affect the distribution and frequency of crime in New South Wales; to identify factors that affect the effectiveness, efficiency or equity of the New South Wales criminal justice system and to ensure that information on these factors and on crime and justice trends is available and accessible to its clients (New South Wales Bureau of Crime Statistics and Research 2016). He worked alongside Ross Homel and Adam Sutton as Research Officers—both of whom went on to have successful careers in criminology—with Adam Sutton later becoming Director of the South Australian Office of Crime Statistics & Research in 1982. Adam, who died in September 2010, was also the South Australian representative on the AICs Board and Criminology Research Council (CRC) between 1984 and 1995 (Plate 2.5). Adam Sutton was an example of a criminologist who bridged the gap between public sector policy-related work and the academic world. As Professor Fiona Haines wrote in his obituary (2010, p. 613), 'he eschewed a critical criminology that resulted only in the denunciation of authority, and argued that the criminologist must work with authorities to develop programs that could be effective in preventing crime'.

The South Australian Office of Crime Statistics (later the Office of Crime Statistics and Research—OCSAR) was established within the Attorney-General's Department in 1978. Peter Grabosky recalled in his interview (2 December 2020) that Greg Woods, who at the time was teaching criminology and criminal law in the Faculty of Law at Sydney University, spent a year in Adelaide as Ministerial Adviser to the Dunstan Labor government. Among the many socially-progressive reforms of

Plate 2.5 Associate Professor Adam Sutton (1950–2010) (*Source* Alessandra Daly-Sutton)

that government, Greg Woods convinced Dunstan that an organisation like BOCSAR was needed in South Australia—leading to the establishment of OCSAR shortly before Dunstan resigned in 1979 due to ill health. OCSAR was responsible for research into and the monitoring of crime trends and the criminal justice system within South Australia. Like BOCSAR, it sought to provide timely, accurate and comprehensive statistical evidence on crime and criminal justice; to conduct research into crime and criminal justice issues; and to disseminate information on crime and criminal justice to government, members of parliament, relevant agencies and the community.

The Office was, however, provided with only a small staff—initially comprising Peter Grabosky, as its foundation director, and a receptionist—owing to a freeze on hiring staff in the South Australian public sector. Interestingly, when Grabosky joined the AIC in 1983 (Plate 2.6), there was also a Commonwealth cap on the number of staff positions at the AIC, and Peter's position was able to be created with the loss of

Plate 2.6 Dr Peter Grabosky, at the AIC, 2001 (*Source* AIC Archives)

a clerical assistant's position (AIC Board Minutes, 25 November 1983, p. 3). In South Australia, the government at the time was in a fluid state as Grabosky recalled in 2004: 'in my first fourteen months there (July 1978 to September 1979), I served (and survived) four successive Attorneys-General and two governments' (Grabosky 2004, p. 19). Nonetheless, Grabosky and his colleagues 'succeeded in establishing the first computer-based system of statistics from lower criminal courts anywhere in Australia, and I chaired an interdepartmental committee on crime victims that charted a course for victim policy in Australia' (Grabosky 2004, p. 19). After Peter left the Office in 1979, it continued with a small staff until it was closed in 2016 with its functions moved to the South Australia Police and Data.SA—the South Australian Government Data Directory. The Directors of OCSAR after Grabosky included Adam Sutton and Joy Wundersitz—both of whom served on the AICs Board of Management—Sutton from 1984 to 1995 and Wundersitz from 1995 to 2006.

In Victoria, prior to 2014, crime statistics had principally been collected by Victoria Police, with a variety of other state agencies, including the Department of Justice, collecting agency-relevant data for their own purposes. For example, crime-related data are collected by and used in connection with the work of Victorian Parliamentary Committees dealing with law reform, road safety, drug control and crime prevention.

After many years of controversy over the handling of crime statistics, matters came to a head in 2011 when Victoria Police released incomplete and misleading data on the eve of the 2010 state election claiming that assaults in the city of Melbourne had declined by 27.5 percent between the July–September quarter 2010 compared to the July–September quarter in 2009 without qualification, based on yet to be validated data—with clear political implications. The Victorian Ombudsman investigated the matter and recommended that 'the Victorian Government create an independent body to manage, collate and disseminate crime statistics' (Brouwer 2011, p. 31). This was an attempt to solve the problem that former AIC Director, Michael Phelan, described as police 'marking their own homework'. Phelan took the view that although criminal justice agencies could collect data, the collation and analysis needed to be done independently (Michael Phelan, Interview, 3 November 2022). After the Ombudsman's report was released, the Chief Commissioner of Police resigned, and after further debate, a new independent Crime Statistics Agency was created by the *Crime Statistics Act 2014* (Vic), at a cost of $8.4 million, with Fiona Dowsley as its Chief Statistician (ABC News 2014; Rance 2015). The Victorian agency's work has been focussed more on gathering and presenting crime statistics than undertaking critical analysis of the data and integrating data with the academic literature for policy purposes.

Western Australia has been the most recent jurisdiction to create a dedicated crime statistics agency in 2020. In the 1980s, and prior to that, the collection of crime statistics was poorly managed leading the Attorney-General and Minister for Prisons at the time, Joe Berinson, to obtain funding of $4 million to create a Crime Research Centre within the Faculty of Arts, Business, Law and Education at the University of Western Australia. After Richard Harding resigned as Director of the AIC in 1987, he was appointed head of the Centre in 1989 and worked to establish the Integrated Numerical Offender Identification System (INOIS) that attracted strong interest internationally. It was one of the most sophisticated data-linking models in the world, providing accurate and detailed statistical data for the long-term study of criminal careers and the evaluation of criminal justice programs (Richard Harding, Interview, 18 November 2021). In 2014, however, the Western Australian government decided to manage crime statistics internally, and the Crime Research Centre was dissolved.

It was not until 2020, that the Western Australian government decided to establish its own Office of Crime Statistics and Research within the Department of Justice. Like some other state agencies, it was set up to provide a whole-of-sector research and evaluation function for the state's crime and justice system. It was also created to provide a policy-relevant research and analytics function to lead initiatives aimed at translating research outcomes into evidence-based law reform and justice initiatives throughout the justice sector. It also administers an annual research grants program that funds research to make a practical contribution to improving the effectiveness of the criminal justice system in Western Australia, and most recently, has taken over the AICs Drug Use Monitoring Australia (DUMA) data collection for Western Australia. This clearly duplicates many of the aims and functions of the AIC—which is not surprising given that the current Director-General of the Department is Dr Adam Tomison, the AICs former Director from 2009 to 2015, and the current Chair of the AICs Advisory Council. Interestingly, when Richard Harding left the Institute as its Director in 1987, he also returned to Perth and sought 'to replicate for Western Australia some of the stuff I'd done in Canberra' (Harding 2015, Interview with Julia Wallis, 8 April 2015).

The Commonwealth government has also shown a willingness to establish other dedicated research institutions to examine a variety of criminal justice-related matters. In addition to the AIC, the Australian Institute of Health and Welfare (AIHW) was established as a statutory authority in 1987 to report to the nation on the state of its health. In 1992, the role and functions of the then Australian Institute of Health were expanded to include welfare-related information and statistics. During its existence, the AIHW has examined a range of crime-related topics including drug abuse, child protection, homelessness, Indigenous disadvantage and youth justice issues. In his interview

(14 November 2022), John Seymour noted the impressive performance of the AIHW due in part to its generous government funding and large staff numbers.

The other principal Commonwealth research agency with functions relevant to crime and justice is the Australian Institute of Family Studies (AIFS) that seeks to increase understanding of factors affecting how Australian families function. The Institute was established in February 1980 and some of its criminological research has related to child protection, family and sexual violence prevention and gambling addiction, through the Australian Gambling Research Centre.

Considerable policy-focussed research has also been conducted by anti-corruption commissions in Australia. The New South Wales Independent Commission Against Corruption (ICAC) was the first anti-corruption agency created in Australia in 1989 and, in addition to investigating alleged corruption, has employed criminologists to conduct research into the nature, extent and prevention of corruption. The other states have also established anti-corruption commissions with varying jurisdictional scope since 2002. There are also dedicated police anti-corruption agencies such as the New South Wales Police Integrity Commission (PIC) that was created in 1996 on the recommendation of the Royal Commission into the New South Wales Police Service, and the South Australian Office for Public Integrity (OPI) that commenced in 2013. At the Commonwealth level, anti-corruption research and research into misconduct in the public sector have been carried out by the Office of the Integrity Commissioner, the Australian Commission for Law Enforcement Integrity, the Australian Public Service Commission, the Commonwealth Ombudsman, the Australian Federal Police and, of course, the AIC and the ACIC. Following the election of the Labor government in May 2022, a Bill to establish a National Anti-Corruption Commission was introduced in September 2022 with investigatory functions but no dedicated research functions contained in the Bill.

Clearly, there are now multiple public sector agencies with an interest in compiling crime-related statistical information. As Fiona Dowsley observed:

> I think that the days of one organisation having the full remit for those
> kinds of statistical collections are well past us. We've been working in
> a very disaggregated statistical system for a good few decades now, and
> I don't see it contracting back – if anything the number of organisa-
> tions holding, organising, releasing data about the criminal justice system
> is expanding, not contracting. (Fiona Dowsley, Interview. 8 December
> 2020)

The difficulty that was present in the 1960s, however, particularly owing
to Australia's federal system of government, was that there was no independent, uniform crime statistics agency at the national level to service
the needs of all jurisdictions, including the Commonwealth government—thus creating an impetus for the establishment of the AIC. As
we shall see below, determining the division of functions between the
AIC and the ABS concerning crime statistics would be difficult and a
problem that would remain to the present time. Former AIC Director,
Adam Graycar, in his interview observed that 'data is the glue that holds
it all together.... I fought very hard to get a good relationship with the
ABS but sometimes it was nearly impossible because they were so rigid'
(Adam Graycar, Interview, 1 March 2021). The questions to resolve
were—who is best equipped and resourced to collect raw crime statistics
(including official criminal justice data and crime victimisation survey
data), and who should be responsible for analysing those datasets, inter-
preting the findings and adding value by integrating the results with the
broader academic and policy literature? Throughout the AICs history,
there have been different views expressed on these questions by members
of the Boards, directors, academics and in the many reviews of the AICs
work. In his interview (14 November 2022), John Seymour encapsulated
the question as follows: 'a Commonwealth agency has an important role
to collect and prepare good statistics but the question is—what do you
do with them?' One of the AICs current Research Managers, Anthony
Morgan, provided an answer to this question (Interview 17 November
2022):

The AIC has a role in adding value to collections through interpretation, analysis and re-analysis of data, ideally at a national level. Our role as criminologists should be to do something with the data that goes above and beyond just reporting numbers.

International Approaches

Internationally, a number of different approaches have been adopted with respect to the location and functions of public sector criminological research activities. Australia was heavily influenced by the model adopted in Britain in which the Home Office was given responsibility for conducting national assessments of crime including the use of large scale, crime victimisation surveys that were novel at the time, but required substantial financing—that the government in the UK was able to provide (see Rock 2019). Some states in Australia, such as New South Wales and much later Western Australia, took up the idea of creating local Institutes of Criminology, located mainly within Faculties of Law—along the lines of the Cambridge Institute and the Centre of Criminology in Toronto that was established in 1963 as a research and graduate teaching institution. In 2011, the Centre in Toronto was renamed the Centre for Criminology and Sociolegal Studies (2022) and is now located within the Faculty of Arts and Science. In Australia, only BOCSAR in New South Wales has really thrived and been able to survive throughout the decades, although newer centres such as those in Victoria and Western Australia are fulfilling some of these functions.

The role of national statistical agencies to collect criminal justice data has been tried in some countries but not always found to be successful—partially due to lack of adequate funding, but also due to difficulties in finding staff with sufficient depth of knowledge both to collect data and to interpret the research findings. In the UK, the US, Canada and the EU, the collection and publication of crime statistics have had variable levels of success—particularly concerning boutique crime types such as white collar crime, transnational crime and cybercrime to name a few. Efforts by the UNODC have also been limited—although the International Crime Victimisation Survey (ICVS) developed by Jan van Dijk (2004) has had success, despite delays in publication during some waves (see van Kesteren 2014). The UN's more important contribution to public sector criminology has been to create the PNI that links crime and justice research institutes throughout the regions of the world—of which the AIC is one long-standing member (see Chapter 13 below). The UNs greatest contribution to improving crime statistics internationally has, arguably, been through its role in creating Conventions and Treaties, such as those relating to Transnational Organized Crime, Corruption, Illicit Drugs and Terrorism that include requirements for signatories to collect and share crime data relating to their specific subject-matter. Again, these have continued to improve the collection of crime statistics over the preceding five decades.

In the US, the NIJ was established in 1968 as the research, development and evaluation agency of the Department of Justice (see Muhlhausen 2019). It began with 35 employees and a budget of US$2.5 million and arose from recommendations in President Lyndon Johnson's Commission on Law Enforcement and the Administration of Justice that reported in 1967 that asserted the need for national research into crime (President's Commission 1967). Its main focus has been to administer a grants program for academic research into crime and justice—with the NIJ setting priorities for the types of research to be conducted. It also keeps a database of the datasets that have resulted from funded projects. The Bureau of Justice Statistics (BJS), within the United States Department of Justice, was established in 1979 to collect, analyse, publish and disseminate information on crime, criminal offenders, victims of crime and the operation of justice systems at all levels of government. This is essentially the crime statistics agency of the US.

Canada has adopted a variety of approaches with Statistics Canada having responsibility for the collection of crime and justice statistics nationally, and two public sector research institutes being affiliated with the UNODC (see Chapter 13, below). In Vancouver, the International Centre for Criminal Law Reform and Criminal Justice Policy (ICCLR&CJP) is an independent, non-profit institute founded in 1991 that focusses on technical co-operation, research, training and advisory services in the field of criminal law, criminal justice policy and crime prevention. It is a joint initiative of the Government of Canada, the

University of British Columbia, Simon Fraser University, the International Society for the Reform of Criminal Law and the Province of British Columbia and, as such, is a hybrid model with national, provincial, public sector and academic elements that focus on legal rather than strictly criminological research.

Canada also has the International Center for the Prevention of Crime (ICPC) that was founded in 1994 in Montreal with both public sector and non-government elements focussing on crime prevention and community safety research. It, too, is affiliated with the United Nations PNI. Even with these various research agencies, there remain gaps in both statistical collections and criminological commentary on crime trends throughout Canada.

There are also various international research and policy institutes affiliated with governments that seek to coordinate the collection and dissemination of crime data. In 2011, for example, the UNODC (2011) inaugurated the Centre of Excellence for Crime Statistics on Governance, Victims of Crime, Public Security and Justice, based in Mexico. This seeks to develop field surveys, share knowledge in the area of crime statistics and organises an annual international conference on statistics—that the AIC has participated in. It has also sought to upgrade the methods used to generate statistics and provide policy-makers in the region with tools to address challenges relating to public security and justice.

Conclusions

This chapter has provided a short review of the development of some public sector criminological research agencies established over the preceding five decades to demonstrate the need for criminological research within government agencies. It has shown that similar drivers existed for the creation of criminological research institutes in Australia and internationally—all of which were created largely in response to perceptions of an increase in the incidence of crime but concern that the level of knowledge about crime and its control was seriously deficient. In particular, the concern over the inadequacy of national crime statistics led to various attempts by governments to control and improve data collection—that would then enable research to be conducted to understand changing trends in crime and how best to respond to emerging problem areas. It also explored the models adopted in different locations for criminological institutes and their relationship to research conducted in academic institutions and private sector organisations. Consideration was also given to understanding the origins of the antipathy that some, but by no means all (Fishwick and Marmo 2018, p. 330), believe still exists between public sector 'administrative' researchers, and academics based in universities in terms of their aims, relationship to public policy outcomes and research methodologies founded in empirically based quantitative, qualitative or theoretically-founded analysis of crime and justice concerns. It seems that never the twain shall meet.

The next chapter explores how this need for criminological research in the public sector was dealt with in Australia in the 1960s—leading to the establishment of the AIC in 1972—and whether the institutional model adopted was appropriate to meet the stated objectives, considering the funding available, and the needs that arose from satisfying competing interests of stakeholders in a federal system of government.

References

ABC News. 2014, March 25. New Independent Crime Statistics Agency To Be Set Up, ABC News. http://www.abc.net.au/news/2014-03-25/new-independent-crime-statistics-agency-to-be-set-up/5342900 Accessed 22 April 2022.

Alvazzi del Frate, Anna. 2012. Statistical Analysis and the United Nations Crime Trends Surveys as Capacity Building, in Redo, Slawomir M. 2012. *Blue Criminology: The Power of United Nations Ideas to Counter Crime Globally: A Monographic Study*, 163–167, HEUNI Publication Series No. 72, Helsinki: HEUNI. https://heuni.fi/documents/47074104/0/Blue_Criminology_www_linked.pdf/0013989d-f932-25ab-ec52-5f21884da6d3/Blue_Criminology_www_linked.pdf?t=1610010139161. Accessed 23 August 2022.

Australian Bureau of Statistics (ABS). 2005. *Informing a Nation: The Evolution of the Australian Bureau of Statistics 1905–2005*, Cat. No. 1382.0. Canberra:

Australian Bureau of Statistics. https://www.ausstats.abs.gov.au/ausstats/subscriber.nsf/0/A8B7911F73578F1ACA2570AA00750101/$File/13820_2005.pdf. Accessed 20 April 2022.

Barry, John Vincent. 1964. *The Life and Death of John Price: A Study of the Exercise of Naked Power.* Melbourne: Melbourne University Press.

Barry, John Vincent. 1958. *Alexander Maconochie of Norfolk Island: A Study of the Pioneer in Penal Reform.* Melbourne: Oxford University Press.

Boys, Harry. 1973. Equality of the Sexes in Crime Too? *The Australian Women's Weekly*, 27 June, pp. 4–5. https://trove.nla.gov.au/newspaper/article/46242128/4975821 Accessed 20 April 2022.

Brouwer, George E. 2011. Investigation into an Allegation about Victoria Police Crime Statistics, Victorian Ombudsman Parliamentary Reports No. 5, Melbourne: Victorian Ombudsman. http://www7.austlii.edu.au/au/other/VicOmbPRp/2011/5.html Accessed 22 April 2022.

Carson, Kit, and Pat O'Malley. 1989. The Institutional Foundations of Contemporary Australian Criminology. *Australian and New Zealand Journal of Sociology* 25 (3): 333–355.

Centre for Criminology and Sociolegal Studies. 2022. Our History, https://www.crimsl.utoronto.ca/about-us/our-department/our-history Accessed 31 October 2022.

Clifford, William. 1981. Foreword. In *Source Book of Australian Criminal and Social Statistics 1900*–1980, ed. Satyanshu K. Mukherjee, Evelyn N. Jacobsen and John R. Walker, p. v. Canberra: Australian Institute of Criminology.

Cottee, Simon. 2005. Sir Leon's Shadow. *Theoretical Criminology* 9 (2): 203–225, 1362–4806.

Cummins, Philip D. 2021. Wig, Gown and Stethoscope. In *The Changing Face of Criminology in Australia and New Zealand*, ed. Russell G. Smith, 15–17. London: Sage Publications.

Finnane, Mark. 2012. The Origins of Criminology in Australia. *Australian and New Zealand Journal of Criminology* 45 (2): 157–178.

Finnane, Mark. 1998. Sir John Barry and the Melbourne Department of Criminology: Some Other Foundations of Australian Criminology. *Australian and New Zealand Journal of Criminology* 31 (1): 69–81.

Fishwick, Elaine and Marmo, Marinella. 2018. Criminology in Australia: A Global South Perspective. In *The Handbook of the History and Philosophy of Criminology*, ed. Triplett Ruth A., pp. 321–333. Oxford: John Wiley & Sons Inc.

Goring, Charles. 1913. *The English Convict: A Statistical Study*. London: HMSO.

Grabosky, Peter N. 2004. Where to Next? In *Lessons from International/ Comparative Criminology/Criminal Justice*, ed. John Winterdyk and Liqun Coo, pp. 8–24. Toronto: deSitter Publications.

Graycar, Adam, and Peter Grabosky. 2002. Trends in Australian Crime and Criminal Justice. In *The Cambridge Handbook of Australian Criminology*, ed. A. Graycar and P. Grabosky, 7–26. Cambridge: Cambridge University Press.

Haines, Fiona. 2010. Obituary: Dr Adam Sutton. *Australian and New Zealand Journal of Criminology* 43 (3): 612–615.

Harding, Richard. 2015. Richard Harding Interview with Julia Wallis. 1 April 2015 and 8 April 2015. *UWA Historical Society: UWA Histories*, Audio Files. https://oralhistories.arts.uwa.edu.au/items/show/89. Accessed 4 January 2021.

Harding, Richard. 2004. Obituary: Gordon Hawkins 1919–2004. *Australian and New Zealand Journal of Criminology* 37 (3): 317–322.

Hawkins, Gordon. 1990. Present at the Creation: The Inception and Development of the Institute of Criminology. *Current Issues in Crime and Criminal Justice* 2 (1): 9–17. http://www.austlii.edu.au/au/journals/CICrimJust/1990/15.pdf. Accessed 3 February 2022.

Hebenton, Bill and Jou, Susyan. 2018. Criminology in China. In *The Handbook of the History and Philosophy of Criminology*, ed. Triplett Ruth A., pp. 377–391. Oxford: John Wiley & Sons Inc.

Hough, Mike. 2018, September 10. Interviewed by Ben Bradford at European Society of Criminology meeting, Sarajevo, Bosnia and Herzegovina. https://www.youtube.com/watch?v=_DLTlrqt_OA&t=7s. Accessed 10 March 2022.

Hough, Mike. 2014. Confessions of a Recovering 'Administrative Criminologist': Jock Young Quatitative Research and Policy Research. *Crime Media Culture* 10 (3): 215–226.

Knepper, Paul. 2018. Laughing at Lombroso: Positivism and Criminal Anthropology in Historical Perspectiv. In *The Handbook of the History and Philosophy of Criminology*, ed. Triplett Ruth A., pp. 51–66. Oxford: John Wiley & Sons Inc.

Lombroso, Cesare. 1911. *Crime: Its Causes and Remedies*. Translated by H. P. Horton. Boston: Little, Brown and Co.

Martin, Randy, Robert J. Mutchnick, and W. Timothy Austin. 1990. *Criminological Thought: Pioneers Past and Present*. New York: Macmillan.

Mayhew, Patricia. 2016. In Defence of Administrative Criminology. *Crime Science* 5 (7): 1–10.

Mayhew, Patricia. 2004. Comparative Research in a Government Environment. In *Lessons from International/Comparative Criminology/Criminal Justice*, ed. John Winterdyk and Liqun Coo, pp. 55–70. Toronto: deSitter Publications.

Morgan, Rod, and Mike Hough. 2007. The Politics of Criminological Research. In *Doing Research on Crime and Justice*, ed. Roy King and Emma Wincup, 45–74. Oxford: Oxford University Press.

Morris, Norval. 1952. The Department of Criminology University of Melbourne. *The Australian Law Journal* 26: 12.

Mukherjee, Satyanshu K., Jacobsen, Evelyn N. and Walker, John R. 1981. *Source Book of Australian Criminal and Social Statistics 1900–1980.* Canberra: Australian Institute of Criminology.

Muhlhausen, David B. 2019. Director's Message, *National Institute of Justice Journal,* No. 281. https://nij.ojp.gov/topics/articles/brief-history-nij. Accessed 27 April 2022.

New South Wales Bureau of Crime Statistics and Research (BOCSAR). 2016. About Us. http://www.bocsar.nsw.gov.au/Pages/bocsar_aboutus.aspx. Accessed 15 June 2020.

President's Commission on Law Enforcement and Administration of Justice. 1967. *The Challenge of Crime in a Free Society.* Washington, DC: President's Commission on Law Enforcement and Administration of Justice. https://www.ojp.gov/sites/g/files/xyckuh241/files/archives/ncjrs/42.pdf. Accessed 27 April 2022.

Radzinowicz, Leon. 1999. *Adventures in Criminology.* London: Routledge.

Radzinowicz, Leon. 1973. *Report of Sir Leon Radzinowicz with Respect to the Australian Institute of Criminology,* New York. Canberra: National Library of Australia (6093/72/4182).

Radzinowicz, Leon. 1965. *The Need for Criminology and a Proposal for an Institute of Criminology.* London: Heineman.

Rance, Carolyn. 2015, May 2. Crime Statistics Hold Mirror to Society, *The Age (Melbourne).* http://www.theage.com.au/business/crime-statistics-hold-mirror-to-society-20150501-1mtx0b.html. Accessed 22 April 2022.

Redo, Slawomir M. 2012. *Blue Criminology: The Power of United Nations Ideas to Counter Crime Globally: A Monographic Study,* HEUNI Publication Series No. 72. Helsinki: HEUNI. https://heuni.fi/documents/47074104/0/Blue_Criminology_www_linked.pdf/0013989d-f932-25ab-ec52-5f21884da6d3/Blue_Criminology_www_linked.pdf?t=1610010139161. Accessed 13 May 2022.

Rock, Paul. 2019. *The Official History of Criminal Justice in England and Wales*, vol. I. London: Routledge.

Smith, Russell G., ed. 2021. *The Changing Face of Criminology in Australia and New Zealand*. London: Sage Publications Ltd.

Smith, Russell G. 2017. Public Sector Criminological Research. In *Palgrave Handbook of Australian and New Zealand Criminology, Crime and Justice*, ed. Antje Deckert and Rick Sarre, 33–49. London: Palgrave Macmillan.

United Nations Office on Drugs and Crime. 2011, October 1. *UNODC Head Inaugurates Centre of Excellence in Statistics in Mexico*. https://www.unodc.org/unodc/en/frontpage/2011/October/unodc-head-inaugurates-statistics-centre-of-excellence-in-mexico.html. Accessed 27 April 2022.

University of Melbourne. 1962. *Handbook: Board of Studies in Criminology*. Melbourne: University of Melbourne.

van Dijk, Jan J. M. 2004. On the Victims' Side. In *Lessons from International/Comparative Criminology/Criminal Justice*, ed. John Winterdyk and Liqun Coo, pp. 71–88. Toronto: deSitter Publications.

van Kesteren, John, van Dijk, Jan and Mayhew, Patricia. 2014. The International Crime Victims Surveys: A Retrospective. *International Journal of Victimology* 20 (1): 49–69.

Walston, Catharine, ed. 2009. *Challenging Crime: A Portrait of the Cambridge Institute of Criminology*. London: Third Millennium Publishing Limited.

Woods, Greg. 2004. Academic Who Swayed Minds and Hearts: Gordon Joseph Hawkins 1919–2004. *Current Issues in Criminal Justice* 15 (3): 272–274.

3

Cooperative Federalism

Foundational Discussions

As outlined in Chapter 2, by the 1960s a movement had begun in a number of countries around the globe to create dedicated research institutes to provide information and policy analysis on the criminal justice research questions facing governments at that time. These issues included concerns over increasing crime victimisation, a lack of crime statistics from criminal justice agencies, a paucity of survey research on crime victimisation generally, a lack of information on crime prevention approaches and their cost-effectiveness in preventing crime and reducing recidivism, a lack of understanding of the role and effectiveness of specific sentences imposed by the courts—particularly capital punishment—and a need for training of criminal justice personnel in understanding the drivers of criminality, how to improve methods of detection and investigation and how to undertake effective and humane correctional practices.

R. G. Smith, *Public Sector Criminological Research*,
https://doi.org/10.1007/978-3-031-28356-7_3

Discussions continued on what type of organisation should undertake the work needed to satisfy these demands, with various models being proposed and tried. These included the creation of stand-alone government entities, embedding research bodies within existing government entities or universities—generally in Faculties of Law—and establishing private sector-funded 'think tanks' or research consultancies to carry out the work. In the UK, EU and the US, examples of each approach were evident during the years preceding the establishment of the AIC in 1972—providing a rich source of possibilities for the direction that Australia should follow.

The other driver of change at the time was the interest demonstrated by the UN in crime prevention and criminal justice, particularly through the establishment of a network of affiliated institutions. The such first institute, UNAFEI, was established in the Tokyo suburb of Fuchu in 1962, followed by the United Nations Interregional Crime and Justice Research Institute (UNICRI) in Rome in 1968 (see Chapter 15, below, and Redo 2012). These developments were followed closely by a number of policy-makers, lawyers and academic criminologists who developed the idea of setting up a criminological research institute in Australia. The work of the UN in reforming criminal justice policy and setting standards for correctional agencies was undertaken at the time during discussions held at the United Nations Congresses on Crime Prevention and Criminal Justice held every five years following the inaugural meeting in Geneva in 1955 (Plate 3.1).

The Australian delegation to these early Congresses included representatives from the Commonwealth Attorney-General's Department (AGD), as well as judges, heads of government agencies and academics with an interest in criminal justice policy-making and law reform internationally. Central among the Australian delegates was Sir John Barry, a Justice of the Supreme Court of Victoria, Chairman of the Victorian Parole Board and Chairman of the Department of Criminology at the University of Melbourne, who led the Australian delegations at both the first and second Congresses held in Geneva in 1955 and in London in 1960, respectively. In the 1961 New Year's Honours List, Barry received and accepted an Imperial Knighthood in recognition of

Plate 3.1 Delegates at the First Crime Congress, Geneva, 22 August 1955 (*Source* UN Photo/SC—UN7517852)

his judicial standing, despite his left-leaning political views (Finnane 2007, p. 236) and his criticism of others who accepted such honours (Teague 1993, n.p.).

Jack Barry (Plate 3.2), as he was known to close associates, was appointed to the Supreme Court of Victoria on 14 January 1947, and was described as 'the one progressive element on an extremely conservative bench' (Teague 1993, n.p.). At the 1960 Crime Congress, Barry was appointed chairman of the section that examined the question of the role and effectiveness of short-term imprisonment. Baroness Wootton of Abinger (1967) wrote of Barry: 'as everyone who knows him must agree, he is one of the most learned, stimulating, vital and kindly men that anyone could ever wish to meet'. Barry's experience of, and attitudes toward the criminal justice system and its reform, helped frame his view that an Australian Institute of Criminology was needed—as Geoffrey Sawer (1972, p. 204) explained in his inaugural Sir John Barry Memorial Lecture delivered at the University of Melbourne in 1972:

Plate 3.2   The Hon. Sir John Barry (*Source* AIC Archives)

My friend Jack Barry was generally and fairly regarded as a man of the Left, a critical observer of the institutions in our society, having no special admiration for, or commitment to, the legal system as it stood or to its institutions. His general stance was shown by such matters as leaving the church of his ancestors and becoming a rationalist, sending his children to an experimental modern school, candidature for the Federal Parliament in the interests of the Australian Labor Party (ALP) and active support as a lawyer and as a judge for what were in his time reforming movements, such as the introduction of a parole system for criminal prisoners and of a curative rather than a retributive approach to the criminal sanction. The readiness with which he made use of scientific information and evidence in the course of his judicial work was likewise characteristic of one strand in the modern criticism of the legal tradition.

Accompanying Barry at the Geneva Crime Congress were Norval Morris who was Associate Professor at the Melbourne Criminology Department and Harold Vagg, Deputy Comptroller of Prisons in New South Wales. At the London Crime Congress in 1960, Barry was joined by Justice John McClemens of the Supreme Court of New South Wales, who was also head of the Australian delegation at the Third Crime Congress in Stockholm in 1965 that included Norval Morris—who was by then Julius Kreeger Professor of Law and Criminology at the University of Chicago.

Jock McClemens, as he was popularly known, was appointed a Justice of the New South Wales Supreme Court on 3 September 1951 and, like Barry, had a keen interest in criminology, the prevention of crime and the care of released offenders. He was President of the Australian Prison After Care Council and of the Australian Crime Prevention Council (ACPC) and a member of the advisory committee of the Institute of Criminology at the University of Sydney. His deep involvement in the preservation of human rights, the safeguarding of civil liberties and the promotion of law reform (D'Apice 2000) led to his advocacy, along with Barry, for establishing an Australian Institute of Criminology in Canberra.

Norval Morris (Plate 3.3), who was born in New Zealand, but lived his early life in Australia, and most of his academic career in Chicago, was among the first lecturers in Criminology at the University of Melbourne in 1951 when Barry had been Chairman of the Board of Studies. Mark Finnane (2004), in his tribute to Norval, who died on 21 February 2004, described Norval's relationship with Barry as 'mutually formative, intellectually and in career terms' (p. 268). Of importance to the current discussion was Morris' appointment in 1962 as foundation Director of UNAFEI in Tokyo.

Attending the UN Crime Congresses provided an opportunity for Barry, Morris and McClemens to develop and to promote their proposal to create an Institute of Criminology in the Asia–Pacific region. As it transpired, in the words of Norval Morris (1973, p. 200) in August 1973, 'the Institute took about 17 years from conception to parturition; with such paternity and such a protracted period of gestation, surely it will flourish'. Richard Fox, who later became Chair of the AICs Board (1973, p. 11), agreed, concluding his enumeration of seven principles

Plate 3.3 Dr Norval Morris, Director of UNAFEI 1962–1964 (*Source* UNAFEI Archives)

that should govern the operation of the CRC with the observation that if these principles are not adhered to, the AICs 'long period of gestation, which has so far even exceeded that of the elephant, [would produce] little more than a mouse'.

In understanding the events that occurred during this lengthy period, we are fortunate in having access to Barry's personal papers lodged in the National Library of Australia (NLA) and the National Archives of Australia (NAA) following his death in 1969, a detailed account of the chronology of events written by Peter Loof (1979) who was intimately involved in creating and promoting the AICs legislation at AGD and then becoming Chairman of the AIC Board over 10 years and the research conducted by Mark Finnane (1998, 2004, 2007, 2008, 2012) aided by John Myrtle, former AIC librarian, who undertook an extensive analysis of Barry's papers and who provided the present author with extracts of correspondence relevant to the establishment of the AIC. Barry's personal correspondence was made available and given to the National Library of Australia by his immediate family in 1976.

Choosing a Location for an Institute

One of the potential solutions to the criminal justice concerns discussed at the UN Congresses was the creation of 'training research institutes' among the UN member countries to conduct research and to provide training for criminal justice personnel. In the Asia–Pacific region, this idea was raised by Dr V. N. Pillai (Plate 3.4), Commissioner of Prisons in Ceylon, who suggested to Manuel Lopez-Rey, then Chief of Social Affairs at the UN in a letter of 21 March 1960, that Australia would be the best location for such an Institute in the region (NLA MS 2505/30/ 1977 addition). Barry and Morris were supportive of the idea and lobbied others in Australia including Professor Geoffrey Sawer, Sir Garfield Barwick and Professor David Derham. Barwick, then Chief Justice of the High Court of Australia, approached Sir Robert Menzies who was Minister for External Affairs (in addition to being Prime Minister) for further support in June 1960. At the same time, Manuel Lopez-Rey wrote to Norval Morris on 13 June 1960, arguing that the Institute should not be located in Tokyo due to the 'language barrier and inadequacy of ways and means' (NLA MS 2505/30/ 1977 addition). By the time of the second UN Crime Congress in London in August 1960, Barry and McClemens were able to discuss the idea further and develop a proposal that the Australian government could consider.

During the ensuing years, negotiations continued among UN officials eventually leading to UNAFEI being established in Tokyo in 1962 with Norval Morris as Director. Norval remained in charge at UNAFEI until June 1964 when he left to take up a position at the University of Chicago—being replaced by Dr Pillai as UNAFEIs Director.

Plate 3.4   Dr V. N. Pillai, Director of UNAFEI, Japan, 1964–1970 (*Source* UNAFEI Archives)

The Preferred Australian Model

Barry was not deterred by this development and, on 28 January 1965, he gave an address to the Third Australian Prison After Care Council conference in Hobart in which he described in detail his proposal for an Australian Institute of Criminal and Penal Science (reproduced in Loof 1979, Annexure A). The essential elements of the Australian Institute reflected those of UNAFEI including training of criminal justice personnel, the conduct of crime prevention research, collation of crime statistics and liaison with government and institutions in the region. The proposal was further developed in a report to the third UN Congress in Stockholm in August 1965 by Justice McClemens as Head of the Delegation supported by Norval Morris (also reproduced in Loof 1979, Annexure B). According to Mr J. H. A. Hoyle, of the United Nations Branch in the Department of External Affairs, Barry was not included in the Australian delegation on the recommendation of Attorney-General Billy Snedden 'on the grounds that he was essentially a divorce lawyer and that his interests in penology were more in the nature of a hobby' (NAA A1838 (A1838/1), 930/4/5 Part 1–5 May 1965)—a somewhat surprising, and ill-informed argument. In the Australian delegation's report, it was argued that an Australian Institute should be a joint initiative of the Commonwealth, the states and New Zealand. The government of New Zealand had previously considered establishing its own Institute, but was agreeable to Australia implementing the idea that would support other Australasian countries. In particular, it was proposed that the Australian Institute could provide training throughout the region, similar to that undertaken pursuant to the Colombo Plan.

By the time of the third UN Crime Congress in 1965, UNAFEI in Japan was operational and, as Loof (1979, p. 5) observed:

> the achievement of the United Nations Institute in Japan supplied convincing proof of the worth of an agency for furthering international amity in promoting the welfare of Asian people. He pointed out that experience at that Institute would furnish a valuable guide in planning of an Australian Institute.

It was also argued that an Australian Institute would not compete with UNAFEI as, at the time, the Tokyo Institute was only able to accept about one-third of prospective trainees, and there was clearly a need for further training capacity in the region. Interest in the proposal from around the region was good with Sir Alan Mann, Chief Justice of the Supreme Court of Papua and New Guinea, for example, supporting the establishment of the Institute in Australia (NLA MS 2505/30/ 1977 addition).

The report of the Australian delegation to the third UN Crime Congress came down strongly in favour of setting-up an Australian Institute with this being 'stressed in virtually every session of the Congress'

(Loof 1979, p. 6). In particular, an Australian Institute was justified on the grounds that it could provide technical training throughout Australia and across Asia. It could also play an important role in the study of crime statistics—the other pressing need at the time.

Consultation Within Australia

Consideration of the proposal was then undertaken by the Attorney-General's Department in 1966 that referred the idea to a Commonwealth Interdepartmental Committee (IDC) that included members from the relevant departments of law, police, finance, education, statistics and immigration. Barry continued his efforts in lobbying for the creation of the Institute but, in a letter to Secretary of Justice, John Robson, in New Zealand on 16 February 1966, he expressed his concern at the lack progress being undertaken:

> I hope your Minister's letter has some effect, but I fear it will not. Canberra simply does not understand the proposal or the need for it; and imagination is a quality sadly lacking in Federal Departments. Canberra and its inhabitants are in a different world from us hewers of wood and drawers of water. (NLA MS 2505/30/ 1977 addition)

After the IDC concluded its work at the end of 1966, it was decided to conduct a pilot seminar with representatives from the Australian states and New Zealand to assess whether the idea was viable. The suggestion to conduct a pilot program was made by Ray Whitrod, who was inaugural Commissioner of the Commonwealth Police Force at the time. Whitrod was an advocate for improving education in policing and had undertaken studies himself at the Cambridge Institute of Criminology in 1965 where he had experienced the benefits of a dedicated criminology research institute. In his autobiography, Whitrod (2001, p. 115) explained how he promoted the idea of a similar institute in Australia.

In 1966 I put together the outline of a campaign to obtain this approval [for an Australian Institute]. One idea was to have a trial run, a residential seminar, with federal and state participants. This would identify the deficiencies in the preparation of senior officials in the Australian criminal justice system, and would demonstrate how a national institute of criminology could overcome these deficiencies at a reasonable cost.

Whitrod's *Seminar on the Control of Deviant Behaviour in Australia* took place at Bruce Hall, ANU with 23 participants, between 30 January and 23 February 1968. He described it as 'a major coup' with all those attending recommending the establishment of a national institute of criminology in Australia (Whitrod 2001, p. 115). The Report of the Seminar outlined the model of an Institute that would satisfy all of the competing interests and fulfil the research and training needs identified by the participants. In addition, Sir John Barry addressed the seminar concerning the importance of developing national uniform crime statistics.

Some of the factors taken into account in supporting the establishment of an Australian Institute included the perceived increase in criminality in society, the estimated cost of crime to individuals—that a Rural Bank survey put at \$350 million a year in 1968, and the growing problems of organised crime and juvenile crime. These factors all supported the argument that a national Institute should be established rather than separate state bodies (Loof 1979, p. 11).

The question also arose as to the proper location of the Institute within Australia. Barry had suggested to David Derham, who was at the time Dean of the Monash University Law School, that the Institute could be based at a University and that Monash would be preferable to the University of Melbourne. Others suggested the Sydney Institute of Criminology and the Police College in the Sydney suburb of Manly. The IDC, however, had considered this question and decided that the Institute should be in a government environment like the Home Office Research Unit in the UK that conducted 'research on a national basis and provide[d] grants of money for research activities' (Loof 1979, p. 12). This, it was argued, would ensure that the research undertaken would be of practical benefit to the government and that access could be provided to internal government resources—some of the same arguments that were advanced in 2015 for merging the AIC with the ACC (see Chapter 14 below).

Development of the Legislation

Peter Loof, who was at the time Principal Legal Officer in the Commonwealth Attorney-General's Department, was given carriage of the Institute proposal, developing a Commonwealth/State scheme and drawing up the legislative model—that originally included New Zealand. It was not, however, until April 1969 that the final model was ready for review. The Attorney-General, Nigel Bowen, wrote to Norval Morris setting out the elements of the model—that included an Institute, a Criminology Research Fund and a Criminology Research Council, with initial staffing of a Director and three or four researchers (NLA 2505/30/39–40). Morris replied on 14 May 1969:

> The idea of a Council, a Fund and an Institute makes very good sense to me. It should provide sufficient autonomy for the Institute, yet also sufficient liaison with the States to give them confidence in the Institute's responsible use of data and a sense of being served by the Institute… The budgets you anticipate are not at all lavish for the necessary duties of the Fund and the Institute; but I appreciate that these are launching budgets. (NLA MS 2505/30/41–42)

The question of funding created considerable tension among the states which it was proposed would be responsible for contributing to the Research Fund. In a report to the Board prepared by the Institute's Director in 1976, Bill Clifford looked back on this question and observed that:

> the Institute had itself been developed as a method of streamlining Federal/State expenditure on the promotion and advancement of crime prevention services with a view to avoiding wasteful and duplicating expenditures on these subjects. (AIC, Board Minutes, 3 February 1976, p. 3)

After protracted negotiations, the Commonwealth agreed to provide $50,000 for the initial Research Fund with a further $50,000 each year coming from the six states on a *pro rata* population basis (CRC Annual Report 1973, p. 1). This sharing of financial responsibilities for the national institute was described by Peter Loof (1979, p. 1) as 'an exercise in co-operative federalism'. At the time, Richard Fox was a Senior Research Associate at the Centre of Criminology in Toronto and was following the progress of the Australian Institute with great interest. In his Interview (15 July 2022), Fox recalled his initial support for the AIC concept because, 'constitutionally, it was bringing everyone together'. Fox argued, however, that 'the Institute was powerful in the sense that it was the product of both the Commonwealth and the states but the biggest battle was who owned the Institute – the Commonwealth couldn't own it because the states were also a party to it' (Richard Fox, Interview, 15 July 2022).

Over time, the model's progress continued slowly until the Coalition government's *Review of Commonwealth Functions* (the so-called Razor Gang proposal) in April 1981 that sought to change the funding allocation to an equal seven-way split—with the Commonwealth providing one-seventh and all of the states contributing on a *pro rata* basis to the remaining six-seventh share. Two states refused to agree to this proposal (Knez 1981) and following the change of government on 11 March 1983, the original model was retained with gradual increases in both Commonwealth and state (and later territory) funding occurring.

By May 1969, the states had agreed in principle to the original proposal and after further discussions a Commonwealth-state meeting of Ministers was held in December 1969. One of the essential requirements requested by the states was that the Institute should *not* be set up within an existing Commonwealth department, but that it should be an independent Commonwealth instrumentality created by Commonwealth legislation. To guarantee an effective partnership between the Commonwealth and the states, a Board of Management was suggested for the Institute with Commonwealth and state representation.

The work of the Institute was intended to entail both criminological research and professional training activities for criminal justice personnel. Although this fulfilled the needs of Australia, in New Zealand, the

Plate 3.5   4th UN Crime Congress, Kyoto, 1970 (*Source* UN Photo—UN7558487)

primary deficiency at the time was for training activities as there were sufficient resources currently available for research in New Zealand. As a result, the New Zealand authorities were unhappy with the idea of providing funding for grants for the conduct of research that was already being undertaken, and, accordingly, decided to withdraw from participation. As Loof (1979, p. 15) noted, however, 'the New Zealand authorities indicated that they would maintain an interest in the training courses proposed to be conducted by the Institute and participation by New Zealand personnel in those courses [would occur]'.

The Australian model was then presented at the fourth UN Crime Congress held in Kyoto, Japan from 17 to 26 August 1970 (Plate 3.5). Peter Loof attended as part of the Australian delegation and Sir Leon Radzinowicz acted as Rapporteur-General of the Congress.

After extensive analysis and discussion based on a Working Paper prepared by the Secretariat to the Congress (United Nations 1970), there was general agreement that the proposed model for an Australian

Institute could resolve many of the requirements for coordinated criminological research. In particular, the model of the Institute was seen as a means of resolving, what Loof (1979, p. 16) called 'a mutual scepticism between policy-makers and researchers'. Peter Loof (1979, p. 16) went on to explain this as follows:

> It was observed that worth-while research was often neglected by policy-makers. However, it was also true that the theoretical framework and technical language used by many researchers provided impediments to the implementation by policy-makers of research. It was considered that, on the one hand, policy-makers should make an attempt to become familiar with the language and methods of research and that, on the other hand, researchers should endeavour to present the results of their research in a manner likely to be of assistance to those concerned with its implementation.

In his Report on the outcomes of the Congress, Sir Leon recounted the discussion of a number of essential elements of effective policy-relevant research—some of which had particular relevance to the debate concerning the Australian model (United Nations 1971, p. 35):

> ... (b) that there was a need to have criminological research carried out in universities, as well as in ministries;
> (h) that the results of research should not be kept secret, but should be published and made the subject of wide discussion and criticism;
> (i) that the researcher and policy-maker were two different kinds of animal; there might be a difference, and indeed sometimes a clash, between their approaches;
> (j) that research should be presented in a readable way so as to be understood and appreciated by those outside a necessarily restricted circle of experts ...

The inclusion of these aspects, it was agreed, could be found in the model being proposed of the Australian Institute that had a Board to monitor the type of research being undertaken, and a Council to allocate funding sought by academic researchers. As we shall see in the following chapters, the AICs approach has not fully resolved the 'mutual scepticism' and although fifty years of bridge-building has been undertaken, the two camps remain at somewhat of a distance. The presence of the AIC, and PNI members, has, however, improved relations and achieved some outcomes that might not, otherwise, have been achievable.

The legislative model finally adopted in Australia provided a balance between public sector, government-focussed research that the Institute would be responsible for conducting, and private sector, academic research that the Council would fund out of the Criminology Research Fund. There would, however, be close contact between the two owing to the fact that the Council membership would be represented on the AICs Board (Loof 1979, p. 18). During 1970, the final draft Criminology Research Bill was distributed to the states for comment and, after further discussion, the states agreed and the Bill was introduced by the Attorney-General, Tom Hughes QC, on 24 February 1971. The Bill was considered by the House of Representatives on 17 March 1971 and by the Senate on 31 March 1971 and was passed by both Houses, receiving Royal Assent on 6 April 1971. Following 18 months' delay, the legislation commenced operation on 6 November 1972, with the official opening almost a year later on 16 October 1973.

Legislative Reform

Apart from some minor legislative changes during the 1970s, the change in the Commonwealth government in March 1983 from the Fraser Coalition to the Hawke Labor party led to a number of proposals for change. In April 1981, the Fraser government had undertaken a substantial Review of Commonwealth Functions that included two recommendations relevant to the AIC—that the states contribute six-sevenths of the costs of running the Institute and that the proposal that the Institute be given a new building not be proceeded with (Fraser 1981, p. 1838). Although the funding change did not occur, a new building was not provided until July 1990 and then only as a leasehold rather than freehold. By the mid-1980s, however, a number of questions had arisen concerning the operation of the Institute that required a legislative solution.

In 1985, the Labor government undertook a Review of Research Bodies in the Attorney-General's Portfolio aiming to reduce costs, avoid duplication of functions and to increase control over research activities by the Attorney-General, Lionel Bowen QC. In December 1986, the Institute's legislation was amended to provide for these and a number of other changes (AIC Annual Report 1986, p. 4):

- the inclusion of the now self-governing Northern Territory by adding a new member to the CRC, and a contribution to the Research Fund;
- the inclusion of the AICs Director as an ex-officio member of the Board;
- the formalisation of the Institute's role in providing information and advice to governments on criminal justice policy matters;
- the clarification of the Institute's right to bid for external contract research funding;
- explicit recognition of the Institute's right to engage in regional and international research and training activities; and
- the clarification of the Institute's role with regard to the collection of statistics.

This last reform was of great importance in resolving the impasse that had developed between the AIC and the ABS in demarcating responsibility for the collection of crime statistics—as outlined in the discussion, above. Matters came to a head during Richard Harding's Directorship when the ABS objected to the AIC conducting work on crime statistics that it argued was outside its legislative remit. The AICs original legislation, it will be recalled, only permitted the Institute 'to give advice in relation to the compilation of statistics relating to crime' (s. 6(g) *Criminology Research Act 1971*) that, arguably, did not extend to data collection, analysis and reporting—the Institute had previously undertaken in publications such as the *Crime Trends in Twentieth Century Australia* (Mukherjee et al. 1981). Harding took the view that the ABS was unwilling and incapable of carrying out the kind of data collection needed for effective criminological work and was able to persuade the Attorney-General, Lionel Bowen and Prime Minister Hawke, that the AIC should be given this function (Richard Harding, Interview, 30 December 2021).

Although the AICs amending legislation recognised the AIC role in the collection of statistics (with the proviso that the AICs function should not detract from, and remain in the context of the overall collecting and co-ordinating role of the ABS), the AICs appropriation was not increased to allow the costly work required to collect and analyse crime statistics—although the amending legislation did permit the Institute to engage in fee-for-service research, thus outsourcing the costs involved. In his interview (18 November 2021), Richard Harding paid tribute to the efforts of Peter Loof in shepherding these amendments through the Department and Parliament, and also in arranging for academics to be represented on the Board. In 1984, for example, the Board membership included: Dr Evan Davies, Senior Lecturer in Psychology, University of New South Wales; Associate Professor Gordon Hawkins, Director of the Institute of Criminology at the University of Sydney; Dr Terry Speed, Chief of the Division of Mathematics and Statistics, CSIRO and Dr Adam Sutton, Director of OCSAR, South Australia—in addition to Professor Harding, himself an academic lawyer and criminologist. This was a period during which the Board and Council had the highest proportion of data scientists as members in the history of the organisation. In 2022, Dr Adam Tomison, Chair of the CRAC, noted the absence of criminologists on the Advisory Council (apart from himself and Fiona Dowsley) and observed: 'I think it's always helpful to have someone with a research background advising what's essentially a research agency' (Adam Tomison, Interview, 26 October 2022).

The collection of crime statistics, as already noted in Chapter 2, continued to be problematic for the Institute. Years later, the Tanzer Review (1994) recommended that the ABS should be regarded as the collector of crime statistics and that the Institute should retain an interpretation role. The Review was, however, persuaded that the ABS was willing to reach arrangements with the AIC which would meet its requirements for access to data and involvement in the design of collection instruments. Tanzer's conclusion was that (1994, p. 22):

we believe that with goodwill and common sense, the AIC and the ABS can overcome the obstacles that have prevented effective collaboration in the past. The reality for the AIC is that in the face of its own budgetary constraints it cannot attempt to maintain any significant statistical collection capacity. It has little choice but to further develop its interpretation capacity.

Taking on the crime statistics function, without a dedicated budget, could be seen as the Institute receiving a poisoned chalice, as it was given responsibility, not only for the costly task of collecting crime data, but for disseminating the findings of its analyses that could, and did, have negative implications for government policy and the work of criminal justice agencies. As Paul Wilson (1990, p. 137) recalled in his memoirs, 'it would be fair to say that the statistical work carried out by the Institute has led to more conflict, with either police or political interests, than has any other single issue'.

The Criminology Research Council

The inaugural meeting of the CRC was held in Melbourne on 20 December 1972 (CRC Annual Report 1973, p. 7) under the chairmanship of Mr Frank Mahony LLB, OBE, Deputy Secretary of the Commonwealth AGD who held the position until his retirement in July 1979 (Plate 3.6). Frank Mahony was the first of many senior bureaucrats from AGD to be involved closely with the AIC and CRC, and represented Commonwealth interests both in Australia and internationally. He showed a keen interest in criminal justice issues in the Asia–Pacific region commenting that 'the Institute can contribute a tremendous amount of criminological material to South East Asian countries even on a shoe-string budget' (Isles 1979, p. 11). The individuals who chaired the CRC are listed in Table 16.1, below.

Plate 3.6 Mr Frank J. Mahony OBE, Chairman of the Criminology Research Council and AIC Board 1973–1979 (*Source* AIC Archives)

The following state members were appointed by the Commonwealth Attorney-General on the nomination of state Ministers:

New South Wales—Mr L. K. Downs, Under-Secretary, Department of the Attorney-General and of Justice
Victoria—Mr A. G. Booth, Director-General of Social Welfare
Queensland—Mr F. N. Albietz, Legal Administrative Officer, Department of Justice
Western Australia—Mr R. M. Christie, Under-Secretary for Law
Tasmania—Dr E. Cunningham Dax, Coordinator in Community Health Services

South Australia—Miss M. C. Doyle, Senior Legal Officer, Attorney-General's Department (who was absent overseas and was represented by Mr G. Muecke, who later became her Deputy).

Following his appointment on 1 February 1973, the Acting Director of the AIC attended CRC meetings from the second meeting as an *ex officio* member. Membership of the CRC was subsequently extended to include a representative from the Northern Territory (pursuant to the *Criminology Research Amendment Act 1986*, s. 21) and a representative from the Australian Capital Territory (ACT) (pursuant to the *Crimes Legislation Enhancement Act 2003*, Schedule 2, ss. 6A–6P). The first Northern Territory Council member appointed on 8 September 1987 was Mr T. O. Fegan, Deputy Secretary, Department of Health and Community Services, Northern Territory, and the first ACT member appointed in July 2003 was Mr Tim Keady, Chief Executive Officer, Department of Justice and Community Safety, Attorney-General's Department, ACT.

Council members were able to appoint Deputies to act on their behalf, with the appointment of both members and deputies having to be approved by the relevant Minister. The Council members were usually heads or senior officers of Departments of Justice or other relevant departments in each jurisdiction and acted to promote state and territory interests in the types of research funded by the Council. With only one, albeit powerful, Commonwealth voice, the Council tended to promote research on crime and justice topics of direct relevance to state and territory criminal conduct, rather than specifically Commonwealth interests.

Following the retirement of Frank Mahony as Chairman of the Council, Peter Loof was promoted from Deputy Chairman to Chairman in 1979, a position he held until 30 June 1991 when Mr Herman Woltring commenced as Chairman. After a year, Mr Laurie Glanfield AM, formerly representative for New South Wales on the Council and Director-General of the New South Wales Attorney-General's Department, became Chair and remained in the position until the merger with the AIC on 1 July 2011—19 years in all. Thereafter, Laurie Glanfield continued as representative for New South Wales for a further year (AIC and CRC, Annual Reports). Laurie Glanfield was the only CRC or AIC

Plate 3.7 (l-r) Laurie Glanfield, Chair CRC, The Hon Brendan O'Connor MP, Minister for Home Affairs and Professor Richard Fox, Chairman, AIC Board, 26 November 2009 (*Source* AIC Archives)

Chairman who was appointed by the Keating Labor government, experienced a Coalition government for most of his term, and ended his term under the Rudd Labor government when Brendan O'Connor was Minister for Home Affairs (Plate 3.7). Glanfield managed to navigate these complex political and financial times for the AIC and CRC well, finishing as the last Chairman of the CRC before its amalgamation with the AIC in 2011.

The Board of Management

As required by the legislative model adopted, the AICs Board of Management consisted, initially, of three Commonwealth members and three state members selected from the CRC on rotation. Frank Mahony was appointed as inaugural Chairman, with Mr R. A. Wilson, Commissioner of the ACT Police Force, and Mr G. E. Parker, Senior Fellow in the

Department of Law at ANU being the Commonwealth members. State representatives were Mr A. G. Booth for Victoria, Mr L. K. Downs for New South Wales, and Dr E. Cunningham Dax for Tasmania. At 9.45am on 18 April 1973, the AICs Board of Management—apart from Cunningham Dax who was an apology—met for the first time. Others present at the meeting were the AICs Acting Director, Judge Muirhead, Peter Loof, Mr P. Baskett, and Mr R. Venables from the Commonwealth Attorney-General's Department (AIC, Minutes, 18 April 1973, p. 1).

Subsequent chairs of the Board until 2011 are listed in Table 16.1, below, along with those who subsequently chaired the CRAC. Prior to 1992, the same person chaired both the CRC and AIC Board, following which there were separate chairs until the establishment of the CRAC in 2011. The two longest-serving chairs were Laurie Glanfield, chair of the CRC from 1992 to 2011 and Richard Fox, AIC Board chair from 1998 to 2011 (Plate 3.8).

Richard Fox's interest in criminology spans the same five decades as the history of the AIC. In 1960, Richard was a student in the subject, Criminology B, in the Graduate Diploma in Criminology course at the University of Melbourne, along with other luminaries including Dr Allen Bartholomew (1925–2004), former Psychiatrist Superintendent, H.M. Prison, Pentridge, Melbourne (Smith 2018). Fox graduated from the University of Melbourne with a Bachelor of Laws in 1962 and in 1965 worked as a Research Assistant to Stanley Johnston, Head of the Melbourne Criminology Department, leading to the publication of their jointly-authored *Corrections Handbook of Victoria* (Johnston and Fox 1965). Richard Fox completed the Graduate Diploma in Criminology in 1967 and then undertook a Master of Laws at Melbourne in the same year with a thesis entitled *The Concept of Obscenity*. Professor Bob Williams, the Sir John Barry Chair of Law at Monash University, commented on his retirement that he had 'a remarkable combination of the skills of a criminologist and an analytical lawyer' (Williams 2006, p. 1).

Although Richard never worked at the AIC as a researcher, he participated in many of its events, received funding from the CRC and published in the AICs *Trends and Issues* series with a paper on Infringement Notices or 'on the spot fines' (Fox 1995). He is internationally

Plate 3.8   Emeritus Professor Richard Fox AM, Chair, Board of Management 1998–2011 (*Source* AIC Archives)

known for his work on criminal procedure and sentencing law with his publication, *Sentencing: State and Federal Law in Victoria* (Fox and Freiberg 1985, 1999), written with Arie Freiberg. This publication arose from a CRC-funded study by Fox and Freiberg (No. 2 of 1979). A third edition continued the work in 2014 as *Fox & Freiberg's Sentencing: State and Federal Law in Victoria*, by Arie Freiberg (2014) on the retirement of Fox. Freiberg worked at the AIC between 1974 and 1976 and later became Foundation Professor at the Melbourne Criminology Department in 1991, Dean of Arts at Melbourne in 2003 and Dean of Law at Monash in 2004. In 2009, he was made a Member of the Order of Australia for service to the law, particularly in the fields of criminology and reform relating to sentencing, to legal education and academic leadership (Plate 3.9).

Richard Fox was present at the official opening of the AIC in October 1973 and spoke on a Panel at the accompanying *Residential Conference on Research Resources and Programmes in Victoria*, chaired by Mr A. G. Booth who was the inaugural Victorian representative on the CRC. Fox also spoke at another session at the conference on crime statistics—focussing on the need for a Commonwealth Bureau of Census and Statistics (AIC 1973).

Fox's contribution to criminology followed the conventional path established by the foundation members of the AIC who were mainly legal or corrections practitioners and academics rather than empirical researchers and social theorists. With considerable knowledge of the

Plate 3.9 Arie Freiberg, Senior Research Officer, 1974–1976 (*Source* Arie Freiberg)

criminal justice system, however, and a keen awareness of how the Institute and CRC operated, Fox was an appropriate and worthy candidate for the chairmanship of the AIC Board when he was appointed in April 1998. He became the longest-serving Board chairman until the Board was abolished and the Advisory Council created in July 2011.

Criminology Research Advisory Council

Although the composition of the Council and Board changed regularly with deputies often participating instead of their principals, the structures remained largely unaltered—apart from adding representatives of the two territories—until 1 July 2011, when the *Criminology Research Act 1971* (Cth.) was amended by the *Financial Framework Legislation Amendment Act 2010* (Cth) to merge the CRC with the AIC and to move the merged body to the *Financial Management and Accountability Act 1997* (Cth–FMA Act). This was, arguably, the most substantive governance and administrative change the AIC and CRC had experienced, becoming a Prescribed Agency subject to the FMA Act and a Statutory Agency under the *Public Service Act 1999* (Cth). The transfer to the FMA Act and *Public Service Act 1999* led to a large increase in compliance and accountability reporting and significant governance, financial, procurement and recruitment policy changes. These legislative changes also established the CRAC (Advisory Council) that comprised representatives from each Australian jurisdiction who had previously been members of the CRC. The Advisory Council's role was to advise the Director of the AIC on strategic research priorities, communications and research dissemination strategies and to recommend which grants should be made under the annual CRG Program.

The Advisory Council held its first meeting on 1 July 2011 (AIC Annual Report 2012, pp. 8–9) with Penny Armytage AM, then Secretary of the Department of Justice in Victoria, as Chair. Since then, the AICs Director has had responsibility for administering the funding program taking into account the advice and recommendations of the Advisory Council. This model created a number of tensions that the AICs Directors and Advisory Council members had to manage, principally to do with providing value for money for those who had contributed funding for the Program. As the financial contributions from the states and territories declined, the importance of the Advisory Council could be said also to have declined. Although there is a clear role for state and territory participation in the Institute's administration, questions have arisen as to the composition of the Council. The AICs Director in 2022, for example, 'wondered whether the Advisory Council should have a much more academic focus than a public service focus' (Michael Phelan, Interview, 3 November 2022). Following Penny Armytage's resignation as Chair of the Advisory Council in July 2013, and her controversial departure from the Department of Justice (Sexton 2012), there have been four CRAC chairs, with Dr Adam Tomison, Director General of the Department of Justice in Western Australia, and former AIC Director, occupying the position at the time of writing.

Official Opening

Although the AIC's legislation commenced on 6 November 1972, it took a further two months before the Judge James Muirhead began work as Acting Director, as we shall see in Chapter 4. After a further six months, the Institute was officially opened on 16 October 1973 marking the five decades commemorated in the present volume. The opening ceremony took place at the National Library of Australia Theatrette in Canberra with 400 attending (Plate 3.10). Senator the Honourable Lionel Murphy QC, Attorney-General, officially opened the Institute and addressed the many politicians, judges, academics and departmental officers from across Australia as well as Mr Minoru Shikita, Deputy Director of UNAFEI in Japan. An official luncheon followed at the Hotel Canberra.

Peter Loof (Plate 3.11), as Deputy Chairman of the Board, welcomed those present—in the absence of Mr Frank Mahony who was absent overseas attending a conference. Loof acknowledged a number of those attending who were supporters of the formation of the Institute including Justice Nigel Bowen QC who, as Attorney-General, supported

Plate 3.10 Official opening of the AIC, 16 October 1973. (l-r) Judge J. H. Muir-head, Acting Director; Senator Lionel Murphy QC, Attorney-General; Justice J. H. McClemens; Mr M. Shikita, Deputy Director, UNFEI; the Hon M. G. Everett QC, MHA, Attorney-General Tasmania; the Hon. T. D. Evans MLA, Attorney-General of Western Australia; the Hon Justice Nigel Bowen QC, Shadow Attorney-General (*Source* AIC Annual Report 1974, facing p. 1)

the introduction of the Institute's legislation in parliament and Lady Barry, Sir John's widow, among others. Peter began his address as follows:

Like the Sydney Opera House, the Institute has been open for business a little in advance of its official opening. There are perhaps some other similarities between the two institutions. Each has been futurist in conception. Both have been difficult of construction. The Institute itself has not been as costly a venture, but indeed the phenomenon of crime, which is its target, involves social and economic costs of proportions not generally appreciated. But here the similarity ceases. The one institution exalts the arts and human achievements. The other is concerned with social deviance and human tragedy. (AIC 1973, p. 2)

Plate 3.11 Peter Loof (1930–2016), former Board and CRC Chairman (*Source* AIC Archives)

Immediately following the official opening, the Institute conducted its First Residential Conference from 16 to 19 October 1973, entitled *Australian Crime Prevention and Treatment: Research Resources and Needs—An Exercise in Co-ordination*. In concluding this introductory chapter, it is appropriate to recall Acting Director Judge Muirhead's reference to 'cooperative federalism' in his opening notes (AIC 1973, p. 6):

Ladies and Gentlemen, we will in the future rely completely on the co-operation of the States and in fields of national importance, be it in seeking uniformity of criminal statistics or in combating delinquency, or in examining the effectiveness of penal methods, we must work in harmony with State instrumentalities and universities. In our association with the Criminology Research Council, which by funding, encourages research elsewhere in this country, through our library and information facilities we will, I hope, become a centre which will prove of continuing value to those who, in their daily work attempt to maintain our domestic security.

References

Australian Institute of Criminology (AIC). 1973. *Proceedings of the Australian Institute of Criminology, First Residential Conference.* Canberra: Australian Institute of Criminology.

Australian Institute of Criminology (AIC). 1974. *2nd Annual Report 1974.* Canberra: Australian Institute of Criminology.

Australian Institute of Criminology (AIC). 1986. *14th Annual Report 1986.* Canberra: Australian Institute of Criminology.

Australian Institute of Criminology (AIC). 2012. *Annual Report 2011–2012.* Canberra: Australian Institute of Criminology.

Criminology Research Council (CRC). 1973. *Annual Report.* Canberra: Australian Institute of Criminology.

D'Apice, Richard J.W. 2000. *McClemens, John Henry (1905–1975).* Australian Dictionary of Biography, vol. 15. Melbourne: Melbourne University Press. https://adb.anu.edu.au/biography/mcclemens-john-henry-10912. Accessed 6 February 2022.

Finnane, Mark. 1998. Sir John Barry and the Melbourne Department of Criminology: Some Other Foundations of Australian Criminology. *Australian and New Zealand Journal of Criminology* 31 (1): 69–81.

Finnane, Mark. 2004. Tributes: Norval Morris (1923–2004). *Current Issues in Criminal Justice* 15 (3): 267–271.

Finnane, Mark. 2007. *J V Barry: A Life.* Sydney: University of New South Wales Press.

Finnane, Mark. 2008. Promoting the Theory and Practice of Criminology: The Australian and New Zealand Society of Criminology and Its Founding Moment. *Australian and New Zealand Journal of Criminology* 41 (2): 199–215.

Finnane, Mark. 2012. The Origins of Criminology in Australia. *Australian and New Zealand Journal of Criminology* 45 (2): 157–178.

Fox, Richard G. 1995. *Infringement Notices: Time for Reform?* Trends and Issues in Crime and Criminal Justice no. 50. Canberra: Australian Institute of Criminology. https://www.aic.gov.au/publications/tandi/tandi50. Accessed 26 June 2022.

Fox, Richard G., and Arie Freiberg. 1985. *Sentencing: State and Federal Law in Victoria*, 1st ed. South Melbourne: Oxford University Press.

Fox, Richard G., and Arie Freiberg. 1999. *Sentencing: State and Federal Law in Victoria*, 2nd ed. South Melbourne: Oxford University Press.

Fraser, Malcolm. 1981. Ministerial Statement on the Review of Commonwealth Functions. *Parliamentary Debates*, Commonwealth House of Representatives, 30 April, p. 1838.

Freiberg, Arie. 2014. *Fox and Freiberg's Sentencing: State and Federal Law in Victoria*, 3rd ed. Pyrmont: Law Book Co Ltd.

Isles, Tim. 1979. Institute Chairman Retires. *AIC Reporter* 1 (1): 11.

Johnston, Stanley W., and Richard G. Fox. 1965. *The Corrections Handbook of Victoria*. Melbourne: Criminology Department, University of Melbourne.

Knez, Ted. 1981. States Revolt on Crime Research. *The Australian*, 22 July.

Loof, Peter R. 1979. *Establishment of the Australian Institute of Criminology and the Criminology Research Council: Proposals, Criteria and Negotiations Associated with the Establishment of the Institute and the Council.* Canberra: Attorney-General's Department.

Morris, Norval. 1973. The Future of Imprisonment. *Australian and New Zealand Journal of Criminology* 6 (4): 200–213.

Mukherjee, Satyanshu K., Evelyn N. Jacobsen, and John R. Walker. 1981. *Source Book of Australian Criminal and Social Statistics 1900–1980.* Canberra: Australian Institute of Criminology.

National Library of Australia (NLA). 1969. *Papers of Sir John Vincent Barry, 1917–1969.* MS 2505, MS Acc03.094, MS Acc03.143, Manuscript ID 3025354. Canberra: National Library of Australia.

Redo, Slawomir M. 2012. *Blue Criminology: The Power of United Nations Ideas to Counter Crime Globally: A Monographic Study.* HEUNI Publication Series No. 72. Helsinki: HEUNI. https://heuni.fi/documents/47074104/0/Blue_Criminology_www_linked.pdf/0013989d-f932-25ab-ec52-5f21884da6d3/Blue_Criminology_www_linked.pdf?t=1610010139161. Accessed 13 May 2022.

Sawer, Geoffrey. 1972. The Criminal Law Cannot Stand Still. *Australian and New Zealand Journal of Criminology* 5 (3): 137–145.

Sexton, Reid. 2012. Justice Chief to Quit Over Controversies. *Sydney Morning Herald*, 26 June. https://www.smh.com.au/politics/federal/justice-chief-to-quit-after-controversies-20120625-20yla.html. Accessed 28 June 2022.

Smith, Russell G. 2018. Stanley William Johnston: 10 November 1932 to 17 August 2018: A Personal Reflection. *PacifiCrim: ANZSOC Newsletter* 15 (2): 17–18.

Tanzer, Noel, Des Hill, and Grant Wardlaw. 1994. *Review of the Australian Institute of Criminology: Report.* Canberra: Australian Institute of Criminology.

Teague, Bernard. 1993. *Barry, Sir John Vincent (1903–1969).* Australian Dictionary of Biography. Canberra: National Centre of Biography, Australian National University. https://adb.anu.edu.au/biography/barry-sir-john-vincent-9442/text16601. Accessed 6 June 2022.

United Nations. 1970. Organization of Research for Policy Development in Social Defence: Working Paper. Fourth United Nations Congress on the Prevention of Crime and the Treatment of Offenders, Kyoto, 17–26 August 1970, A/CONF.43/4. https://www.unodc.org/documents/congress//Previous_Congresses/4th_Congress_1970/009_ACONF.43.4_Organization_of_Research_for_Policy_Development_in_Social_Defense.pdf

United Nations. 1971. *Report of the Fourth United Nations Congress on the Prevention of Crime and the Treatment of Offenders*, Kyoto, 17–26 August 1970, A/CONF.43/5. https://www.unodc.org/documents/congress//Previous_Congresses/4th_Congress_1970/010_ACONF.43.5_Fourth_United_Nations_Congress_on_the_Prevention_of_Crime_and_the_Treatment_of_Offenders.pdf

Whitrod, Ray. 2001. *Before I Sleep: Memoirs of a Modern Police Commissioner.* St Lucia: University of Queensland Press.

Williams, C.R. (Bob). 2006. Minute of Appreciation: Professor Richard G Fox. *Monash University Law Review* 32 (1): 1–3. https://doi.org/10.26180/5db7f86e7cb69. Accessed 1 July 2022.

Wilson, Paul. 1990. *A Life of Crime.* Newham: Scribe Publications.

Wootton, Barbara. 1967. *In a World I Never Made: Autobiographical Reflections.* London: Allen and Unwin.

4

Caught Between a Rock and a Hard Place

Tensions Within Public Sector Criminological Research Institutes

As we have seen, criminological research was first undertaken in the Italian and French public sectors using government resources to collect statistics on crime and its control in military and correctional settings in the nineteenth century. This positivist, empirical model of research still permeates much of public sector criminology today and continues to attract criticism from some academic circles (for example, Carson and O'Malley 1989). With the development of sociology and social theory in academic institutions in the mid-twentieth century, however, scholars working within government agencies were required to navigate a difficult course between conventional academic research undertaken in universities and research that could inform and provide an evidence-base for government policy-making. At the heart of this lay difficult questions of human research ethics, confidentiality and publicity of research findings, particularly where the outcomes of research might not accord with government policy agendas—that Geis (1994, p. 282) referred to as

R. G. Smith, *Public Sector Criminological Research*, https://doi.org/10.1007/978-3-031-28356-7_4

'being caught between a rock and a hard place' (see Chapter 1, above, and also Chapters 10 and 11, below).

These tensions, that continue to resonate today, are not unique to the AIC and have been faced also by the UK Home Office (Hough 2014; Mayhew 2016) and research agencies in the US and EU (Tonry 2010). One salient example of the risks faced by criminology schools in moving too far away from the needs and control of their political masters was the closure of the Berkeley School of Criminology in California in 1976 (Koehler 2015; Editors 1976). Like the AIC, the Berkeley School was established to provide training and resources to criminal justice personnel, in the case of Berkeley, having been established by August Vollmer in 1931, to professionalise and teach police science to California police officers. In the 1960s, however, a faction of radical criminologists took over the school leading to its alienation from the police and criminal justice agencies that had previously provided support. During the student protests of the late 1960s, the school eventually drew the ire of Ronald Reagan, then Governor of California. Hardman (2016, n.p.) explained this as: 'having strayed from its origins as a "professional" program toward a more academic and critical focus, the School was no longer able to solicit legitimacy from its historical sources, and on the wishes of the Berkeley administration it was closed on July 15th, 1976'. This demonstrates the fine line that must be navigated by an agency that strives for academic freedom and the ability to be critical of public sector interests, while also seeking to maintain good relations with those who provide its funding and support.

The AICs Director, Bill Clifford, in his opening address to the second AIC research seminar, *Review of Australian Criminological Research*, in February 1981 explained the complexity of the Institute's role and functions as follows:

> Australia has come late on the criminological scene – and this despite the fact that it arrived early at the centre of penal policy and penal reform. Following the British more than the American traditions in tertiary education, Australia took a long time to accept criminology as an academic discipline. When it did swing into operation, however, Australia sought to learn from the mistakes made elsewhere; the fact that we are

able to meet here and share knowledge of the research which is going on in an Institute which straddles federal and state boundaries and services a Research Council which makes grants for any methodologically sound project, is an indication that we are doing something rather different to many other countries. In some countries the state and federal levels are more decisively separated. In no country is there an Institute like this, which is a public, i.e. statutory, authority, with the capacity to bring academic and professional workers together, which is free to determine its own program, committed to no one government but in the service of all governments, as well as all universities, all criminal justice services and, of course, the public. The range of subjects which you are covering is, in itself, testimony to diversity. The fact that we are doing this together is testimony to unity within that diversity. (Clifford 1981, pp. 4–5)

This chapter assesses how the AIC sought to satisfy competing interests of stakeholders while ensuring that it fulfilled its statutory aims and did not unduly alienate sitting governments by presenting the results of research that might detract from their policy agendas. Central to this approach was the need for the Institute to be independent of political influence and not subject to budgetary pressures that could be used to stifle academic freedom or colour how research findings were presented. This chapter also examines the vexed question of how confidential and classified material was used in research and the proportion of research that was undertaken for government in confidence but not publicly-released and how this proportion changed over time—particularly, in the case of the AIC, since its relationship with the ACIC became closer. Reference is also made to the tensions of a similar nature that existed in comparable public sector criminological research organisations, as well as in academic criminological research institutes and private sector think tanks and consultancy firms.

Stakeholder Relations

Effective management of stakeholders was critical for the AICs Directors. As Director Adam Graycar noted during his interview, 'you need to map who your key stakeholders are, to keep them very close and to keep them supplied with good information' (Adam Graycar, Interview, 1 March 2021). Apart from holding regular meetings with ministers and departmental heads, Graycar established a group of directors of eight comparable research agencies who met twice a year to discuss common issues and to develop collaborative solutions to them. This group included Directors of the Australian Bureau of Agricultural and Resource Economics (ABARE)—the largest of the eight—the Australian Institute of Family Studies (AIFS), the Australian Institute of Health and Welfare (AIHW) and the Australian Bureau of Statistics (ABS) among others. Half of the group were public service entities and the other half statutory authorities like the AIC. The aim was to ensure that all Directors were aware of common issues that could affect them and to identify collaborative practices could reduce costs and create efficiencies. Potential initiatives included sharing of publication processes such as editing and the sharing of conference administration processes.

Ministers

More problematic was the maintenance of good relationships between the Institute and government ministers and departmental heads. During Adam Graycar's term as Director in the 1990s, he recalled that 'we were always under risk of being abolished' and that 'the Institute for every minute I was there was under threat–you just couldn't take anything for granted' (Adam Graycar, Interview, 1 March 2021). To deal with these threats, it was essential to meet regularly with ministers—which some Directors did more effectively than others. The Tanzer Report in 1994, for example, found that 'the roles and responsibilities of the Minister, the Board of Management and the Director of the AIC are inadequately defined and poorly understood' and recommended 'that Ministerial involvement with the AIC should include regular scheduled meetings between the AICs Director and the Minister and the attendance of the Minister at, at least, part of two meetings each year of the Board of Management' (Tanzer et al. 1994, p. 17). In addition to meeting with the Institute's own Minister, directors were also advised to attend meetings of the Standing Committee of Attorneys-General and the Ministerial Council on the Administration of Justice that comprised police and corrections Ministers of the states and territories.

Over time, governments, responsible departments and their ministers changed regularly (see Table 16.1, below) and it was necessary constantly to establish relationships with the new incumbents. Over the Institute's five decades, the Liberal/National coalition was in government on four occasions over 29 years with 6 different Prime Ministers and 12 Ministers responsible for the AIC (noting that Scott Morrison was appointed as Minister for Home Affairs from 6 May 2021 until 23 May 2022, in addition to being Prime Minister—at the same time that Karen Andrews was Minister for Home Affairs). In August 2022, the Solicitor-General gave advice concerning the concurrent appointment of the then Prime Minister to another Ministerial position, finding that although this was legally valid, the failure to publicise the appointment was inconsistent with the principle of responsible government (Donaghue 2022, p. 14).

The ALP was also in government on four occasions over 23 years with six different Prime Ministers and eleven Ministers responsible for the AIC. This provides, to some extent, a natural experiment to test some of the influences which each government had exerted on the AICs functions and fortunes.

The Institute's legislation was introduced by the Gorton Liberal/Country Party coalition in 1971 and fell within the Attorney-General's portfolio. Early Attorneys-General demonstrated an interest in black-letter legal reforms to criminal law and procedure and the Institute undertook a good deal of research in these areas to satisfy their demands.

Although the Institute's legislation was enacted during the currency of a conservative government, it began work during the term of the Whitlam Labor government (from 1972 to 1975) and continued to fall within the Attorney-General's Portfolio during subsequent administrations including the Fraser coalition (from 1975 to 1983) and the Hawke-Keating Labor Party (from 1983 to 1996)—although each of these governments raised new and diverse research requirements for the Institute.

When the Howard coalition took office in 1996 (Plate 4.1), the responsible portfolio for the Institute changed from that of the

Plate 4.1 (l-r) Director, Dr Adam Graycar, Attorney-General and Minister for Justice, The Hon. Daryl Williams and AIC Board Chair, The Hon. Justice Sally Brown, at the opening of the Griffith building, 24 July 1996 (*Source* AIC Archives)

Attorney-General to the newly-styled Justice Department under Coalition Minister Daryl Williams, and then to the Department of Justice and Customs from 1998 to 2007 under Coalition Ministers Amanda Vanstone, Chris Ellison and David Johnston, sequentially. When the ALP took office in 2007, the Institute became the responsibility of Bob Debus MP, Minister for Home Affairs, who was followed by Brendan O'Conner MP from June 2009, and Jason Clare MP who was Minister for Home Affairs and Minister of Justice from December 2011 until Labor lost government to the Coalition in September 2013. Since 1 June 2022, following the election of the Labor government on 23 May 2022, the Institute has once again fallen within the portfolio of the Attorney-General (pursuant to Commonwealth Administrative Arrangements Orders, C2022Q00006 and C2022Q00007).

Plate 4.2 Child Exploitation Material Reduction Research Program Roundtable, Brisbane, 1 November 2018. (left to right) Dr Rick Brown, AIC Deputy Director; Neil Gaughan, AFP Deputy Commissioner Operations; former Minister for Home Affairs, the Hon Peter Dutton MP and Michael Phelan APM, ACIC CEO and AIC Director (*Source* AIC Annual Report 2018, p. 77)

These changes in governments and administering departments resulted in various alterations being made to the type of research being undertaken by the Institute as well as to its budgets, staffing and accommodation. Some Ministers, for example, had particular criminal justice or crime prevention initiatives that they wished the Institute to pursue. Attorney-General Lionel Murphy QC, for example, promoted the ALP social reform agenda that included abolition of capital punishment, establishment of the Australian Law Reform Commission (ALRC), the Family Court, the Australian Legal Aid Office and the Trade Practices Commission that all provided new research opportunities for the AIC. More recently, former Minister of Home Affairs, Peter Dutton's concern over child exploitation and abuse between 2017 and 2021 (AIC Annual Report 2019, p. 77) led to the establishment of the Australian Centre to Counter Child Exploitation (ACCCE) and a range of research projects being undertaken by the AIC concerning child abuse and sexual exploitation. The AIC also chaired the Research Working Group of the ACCCE that was established on 1 April 2019 with 18 stakeholder members (Plate 4.2).

When Karen Andrews was appointed as Minister for Home Affairs in 2021, she continued to support the Institute's focus on child abuse and family violence as well as the Institute's ongoing work on serious and organised crime. Throughout the fifty years, only two Ministers have been women, both Liberals, Amanda Vanstone from 1997 to 2001, and Karen Andrews from March 2021 to May 2022. Both agreed to the Institute promoting Commonwealth interests in its research agenda but have shown, arguably, less interest in re-framing the research agenda to address their own personal interests than some other Ministers. The return of the Labor government in May 2022 promises to reinstate some of the social justice research agendas that existed when it began life fifty years previously—along with new ones that have taken on currency in recent times such as climate change, corruption and cybercrime.

Other Public Sector Stakeholders

The Institute's stakeholders, however, go far beyond Commonwealth government ministers, their staff and public officials within their departments. The members of the Institute's Board of Management, the CRC and CRAC have been equally important stakeholders as they represent the interests not only of Commonwealth concerns, but also those of the states and territories—recalling that most conventional crime is predominantly a state and territory matter. Ensuring that these representatives were made aware of the Institute's research activities and happy with their focus and breadth, were essential in guaranteeing financial and political support for the Institute as a whole. Failure to obtain adequate approval from such stakeholders led to the possibility of governments losing confidence in the need for the Institute, and contemplating ways in which its influence (and even existence) could be curtailed.

In 1981, for example, recommendations were made by the so-called Razor Gang, the Coalition Government's Cabinet *Review of Commonwealth Functions*. These suggested that the federal public service should be reduced in size by two percent with administrative costs cut by three percent. Included in the plans were that the AICs proposed new building should not proceed and that the states should meet six-sevenths of the annual appropriation of $1.2m provided to the AIC by the federal government (Fraser 1981). Two unnamed states declined to pay the estimated $200,000 each to maintain the work of the Institute in addition to their normal contributions to the Criminology Research Fund. This situation led to considerable instability in the Institute with the Board writing to the Attorney-General in June 1981 expressing its concern over the impact of the government's proposals:

> The Board stresses the irreparable damage likely to be inflicted upon the Institute if the present uncertainty continues. Years of work in building up an expert team will be lost as the staff are already leaving. (AIC Board Minutes, 9 June 1981, p. 5)

Because the states were aware of the work of the Institute and supported the continuation of the Institute's research activities supported by Commonwealth funding, the proposed re-allocation of funding was not pursued—although the rejection of funding for a new building was affirmed—leading to the Institute remaining at Colbee Court for almost another decade (Knez 1981). Although the federal government decided not to close the Institute, it required the Institute's staff and organisational structure to be reviewed by the Management and Special Services Division of the Attorney-General's Department. This review was carried out by Mr D. I. McDonald and Mrs C. Moore in December 1981, and included lengthy discussions with Institute staff (AIC Board Minutes, 14 December 1981, p. 4).

Relations with Law Enforcement

During the early years of the Institute, there was little research undertaken on law enforcement, with only occasional projects dealing with police and other law enforcement agencies. When Director Adam Graycar attended his first meeting of the Ministerial Council on the Administration of Justice, he experienced general hostility from the Police Commissioners who believed that 'the AIC thought all police were evil and the only role of police was to oppress the poor and harass indigenous people' (Adam Graycar, Interview, 1 March 2021). Adam sought to address this perception by visiting all the Commissioners in their home states and territories shortly after his arrival. As a result of this, and further efforts, the relationship of trust between the police and the AIC gradually improved over time.

One important stakeholder that the Institute had a close, but sometimes variable, relationship with, was the Australian Federal Police (AFP 2009). As the principal Commonwealth law enforcement agency, it was inevitable that the Institute's research would touch on how the AFP undertook its activities and the level of satisfaction that the community had with its achievements. Research findings that were seen to be critical of the AFP had to be managed carefully in order to ensure the continuation of a congenial relationship between the AIC and the AFP such that AIC researchers would have ongoing access to AFP personnel and information for future research projects.

Since the AFP had been established in 1979, following the recommendations of Sir Robert Mark (1978) that there should be a single federal police agency in Australia, questions arose as to the necessity for and effectiveness of the new agency. At the AIC, Bruce Swanton (Plate 4.3) had been appointed as a Senior Research Officer to work on a range of projects including a number relating to law enforcement. Bruce had extensive experience of policing having served with the London Metropolitan Police, the New Zealand and New South Wales Police Forces and the Royal Papua New Guinea Constabulary. He also had experience with the Royal Military Police and the Royal Australian Army Provost Corp. As such he was well placed to lead the Institute's policing research. When it came to Commonwealth policing by the AFP, Bruce had published numerous articles on police conduct and integrity in various journals, including a regular column, 'Offbeat', in the *Australian Police Journal*. These opinions attracted a good deal of attention, some coming to the attention of the Attorney-General and the AICs Board. In response, the following advice was recorded by the Board:

> [Acting Director] Professor Harding felt that more care should be taken in phrasing any introduction to Bruce Swanton to ensure his Institute connection was not mentioned. The Chairman suggested that if Mr Swanton could not guarantee this, he should be instructed not to submit this material for publication. After some discussion, the Board of Management decided that the Acting Director should take appropriate steps to ensure that any member of staff who prepared material for publication in a private capacity should not be described as associated with the Institute of Criminology in the eventual publication of that material. (AIC Board Minutes, 25 November 1983, p. 6)

Relations between the AIC and the AFP fluctuated over time, with criticisms of the AFP, overt or implied from the Institute's research findings or staff, resulting in some offers of research consultancies ceasing, and then re-commencing after efforts were made to repair any damage caused to the relationship. In December 1987, the Deputy Commissioner of the AFP, John Johnson, replaced Norman Reaburn on the AICs Board, which was indicative of an improvement in AIC-AFP relations (Grant Wardlaw, Interview, 30 November 2020). Since the development of the AICs association with the ACIC, the relationship with the AFP has improved further, leading to close collaboration on various research projects such as those relating to online child abuse, organised crime and economic crime. This, of course, has not solved the question of the AICs independence from public sector agencies, some of which have been criticised for their conduct, particularly concerning Indigenous Australians.

Another member of staff whose criticism of law enforcement agencies created difficulties for the Institute was Dr Jocelynne Scutt (Plate 4.4), who had worked at the Institute between 1976 and 1981 as a Research Criminologist (Legal). Dr Scutt had graduated in law from the University of Western Australia in 1969 and undertook postgraduate studies in law at the University of Sydney, at both Southern Methodist University and the University of Michigan in the US and Cambridge University in England.

Plate 4.3   Bruce Swanton, c. 1983 (*Source* AIC Archives)

Dr Scutt was one of a highly qualified and respected group of researchers who had worked at the AIC during the 1970s and whose work enhanced the Institute's reputation greatly. These individuals—including John Braithwaite, Andrew Hopkins, Arie Freiberg, Grant Wardlaw, John Seymour, John Walker and Jocelynne Scutt—to name a few, each had highly successful University and government careers after leaving the Institute. Dr Scutt had undertaken considerable work on victims of crime and had impressive publication and presentation records as well as a high media profile. On 29 June 1981, Dr Scutt's contract with the AIC ended, but the Board agreed to extend her term for a further six months, noting that 'this six months being notice of termination'

Plate 4.4   Dr Jocelynne Scutt, c. 1981 (*Source* AIC Archives)

(AIC Board Report, 9 June 1981, p. 2). Shortly after this Board meeting, Dr Scutt's report, *Restoring Victims of Crime: A Basis for the Reintroduction of Restitution into the Australian Criminal Justice System*, was released (Scutt 1980). Her departure on 19 August 1981, prior to the end of the six-month extension of her contract, was apparently also hastened by a decline in her professional relationship with the Director. She recounted the circumstances of this in an interview in 2006 for the *Women's Web* (2006, n.p.):

> [In 1981] I did a conference on criminal assault at home and other forms
> of domestic violence at the Australian Institute of Criminology. I made

sure that conference had women from the refuges, women from sexual assault reform centres, the police, academics, social workers etc. … What was really hilarious about that conference (it was a very good conference but of course there was some agitation because of these people with competing views, who had never discussed things before) was that it got on to the front page of the *Canberra Times*. At the time the head of the Australian Institute of Criminology, Bill Clifford, had been overseas. He came back to find all this action emblazoned on the front page. He was quite upset. He was also upset because we had used the funding from the budget for this conference. … I think that money, for Bill Clifford at least notionally, had been allocated for a new vehicle for the Australian Institute of Criminology – his vehicle. … The next year I decided that what we had to do was have a conference on rape law reform. He said we weren't going to have it at the Institute, because we weren't going to use the money on bringing all these women to Canberra again.

After leaving the Institute, Dr Scutt practised at the Sydney Bar and also became Associate to Justice Lionel Murphy of the High Court, whom she described as 'having an acute legal and political brain' (Women's Web 2006, n.p.). She then went on to hold a number of senior government and private sector roles including as a Judge in Fiji. She later moved to England where she is currently a local Councillor in Cambridge, a Senior Fellow at the University of Buckingham, an author and filmmaker. She was appointed an Officer of the Order of Australia in 1996, for service to feminist jurisprudence and issues affecting women. Dr Scutt's departure from the Institute in 1981 was followed by a number of other resignations by senior research staff, leading to a general decline in morale, caused principally by the uncertainty over the Institute's future resulting from the 'Razor Gang's' recommendations. The departure of both Drs Scutt and Seymour in 1981 left the Institute 'in the parlous state of having no person with legal training in any of the senior research positions' (AIC Annual Report 1982, p. 6). The Director then raised this matter with the Attorney-General who 'indicated that he would be unable to take any decision on replacement until receipt of the report on the staff and organisational structure of the Institute'. He also indicated 'that he was aware that the Institute had suffered greatly from staff ceilings and the cuts which had been imposed' (AIC Board Minutes, 9 March 1982, p. 2).

Constraints of Working Within Government

A major difference between academic research and that engaged in by government criminologists is the necessity for Ministerial approval for the release of research reports. Although some University consultancy reports may never be published owing to the terms of funding contracts, there is an ever-present possibility that research conducted within government will not be publicly-available owing to its sensitivities. This has happened to AIC research reports on a number of occasions, including instances in which, objectively, the findings being reported were innocuous, simply presenting information already available to the public. The same issue also arose for the Home Office Research Unit in the UK (Hough 2014, p. 217). Former AIC director, Adam Graycar, described the problem as follows (Graycar 2016, p. 2):

> While I was Director of the AIC I had a 'top secret' security clearance. From time to time I would see classified material, and often would have no idea why it was classified, because there was nothing special or secret in it. Not only that, there were times when material came marked as classified, which was entirely plagiarised. The material which I recall, produced by the former NCA and other agencies, was on occasion an AIC or other public research document, word for word, but re-titled and classified.

Until recently, the fact that the AIC was an independent statutory authority carried with it the expectation that the bulk of its research would be available for public scrutiny, but now that the Institute is embedded within the Commonwealth public service, this might not continue to be the case.

The need for independence from government was identified from the earliest days of the Institute's existence. Sir Leon Radzinowicz (1973, p. 2), in his Report to the Commonwealth on 17 November 1973, observed:

The Institute is expected to function under the authority of the Attorney General and in this sense may be regarded as part of the Department of Justice. Yet it is also expected to serve the needs of the other States, and last, but not least, to preserve an independence in research and in its other activities which would make it appear, neither in substance nor in form, as a purely administrative adjunct of the Ministry... I cannot say that these concerns have been fully secured in the structure of the Institute as it is presently envisaged. ... It is essential that the institute should preserve its managing committee wherein the various States are represented by senior civil servants of their respective Departments of Justice.

Conducting research within government also means that the time for public release of findings has to fit within the government's policy agenda. This can result in some reports waiting many months, or even years, before they are released in order for the government to be confident that the findings can be explained in terms of existing or planned policies and any criticism minimised.

An example of this concerned the cost of crime research undertaken by the Institute since its establishment. Governments, and particularly criminal justice agencies, have a keen interest in estimating the cost of crime to the community as this can indicate, on the one hand, their effectiveness in controlling crime and reducing government expenditure, or, on the other hand, their need to increase resources to control increasing incidence of crime and its associated cost. The Institute has embarked on research to estimate the incidence of crime and its associated costs each five years or so since the mid-1970s. On each occasion, completed reports remained under embargo for many months until the government considered it appropriate to make the findings public.

The first piece of AIC research that estimated the cost of maintaining the criminal justice system was published in May 1976 (Kononewsky 1976). It arose out of interest in this policy question shown during the Fifth UN Crime Congress held in Geneva in September 1975. Although limited to the costs of law enforcement, courts and correctional administration, the study estimated the expenditure on law, order and public safety at $569 million for 1975–1976 and $740 million for 1977–1978. This, however, did not take into account the economic losses associated with individual criminal victimisation which, when added to the cost of law, order and public safety, were estimated to amount to more than $2 billion for 1977–1978 (Clifford 1979). Between 1990 and 2011, the Institute carried out more detailed and extensive assessments of the cost of all crime to the Australian economy. Between 2014 and 2021, further research was undertaken to estimate the economic impact of serious and organised crime only—following the Institute's developing association with the ACIC. Over the thirty-one years from 1990 to 2021, the research showed a general increase in these costs of crime, with the total cost as a percentage of GDP fluctuating over the same period (Fig. 4.1). Appropriate selection of either net cost or cost as a percentage of GDP has been used by governments for media publicity depending on the position to be adopted by the agency in question. Paul Wilson, former Assistant Director (Research and Statistics), noted this when he observed that [the Institute researchers] 'work very hard at maintaining intellectual integrity and independence despite occasional pressures from outside to conduct the research process or present results in a particular manner' (Wilson 1987, p. vi). The most recent cost estimation for 2020–2021 (Smith and Hickman 2022) was written in August 2021 but only released in April 2022 during debate on the budget that preceded the federal election on 21 May 2022.

Two other limitations on conducting research within the public sector relate to the level of funding available and the timelines during which research must be conducted. Although criminological research conducted in universities and by consultancy practices is also subject to these constraints, the demands within government are sometimes extreme—with major research activities being required within months as opposed to years, and for tens of thousands of dollars rather than hundreds of thousands. Public sector criminologists, as government employees, are invariably required to adhere to these requirements, occasionally resulting in research outputs being of limited sophistication and scale—thus justifying some of the criticisms from academics levelled against 'administrative' criminology (see Hough 2014; Mayhew 2016).

Finally, the demands of government often require public sector criminological research to be conducted on new and developing crime problems. Often, such topics are so new that little is known about them,

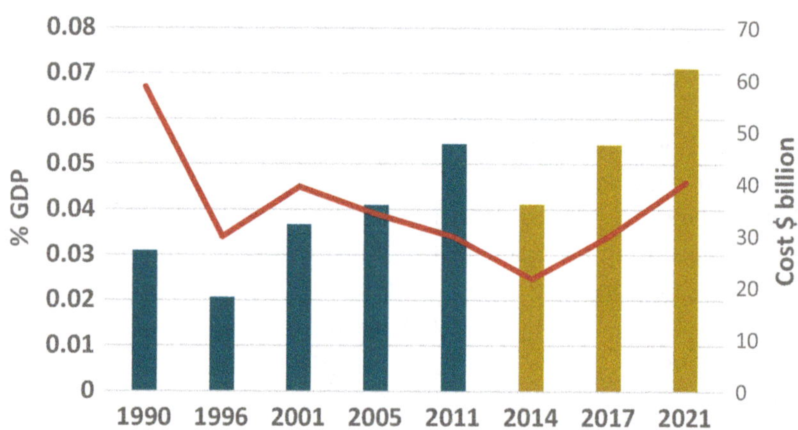

Fig. 4.1 AIC cost of crime estimations, 1990–2021 (*Source* **Cost of all crime** [Walker 1992, 1997; Mayhew 2003; Rollings 2008; Smith et al. 2014]. **Cost of organised crime** [ACC 2015; Smith 2018; Smith and Hickman 2022])

no statistics are available to assess their extent, and no legal jurisprudence has developed to support legal analysis. Research into cybercrime, environmental crime, human trafficking, terrorism and crime during pandemics are cases in point leading to research sometimes being somewhat descriptive and tentative in its solutions.

Conclusions

Throughout the Institute's fifty years, relations with governments have been torrid, with regular reviews conducted of the Institute and its activities by the four Coalition governments and three Labor governments (see Chapter 5 below). When each new government commenced, Ministers saw this as an opportunity to review the Institute's operations and funding with reductions in funding occurring usually within years of a new government taking office, resulting in deficits being experienced.

New Ministers also sought to institute changes in the focus of research, some more profoundly than others—with most leading to a need for the Institute to enhance its Commonwealth research focus.

Although the Institute was established as an independent statutory authority, where its research disclosed critical questions for governments to address concerning crime and justice policies or agendas, the Institute found itself, indeed, 'between a rock and a hard place', facing the challenges of maintaining its role as a provider of independent, evidence-based research and its need to satisfy ministers and their governments in minimising public sector costs and not raising difficult issues for which governments needed to respond. On occasions, the balance shifted one way or the other, and it is a tribute to the efforts of many Directors and Boards that the Institute survived attempts to silence it or reduce its impact. Peter Grabosky, in his interview (3 December 2020), noted 'the vulnerability of the AIC to public sector reform', and to fend this off, Directors sought to 'stake out a claim' for research projects that others, such as the ABS, were not willing to undertake—such as the Deaths in Custody and National Homicide Monitoring programs—that remain current today.

During the 1980s, Director Richard Harding was supportive of research that raised the hackles of government officials by disclosing inadequacies in public administration. An example cited by John Braithwaite in his interview (30 January 2021) was the politically sensitive research he undertook with Peter Grabosky into the 'Bottom of the Harbour' tax fraud schemes and the lack of action taken by the Australian Taxation Office to address these at the time (Grabosky 1989). Braithwaite recalled: 'in a meeting we had with the then Deputy Commissioner of Taxation, he was so angry with us I thought he was going to have a heart attack':

In another era, that kind of robust critique of a Commonwealth government agency for allowing major criminality to occur on their watch that was just unacceptable and should be exposed by an agency like the Institute of Criminology, just wasn't on–after the Harding era. (John Braithwaite, Interview, 30 January 2021)

Threats of merger have loomed large on a number of occasions as we shall see below, and these were often used to remove a contentious public sector voice, without being seen to silence it entirely through dissolution. The Institute has come close to destruction on a number of occasions, but survived by reducing its costs or changing its research or publication focus—while just being able to continue with its independent research. Overseas, other similar organisations have faced the same tensions—with some suffering the consequences of merger with larger entities, others changing their research focus, and still others ceasing to exist. On balance, it appears that allowing public sector criminological research bodies to exist as separate entities, with ring-fenced budgets and funding sufficient to meet their stated aims, results in the greatest degree of stability, productivity and utility of the work, both for governments and the communities they serve.

References

Australian Crime Commission (ACC). 2015. *The Costs of Serious and Organised Crime in Australia 2013–14*. Canberra: Australian Crime Commission. https://acic.govcms.gov.au/publications/intelligence-products/costs-ser ious-and-organised-crime-australia. Accessed 6 October 2021.

Australian Federal Police (AFP). 2009. *Australian Federal Police: The First Thirty Years*, 2nd rev. 2012. Canberra: AFP. https://www.afp.gov.au/sites/default/ files/PDF/afp-the-first-thirty-years.pdf. Accessed 6 March 2022.

Australian Institute of Criminology (AIC). 1981. *Minutes of the 34th Meeting of the Board of Management.* 9 June, Canberra: Australian Institute of Criminology.

Australian Institute of Criminology (AIC). 1981. *Minutes of the 36th Meeting of the Board of Management.* 14 December, Canberra: Australian Institute of Criminology.

Australian Institute of Criminology (AIC). 1982. *10th Annual Report 1982.* Canberra: Australian Institute of Criminology.

Australian Institute of Criminology (AIC). 1982. *Minutes of the 37th Meeting of the Board of Management.* 9 March, Canberra: Australian Institute of Criminology.

Australian Institute of Criminology (AIC). 1983. *Minutes of the 44th Meeting of the Board of Management*. 25 November, Canberra: Australian Institute of Criminology.

Australian Institute of Criminology (AIC). 2018. *Annual Report 2017–18*. Canberra: Australian Institute of Criminology.

Australian Institute of Criminology (AIC). 2019. *Annual Report 2018–19*. Canberra: Australian Institute of Criminology.

Carson, Kit, and Pat O'Malley. 1989. The Institutional Foundations of Contemporary Australian Criminology. *Australian and New Zealand Journal of Sociology* 25 (3): 333–355.

Clifford, William. 1979. Director's Digest: The Cost of Crime. *Australian Institute of Criminology Reporter* 1 (2): 3–4.

Clifford, William. 1981. Criminological Research in Perspective. In *Review of Criminological Research: Papers from a Seminar 24–27 February 1981*, ed. David Biles. Canberra: AIC Archives.

Donaghue, Stephen. 2022. *Opinion in the Matter of the Validity of the Appointment of Mr Morrison to Administer the Department of Industry, Science, Energy and Resources*. SG No. 12 of 2022. Canberra: Office of the Solicitor-General. https://www.pmc.gov.au/sites/default/files/sg-no-12-of-2022.pdf. Accessed 25 August 2022.

Editors. 1976. Editorial: Berkeley's School of Criminology, 1950–1976. *Crime and Social Justice* 6 (1976): 1–3. https://www.socialjusticejournal.org/SJE dits/06Edit-1.html. Accessed 13 August 2022.

Fraser, Malcolm. 1981. Ministerial Statement on the Review of Commonwealth Functions. Parliamentary Debates, House of Representatives, 30 April, p. 1838.

Geis, Gilbert. 1994. 'This Sort of Thing Isn't Helpful:' The Dilemmas of the Australian Institute of Criminology. *Australian and New Zealand Journal of Criminology* 27 (3): 282–298.

Grabosky, Peter N. 1989. *Wayward Governance: Illegality and its Control in the Public Sector*, Canberra: Australian Institute of Criminology.

Graycar, Adam. 2016. Submission to the Senate Legal and Constitutional Affairs Legislation Committee on the Australian Crime Commission Amendment (Criminology Research) Bill 2016. Canberra: Parliament House.

Hardman, Josh. 2016. UC Berkeley: The Closure of the School of Criminology, 1976. In *A History of Repression at UC Berkeley*. https://www.fou ndsf.org/index.php?title=UC_Berkeley:_The_Closure_of_the_School_of_ Criminology,_1976. Accessed 13 August 2022.

Hough, Mike. 2014. Confessions of a Recovering 'Administrative Criminologist': Jock Young, Quantitative Research and Policy Research. *Crime Media Culture* 10 (3): 215–226.

Knez, Ted. 1981. States Revolt on Crime Research. *The Australian*, 22 July.

Koehler, Johann. 2015. Development and Fracture of a Discipline: Legacies of the School of Criminology at Berkeley. *Criminology* 53 (4): 513–544.

Konenewsky, Anatole. 1976. *The Costs of Criminal Justice: An Analysis.* Canberra: Australian Institute of Criminology. https://www.aic.gov.au/publications/archive/archive-42. Accessed 4 January 2021.

Mark, Sir Robert. 1978. *Report to the Minister for Administrative Services on the Organisation of Police Resources in the Commonwealth Area and Other Related Matters.* Canberra: Australian Government Publishing Service. https://nla.gov.au/nla.obj-2720249015/view?partId=nla.obj-2721138600. Accessed 6 March 2022.

Mayhew, Patricia. 2003. *Counting the Costs of Crime in Australia.* Trends & Issues in Crime and Criminal Justice, no. 247. Canberra: Australian Institute of Criminology.

Mayhew, Patricia. 2016. In Defence of Administrative Criminology. *Crime Science* 5 (7): 1–10.

Radzinowicz, Leon. 1973. *Report of Sir Leon Radzinowicz with Respect to the Australian Institute of Criminology*, New York. Canberra: National Library of Australia (6093 / 72/4182).

Rollings, Kia. 2008. *Counting the Costs of Crime in Australia: A 2005 Update.* Research and Public Policy Series, no. 91. Canberra: Australian Institute of Criminology.

Scutt, Jocelynne A. 1980. *Restoring Victims of Crime: A Basis for the Reintroduction of Restitution into the Australian Criminal Justice System.* Canberra: Australian Institute of Criminology. https://www.aic.gov.au/publications/archive/archive-64 Accessed 28 May 2021.

Smith, Russell G. 2018. *Estimating the Costs of Serious and Organised Crime in Australia 2016–17*. Statistical Report no. 9. Canberra: Australian Institute of Criminology. https://www.aic.gov.au/publications/sr/sr9. Accessed 6 October 2021.

Smith, Russell G., and Amelia Hickman. 2022. *Estimating the Costs of Serious and Organised Crime in Australia 2020–21*. Statistical Report. Canberra: Australian Institute of Criminology. https://www.aic.gov.au/publications/sr/sr. Accessed 1 May 2022.

Smith, Russell G., Penny Jorna, Josh Sweeney, and Georgina Fuller. 2014. *Counting the Costs of Crime in Australia: A 2011 Estimate.* Research and Public Policy Series, no. 129. Canberra, Australian Institute of Criminology.

Tanzer, Noel, Des Hill, and Grant Wardlaw. 1994. *Review of the Australian Institute of Criminology: Report.* Canberra: Australian Institute of Criminology.

Tonry, Michael. 2010. 'Public Criminology' and Evidence-Based Policy. *Criminology and Public Policy* 9 (4): 783–797.

Walker, John. 1992. *Estimates of the Costs of Crime in Australia.* Trends & Issues in Crime and Criminal Justice, no. 39. Canberra: Australian Institute of Criminology.

Walker, John. 1997. *Estimates of the Costs of Crime in Australia in 1996.* Trends & Issues in Crime and Criminal Justice, no. 72. Canberra: Australian Institute of Criminology.

Wilson, Paul. 1987. Introduction: Review of Australian Criminological Research. In *Review of the Australian Criminological Research*, ed. Paul Wilson and Vicki Dalton, v–vii. Canberra: Australian Institute of Criminology. https://www.aic.gov.au/sites/default/files/2021-09/review-australian-criminological-research-1987.pdf. Accessed 25 March 2022.

Women's Web. 2006. Interview with Dr Jocelynne Scutt, 11 September. https://web.archive.org/web/20060224081647/http:/home.vicnet.net.au/~womenweb/sources/Later%20Narratives/Dr%20Jocelynne%20Scutt.htm. Accessed 4 June 2021.

5

Balancing the Books

Introduction

When the AIC was established, the model of public sector criminological research adopted in Australia had two approaches to improving the level and quality of research being conducted: on the one hand, it provided for the employment of internal staff to undertake research on topics determined by the Board of Management, directors and stakeholders and, on the other, it provided funding for researchers external to the agency to undertake research on topics they proposed that had been approved by the CRC. These have been called, respectively, proactive and reactive approaches to conducting public sector research.

Funding for the Institute came from both Commonwealth appropriation, state and territory contributions to the Criminology Research Fund and from revenue raised by the organisation itself (own-source funding). Own-source funding included revenue from fee-for-service research activities conducted by the AICs own research staff, revenue from publication and training activities, income from royalties and investments and revenue derived from special government funds—such

© The Author(s), under exclusive license to Springer Nature
Switzerland AG 2023
R. G. Smith, *Public Sector Criminological Research*,
https://doi.org/10.1007/978-3-031-28356-7_5

as the Proceeds of Crime Fund—that permitted the Institute, and others, to apply for funding for specified crime prevention activities out of money confiscated from offenders.

Comparing this model, with those adopted in other countries, it is clear that the local Australian approach carried with it a number of problematic aspects. In some other countries, criminological research was undertaken largely either within relevant government departments, such as the Home Office in the UK, in Universities or in dedicated criminological research agencies, such as the PNI agencies affiliated with the UN (see Chapter 12). Funding came from conventional, internal sources and the scope and type of research undertaken were clearly required to fulfil the mandate of the entity concerned. Where criminological research was conducted within a large government entity, such as the UK Home Office, access could be provided to substantial resources for projects that fell within the policy agenda of the government. In his Interview (17 October 2022), former Home Office employee, Dr Rick Brown, recalled that the Home Office Crime Reduction Program was initially provided with funding of £250 million with a further allocation of £150 million for closed-circuit television research. Ten percent of the original budget had been allocated for evaluation work. Another former Home Office employee at that time, Mike Hough (2018), argued that the outcomes of the evaluation work were 'pretty disappointing'.

In the US, the NIJ was charged with administering government funding to external researchers who applied for grants or consultancies to undertake specified work. In Australia, however, these roles were created by the same legislation, but administered separately by the AIC in respect of internal research, and the CRC in respect of external research. After legislative changes that merged the AIC and CRC took effect on 1 July 2011, both internal and external research was managed by the one administrative entity—the AIC. As a small statutory authority, core funding had to provide for infrastructure such as rental and information technology, personnel costs and the costs of undertaking and disseminating research.

Finance Managers

As shown in Table 16.2, the management of the AICs finances and other business administrative functions were undertaken by senior managers, variously designated over time as Executive Officer, Assistant Secretary, Corporate Manager, Manager of Administration and Finance, Deputy Director (Corporate) and Chief Financial Officer (CFO). Each was supported by Finance Officers and a team of clerical and accounting staff. William Miller was the first and longest serving Executive Officer from 1974 to September 1987, supported by Joseph Millar AASA, CPA, as Finance Officer, who took over when Bill retired, and served from 1987 until 1995. Bill Miller (Plate 5.1) was born in Scotland and had served in the Black Watch Regiment during the Second World War prior to working for the British Colonial Service. Before joining the AIC, he worked in the Fiji High Commissioner's Office in Canberra. Lionel Murphy QC, as Attorney-General, had opposed Bill's appointment as Executive Officer owing to his having been born outside Australia, but Jim Muirhead, as the AICs Acting Director, insisted that he be appointed—which Murphy subsequently agreed to (Muirhead 1996, p. 94).

When Adam Graycar became Director in 1994, a new Administrative Services Group was established that included general administration, human resources and financial operations. At this time, the Corporate Manager was Michael Brown who was supported by Carole Hunt as Head of Administration, François Debaecker as Manager of Information Technology, Merril Thompson as Publications Manager, Garry Raffaele as Communications Manager and John Myrtle as Principal Librarian. Including Executive personnel, there were 28 staff engaged in these corporate and administrative functions, 64% of the total 44 staff members in 1996. Salaries for these individuals represented a large financial burden on a small government agency established primarily to conduct criminological research. Over time, the balance between research and administrative staff altered with research personnel gradually representing a higher proportion of total staffing. In his interview

Plate 5.1   Bill Miller, Executive Officer, 1974–1987 (*Source* AIC Archives)

(10 June 2022), Rick Brown noted that when he joined the AIC in 2011, there was 'a perception that the corporate side had grown while the research side had not'. He argued that 'non-research functions are a peripheral cost that should service the delivery and dissemination of research', and currently, he keeps his eye more on the research side than corporate functions that are monitored by the ACIC/AICs Director.

Michael Brown's appointment as Corporate Manager was short, being replaced by Geoff Chapman, as Manager of Administration and Finance in 1998, supported by Raju Mahen as Finance Officer. During Toni Makkai's term as Director, Administrative Services were re-named, Corporate Services, and Tony Marks FCPA, FFin, FTIA was appointed as CFO, later taking on the position of Acting Director from 3 May 2008. The AICs new Director, Adam Tomison, also re-structured the Institute in 2009, with Tony Marks becoming Deputy Director (Corporate) and CFO. Upon the legislative change to FMA Act governance in 2011, Tony Marks's assistant, Brian Russell CPA, became Deputy Director (Corporate) and CFO. The most recent re-structure occurred following the Machinery of Government change in 2015 in which the ACIC began to provide corporate services to the AIC that included having Yvette Whitaker CPA, as CFO of both the ACIC and AIC, supported by the ACICs Finance Team. This most recent version was not always the most efficient arrangement as the AICs business needs were often subsumed within the heavy workload required of finance and accounting staff of the much larger entity, leading to delays and some instances of mis-communication and error in servicing the AIC.

Trends in Income and Expenditure

Between 1972–1973 and 2020–2022, the AICs total government appropriation amounted to $180 million. In addition, a further $62.3 million was received from own-source income such as fee-for-service consulting and other sources. Total operating revenue amounted to $242 million over the five decades while total current annual expenditure totalled $241 million, or 99.4% of total operating revenue over the same period.

During the AICs first fifteen years, the Commonwealth provided funds that largely met all these expenses as shown in Fig. 5.1.

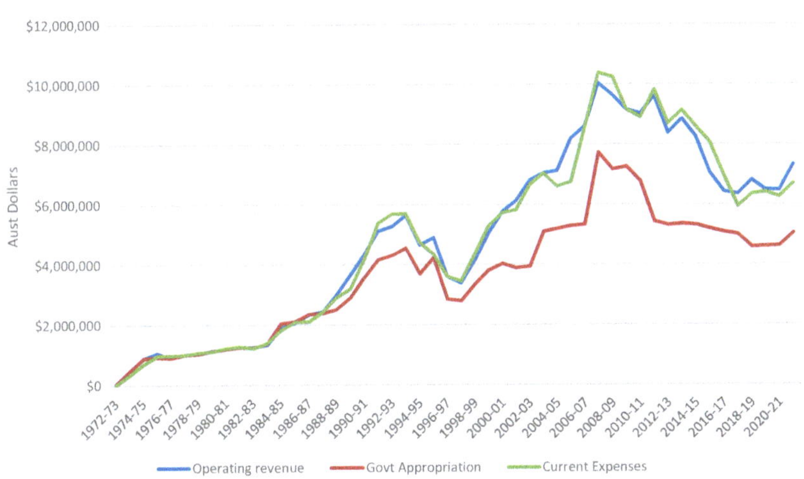

Fig. 5.1 AIC revenue and expenses, 1972–1973 to 2021–2022 (Aust$) (*Source* Derived from Financial Statements in AIC *Annual Reports* 1972–1973 to 2021–2022)

From the late 1980s, however, expenditure began to exceed government appropriation with the shortfall being largely met from other sources including fee-for-service consulting work undertaken for other government entities and the private sector. In some years, a substantial deficit was recorded, such as in 2008–2009 when current expenses exceeded operating revenue by almost $600,000. By contrast, however, in 2005–2006, a surplus of more than $1.4 million was recorded (Fig. 5.2).

To understand the changing value of funds provided by government and from other sources to the AIC over the five decades, it is useful to consider the funds provided as a percentage of national GDP. Apart from a small increase in the early 1990s, there was an overall decline in funding as a percentage of GDP between 1973 and 2022 (Fig. 5.3).

Revenue as a percentage of GDP declined during the first decade and then increased gradually to peak in 1991–1992 to 1993–1994. The Institute then experienced a substantial decline in government appropriation following a review of its operations (see Geis 1994; James and Sutton 1994) with funding never returning to the same level as a percentage of GDP. The Institute continued to expand, however, owing to a large increase in fee-for-service revenue until this, too began to decline in

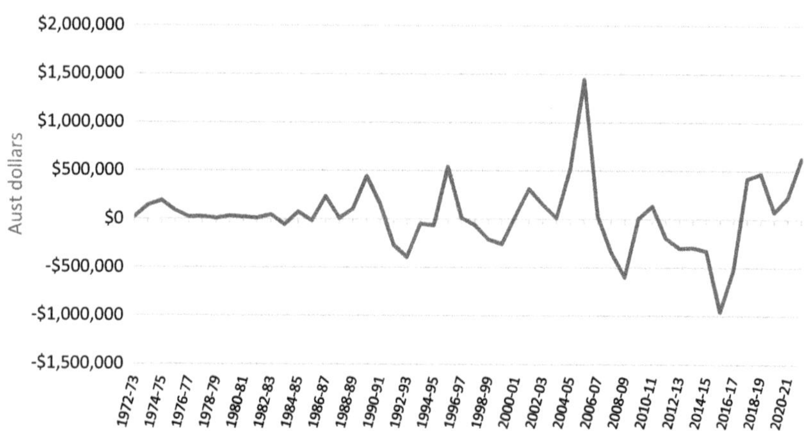

Fig. 5.2 AIC surplus/deficit, 1972–1973 to 2021–2022 (Aust$) (*Source* Derived from Financial Statements in AIC *Annual Reports* 1973–2022)

Fig. 5.3 AIC revenue and expenses, 1972–1973 to 2021–2022 as a percentage of current price annual GDP (% A$/1,000,000) (*Source* Derived from AIC *Annual Reports* 1973–2022; GDP derived from OECD [2022])

2007–08. In 2021–2022, government appropriation as a percentage of GDP was the lowest ever, although total operating revenue as a percentage of GDP increased between 2020–2021 and 2021–2022.

Trends in current expenditure of the AIC followed closely annual operating revenue, with expenses as a percentage of GDP declining during the first decade and then increasing gradually to peak in 1991–1992 to 1993–1994. The Institute then experienced a substantial decline in current expenditure as a percentage of GDP until 1997–1998. Expenditure as a percentage of GDP then increased until 2007–2008 following which it has continued to decline until 2021–2022—this being due, largely, to a general reduction in staffing numbers until staffing began to increase since 2016–2017.

Influences on the Institute's Finances

As we have seen in previous chapters, the Institute's operations were subject to a number of administrative, procedural, legislative and governance changes over the five decades—a number of which had financial implications. During this time, the Institute was subject to more than a dozen internal and independent reviews, some leading to major legislative or governance reforms (see Chapter 14). These were often provoked by a change in government or a perceived need to reduce expenditure, or to minimise or avoid activities that the government or reviewers believed were unnecessary, or not cost-effective. Some reforms were also based on more general economic reform strategies such as implementation of the concept of small government favoured by Coalition governments (see Kelly 2000). Table 5.1 lists the major internal and external reviews that were undertaken of the Institute's operations. Interestingly, almost equal numbers were instigated by either Coalition or Labor governments, often with the objective of reducing costs or streamlining administration. The reviews with the most profound impact on the AICs budget were the Coad/Tanzer reviews of 1994, and the incomplete merger with the ACC following the National Commission of Audit Report (Shepherd et al. 2014) that led to the MoG changes in 2015. The AICs Directors were able to fight-off other plans to abolish, diminish or merge the Institute in earlier years.

One of the most prominent changes to the Institute's financial management occurred when the *Criminology Research Act 1971* (Cth.) was amended by the *Financial Framework Legislation Amendment Act 2010* (Cth) to merge the CRC with the AIC and to move the merged body to the *Financial Management and Accountability Act 1997* (Cth—FMA Act). This arose from the findings of the Behm Report (2006) that decided against merging the AIC with the Attorney-General's Department, but led to the eventual merger of the AIC and CRC through the FMA Act reforms in 2011. These amendments also established the Criminology Research Special Account which is a ledger account in which all payments (debits) and receipts (credits) are recorded that relate to a particular activity or body. They included budget appropriations and items that could be debited to the special account such as the cost of running the AIC (s. 46(4)(a)).

Table 5.1 Inquiries and reviews of the AIC and CRC

Date	Government	Author	Title	Scope/Recommendations
6 April 1971	Lib/Nat		Establishment of AIC	
6 July 1979	Lib/Nat	Loof (1979)	Internal review of AICs establishment	AICs role and scope
30April 1981	Lib/Nat	Fraser (1981)	Review of Commonwealth Functions (Razor Gang) Sir Philip Lynch (Chair)	Increase state funding of AIC to 6/7 share; No new AIC building—see Cope (1981)
27 November 1981	Lib/Nat	McDonald and Moore (1981)	Internal AGD Review of Staff and Organisational Structure	AGD review of AIC following Razor Gang—Publications Division to be removed; staff ceiling of 26 imposed
16 August 1982	Lib/Nat	Gosling (1982)	Internal JV Barry Memorial Library Review	Internal review of functions and policy of library due to staff cuts
January 1987	ALP	Biles (1987)	Internal review of the work of the Criminology Research Council	Internal review of the CRCs funding, policies and outputs 1972–1986
April 1987	ALP	Wilson and Nixon (1987)	Internal policy-related research review	Internal review of AIC policy research 1974–1987
1990	ALP	CPMC	Review of AIC Corporate Plan	Management and administration review commissioned by AIC Board

(continued)

Table 5.1 (continued)

Date	Government	Author	Title	Scope/Recommendations
24 February 1994	ALP	Coad et al. (1994)	Review of Law Enforcement Arrangements	Abolish AIC Board; Report to CLEB; abolish CRC; save $1.5m per annum
23 May 1994	ALP	Tanzer et al. (1994)	Review of the AIC	Change building; new corporate goals and priorities by Minister; new Director and Research Director; new IT program; Library and publications reform; reduced international travel and work; 37 FTE staffing; CRC admin cost sharing
June 2003	Lib/Nat	Uhrig (2003)	Review of Statutory Authorities	Corporate governance recommendations
November 2006	Lib/Nat	Behm (2006)	Review of CRC Act, governance of AIC/CRC	Potential absorption of AIC/CRC into AGD, or transition to FMA Act
May 2006	Lib/Nat	Quay Connection (2006)	Communication Review	Internal review of AIC publications, website and dissemination activities
March 2008	ALP	Libraries Alive!	Review of JV Barry Library	Internal management review of Library's aims, procedures and outputs
1 July 2011	ALP	Act No 148/2010	Transfer of AIC from a CAC Act to FMA Act Agency	Merger of AIC and CRC and creation of CRAC

Date	Government	Author	Title	Scope/Recommendations
January 2012	ALP	Skehill (2012)	AGD Small and Medium Agencies Review	AIC to continue, but consider use of AGDs corporate services business offering
1 February 2014	Lib/Nat	Shepherd et al. (2014)	National Commission of Audit—Phase 1	AIC to be reviewed for possible merging, abolishing or transferring to a University
31 December 2015	Lib/Nat	APSC	Machinery of Government change	Movement of AIC staff to ACC and sharing building and some corporate services; staff seconded to work for AIC
June 2017	Lib/Nat	PM&C (PM&C)	Independent Intelligence Review	Need for better coordination of research with Innovation Fund and Hub

Income Considerations

In relation to the Institute's income, a number of aspects are worthy of further examination, although space does not permit a complete review of the many debates concerning the derivation of revenue over the five decades from each of the Institute's differing activities.

Fee-for-Service Work

As we have seen in Fig. 5.1, during the first fifteen years of the Institute's life, expenditure closely matched income from government. Since then, some directors sought to enhance the Institute's income by undertaking a range of profit-making ventures—some being more successful than others. There was also a debate among Boards, directors and staff about the propriety of a government agency undertaking profit-generating activities—with some being singularly opposed to the idea. Both Richard Harding and Dennis Challinger, for example, thought that fee-for-service work was generally inappropriate. In his interview, Harding argued that 'this was the wrong path for the Institute to follow as it prevented setting one's own agenda, and you were always a step behind the current trend—having to follow rather than lead' in producing research for the government (Richard Harding, Interview, 18 November 2021). During Duncan Chappell's time as Director, there was a general increase in fee-for-service work, which Dennis Challinger—who was at the time in charge of training activities—considered to be inappropriate. When his staff were told to do fee-for-service work instead of training activities that were funded out of appropriation, Challinger objected and eventually resigned from his position arguing that the 'move towards generating extra money to do additional research was something that I saw as slightly problematic' (Dennis Challinger, Interview, 18 February 2022).

On occasions, external funding provided the impetus to develop new and often lucrative lines of research. An example was Grant Wardlaw's work on drug indicators in the ACT in the late 1980s (Stevens et al. 1988). Funding for a three-year demonstration project was obtained that eventually led to the Institute's DUMA research that attracted government funding of many millions of dollars until it ceased in 2021. In his interview, however, Grant Wardlaw noted that it was preferable for the Institute to secure core funding rather than to seek out external funds, as 'staff would often spend more time looking for external money than undertaking the research they were employed to do' (Interview, 30 November 2020).

Following the legislative changes in 2010, section 47(1) of the *Criminology Research Act 1971* (Cth) now specifically allows the Institute to charge for its services as long as the charges are reasonably related to the cost of providing those services. Since 2000, the Institute received income from the sale of goods and services totalling over $45 million, or approximately $2 million a year (AIC, Annual Reports 2000–2022, Financial Statements). This came from research contracts entered into with a wide range of government entities as well as private sector bodies and non-profit organisations. Some were in response to requests for tenders, others were by direct invitation, and others formed part of official New Policy Proposals developed by other Commonwealth entities. Reliance on fee-for-service work was also evident in other Commonwealth entities including the AIHW where the agency undertook paid research regularly for the Department of Health, other government agencies and the private sector (Samantha Bricknell, Interview, 21 November 2022).

Following the AICs partial merger with the ACC in 2015, however, the decision was made to reduce substantially the amount of fee-for-service work undertaken. In his Interview (4 November 2022), Rick Brown explained this as being mainly to change the research focus away from research on the operation of criminal justice system entities in the states and territories, to research on more national concerns of relevance to the Commonwealth. This change was also made in recognition of the need to acknowledge that it was the Commonwealth that provided the bulk of the funding for the AICs activities.

Despite this, the Institute continued to undertake some fee-for-service work. Until 2022, the Institute had regularly collaborated in the presentation of ANZSOCs annual conference program. As the principal professional association for criminologists in Australia and New Zealand, it was appropriate for the AIC to have a close involvement with the society's activities. A number of directors and senior research staff held unpaid administrative positions on ANZSOCs Committee of Management, including positions as President and Fellow, Secretary and Treasurer, and the Institute co-hosted a number of ANZSOC conferences—especially those conducted in Canberra. Often, the Institute provided sponsorship funding or in-kind support by offering the services of its staff to assist with conference organisation. Since 2022, however, financial constraints, and a change of priorities, meant that the AIC would no longer provide sponsorship for ANZSOC events. This was also a reflection of the change in research emphasis away from state and territory concerns.

From 2011 to 2022, the Institute established a fee-for-service arrangement that enabled one of its administrative staff to work as the ANZSOC Secretary for two days a week with the Society paying an annual services fee and related expenses. This role was undertaken since 1 December 2016 by Katalina Foliaki (Plate 5.2). The benefits of the Institute's association with ANZSOC were, however, principally intangible in terms of publicity, advertising and promotion, rather than purely financial. Nonetheless, it was beneficial to have access to ANZSOC members who could act as referees for publications and speak at AIC events. In 2022, the AICs Director decided that allowing an AIC/ACIC staff member to work for ANZSOC on a fee-for-service basis was no longer appropriate and the arrangement ceased at the end of 2022.

Sale of Publications

One potential solution to the cost of producing printed publications was to charge users for access to works. In 1974, the Board approved a recommendation that Institute publications be sold in order to recover the cost of production and postage, other than for the Newsletter, Information Bulletins and Conference Proceedings—that were to be free to participants only—and that all publications would be free for libraries and government departments and other organisations with reciprocal arrangements (AIC, Minutes 25 February 1974, p. 33). This policy

Plate 5.2 Katalina Foliaki, ANZSOC Secretary, 2017–2022 (*Source* AIC Archives)

continued throughout the 1970s with books costing between $2.00 and $5.00 each, research reports generally $2.00 and other publications up to $5.00 (excluding postage) (see the full list of prices in the *AIC Reporter*, 1979 1(1), p. 1).

During the 1980s, only a small number of stakeholders continued to receive publications for free, with others either paying in full or, in the case of some libraries, having publication exchange agreements in place that allowed for reciprocal access to publications for free among certain agencies. Between 1988 and 1996, almost $100,000 a year was received by the Institute from the sale of publications, totalling $766,733 for these years alone (AIC, Annual Reports, 1988–1996, Financial Statements).

In more recent times, however, directors have all been opposed to the idea of charging for AIC publications, arguing that a publicly-funded government entity should make its research output freely available to all. This, of course, reflected the fact that most publications were available online rather than being printed, thus vastly reducing publication costs. Shortly before she retired from the AIC as Manager of the JV Barry

Library, Jane Shelling agreed, arguing that the demand would not be large enough to cover the administrative costs involved in collecting the fees and that other agencies such as AIHW, ABS and Australia's National Research Organisation for Women's Safety (ANROWS) did not sell their reports. Jane went on to say that 'it might, however, be possible to charge for enhanced access that includes searching for resources, but this might not be cost effective... The aim is for our material to be disseminated as widely as possible, and I think that would be impeded if it was for sale' (Jane Shelling, Interview, 23 March 2021).

Royalties

On occasions, commercially-published books written by Institute staff were offered for sale to the public by publishing houses. This, however, created a new policy challenge for Institute directors as current and former Institute staff who had authored such works, became entitled to receive contractual fees, royalties and other copyright fees from Collecting Agencies and elsewhere, in the absence of specific arrangements with the Institute. The matter first achieved prominence in the early 1980s in a number of cases in which former AIC staff had published books based on, or dealing with research undertaken during their tenure as AIC employees. After considering the circumstances of one case, the Board resolved to waive its entitlement to any copyright or royalty payments made to the staff member provided that the Institute was acknowledged in the publication and it received 100 copies of the work in question (AIC Minutes, 8 June 1982, pp. 3–4).

Similar arrangements were entered into with other former staff members who were permitted to retain all royalties on condition that the 100 copies of the book were provided to the Institute free of charge (AIC, Minutes 13 December 1982, p. 4). During his interview, Richard Harding was unable to recall knowing of this policy, observing that 'I didn't know that – nobody ever told me that – and I've no idea whether we did keep a hundred copies' (Richard Harding, Interview 18 November 2021). In one case, only six copies of the book in question were delivered (AIC, Minutes 25 November 1983, p. 5) leading to further discussion of the policy by the Board, and eventually to the adoption of a revised policy that 'no royalties shall be payable to Institute staff members for books or other publications written in the course of their employment' but that the director would have a discretion to decide how such income should be dealt with (AIC, Minutes, 11 December 1986, p. 7). This, of course, led to debate about the entitlement to retain royalties where the research for publications had been undertaken partly during Institute work time and partly during staff members' non-work time.

Over time, the policy was relaxed as it became clear that it was administratively difficult to monitor receipt of copyright payments made to current and former staff. In the case of five staff members, for example, each had published over 100 AIC or external books or articles during their time at the AIC, with one individual publishing almost 250 works. Accounting for copyright payments well into the future became unworkable, especially as payments had to be made to named authors rather than an employer such as the Institute. As a result, it was determined that if the net receipts were less than $500, then the author could retain the income subject to due acknowledgement of the Institute in the publication. The requirement to supply 100 free copies of any book published was later ignored (in 2022 this could have amounted to books worth tens of thousands of dollars being given to the Institute by each author), although a single copy for the JV Barry Library was invariably provided. Although only a small number of research staff were prolific, published authors, the publicity that the Institute received following the publication of their works was more than adequate recompense—particularly given that a good deal of the work was undertaken out-of-work hours or following departure from the Institute, and that many books were published with world-class academic publishing houses including Oxford, Cambridge, State University of New York, Elgar, Routledge and Palgrave Macmillan.

Nonetheless, between 1990 and 2022, it can be estimated that approximately $1.3 million in royalties was received by the Institute, with $54,000, on average, each year being received in the most recent decade. This is based on reported royalty revenue in the AICs financial statements (AIC, Annual Reports, 1989–2022). Between 1997 and 2006, royalty income data were omitted from annual reports, and these were estimated based on the mean reported annual increases present in the reports that did include these data.

Income from Training Activities

Chapter 12, below, describes the Institute's early training activities that were largely undertaken within the scope of government appropriation provided—without seeking fees from participants. Once the training program had formally ceased in the mid-1990s, the Institute continued to provide occasional training courses on a profit-making basis. An example of this arose out of Peter Grabosky's telecommunications/cybercrime research carried out with the present author and funded by a grant from the Telstra Fund for Social and Policy Research in Telecommunications in 1996. This resulted in a commercial publication, *Crime in the Digital Age* (Grabosky and Smith 1998) that Adam Graycar described as being 'monumentally innovative – and put us on the map' (Adam Graycar, Interview, 1 March 2021) (Plate 5.3). Since publication, this book has been cited on 212 occasions.

Research on what later became known as 'crime science' and 'environmental criminology', created many opportunities for the Institute to develop fee-for-service courses for the business sector and others. An example of this was the Institute's 'Identity-related fraud training for managers and supervisors of employees whose duties include establishing and/or recording the identity of their clients' that was provided to a number of state and federal agencies as part of the Institute's Learning and Knowledge Development Division managed by Stephen Bond between 2002 and 2005 during Toni Makkai's term as Director. Although widely marketed, the courses were expensive to develop and, after paying the fees of consultants to present the material, little profit resulted and the concept was eventually discontinued. As Adam Graycar noted, 'Training is a very hard thing to make money on and also to get credibility on' (Interview, 1 March 2022).

In June 2004, for example, the Institute conducted six half-day courses on identity-related fraud for counter staff of a state Registry of Births,

Plate 5.3 Crime in the digital age (Grabosky and Smith 1998) (*Source* The Authors)

Deaths and Marriages. The preparation and printing of course materials, payment of the course presenter's fees and travel expenses amounted to more than $10,000 with participants' fees totalling just $13,650—resulting in a net profit of slightly in excess of $3,000. The work undertaken to develop the training materials was, however, later used in the Institute's Identity Crime Monitoring Program that received funding of more than $400,000 from the Commonwealth Attorney-General's

Department and, after 2012, from the Department of Home Affairs. Those attending the program in 2004 found it to be of practical benefit for their daily work, with one commenting that the course was 'informative, detailed but not too detailed, and with practical suggestions for use in the workplace' (AIC, Program Evaluation, Archives, 6 August 2004).

Conference-Related Income

Another potential source of revenue for the Institute came from commercially-based conferences that could, if well-managed, return a profit where income exceeded expenses. In the early years, the Institute conducted a regular program of conferences and seminars, but these in most cases were provided at no cost to delegates as a service to stakeholders. This work was, however, costly to conduct with the Institute having a small staff to manage the promotion and organisation of events, but also requiring research staff to develop programs and to present their own conference papers on selected topics.

On the whole, the AICs Board and Directors considered that the provision of public seminars and conferences, was generally uneconomic as the time required for Institute staff to develop and manage events, as well as the fees incurred in providing suitable venues and catering, left little over in terms of net profit. When Adam Graycar commenced as director in 1994, he considered if it was worthwhile maintaining a staff of five to manage the Institute's conference program. He also noted the Tanzer Report's (1994, p. 28) recommendations:

> The Review recommends that the AIC conference program be much more closely aligned to the ongoing research program and certainly to the AICs agreed priority list. In devising conferences the program will rely much more heavily on the expertise of AIC research staff. In addition, the conferences program should seek to use a wider range of vehicles (seminars, briefings, etc) for its information dissemination activities. All such activities should be driven by a clearly stated set of objectives and anticipated outcomes, including the need for each conference to cover its full costs, including assigned overheads.

Adam Graycar (Interview, 1 March 2021), however, considered that the Tanzer Report (1994) made a 'fundamental and bizarre error' in its revenue assumptions that required the AIC to conduct four conferences a year with 170 attendees each, at $500 per person ($340,000), owing to the fact government budget cuts at the time meant that conferences and travel had a low priority on departmental budgets. Graycar argued to the Board that 'conferences are being run in an era of no money–an era in which agencies have had budget cuts which have placed conferences and travel low on expenditure priorities' (AIC, Minutes, 11-4-1997, p. 4).

In 1995–1996, when the Institute still had its in-house conference staff, $216,292 was earned from seminars, with $52,180 spent on seminars, resulting in a net profit of $164,112—apart from relevant salaries (AIC, Annual Report 1995–1996, pp. 34–35). If the salaries of administrative and research staff were included, conferences almost always ran at a loss. In order to reduce costs, Adam Graycar arranged for KPMG to conduct a review of the conference program in November 1996. It found that it was approximately 40% more expensive for the Institute to run conferences internally, than with external conference organisers (AIC, Minutes 11 April 1997, p. 4). As a result, the AICs internal conference staff were moved to other duties and conference organisation was outsourced to private companies. In 2008, when the Institute conducted a conference in Canberra for ANZSOC using a professional conference organiser, income of almost $200,000 was obtained with total expenditure being only $152 in excess of income. The conference organiser's fees alone cost approximately 12% of total expenditure (AIC, Archives 1 May 2009).

In recent years, large amounts of income from conferences were recorded in the Institute's financial statements. Between 2016 and 2019, for example, conference income approached $1 million, or over $300,000 a year (AIC, Annual Reports, 2016–2019, Financial Statements). This did not last, however, with income in 2019–2020 being only $3,881 and zero income the year after—due to the effects of the Coronavirus pandemic. Since then, it became usual for meetings, seminars and conferences to be conducted online, with directors and staff rarely attending face-to-face events. With the relaxation of many public health measures, in-person conferences have re-commenced, although risks of spreading the virus remain present creating many questions about the health and safety implications of attending such events as well as liability for scheduling events and having to cancel them due to emergency health provisions. In 2021–2022, just $27,000 was earned through conferences (AIC, Annual Report 2022, Financial Statements).

Expenditure Considerations

The primary categories of expenditure identified in the annual Financial Statements were employee expenses and various supplier expenses relating to building rental and related costs, travel expenses and conference expenditure. Financial reporting standards differed over the five decades and expenses were only consistently reported in respect of employee expenses. Other expense items were reported separately until the mid-1990s and were thereafter generically reported as general supplier expenses.

Employee Expenses

Employee expenses including salaries and allowances, and later superannuation, represented more than half (52%) of the entire AIC expenditure over the five decades. Total employee expenses amounted to more than $125 million and increased gradually until the restrictions imposed by the reviews in 1994 and, after five years of restraint, increased again until a peak in 2009–2010 of $5.4 million for that year. A vast reduction in employee expenses occurred following the MoG change in 2015 that resulted in staff resignations and the transfer of most non-research staff to the ACIC as part of the shared corporate services arrangement. These trends are shown in Fig. 5.4.

Controlling employee expenses was one of the more difficult duties imposed on Boards and directors, with staffing numbers, salary levels and opportunities for promotion leading to many disputes with management, staff and union delegates. Although salary levels were set in negotiated Agency Agreements, and these generally reflected salaries paid

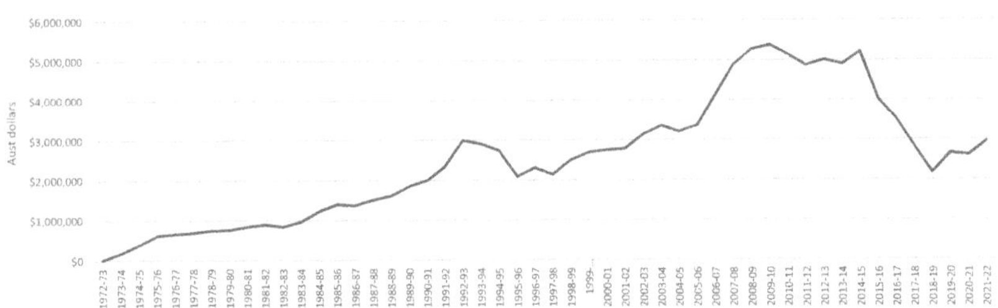

Fig. 5.4 AIC employee expenses, 1972–1973 to 2021–2022 (*Source* AIC *Annual Reports* 1972–1973 to 2021–2022)

in comparable government research bodies as well as in the University sector, many staff resigned in order to advance their careers and obtain salaries higher than those available at the Institute. Staffing number ceilings imposed by governments, and salary scales that failed to increase, led to low staff morale in the Institute on a number of occasions and associated resignations. Many talented researchers left the Institute to advance their income and careers including Satyanshu Mukherjee in the 1980s (AIC, Minutes, 13 December 1982, p. 2).

To minimise staff losses, various devices were used on occasions, including the payment of performance bonuses, provision of secondments or leave of absence to enable staff to work elsewhere, sometimes with higher salaries, the use of flexible working arrangements and allowing staff to undertake overseas travel or retain remuneration from other sources. These proved to be attractive on occasions, but created difficulties in ensuring that such benefits were made available equitably to all staff.

Building

The second-largest expenditure item each year was in connection with leasing of accommodation and maintenance, repair and renovation of offices. Over the five decades, this amounted to more than $20 million. As shown in Fig. 5.5, the costs of the premises at Colbee Court were modest, but following the move to Marcus Clarke Street in 1990, expenses approached one million dollars annually, leading to the severe

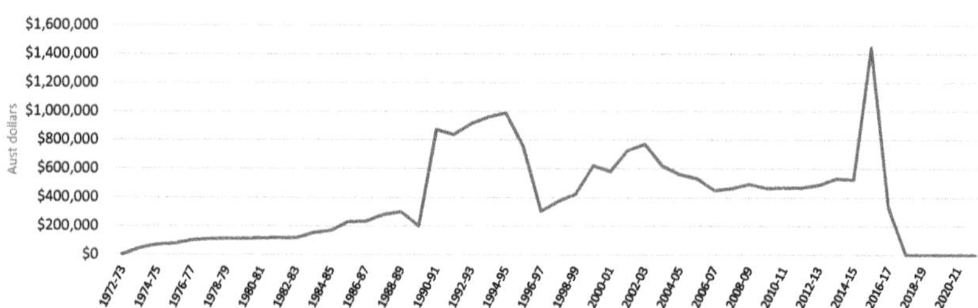

Fig. 5.5 AIC building expenses, 1972–1973 to 2020–2022 (*Source* AIC *Annual Reports* 1972–1973 to 2020–2022)

criticism of such costs in the Tanzer Report (1994). Following the move to the Leichhardt Street building in 1995, costs remained manageable, although renovations on two occasions led to large financial outlays. The move to National Circuit in 2015 entailed a substantial financial impost of having to bear the costs, not only of moving to the new office, but also of servicing the lease of the Leichhardt Street building until it expired while also paying rental for the offices provided by the ACIC as part of its corporate services agreement. Once the Leichhardt Street lease finished, accommodation costs again became manageable. With the onset of the Coronavirus pandemic, however, that enabled staff to work remotely from home, the need for office accommodation came under scrutiny with the future remaining uncertain. Further detail of the Institute's office accommodation over the five decades is presented in Chapter 8. After 2015–2016, rental costs were included in the global sum paid to the ACIC as part of the AICs corporate services agreement, that in 2021–2022 amounted to more than $1.6 million for all services provided including accommodation costs (AIC, Annual Report, 2022, Financial Statements).

Travel

As we have seen, one of the more contentious items of expenditure incurred by the Institute is related to staff travel expenses—particularly those involving overseas travel. Although travel costs were not separately reported in Financial Statements between 1996 and 2009, it can be estimated that approximately $5 million was spent on travel over the five decades. Despite the first director travelling first-class overseas regularly, travel costs generally remained under $100,000 a year during the early years until they doubled in 1992. Following the Tanzer Review (1994), Director Adam Graycar managed to reduce travel expenses considerably. In 1994–1995, for example, travel costs halved and remained well under $100,000 a year for some time. When travel expenses were again separately reported in accounts in 2009, expenditure again began to approach $200,000 a year until a large reduction took place following the Machinery of Government changes in 2015. Since the onset of the Coronavirus, travel costs have declined to minimal levels ($7,062 in 2020–2021), although have begun to increase again as the impact of the pandemic has eased ($32,838 in 2021–2022–AIC, Annual Reports, 2020–2021, 2021–2022).

Conferences

Throughout the fifty years, considerable resources were devoted to conducting conferences, seminars and other events. During the first full year of operations, 1973–1974, the two most costly items of expenditure apart from building costs and salaries were seminar expenses ($36,125) and travelling expenses ($45,018) (AIC, Annual Report 1973–1973, p. 22). As conferences became larger and more time-consuming to manage, professional conference organisers were used which, although charging high fees, were more efficient and arguably less expensive than maintaining full-time conference staff on the payroll—as we have seen in connection with conference revenue.

Prior to the 1990s, conference expenditure remained fairly constant and low, but during Duncan Chappell's tenure, expenses more than doubled reaching $441,657 in 1991–1992, before being substantially reduced following the Tanzer Review (1994). In more recent times, following the MoG in 2015, conference expenditure has again increased substantially—although declined to $10, 954 in 2020–2021 during the pandemic and has begun to increase in 2021–2022 ($70,801–AIC Annual Reports, 2020–2021 and 2021–2022).

Debate over the level of expenditure on travel and conferences endured throughout the Institute's history with some directors seeking to enhance the Institute's reputation by increasing visibility, while others sought to rely on the quantity and quality of publications to attract attention and resources. The preferred model represents a balance between the two as we shall see in Chapter 11, that examines how research was disseminated.

Outsourcing

One of the enduring debates that occupied directors throughout the Institute's history was whether, and the extent to which, research and other services should be contracted-out to external suppliers. Outsourcing could be, and was, undertaken for many of the services that the Institute needed including corporate administration, research, library services, information technology, conference administration and training activities. On the one hand, engaging external providers can be efficient where short-term work is required and where existing staff are fully committed with work and unable to take on new tasks. On the other hand, unless contractors are recruited carefully, and their work monitored and evaluated, the net benefits might not be clear and the work may have to be re-done by more experienced workers—usually in-house. External contracting also carried with it administrative costs and overheads that may make the total cost prohibitive.

Some of the AICs Directors were willing to engage contractors for many of the services needed, while others were sceptical and used outsourcing infrequently or on a trial basis. In some cases, such as the use of external information technology services, it was found to be preferable to have skilled staff employed who were familiar with the specific needs of the Institute, rather than external contractors who were used to working with their familiar applications—even if these were not entirely satisfactory for the needs of the organisation. External contractor rates could also be much more expensive than in-house salary rates. Adam Graycar, for example, found outsourcing of information technology services, conferences and publications to be overly costly (Interview, 1 March 2021), despite that fact that KPMGs review that he commissioned found that internally-run conferences were more expensive than having them outsourced to a private company (AIC, Board Minutes, 11 April 1997, p. 4).

In the 1980s, during the era of Thatcherism, outsourcing was, as John Walker recalled, 'all the rage' (John Walker, Interview, 30 November 2020). John witnessed the decline of Home Office research division internal staffing and its replacement with contracted academics—some of whom were not as successful in producing government research publications in the style required and in accordance with timelines. It also led to many talented staff leaving—some of whom came to the Institute in Canberra (John Walker, Interview, 30 November 2020). Mike Hough (2018), in his interview with Ben Bradford in 2018, noted, however, that most academic criminologists were unsuited, or unwilling, to engage in applied criminological research such as that undertaken by the Home Office. The same could be said of Australian academic criminologists, as discussed in Chapter 2.

In relation to outsourcing research work, Rick Brown noted that sometimes 'consultants are more trouble than they're worth'. He explained that 'if they are engaged to undertake work on research questions relating to general themes and programs, then you can get insightful research and it works well; when it relates to very specific research questions then it's more painful' (Rick Brown, Interview, 10 June 2022). During a secondment to the NIJ in Washington, Rick observed that there was a lot of dissatisfaction among research staff whose daily work mainly involved contract management rather than doing research themselves. At the AIC, Rick sought to avoid this problem by limiting outsourced research work to topics where the AIC researchers did not have relevant expertise (Rick Brown, Interview, 10 June 2022).

Nonetheless, the AIC spent considerable amounts on contractors over its history. Since 1996, for example, supplier expenses have amounted to more than $82 million, including the cost of corporate services outsourced to the ACIC since 2015. This represents, 45% of total current annual expenses for the years 1996–2022 (Fig. 5.6).

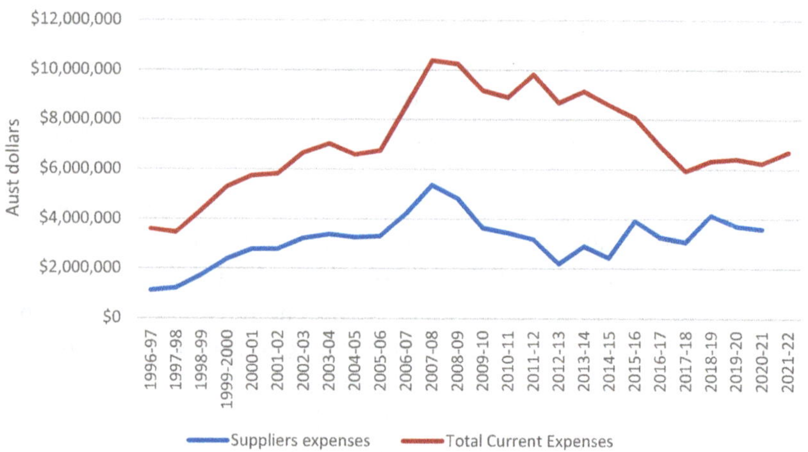

Fig. 5.6 AIC supplier and total current expenses, 1996–1997 to 2021–2022 (*Source* AIC *Annual Reports* 1972–1973 to 2020–2021)

Conclusions

This chapter has provided a brief outline of how the Australian government funded the criminological research undertaken by the AIC, and how directors and Boards approached their task of spending the funds appropriately, so as to demonstrate value for money, and cost-effectiveness. During the five decades, governments of both political persuasions maintained close scrutiny over the Institute and its activities and used staffing level caps, efficiency dividends and actual reductions in appropriation to ensure that spending did not become too great. Directors showed different approaches to managing the finances of the Institute with some favouring fee-for-service research to enhance budgets, while others sought to engage in outsourcing of services with the intention of reducing expenditure. There was also a continual tension between show-casing the Institute's work, both within Australia and internationally—that increased travel and conference expenditure—and using income to enhance the Institute's research output—in terms of both volume and quality.

As funding declined as a percentage of GDP, directors had to adjust the focus of the Institute's work in order to achieve cost-effectiveness. This resulted in some performance indicators changing in order to match the ability of staff to produce the necessary research outputs. One consequence of this was a reduction in the physical—but perhaps not virtual—profile of the Institute with media, print publications and face-to-face conference activities declining, as shown in Chapter 11. On the whole, however, the Institute's directors and Board were able to manage budgets carefully and use the relatively small resourcing provided by government to produce an impressive and diverse range of outputs.

References

Behm, Allan. 2006. *Review of the Criminology Research Act 1971*, Unpublished, November 2006. Canberra: Attorney General's Department.

Biles, David. 1987. *A Review of the Work of the Criminology Research Council, 1972–1986*. Canberra: Australian Institute of Criminology.

Coad, William J., Prudence Ford, Malcolm Hazell, Peter Lamb, Norman Reaburn, and Adrian Whiddett. 1994. *Report of the Review of Commonwealth Law Enforcement Arrangements*. Canberra: Australian Government Publishing Service.

Cope, R. L. 1981. Commonwealth Official Publications and the Razor Gang: Some Thoughts. *The Australian Library Journal,* 30 (3): 73.

Fraser, Malcolm. 1981. Ministerial Statement on the Review of Commonwealth Functions, *Parliamentary Debates*, House of Representatives, 30 April, p. 1838.

Geis, Gilbert. 1994. 'This Sort of Thing Isn't Helpful:' The Dilemmas of the Australian Institute of Criminology. *Australian and New Zealand Journal of Criminology* 27 (3): 282–298.

Gosling, Mary E. 1982. *The J. V. Barry Memorial Library: A Review of Its Functions and Policy*, Unpublished Report, 16 August. Canberra: Australian Institute of Criminology.

Grabosky, Peter N., and Russell G. Smith. 1998. *Crime in the Digital Age: Controlling Telecommunications and Cyberspace Illegalities*. Sydney: Federation Press, New Brunswick: Transaction Publishers.

Hough, Mike. 2018. Interviewed by Ben Bradford at European Society of Criminology meeting, Sarajevo, Bosnia and Herzegovina, 10 September 2018. https://www.youtube.com/watch?v=_DLTlrqt_OA&t=7s. Accessed 10 March 2022.

James, Steve, and Adam Sutton. 1994. Criminology and Crime Control in Australia. *Australian and New Zealand Journal of Criminology* 27 (3): 299–308.

Kelly, Paul. 2000. The Politics of Economic Change in Australia in the 1980s and 1990s. In *The Australian Economy in the 1990s*, ed. David Gruen and Sona Shrestha. RBA Conference, 24–25 July 2000. Sydney: RBA https://www.rba.gov.au/publications/confs/2000/kelly-address.html. Accessed 30 June 2022.

Libraries Alive!. 2008. *Review of the JV Barry Library, Australian Institute of Criminology: Final Report*. Canberra: Libraries Alive!

Loof, Peter R. 1979. *Establishment of the Australian Institute of Criminology and the Criminology Research Council: Proposals, Criteria and Negotiations Associated with the Establishment of the Institute and the Council*. Canberra: Attorney-General's Department.

McDonald, D.I., and C. Moore. 1981. *Review of the Staff and Organisational Structure of the Australian Institute of Criminology*, Management and Special Services Division, Canberra: Attorney-General's Department (Referred to in AIC, Minutes, 14 December 1981, p. 4).

Muirhead, James Henry. 1996. *A Brief Summing Up*. Northbridge: Access Press.

Quay Connection. 2006. *Australian Institute of Criminology: Communication Review, Final Report*. Annandale: Quay Connection.

Shepherd, Tony, Peter Boxall, Tony Cole, Robert Fisher, and Amanda Vanstone. 2014. *Towards Responsible Government: The Report of the National Commission of Audit: Phase One*. Canberra: National Commission of Audit. https://web.archive.org.au/awa/20140501135754mp_/http://pandora.nla.gov.au/pan/143632/20140502-0001/www.ncoa.gov.au/report/docs/phase_one_report.pdf. Accessed 3 August 2022.

Skehill, Stephen. 2012. *Strategic Review of Small and Medium Agencies in the Attorney-General's Portfolio: Report to the Australian Government*. Canberra: Department of Finance and Deregulation.

Stevens, Adele, Grant Wardlaw, Stephen Mugford, and Heather Deane. 1988. *ACT Drug Indicators Project: Quarterly Report, January to March 1988*. Canberra: AIC. http://elib/scan/218927.pdf. Accessed 8 August 2022.

Tanzer, Noel, Des Hill, and Grant Wardlaw. 1994. *Review of the Australian Institute of Criminology: Report*. Canberra: Australian Institute of Criminology.

Uhrig, John. 2003. *Review of the Corporate Governance of Statutory Authorities and Office Holders*, Parliamentary Paper No. 352. Canberra: Commonwealth of Australia. https://nla.gov.au/nla.obj-922761191/view?partId=nla.obj-924 650826#page/n135/mode/1up Accessed 3 August 2022.

Wilson, Paul, and Christine Nixon. 1987. *Practical and Policy Related Research Conducted by the Australian Institute of Criminology, 1974–87*. Canberra: AIC.

6

Funding Criminological Research

Introduction

As we have seen, when the AIC was established, in addition to providing funding for research conducted by the AICs staff, the *Criminology Research Act 1971* (Cth) provided funding for researchers external to the agency to undertake research on topics they proposed that had been approved by the Criminology Research Council (CRC). The original level of funding provided to the CRC was $100,000 that comprised $50,000 from the Commonwealth government and $50,000 from state governments—with each state's contribution calculated on a popula-tion *pro-rata* basis. This funding was able to be used to pay for the administration of the Council and to make other payments:

> for such purposes of, or related to, criminological research (including the dissemination of information and advice, and the publication of reports, periodicals, books and papers, in connexion with criminological research and the results of criminological research) as are determined by the Council (s. 47(1)(a)).

© The Author(s), under exclusive license to Springer Nature Switzerland AG 2023

R. G. Smith, *Public Sector Criminological Research*,
https://doi.org/10.1007/978-3-031-28356-7_6

In relation to the CRC and later CRG Programs, the funding provided was made available for academics and others to apply for funding to conduct criminological research on approved projects. Once again, 'being caught between a rock and a hard place', the CRC had many, competing interests to satisfy in deciding how to allocate this research funding. Particular complexity arose because the funding came from the Commonwealth, state and later territory governments—each of which had its own research agenda and policy objectives. In addition, because crime was, on the whole, constitutionally within the jurisdiction of the states, the Commonwealth often felt that its own crime-related interests were being neglected if state-focussed research was being undertaken. This created an environment in which the Commonwealth sought, on the one hand, to limit funding for research, while, on the other to change the focus of research to more Commonwealth-oriented topics that had a national, or cross-border emphasis. The change in emphasis from street-based, volume crime to organised, transnational and cybercrime is an illustration of this, particularly after 1990. This transition in focus was also evident internationally, as Joutsen (2022) has observed in connection with the UNODCs crime program.

Since 2000, changes in the Commonwealth regulatory environment also led to a change in the nature of research funding provided by the government. In 2019, the research funding process was changed to a contract-based procurement system rather than one involving government grants. This meant that CRG funding had to comply with all the Australian Public Sector's procurement policies and procedures, resulting in AIC staff not being able to be involved in CRG-funded research as in the past and meaning that the AIC could not provide in-kind funding to support applications. The CRC, and later the Advisory Council, could, however, engage AIC staff to undertake research work directly. Thus, although the CRG Program is described as a grants program, funded projects now involve contracts procured through a competitive approach to market using the Commonwealth's AusTender procedures. The term 'grant' is, however, still used in the title to the program for historical reasons that derive from the *Criminology Research Act 1971* (Cth.)(AIC, Annual Report, 2021, p. 27) and to make the process more understandable to applicants.

Assessing Applications for Funding

Originally, applications for funding were made to the CRC which assessed applications based on a merit-based, internal review process. More recently, applications for funding are reviewed initially by a panel of at least two individuals who are senior criminologists selected by the Advisory Council from among potential candidates recommended by the President of ANZSOC. Panel members evaluate all proposals independently of each other and their evaluations are discussed with the Academic Adviser to the CRG Program (an AIC-employed senior researcher), who submits final recommendations to the Advisory Council for consideration. Where applications involve questions beyond the expertise of the Panel members, they may be sent for external, independent peer review by academic referees experienced in the subject matter of the application and the specific methodologies proposed. Advisory Council members, often acting on the advice of officers within the Council members' departments, examine the proposals, advice and recommendations of the Selection Panel and determine which proposals to fund, and at what level of funding.

This selection process has generally worked well, although on occasions funding has been provided for projects that the Selection Panel did not recommend highly, usually owing to the perceived desirability of funding research into a particular topic at the time in question. It has also been apparent that a relatively small cohort of successful applicants for funding are more likely to be successful than others who occasionally have submitted novel and worthy projects but who fail to have an established track record. Related to this, is the tendency for particular methodologies to be preferred—mainly those involving empirical, quantitative research rather than theoretical, or 'green-fields' studies that seek to explore new, untried topics or novel methodologies.

Over time, the selection process has become increasingly competitive. Glanfield and Jobes (2004, p. 262), in their review of the success rates for applications made between 1973 and 2002, found that during the first five years of the CRC, 38% of proposals submitted were funded while in 2002, this had fallen to 20%. The lowest rate was in 1999 when only 10% were funded. The success rate in more recent years has fluctuated but has been approximately 20% on average during the most recent decade, which is comparable with other national grants funding programs for social science research and also criminology journal acceptance rates.

At its first meeting, the CRC noted that a flexible outlook would be maintained with respect to funding with the following considerations taken into account when assessing applications:

> National importance of the problem; the subject of investigation; its particular importance within a state or territory; urgency; novelty of area of research; practical benefit; cost in relationship to the fund; parity between states; experience of applicant and practicability of method. (CRC, Annual Report, 1973, p. 3)

Applying these criteria, the Council first approved two grants, one to Dr Eric Cunningham Dax for $7,900 for an 'Investigation into the background of successful members of a series of families with multiple criminal records and social problems'; and another to Malcolm McCouat for $2,057 for a study of 'Prisoners and their families: Processes of family relationships and adaptation to the imprisonment' (CRC, Annual Report 1973, p. 3). Apart from the clear conflict of interest in funding Dr Cunningham Dax—one of the members of the Council—these two topics were among those that received funding on a number of occasions over the fifty years in different contexts and by various researchers. Eric Cunningham Dax, who was Coordinator in Community Health in Tasmania, applied for and received further funding of $13,000 on 25 February 1974 for the same project and submitted his final report in 1978 (Cunningham Dax et al. 1978).

Parity between the states was a matter of particular importance, but the concept was difficult to apply in practice. Glanfield and Jobes (2004, p. 260) explained this as follows:

> There is also a requirement that the research funded by the CRC must produce results that will have relevance at either a national level or across a number of states. Research that is likely to yield results that are pertinent only to one particular state is unlikely to be funded unless the findings have broader implications that could be implemented by other states. For

example, research investigating child abuse in Queensland was recently funded because it was broadly applicable to other states in addition to meeting certain other criteria.

The first CRC Report to be published was by Dennis Challinger (1974) who later became the Assistant Director, Information and Training between 1986 and 1989. Dennis, who was at the time a Lecturer in Criminology at the University of Melbourne, received a grant of $1,766 on 15 August 1973 for a study based on a detailed analysis of Children's Court records in Victoria (CRC, Annual Report, 1973–1974, p. 3). He recalled the procedure for gaining the funding during his interview:

> I had made an application for a research grant from the Criminology Research Council in its first round for a statistical study on... youthful offending. I got a phone call saying that I had to go up to Canberra to meet the Director to talk about that research. I flew up to Canberra and was met at the airport by Harold Weir in the Institute car and he drove me into the centre of Canberra to Ethos House, a most unprepossessing office building. I was introduced to Jim Muirhead and we talked about the research I was going to do... and I subsequently got the grant. (Dennis Challinger, Interview, 18 February 2022)

This somewhat informal process reflected the operation of the public sector prior to the digital age, and the modest level of funding for research that was provided. In 1973–1974, however, almost 90% of funding available was allocated to research grants, with the Council's administrative costs totalling only $330. As is apparent from Fig. 6.1, the proportion of administrative costs increased substantially over time.

Some of the considerations taken into account when awarding grants received differing levels of prominence at various times in the Council's history. In 2002, for example, when the current author was the Council's Academic Adviser, they were revised to include the following factors:

> Public policy relevance; the extent to which the proposed research will have practical application and contribute to the understanding, preven-tion or correction of criminal behaviour; the likelihood of the proposed

research making a substantial and original contribution to criminological knowledge; the cost-effectiveness of the research; the soundness of the design and methodology; the feasibility of the research; the competence of the applicant(s) or principal investigator(s) to undertake the proposed research; the presence of Human Research Ethics Committee approval, where appropriate; the availability of data, where required; and the extent of funding or in-kind support obtained from relevant agencies. (CRC 2002, p. 8)

The application kit at the time also emphasised that: 'the Council does not encourage applications for research projects which, in its view, are the normal operational responsibilities of Government departments, or institutions, or which are more appropriately funded by other research bodies' (CRC 2002, p. 8). This criterion was used regularly in the selection process to exclude applications from other government entities or projects that would have been likely to receive funding from other funding bodies—particularly those dealing with health-related topics or addictions.

Since the transition to a procurement process, these instructions appear on the AusTender website in highly reduced form, simply stating that proposals should 'make a valuable contribution to knowledge and address policy-relevant needs in the area of crime and criminal justice' and that they should be 'relevant to the public policy of the Commonwealth, the states, the Australian Capital Territory and the Northern Territory and activities related to that research (including, for example, the publication of that research)' (AusTender 2021). In addition, targeted areas for research are now specified on the Website which enables the Advisory Council to indicate its preference for topics to be funded in the current round of funding. In 2021, for example, the following topics were indicated as reflecting the Council's research priorities for that year:

- coercive control within abusive intimate relationships;
- over-representation of Aboriginal and Torres Strait Islander people in the criminal justice system; or

- sexual offence victim/survivor experience of the criminal justice system.

Decisions are made in closed meetings and discussion of the reasons for funding (or not funding) specific proposals are rarely entered into with applicants.

In David Biles's review of the CRC in 1987, he noted that:

> The underlying theme that has dominated the Council's decision making since its establishment has been the desirability of research being supported that potentially is of practical value to the prevention of crime and the humane and efficient operation of criminal justice throughout the country. This emphasis on the practical value of projects has led the Council to be disinclined to support proposals of a purely theoretical or scholarly interest. (Biles 1987a, p. 24)

David Biles (Plate 6.1) also observed that the Council's approach to funding was almost exclusively reactive—in that it primarily considered applications submitted to it for funding, rather that providing funding on its own initiative (Biles 1987a, p. 24). From November 1999, however, the Council decided to engage its own Post-doctoral Research Fellow—later known as the CRC Research Fellow—the first of whom was Dr Emma Ogilvie, whose appointment lasted from November 1999 to August 2001. During that time, she conducted research on topics specifically chosen by the CRC members. Dr Ogilvie's initial tasks were to conduct research on knives and armed robbery, post-release and community corrections and chronic offenders. The Research Fellows were criminologists appointed for a three-year term to carry out research and to support the work of the Council in planning and overseeing funded research and consultancies. They also developed and undertook research proposals as directed by the Council and assisted in management of the Council's consultancies. Research Fellows also provided advice to Council members on criminal justice research matters and assisted in the preparation of policy documents on areas of specific criminal justice topics as directed by the Council.

Plate 6.1   John Braithwaite, David Biles and the Hon. Gareth Evans QC, MP at the launch of 'Occupational Health and Safety Enforcement in Australia' 1985 (*Source* AIC Archives)

Research Fellows were appointed between 1999 and December 2013 when the last CRC Fellow, Jacqueline Joudo-Larsen, resigned from her position (AIC, Annual Report, 2014, p. 36). Since then, the AICs research staff have taken on some of the self-initiated tasks that the Council previously engaged the Research Fellow to perform. Although CRC Fellowships were for three years, most Fellows, who were often relatively junior academics, resigned early from their positions to take up other employment opportunities, usually in universities. Locating candidates willing to come to Canberra for a maximum of three years was generally difficult, as there was no opportunity to extend Fellowships for a second term.

In addition, the CRC also determined to spend a proportion of its budget on so-called consultancies in which the Council provided funding for selected external academics or AIC researchers to conduct research on topics specifically chosen by the Council members. The Council originally sought to control its allocation of funding by developing targeted areas for research in respect of which applicants would be invited to submit proposals. Consultancy topics varied widely, although they tended to focus on state and territory crime and justice issues, particularly relating to Indigenous justice, victims of crime and the operation of the criminal justice system. Prior to determining topics, the Council sometimes held consultation meetings with stakeholders from across Australia who were invited to attend a meeting in Canberra to present their ideas on what research should be undertaken by the CRC. This invariably generated a substantial, potential work program, that was generally unable to be satisfied. It did, however, elicit some novel ideas for research.

This proactive approach to funding criminological research was similar to that undertaken in Canada and the US as well as by the Home Office in the UK. Originally, the CRC in Australia preferred the reactive approach in which applicants simply applied for funding of topics of their own choosing, which the CRC believed was more appropriate for predominantly low-value grants (Biles 1987a, p. 24). Over time, as more funding became available, the CRC decided to allocate more funds to topics of its own choosing in addition to providing conventional grants to academic applicants.

Funding Provided

Throughout the history of the CRC, net funding from government increased from an initial annual amount of $100,000 during the early years to around $500,000 in 2021–2022. Matched funding was provided from the Commonwealth and the states and territories collectively, with state and territory contributions calculated in accordance with a population-based formula used since the program commenced in 1973 (rates of non-Commonwealth contributions were in 2022—New South Wales 32%, Victoria 26%, Queensland 20%, Western Australia 10%, South Australia 7%, Tasmania 2%, ACT 2%, Northern Territory 1%). In some years, total state and territory contributions were increased to take account of inflation—for example, between 2018–2019 and 2019–2020 a 2.0% increase was made. In addition, the AIC provided funding to cover the administration of the research program that amounted to $76,500 in 2021–2022. The total cost of administering the program was, therefore, approximately one-third of total annual income—a proportion that Director, Adam Graycar, for one, was embarrassed about (Interview, 1 March 2022). In 1994–1995, the year before the Institute's budget had been reduced substantially, the largest amount of funding for the Council's research fund in one year was provided amounting to $636,163 out of a total income for the CRC of $693,439. The following year, the CRCs total income was reduced to $244,469, with grants of $152,833 funded in 1995–1996. This was the lowest level of grants funded since 1983–1984.

In some years, the CRG Program allocated funding for AIC research staff to undertake specific projects recommended to the Director by the Advisory Council. For example, in 2014–2015, $123,000 was allocated for a project to be conducted by AIC staff. In that year, approximately one-quarter of funds available for research were provided back to the AIC, leaving only $324,009 paid to grantees (AIC, Annual Report, 2015, p. 44). Some unsuccessful grantees may have felt aggrieved at funds going to the AIC rather than academic criminologists—although it was the Council members who made this determination of how funding should be allocated. Figure 6.1 shows the total income received by the CRC and CRG Program and the amounts provided for research grants and/or contacts each year.

Following the large reduction in funding in 1994–1995, the gap between total income and funds provided for research grants widened, as CRC administrative costs increased. Total CRC/CRG Program income from all sources between 1972–1973 and 2021–2022 amounted to $18.0 million, with $12.6 million in grants and research contracts

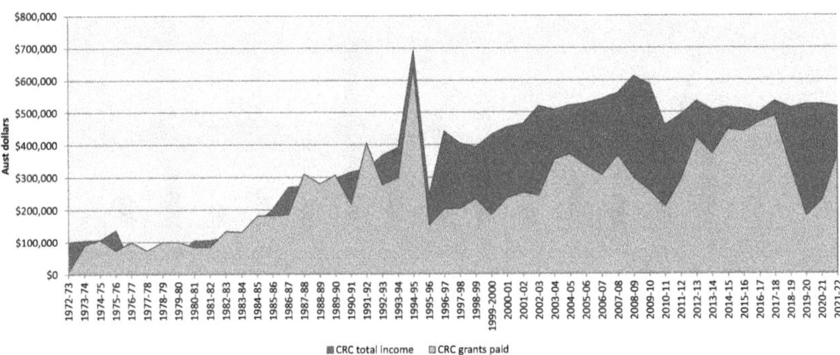

Fig. 6.1 Criminology Research Council income and grants funding provided, 1972–1973 to 2021–2022 ($) (*Source* Derived from CRC *Annual Reports* 1973–2022)

provided. The difference of 30% of total income was spent on administration costs and other expenses. This proportion spent on administration led some academics (who had not received funding) to question the value for money being provided (James and Sutton 1994). Another cause for concern arose in 2016–2017, when, due to an administrative mistake by the ACICs finance officers, funding of almost $900,000 was allocated despite income for that year only amounting to $500,000. This pleased applicants in that year, but led to a vast reduction in funding being allocated each year thereafter (Fig. 6.2).

Some academics expressed concern about the average amounts provided for individual projects which in recent years has been insufficient to support major research work. Since 2009, the mean annual funding provided for all new projects was $335,241, but the mean for each funded project was only $51,166. This would currently fund only a junior research assistant, or cover minor travel costs. As a result, other sources of funding were required for projects. In addition to Australian Research Council (ARC) funding, external funding was often provided from university-based sources, either as cash contributions for travel or in-kind support. State and territory government agencies also supplied additional funding to support these projects, either in cash or in-kind by providing access to data. Rick Brown observed in his Interview (4 November 2022), 'we get very good value for money from those projects.

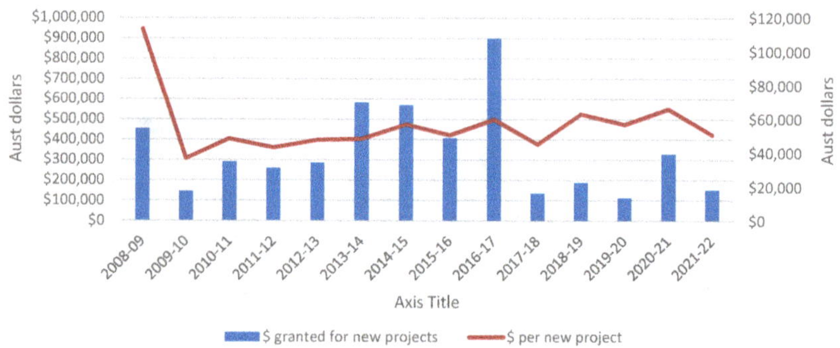

Fig. 6.2 Criminology Research Council funding provided—mean amount per project, 2008–2009 to 2021–2022 ($) (*Source* Derived from CRG *Annual Reports* 2008–2022)

Some departmental policy-makers say that they have been surprised how little CRG projects cost compared to what they are charged when they commission a piece of research directly'.

The exception to the generally low level of mean funding provided for individual projects was one application by John Braithwaite and Lawrence Sherman in 1993 (No. 47/93-94) that received funding of $300,000 over three years. Its aim was to test, empirically, Braithwaite's theory of reintegrative shaming by comparing diversionary conferences with court processing (CRC Annual Report 1995, p. 63). This led to 'long-standing resentment [that this project had] severely diminished funding that would otherwise have been available to smaller deserving grants' (Glanfield and Jobes 2004, p. 263). Braithwaite, in his interview (30 January 2021), recalled this and noted his decision not to apply for further CRC funding 'given the feeling at the time that he'd had more than his fair share'. In the event, John made no further applications for CRC funding at all. Nonetheless, as Glanfield and Jobes (2004, p. 263) observed, this grant funded research 'on one of the monumental theoretical and policy-based contributions of Australian criminology'. John Braithwaite went on the receive the inaugural Stockholm Prize in Criminology (2006), jointly with Friedrich Lösel for theoretical and empirical research on programs and policies to prevent reoffending—in the case of

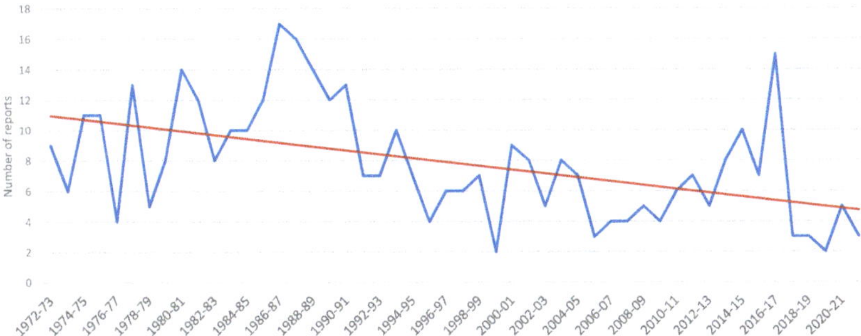

Fig. 6.3 Number of published reports by year funded, 1972–1973 to 2021–2022 (*Source* Derived from CRG *Annual Reports* 1973–2022)

Braithwaite, his theories of reintegrative shaming and responsive regulation. The CRCs funding contributed not only to the initial CRC Report (Sherman et al. 1997), but also to an ongoing series of influential books and research publications that have continued to the present.

The CRC and CRGs Program funding has, in all, enabled more than 400 publications from research projects to be released, with substantial outputs being present in some years (17 separate reports released in 1986–1987 and 16 in 1987–1988—the top two years for published CRC reports). Figure 6.3 shows, however, a general decline in the number of reports being published throughout the 50 years, noting that for the last few years some research projects are still being undertaken and so the numbers shown underrepresent the total number of reports that will eventually be completed.

Types of Research Funded

In the case of both the AIC and the CRC, an extensive range of criminological topics has been examined that have reflected not only the interests of stakeholders, but also changes in crime and justice problems in the community and the interest of individual researchers to embark on such research. Fashions of criminological research, theories and methodologies all changed over time, although some topics maintained their topicality, interest and importance. In Chapter 10, data are presented on the principal topics addressed in *Trends and Issues in Crime and Criminal Justice* publications since 1986 (Fig. 10.1). In Fig. 6.4, a comparable chart shows the principal topics examined in CRC-funded research published in *Trends and Issues* papers over the five decades (counted until the publication of the research in application no. 04/19-20 released in November 2022 in *Trends and Issues* paper No 659). Data for the most recent decade (2010s and beyond) will underrepresent the actual number of publications because some recent CRC projects have not yet been published, Fig. 6.4 shows the principal topics examined grouped in 21 categories during the five decades.

In reading Figs. 6.4 and 10.1, it needs to be noted that the two datasets are not mutually exclusive as those who receive CRC funding are required as part of their contractual obligations to submit a *Trends and Issues* paper for consideration—not all of which are published. Comparing the principal topics of *Trends and Issues* papers with those of CRC-funded projects, it is apparent that some topics such as economic crime, drugs, policing and cybercrime, in particular, were published as *Trends and Issues* papers much more frequently than CRC publications. In some other cases, the reverse was the case with the number of CRC reports being less than the number of *Trends and Issues* papers, for example, research on the courts, statistics, juvenile offending, Indigenous topics and environmental crime. Part of the reason for this is that *Trends and Issues* papers only commenced in 1986, whereas CRC grants were made from 1973. It is apparent, however, that the AICs own research into some topics such as economic crime, drugs, cybercrime and organised crime was much more prolific than CRC-funded research on these topics.

In order to understand how research topics funded by the CRC changed over time, an analysis was made of the number of CRC-funded publications completed each decade that related to the 21 categories (see also Fig. 10.2). Figure 6.5 presents these findings for the CRC publications.

From Fig. 6.5, it is apparent that some topics were more prevalent in the early years of the CRC such as juvenile offending, prisons research,

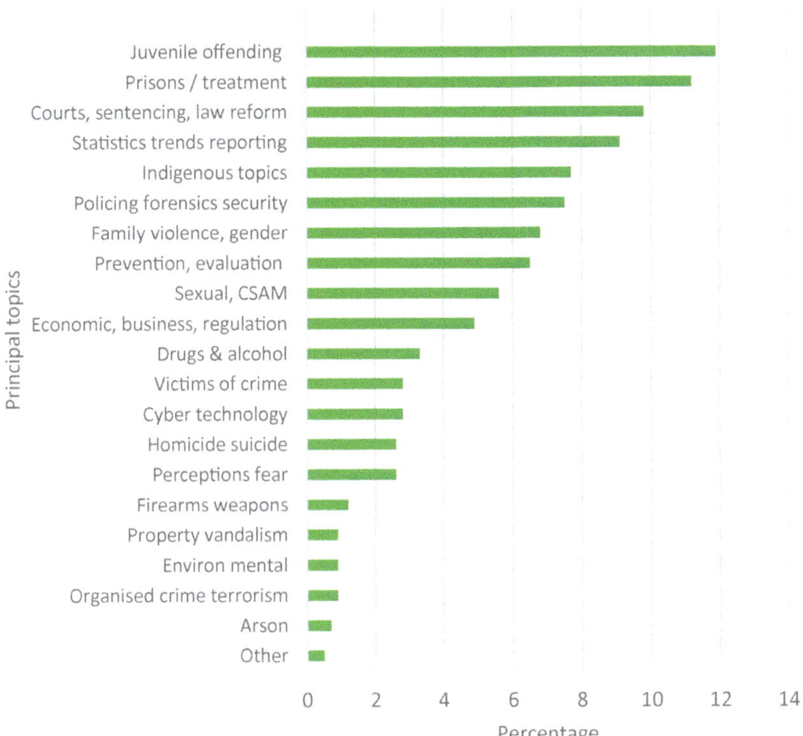

Fig. 6.4 Principal topics in CRC-funded research publications (*Note* The full topic categories were: Economic, business, white collar crime & regulation; Drugs & alcohol research; Statistics, trends & reporting; Policing, forensics & security; Sexual offending, child abuse and child sexual abuse materials; Corrections & treatment of offenders; Prevention of crime & evaluation studies; Courts, sentencing, legal issues & law reform; Juvenile offending & responses; Cybercrime & technology; Family violence & gender research; Indigenous offending, victims & responses; Homicide & suicide research; Organised crime & terrorism; Trafficking people & commodities; Firearms & weapons; Victims of crime; Perceptions & fear of crime; Arson; Property crime & vandalism; Crimes against the environment; Other topics. *Source* Derived from CRC/CRAC Publications listings, noting that the topic categories used on this website were not used in order to make the current analysis comparable with the analysis of *Trends and Issues* publications used in Chapter 10. https://www.aic.gov.au/crg/reports-year)

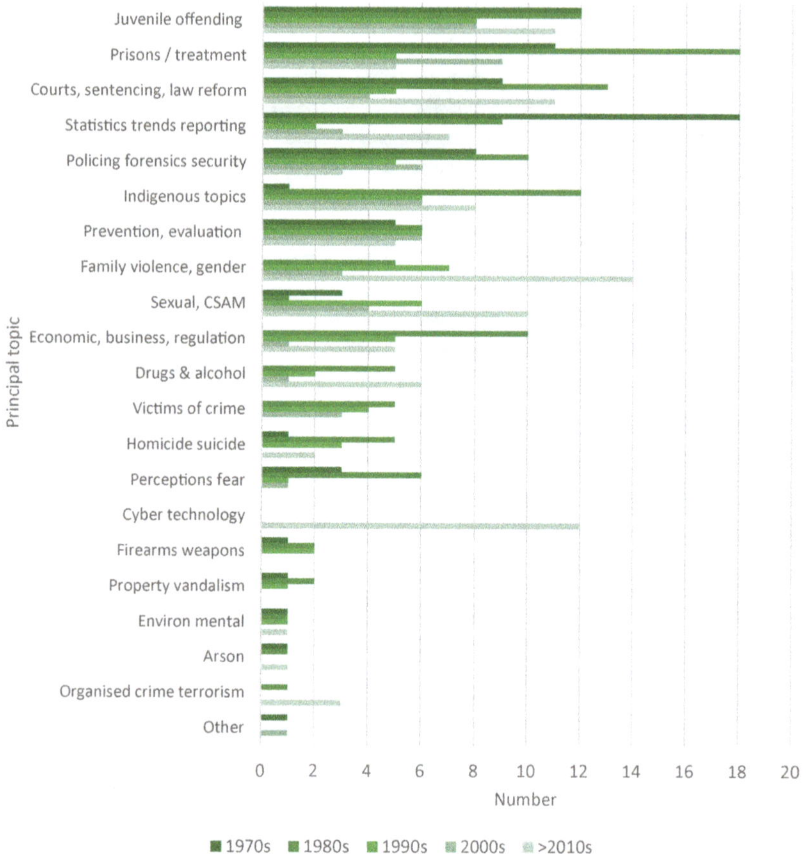

Fig. 6.5 Principal topics of CRC publications by decade (*Note* Decade periods relate to the years in which grants were made, not years of publication, commencing in 1972–1973 and including projects funded in 2021–2022. Results have been arranged from most frequently occurring to least over the 50 years)

courts and statistics. Research into Indigenous issues was largely overlooked in the 1970s until Director Richard Harding took office and made it a priority. He observed during his interview:

[O]ne of the stand-out problems [was] absolutely no research or conference presence in the area of Aboriginal crime and punishment... it's stunning in retrospect that you could go to a national institute of criminology in 1984 and there wasn't stuff being actively researched and published on the problems of the Indigenous population. (Richard Harding, Interview, 18 November 2021)

Other topics such as family violence and sexual offending were funded throughout the CRCs history, but have increased greatly since 2010. There was also an interest in funding drugs-related research in the 1970s, that was only taken up again since 2010. Of course, cybercrime research has only been funded in recent years, sometime after Grabosky and Smith (1998) published their first book on the topic while at the Institute.

Although some topics were funded in the early years of the CRC, such as perceptions of crime, firearms and property crime, these have no longer been funded—perhaps because no applications have been made in recent years, or because their policy priorities were low, or data difficult to find. Some gaps in funding include research on human trafficking and slavery and cost of crime research—although both of these topics were funded internally by the AIC or by other Commonwealth entities. In four areas—arson, drugs, organised crime and economic crime—the CRC provided considerable funding during the 1970s, but little between then and the 2010s when funding for these topics was again provided more often.

The reasons for these trends are complex and are partially explicable by the specific research interests of academics and universities, but also due to the policy needs of CRC/CRG members who make the final decisions concerning funding. Further research could be undertaken to compare topics present in applications with topics of funded projects to determine the extent to which the Council's decision-making affected the nature of published research.

On occasions, the Selection Panel and CRC members were presented with research proposals that were unusual, unique and occasionally extraordinary, to say the least. Glanfield and Jobes (2004, p. 259), for example, recalled a proposal submitted in 1975 entitled: 'An Investigation into the Use of Mandalic Civilization for the Harmonization of Planetary Society and the Obviation of Criminality' that was not listed as a high priority. In addition, during his time as Academic Adviser to the CRC, the present author encountered the following memorable applications—that were similarly not funded. In one, over $30,000 was sought to conduct an analysis of the contents of 500 rubbish bins from households in New South Wales to see what kinds of sensitive personal documents were being disposed of, in order to assess the householders' risk of victimisation by identity thieves. Another application sought funding of almost $60,000 to examine the problems of extracting DNA from the teeth of bodies which had been buried or exposed to water. One terrorism-related project sought funding of almost $140,000 to film simulated terrorist attacks on individuals to determine which types of martial arts self-defence responses are most effective in disarming the assailant. Although of some practical forensic value, these can hardly be considered as conventional, criminological research.

Evaluation and Conclusions

Evaluating the contribution of funding for criminological research provided by the CRC and AIC is difficult for a number of reasons. As shown above, the mean amount of funding provided was relatively small, often being used to add to funds provided by other funding bodies, thus making the separate contribution of the CRCs funds difficult to disaggregate and assess. In addition, CRC funding often enabled pilot studies or background literature reviews to be conducted that produced reports and publications that could be used to obtain further funding of a more substantial nature from other sources. Finally, CRC funding sometimes simply demonstrated that early career researchers were capable of obtaining competitive funding, thus enhancing their chances of succeeding in other funding applications, and improving their career progression.

One example of how CRC funding led to the establishment of an enduring and important social support program in Victoria, Jesuit Social Services, was described by its founder, Peter Norden (2020) in his history of the Brosnan Centre. Norden recalled how the Centre developed from a half-way house for young men recently released from Youth Training Centres or Prisons in Victoria, founded in 1977 using four flats in the house at 56 Power Street in the leafy suburb of Hawthorn in Melbourne. The Centre grew over time to become Jesuit Social Services. In 1976, Norden obtained funding from the CRC, with the encouragement of the AICs Director Bill Clifford, to evaluate the half-way house project, known as 'The Four Flats Hawthorn'. 'Elery Hamilton-Smith was engaged to undertake the independent evaluation and he began work monitoring the planning stage in mid-1976. Elery had been a very experienced practitioner in the field of youth work and community development' (Norden 2020, p. 2). The grant was for a three-year period that included a two-year demonstration project, followed by the preparation of the evaluation report (Hamilton-Smith 1983). The evaluation consisted of a detailed description of the program in operation with a comparison being made between 53 young men who were residents in the hostel and 37 controls who had similar characteristics. A follow-up 12 months after release compared these two groups in terms of recidivism, ability to cope and self-esteem. The evaluation report found the program to be a success in terms of reducing recidivism, enhancing the ability of the young men to live independently and ensuring they were treated with dignity and compassion. The provision of funding by the CRC for this research provides an example of how even small-scale resourcing can support the development of a crime-reduction program that led to a much larger social welfare initiative being established. It is also an example of the importance of program evaluation that the psychologist Donald T. Campbell (1969) promoted in the 1960s and led to the creation of the Campbell Collaboration that had an AIC officer among the founding members of its Crime and Justice Group in 2000 (see Petrosino 2013).

In 1987, the Deputy Director of the AIC, David Biles, carried out a review of research projects funded by the CRC between 1972 and 1986 (Biles 1987b). Letters were sent to all successful grantees who could be contacted asking them to provide information about the extent to which their research projects had resulted in changes to criminal justice practice or policy. Of the 45 replies received (68% of those contacted), there was some element of positive impact or influence in over 86% of the cases: 11.1% provided evidence which showed that the project definitely influenced changes in legislative or criminal justice policy; 26.7% showed that the project had some indirect impact which led to changes in legislation or criminal justice policy and a further 48.9% saying that the report or results of the project have been cited in court cases, by practitioners or in the literature. One respondent, for example, said: 'there is no doubt in my mind that the Council has had a major effect on the criminal justice scene through its support of a far-reaching range of studies' (Biles 1987a, p. 21).

References

AusTender. 2021. Approaches to Market: Criminology Research Projects Round 2021. https://www.tenders.gov.au/Atm/ShowClosed/73447a67-a22f-4b93-8913-eb5a1c691143?PreviewMode=False Accessed 28 January 2022.

Biles, David. 1987a. *A Review of the Work of the Criminology Research Council, 1972–1986*. Canberra: Australian Institute of Criminology.

Biles, David. 1987b. The Funding of Criminological Research in Australia. *Australian and New Zealand Journal of Criminology* 20 (2): 67–77.

Campbell, Donald T. 1969. Reforms as Experiments. *American Psychologist* 24 (4): 409–429.

Challinger, Dennis. 1974. *The Juvenile Offender in Victoria*. Criminology Research Grant 17/73. https://www.aic.gov.au/crg/reports/crg-16-73 Accessed 23 February 2022.

Criminology Research Council (CRC). 1995. *23rd Annual Report 1995*. Canberra: Australian Institute of Criminology.

Criminology Research Council (CRC). 2002. *CRC Application Kit*. Canberra: Criminology Research Council.

Cunningham Dax, Eric, Sylvia Gosden, and Rona Hagger. 1978. *A Comparison Between Recidivists from Problem Families and Recidivists Currently in the Tasmanian Prison*. Criminology Research Council Grant 1/73. https://www.aic.gov.au/crg/reports/crg-1-73. Accessed: 23 February 2022.

Glanfield, Laurie, and Patrick C. Jobes. 2004. Understanding the Criminology Research Council. *Current Issues in Criminal Justice* 16 (2): 258–266.

Grabosky, Peter N., and Russell G. Smith. 1998. *Crime in the Digital Age: Controlling Telecommunications and Cyberspace Illegalities*. Sydney: Federation Press, New Brunswick: Transaction Publishers.

Hamilton-Smith, Elery. 1983. *Four Flats Hawthorn: An Evaluation*. Criminology Research Grant 11/76, Canberra: Australian Institute of Criminology. https://www.aic.gov.au/sites/default/files/2020-10/CRG-11-76-FinalReportb.pdf. Accessed 4 January 2021.

James, Steve, and Adam Sutton. 1994. Criminology and Crime Control in Australia. *Australian and New Zealand Journal of Criminology* 27 (3): 299–308.

Joutsen, Matti. 2022. Creating Inclusive Societies: The Reduction of Reoffending in the Context of the UN Crime Programme. *Address at UNAFEIs 60th Anniversary Event: Creating Inclusive Societies: Approaches to Reducing Reoffending*. Tokyo: Ministry of Justice.

Norden, Peter. 2020. *The Brosnan Centre: From Community Service to Social Action*, 2nd ed. Bentleigh: Norden Directions.

Petrosino, Anthony. 2013. Reflections on the Genesis of the Campbell Collaboration. *The Experimental Criminologist* 8 (2): 9–12. https://www.campbellcollaboration.org/images/pdf/plain-language/Petrosino_2013_EC_Reflections_Genesis_of_the_Campbell_Collaboration.pdf Accessed 6 November 2022.

Sherman, Lawrence, John Braithwaite, and Heather Strang et al. 1997. *Reintegrative Shaming of Violence, Drink-driving and Property Crime: A Randomised Controlled Trial*. Final CRC Report. Canberra: Criminology Research Advisory Council. https://www.aic.gov.au/crg/reports/crg-4793-4. Accessed 30 April 2022.

Stockholm Prize in Criminology. 2006. The First Winners of the Stockholm Prize in Criminology. *Press Release* No. 2, 2005-03-29.

7

Punching Above Its Weight

Seeking the Ideal Criminologist

In order to have an effective and productive public sector criminological research institute, it is essential to recruit and retain a qualified, motivated and satisfied group of individuals led by an experienced director and senior management team. Adam Graycar, the Institute's Director between 1994 and 2003, observed that during his tenure he had engaged 'good, solid people who were highly respected for their work' and that the Institute had more PhDs than any criminology department in an Australian university at the time (Adam Graycar, Interview, 1 March 2021).

There is, however, no pre-determined formula for the attributes required of the ideal candidate. Applicants for research positions at the AIC came from various backgrounds—including universities from where middle-level academics with doctorates were often recruited, while others came from government positions where higher academic qualifications were less likely to be present—particularly in the Institute's earlier years. Disciplinary backgrounds varied considerably with some having qualifications in law, psychology, sociology, political science, anthropology

R. G. Smith, *Public Sector Criminological Research*, https://doi.org/10.1007/978-3-031-28356-7_7

and criminology—once such courses became available. Methodological experience also varied with staff having training in both quantitative and qualitative research methods as well as historical and legal research techniques. On occasions, research staff had qualifications and experience in multiple disciplines and methods that proved to be beneficial for those managing across projects.

Because of its unique position that crossed disciplinary and administrative boundaries, staff conditions of employment had some elements of public sector employment but other characteristics of a University position. This created difficulties for some of those who came from universities where salary levels and conditions—such as study leave, travel and conference leave—were not always available at the Institute. Grant Wardlaw (Interview, 30 November 2020) recalled experiencing this tension during his time at the Institute in the 1970s, observing that 'moving to a public service model was seen as a threat to academic freedom'. Satisfying individuals who came to the Institute from differing backgrounds provided a challenge both for directors and those in the Commonwealth and Public Sector Union (CPSU)—that was active during the Institute's early decades.

Similar questions arose concerning the ideal attributes of the Institute's Directors. One enduring question was whether or not directors should be experienced criminologists or, rather, public sector administrators who could effectively manage a government agency. Some, such as Sir Leon Radzinowicz (1973, p. 2), in his *Report to the Commonwealth* of 17 November 1973, was clearly of the view that 'the director should be a criminologist'. This, however, was problematic in the 1970s in Australia when the discipline was in its infancy and there were few graduates who could claim to be 'criminologists'. Rick Brown (Interview, 10 June 2022) argued that 'the ideal scenario is having someone who understands and knows good quality research when they see it, but at the same time has connections with government so as to know what's driving the research agenda and what's valuable to government'.

Over time, the Institute has seen directors appointed who had academic credentials akin to modern criminology—including training in social science research methods, an understanding of theories of criminology and an appreciation of the socio-political context in which criminal justice research exists. Having subject-matter knowledge also made many of the tasks of a director somewhat easier, as conversations with the media, the academy and government could be undertaken with an understanding of both the theory and practice of criminology. Of course, such knowledge could be acquired 'on the job'—but this takes time, leaving unqualified individuals at risk of providing information that was incorrect or misleading.

The Institute's first four directors/acting directors had a legal background (Muirhead, Clifford, Harding, Chappell), while later directors/acting directors had their primary training in psychology (Davies, Biles, Wardlaw, Tomison), public policy/drug policy (Graycar, Makkai), finance (Marks, Rose) and policing (Dawson, Phelan)—see Timeline 16.2 for each of their periods of office. The Institute's first Acting Director, Judge James Muirhead (1973, p. 116), admitted: 'speaking personally, I assert no specialised qualification other than a broad understanding of the social problems we face, an interest in people and an enthusiasm to play a small part in a critical sphere'. Similarly, Adam Graycar observed in his Interview (1 March 2021):

> I was not a criminologist, I had no criminological knowledge at all… It is not necessary to be a subject matter expert. You need an understanding of social science, an understanding of research, an understanding of policy and some management and public service experience.

Of primary importance was the need for the director to be well-connected with those in government, as well as the academic world—both locally and internationally. Director Richard Harding emphasised this during his Interview (18 November 2021): 'If you're running one of these places the ability actually to be in touch with the people who can make decisions is a bonus'. Harding confessed to being 'a political animal' at the time who was 'tuned into' what was taking place in Canberra (Interview, 18 November 2021). Although he found Canberra 'a stultifying kind of place in many ways', he argued that it was necessary to be close to the seat of government to understand what was taking place and to make greatest use of political contacts. And, of course, if one fell out of favour with those in power, then continuing as director could be problematic—as both Bill Clifford found in 1983 and Duncan Chappell found in 1994.

Finding a Director

As we have seen in Chapter 3, above, the negotiations concerning the creation of the Institute took place throughout the 1960s, with the question of its location—in Japan or Australia—being closely linked to the engagement of its inaugural director. Had Japan been chosen, then Manuel Lopez-Rey, Chief of Social Affairs at the UN, could have become director of an Asia-Pacific Institute. Support for Lopez-Rey was, however, lacking and Norval Morris was eventually appointed director of UNAFEI in Tokyo in 1962. Morris was clearly well-qualified for the comparable position as director of the Australian Institute, having been one of the first lecturers in criminology at the University of Melbourne as well as being familiar with the regional context of criminal justice through his work for the UN. However, owing to the length of time that the negotiations took regarding the establishment of the AIC in Canberra, Morris elected to move to the prestigious, University of Chicago in 1964, allowing Dr V. N. Pillai to replace him as UNAFEI director.

Appointments to the position of director of the AIC had to be made by the Australian Governor-General and were for a seven-year term (s. 15 *Criminology Research Act 1971* (Cth)). The appointee had to be aged under 65 years by the time of the end of the term as director (s. 17), and the remuneration was to be determined by Parliament (s. 18). In the event, the question of salary took on some importance in attracting a candidate with suitable experience and standing. In accordance with the *Salaries (Statutory Offices) Adjustment Act 1971* (Cth), the director's salary was set at \$15,370 plus allowances. This was less than the salary of a Judge at the time, making the position problematic for some potential candidates. Over time, the level of salary was set by the Commonwealth Remuneration Tribunal that had been established by the *Remuneration Tribunal Act 1973* (Cth) to ensure that salaries for public officials were not subject to political considerations. The AIC was cited as an example, with Senator Lionel Murphy QC (1974, p. 512) arguing:

I can give honourable senators an illustration coming within my own Department to point up the implications of the proposed rejection of the Tribunal. Negotiations are currently being carried out for the appointment of a suitable person as the director of the Australian Institute of Criminology. We need a first class man for the job. But if this determination is not allowed to stand, no satisfactory salary would be available for the position. The level of salary will be one consideration but in point of principle what may be a greater disincentive will be the spectacle of decisions of responsible tribunals on wage fixation—an established and desirable method of removing wages from contentious debate—being set aside by the votes of either House of Parliament for insufficient or extraneous considerations.

The Attorney-General, Nigel Bowen, formed the opinion that the 'man for the job' was Norval Morris and he wrote to him with an offer on 22 January 1969, acknowledging that the position would not attract 'the facilities and support' that he was enjoying in Chicago (Finnane 2004, p. 270; NLA MS 2505/30/34–35). The offer was considered by both Barry and the recently appointed Minister for External Affairs, Paul Hasluck (NLA MS 2505/30/1977 addition). Morris, however, replied with an inconclusive response due to the likely nature of the Australian Institute, and also due to concern that he might be regarded as unsuitable in some circles (Finnane 2004, p. 270).

At the time, Morris, and his collaborator Gordon Hawkins had just published their book *The Honest Politician's Guide to Crime Control*—that sold over 100,000 copies—in which they sought to 'strip off the moralistic excrescences on our criminal justice system so that it may concentrate on the essential' (Morris and Hawkins 1970, p. 2). Their attack on the 'over-reach of the criminal law' identified eight 'ukases' such as 'abortion performed by a qualified medical practitioner in a registered hospital shall cease to be a criminal offence' and 'sexual activities between consenting adults in private will not be subject to the criminal law' (p. 3). Other targets for de-criminalisation included public drunkenness, illicit drug use, gambling, vagrancy and juvenile delinquency. These proposals were unlikely to be palatable to the government, and Morris himself thought that the 'police might blackball him' if he were proposed as the AICs Director (Finnane 2004, p. 270).

Richard Harding in his Interview (18 November 2021) believed that Norval's appointment fell through because 'someone in the government had found some inappropriate behaviour in his background'. Gideon Haigh (2008) in his account of the history of abortion law reform in Victoria provided the answer. In the early 1970s, Norval was closely aligned with the pro-choice abortion law reform movement, and years earlier had associated with practitioners who provided such procedures. He also had some personal experience of this in 1953, after forming a relationship with Margaret (Peggy) Berman, whom he had met when she was running a sandwich bar at University House at the University of Melbourne, when Norval was at the Criminology Department (Fenwick 2022). Peggy described Norval as 'handsome, with dark wavy hair and tremendous intellectual and physical vitality' (Berman and Childs 1972, p. 20). When she became pregnant, Norval helped arrange for her to have an abortion by a Melbourne city practitioner for £45—that was, fortunately, performed without complications. After the procedure, the doctor offered Peggy a job as his receptionist/assistant which she accepted in January 1954 at £25 a week. This led to her later being a witness to a pattern of police corruption in connection with illegal abortions in Melbourne that she recounted in evidence to the subsequent Kaye Inquiry (1971). Norval and Peggy had remained involved until he became Dean of Law at Adelaide University in 1955, but he kept in contact with her up to and during the Kaye Inquiry in 1971 (Haigh 2008, p. 71; Berman and Childs 1972, pp. 108–109). Mark Finnane noted in his obituary of Norval that '[Adelaide's] legal establishment was not friendly to a criminal law expert who became involved in controversial cases' (2004, p. 268), and for similar reasons, he was unsuccessful in becoming the AICs first director. John Braithwaite recalled in his Interview (30 January 2021) that 'the reason that the job was never offered to Norval was that Gough Whitlam vetoed it'. Gough admitted this to Professor Gil Geis during Gil's visit to Australia—'there was too much scandal around him' referring to Norval's prominent involvement in abortion law reform and his affair with Peggy. The result was that Norval remained in Chicago where he pursued a successful academic career; rather than heading-up the Institute in Canberra.

Norval continued to show interest in Australian criminology, and in 1974 became a Visiting Expert at the Institute—a position that included payment of 'a first class return air fare from Chicago to Canberra, payment of a $3000 consultancy fee, provision of a furnished apartment or flat in Canberra during his appointment and the cost of internal first class travel in Australia' (AIC Minutes, 13 August 1974, pp. 1–2). Norval was one of the first to stay in the Institute's leased flat in Kingston that was 'provided for the convenience of visiting experts and scholars' (AIC Minutes, 19 February 1975, p. 7). Col Bevan (2005, p. 294), Assistant Director of Training, also stayed in this flat with his fiancée for a fortnight when he first came to Canberra in 1975.

Further investigations were undertaken to locate a suitable director including advertising the position early in 1972. Expressions of interest were made to AGD that was responsible for the selection process and for submitting a recommendation to the Governor-General. The Selection Committee comprised Messrs. L. J. Curtis and Peter Loof from AGD, Mr B. A. J. Keddie, Deputy Director of Social Welfare in Victoria and Professor A. H. Pollard from Macquarie University. Of the eleven applicants, Mr R. S. Watson QC, who had been called to the Sydney Bar on 7 May 1948, was considered the most suitable candidate, although Judge J. Clarkson from Papua New Guinea and Judge James H. Muirhead from Adelaide were also under active consideration.

Jim Muirhead Q.C. had just been appointed to the newly formed South Australian Local and District Criminal Court in 1970 and, over time, became 'interested in the ramifications of the criminal justice system outside the courts, especially in the area of corrections' (Muirhead 1996, p. 71). This led to him being invited to join the Australian Crime Prevention Council (ACPC) by Jock McClemens who was then its National President. In 1971, Muirhead was invited to fill a temporary vacancy for five months on the Supreme Court of Papua New Guinea. Apart from experiencing death-defying flights to regional village courts, Muirhead presided over a range of criminal cases involving serious violence that fuelled his interest in criminology (Muirhead 1996, p. 82). By the time he had returned to Adelaide, he had taken over from McClemens as National President of the ACPC that eventually contributed to his being recommended for appointment as Acting Director of the AIC in 1972.

In his autobiography, Muirhead (1996, p. 90) described his conception of the functions of the Institute as being 'to present unified national support and statistical information to those who had the responsibility of containing crime and minimising destructive deviance'. His decision to take on this position was, however, problematic for his family as he had to leave his two sons in Adelaide to continue their studies—like many other subsequent members of the Institute's staff who relocated from other cities to Canberra and experienced domestic upsets as a result. Jim's wife, Margaret, found the move devastating.

Jim's initial tasks were to appoint staff and to find better accommodation for the Institute than the small office that had been provided at Ethos House in Canberra. Employing staff was difficult as all appointments had to be made with the approval of the Attorney-General. The first appointment, of Bill Miller as Executive Officer, led to conflict with Lionel Murphy as Attorney-General, as noted in Chapter 5, above. Jim admitted to 'making a couple of blunders' in appointing staff, 'little realising that some with apparent free thinking academic minds may be both arrogant and unreliable'. Other appointments such as his 'efficient secretary' Joan Swann and senior managers, Harold Weir and David Biles, were 'towers of strength and enthusiasm' (Muirhead 1996, p. 96).

After a year as Acting Director, Muirhead encountered serious personnel problems with some of the staff he had appointed. The problem, essentially, arose from a disjunction between his objectives in managing the Institute's research program, and the expectations of the research staff who had come from a quite different academic environment. With such a small number of staff, it seems hard to imagine that conflicts between groups and individuals in the organisation were generated so quickly. Shortly after he began work, he outlined what he expected of the research staff: 'I do not anticipate that the Institute will indulge in research for the sake of research. It will, I think, direct its investigations into areas of need or concern to government and to those vested with the responsibility of working in the realms of social deviance' (Muirhead 1973, p. 115). By April 1974, however, he said in a Memorandum to Research Staff that his 'hopes were not fulfilled. I have sensed and experienced hostility to others, hasty uninformed criticism and resentment of the efforts of others. I have heard talk of "bureaucracy" and the Research Division is now fragmented and thus unhappy' (Muirhead 1974, n.p.). He then went on to exhort the research staff to be more willing to accept direction from management and to communicate their concerns openly rather than dwelling on dissatisfactions. After Muirhead left, the main offender resigned and relations with the other research staff improved.

Most of the staff during Muirhead's term of office, however, worked harmoniously together. Harold Weir, for example, as Head of Training and Information received a glowing report from the Acting Director:

> Mr Weir is ambitious for the Institute and his staff. He works day and night, is efficient and seems to get the best out of his team. He is a little quick to take offence and 'a little over formal'. However I have every confidence in him and I can only suggest that he be given every encouragement in pursuing our training program. He is well regarded generally and has a significant international reputation following his overseas experience with UNAFEI and at other conferences. His efforts are largely responsible for our successful development. (Muirhead 1974, n.p.) (Plate 7.1)

The Acting Director's appointment was cut short at the end of April 1974 when Lionel Murphy directed him to be appointed as the second resident Judge of the Supreme Court in Darwin. Again, his wife, Margaret was not impressed with the decision not to return to Adelaide. This appointment did, however, provide Muirhead with an informed understanding of Indigenous disadvantage that served him well as Royal Commissioner of the Inquiry into Aboriginal Deaths in Custody in 1987.

Plate 7.1   Harold Weir, c. 1974 (*Source* AIC Archives)

The Institute's Organisational Structure

One of Judge Muirhead's first duties as Acting Director of the Institute was to establish an organisational framework and to appoint staff to manage the various work units. As we have seen, the *Criminology Research Act 1971* (Cth) created two bodies, the Institute and the Criminology Research Council (CRC)—each with its own management and administrative arrangements. Secretarial services for the CRC were provided by AIC staff who assisted with the administration of the grants program.

After January 1974, David Biles acted as the Institute's Adviser to the CRC (CRC Annual Report 1974, p. 8) with senior AIC researchers continuing this tradition over the ensuing decades.

On 26 April 1973, the Attorney-General approved the appointment of the Institute's first research staff: Harold Weir as Senior Criminologist (Information and Training) who was previously director (Education and Welfare) with the Australian Parliamentary Research Service, and before that Advisor at UNAFEI in Tokyo; David Biles as Senior Criminologist (Research) who was previously Senior Lecturer at the Criminology Department of the University of Melbourne; and Mary Daunton-Fear as Senior Criminologist (Criminal Law) who was previously a Senior Lecturer in Law at the University of Adelaide. Other staff were Diana Solman as Librarian, Bill Miller as Executive Officer and Michael Cass as a Senior Research Officer (AIC Annual Report 1973, p. 7) (Plate 7.2).

By 30 June 1974, the Institute has three main Divisions: Executive, managed by Bill Miller with eight other secretarial and finance staff; Research, managed by David Biles with three research criminologists and four clerical staff; Training and Information, managed by Harold Weir with four staff in the Training Branch, four staff in the Publications Branch and the J V Barry Memorial Library with five staff managed by Sylvia Blomfield. The total staff at this date numbered 34 including the Acting Director. By 30 June 1979, this had risen to 46.

Table 16.2, below, lists the names of the principal managers of the Institute's Divisions along with the senior research staff employed at 30 June each year, excluding secretarial staff (other than the Director's Executive Assistants), administrative officers and junior research officers. It also provides an indication of the length of each person's service and which researchers had a PhD by the time they ceased their AIC positions (some, such as Jenny Cartwright, née Mouzos, having commenced and completed doctoral studies during their time at the Institute). The total number of individuals named in this Timeline to 30 June 2022 was 197, 53% of whom were women (Plate 7.3). The highest number of all AIC staff was recorded at 30 June 2009, when Tony Marks was Acting Director, numbering 64 individuals. On 30 June 2022, the Institute had 33 staff, the decline largely owing to corporate services having been outsourced to the ACIC.

Plate 7.2   Judge Muirhead and his staff, 1973 (Back from left: Bill Miller, Harold Weir, Diana Solman, Pat Riley, Peggy Walsh, Jean Willoughby, Adam Browne, Peter Kay; Front: Joan Swann, Anne Wright, Judge Muirhead, Robyn Zebo, Mary McLean) (*Source* AIC Archives)

The Institute's First Permanent Director

In anticipation of Judge Muirhead leaving the Institute in 1974, discussions were had about finding an interim replacement as Acting Director, until a permanent appointment could be made. Jim Muirhead and Colin Howard both favoured David Biles, but Peter Loof, then Deputy Chairman of the Board, considered Biles to be insufficiently senior, although having 'maturity and many fine qualities that will make him well fitted to the task'. Tony Vinson was also considered, as was Graeme Newman who was then a Research Expert with the United Nations Social Defence Research Institute (NAA A2130, S1972/155 Part 2, Letter from Peter Loof to Clarrie W. Harders, 6 April 1974). These discussions reflect the importance of the network of individuals involved

Plate 7.3 AIC staff May 2023 ((l-r) Emily Faulconbridge, Hannah Miles, Sarah Napier, Timothy Cubitt, Alexandra Gannoni, Isabella Voce, Samantha Lyneham, Michael Cahill, Laura Doherty, Siobhan Lawler, Heather Wolbers, Megan Whittle, Katy Norman, Alexandra Voce, Yvette Maconachie, Samantha Jackson, Tom Sullivan, Katalina Foliaki, Merran McAlister, Emma Purtell, Samantha Bricknell, Rick Brown) (absent: Anthony Morgan, Hayley Boxall, Christopher Dowling) (*Source* AIC Archives)

with crime prevention, both at the United Nations and at the ACPC, in the appointment of staff. In the event, Dr Evan Davies, a Senior Lecturer in Psychology at the University of New South Wales, acted in the role until Bill Clifford was appointed on 4 October 1974. Davies then replaced Professor Colin Howard as one of the Attorney-General's appointments to the AIC Board for 1975.

The recruitment of the Institute's permanent director involved staff of the Attorney-General's Department liaising with previous candidates and seeking out new ones for the post. The Chairman of the Institute's Board, Frank Mahony, drew on his own list of candidates that included Keith Edmunds, an Acting Judge from Papua New Guinea, and Norval Morris, then in Chicago. Professor Colin Howard, who was at the time General Counsel to the Attorney-General, had planned a visit to Chicago and was asked to speak with Norval to see if he was still interested in the position. Jim Muirhead also reminded Frank Mahony that Bill Clifford would be visiting Canberra in June 1974 and could be approached about the position (NAA A432, 1974/5957). It was clear that the existing Board members, including Frank Mahony as Chairman and Peter Loof as his Deputy, favoured Bill Clifford for the position—given his association with the United Nations and extensive international connections (Plate 7.4). As we have seen, Norval Morris was no longer considered suitable for appointment.

William Clifford was a Yorkshireman with a war service record, extensive experience with the British Colonial Service in Cyprus and Northern Rhodesia and as the 'seventh Chief of the United Nations Social Defence Section in New York from 1968 to 1971 and later as Chief of the Crime Prevention and Criminal Justice Section from 1971 to 1974' (Redo 2012, p. 236). He had previous experience in policing and the probation service in England and had academic qualifications in economics and law from the University of London (Garton 2007). These connections meant that he was well-known and respected among those in AGD who were

Plate 7.4 (l–r) William Clifford, Director (1975–1983) and James Muirhead, Acting Director (1973–1974) (*Source* AIC Archives)

responsible for finding a director for the AIC. Leon Radzinowicz (1999, p. 407) also strongly recommended Clifford for the director's position, observing that:

> He was not a criminological star and he could be somewhat pedantic. But he had a solid appearance and many solid qualities which were badly needed at this stage of the Institute's life. He had wide experience and a gift for establishing good relationships and useful contacts.

When Norval Morris was found to be unsuitable, Clifford became the chosen candidate. However, as noted above, the statutory salary for the AICs Director was fixed at $15,370 plus allowances and because there was a wage freeze on the public service at the time; it was impossible to make an offer at a higher salary. As a result, Clifford agreed to be appointed as Acting Director from 4 October 1974 until the position could be made permanent at a higher salary—which occurred on 5 June 1975 (William Clifford papers, NAA, No. A432, 1974/5957).

Bill Clifford commenced on 20 January 1975 at Colbee Court in Woden—in clearly less salubrious premises than he had been accustomed to at the United Nations in New York and elsewhere. His biographer described him as 'a tall, heavy-set, balding, red-haired, fresh-faced man' (Garton 2007, n.p.), while Dennis Challinger (Interview, 18 February 2022) recalled him as being 'a semi-pompous sort of Englishman who was a career, international public servant rather than a criminologist who had worked extensively with the United Nations and was very keen to help developing countries'. Nonetheless, Clifford came with extensive experience, an impressive record of writing (only a portion of which resulted in refereed academic publications), and a reforming interest in reducing imprisonment of Aborigines, enhancing prisoners' rights, removing the death penalty and conducting research into white collar crime and victimology (Garton 2007). As John Braithwaite recalled in his Interview (30 January 2021), Norval Morris had also recommended Clifford for the position as AIC Director.

The problem with Clifford's tenure as director was that, as Richard Harding observed (Interview, 18 November 2021), 'he was never there—he was running around too much' and 'not really putting his time, effort and skills into developing the Australian significance of the Institute as much as its international significance'. Grant Wardlaw (Interview, 30 November 2020) observed what he called the 'UN gravy train' with Bill inviting, and being invited back by, other United Nations and international guests (Plate 7.5). This eventually alienated Bill from those in AGD who took the view that his ventures, such as the annual meetings of the Asia and Pacific Conference of Correctional Administrators that covered eight nations, were, according to Attorney-General Gareth Evans, 'just a rort' as Richard Harding recalled in his interview. When the next meeting was called for Tonga in 1984, Evans refused permission for the AICs Director to attend—which was unfortunate given that the AIC was the Secretariat for the group. In the event, David Biles and his secretary Marjory Johnson represented the Institute (Richard Harding, Interview, 18 November 2021).

Clifford's work ethic was, however, prodigious, which John Myrtle discovered when Bill's widow sought his assistance to go through his library and papers at his home after he had died (Plate 7.6). The National Library of Australia now holds 12 boxes, six volumes and three folio boxes of the Papers of William Clifford (MS 10133), while the National Archives of Australia holds 87 folders of Clifford's personal correspondence, speeches and official documents (NAA No M3548, 1951–1986).

Prior to his retirement in August 1983, Clifford drew attention to the inadequacy of government funding for the Institute in his last Annual Report, noting that:

> [S]taff reductions have continued through the year. Financial restraints and staff ceilings have reduced the capacity of the Institute to satisfactorily fulfil its functions.... The annual attrition rate of effective resources and personnel has meant that many opportunities for improving crime prevention in Australia have had to be shelved or relinquished. (AIC Annual Report 1983, p. 3)

After recounting the many initiatives undertaken by the Institute that had to be discontinued through lack of staff, Clifford concluded by arguing: 'the significance of the Australian Institute of Criminology as

Plate 7.5 United Nations Training Course at the AIC, 1981 (Standing (l–r): C. R. Bevan (Assistant Director Training AIC); M. A. Arbab (Pakistan); B. Nicholson (New Zealand); D. V. Fariaki (Fiji); M. Wahidi (Afghanistan); K. Nakai (Japan); Jin-Woo Byun (Sri Lanka); M. Budiarto (Indonesia); S. Songsamphant (Thailand); S. M. Hussain (Bangladesh); F. Mwanesalua (Solomon Islands); R. Nieva (Philippines); Seated (l–r): Dr El Augi (UN); B. Pissarev (UN); W. Clifford (Director AIC); K. F. Nyamekye (UN); E. S. S. Palmer (UN); Hon'Akau'ola (Tonga)) (*Source* AIC Archives)

a statistical data bank, as a dispeller of myths, as a reformer of criminal justice systems, and as a mobiliser of community concern for victims and for the treatment of offenders needs to be developed' (AIC Annual Report 1983, p. 4).

On 6 June 1986, less than three years after he had retired from the Institute, Bill Clifford died of a heart attack in Canberra. During his final years, he had continued to work, including as advisor on law and order in Papua New Guinea (Garton 2007), and with his position as 'Honorary Senior Consultant to the Institute' (AIC Annual Report 1984, p. 3).

Plate 7.6   Bill Clifford at the AIC, c. 1981 (*Source* AIC Archives)

Subsequent Directors of the Institute

Richard Harding

Between 1984 and 2022, seven individuals held office as directors, or Chief Executives of the AIC, with another five serving as Acting Directors on various occasions. Information about these people is presented below and in subsequent chapters. During almost four decades, they served under Labor governments on three occasions over 20 years reporting to eight different Ministers, and under Coalition governments twice over 20 years reporting also to eight separate Ministers (see Table 16.1, below, for further details).

Some months after Bill Clifford resigned from the Institute, Attorney-General Gareth Evans announced that Professor Richard Harding, Dean of the Law School, at the University of Western Australia, would be appointed as director. Harding was the first of a number of academics to be appointed as director. Harding arrived during Bob Hawke's term as Prime Minister and, in his Interview (18 November 2021), recalled that the director's position had originally been advertised under the Fraser Coalition government, but because of a falling-out with the then Attorney-General, Peter Durack, over politics, Harding had not applied. Following the change of government on 11 March 1983, Gareth Evans, the new Attorney-General, decided to re-advertise the position and on this occasion, Richard submitted an application, believing that it would be more likely to be successful with Labor in power, and Evans as the Minister—whom Richard knew quite well from their days working together at the Australian Law Reform Commission. In the event, Richard was offered the position, ahead of the other applicants, including David Biles and John Braithwaite, but owing to difficulties in re-locating his family to Canberra, Gareth agreed to him spending one week a month in Perth, prior to moving permanently to Canberra after the first 12 months (Richard Harding, Interview, 18 November 2021). His appointment also could have been assisted due to his having just presented the John Barry Memorial Lecture at the University of Melbourne on gun control and public health on 20 October 1982 (later published as Harding 1983) (Plate 7.7).

On commencing at the Institute on 30 January 1984, Harding discovered the full extent of the work needed to reform its operations including the appointment of more women, increasing research on Indigenous topics, improving library resourcing and changing the management structure (Richard Harding, Interview, 18 November 2021). Richard set to work remedying these problems including by appointing David Biles as Deputy Director and Gael Parr as Librarian. He also engaged Kayleen Hazlehurst to conduct research on Aboriginal affairs and Suzanne Hatty to work on domestic violence. Two years later he appointed Paul Wilson as Assistant Director (Research) and Dennis Challinger as Assistant Director (Information and Training), Dennis noting that it was because Richard was there that he agreed to move to Canberra. Personnel changes, such as these, invariably occurred each time directors changed, sometimes causing disruption to research activities and dissatisfaction among some staff.

Plate 7.7   Richard Harding at the AIC, c. 1984 (*Source* AIC Archives)

Unfortunately, after three years as director, Richard Harding decided to return to Perth as his 'family had never really settled in Canberra, and his wife found it professionally a very frustrating place' (Harding 2015, Interview with Julia Wallis, 8 April 2015). Nonetheless, Harding's time as director was important in the Institute's history. As John Braithwaite recalled in his Interview (30 January 2021), 'Richard was an excellent director who gave bold leadership and had built the Institute very effectively in its profile and impact'. After Harding left as director at the end of January 1987, David Biles became Acting Director for six months until 20 July 1987 when the new director, Duncan Chappell took office.

Duncan Chappell

Chappell was the third English-born; legal academic to be appointed as director and was aged 48 when he took office. At the age of 8, Duncan migrated to Tasmania where he graduated in arts and law with first-class honours from the University of Tasmania in 1962, the year he married his first wife, Susan. He attributed his interest in criminology to having heard an address by Jack Barry when he was a law student (Isles 1979). He then completed a PhD at Cambridge University in 1965 under the supervision of Leon Radzinowicz before taking up a Senior Lectureship in Law at the University of Sydney in December 1965 at around the time the Sydney Institute of Criminology was established. Duncan was also a foundation member of ANZSOC in 1967, Assistant Editor of the Australian and New Zealand Journal of Criminology from 1968 to 1971 (Chappell 2021), and in 2016 received the Society's Distinguished Criminologist Award. Radzinowicz (1999, p. 407) recorded in his memoirs that 'it gave me great pleasure when Dr Duncan Chappell was appointed director of the Canberra Institute'.

In 1969, he left Sydney on a Harkness Fellowship at the School of Criminal Justice in the State University of New York, Albany, becoming an Associate Professor in 1971, after which he was appointed director of the Law and Justice Study Center at Battelle Memorial Institute in Seattle in 1973. He divorced in 1976 and then returned to Australia accepting a visiting professorship in legal studies at La Trobe University in Melbourne and then received his first Commonwealth position with the Australian Law Reform Commission in Sydney in 1978.

He then moved to Canada where he was Professor and Chairman of the School of Criminology at Simon Fraser University at the time he was appointed to the AIC. As such, he was eminently qualified to become director of the AIC as he had both academic achievements as well as extensive experience advising public sector bodies on criminal justice administration and law reform over many years—as noted in the announcement of his ANZSOC Award:

> Some of his key contributions include his work with the International Labour Organisation in Geneva that examined the exposure of work places to violence through criminal events and later in his career he brought his expertise to the NSW Mental Health Review Tribunal. In the early 1990s he spent time in South Africa as a Member, then Chair of the Commonwealth Secretariat Observer Mission to South Africa for the United Nations sponsored peacekeeping mission in the lead up to the post-apartheid elections. During this mission he visited the notorious prison on Robben Island as well as Pretoria prison where at that time there were several hundred prisoners on death row. (ANZSOC 2017, p. 8)

Chappell remained at the Institute for almost seven years, retaining his adjunct status at Simon Fraser until 1990. At the Institute, he presided over some major initiatives including, most famously, the move to the new building in Canberra city and chairing the National Committee on Violence in 1989 (see Chapter 10, below) (Plate 7.8). Towards the end of his time as AIC Director, however, he fell out of favour with Minister for Justice, Duncan Kerr, partly due to the excessive costs of the new building and the Institute's continuing annual deficits that were creating difficulties for the Labor government that was trying to reduce the costs of the public service in Canberra.

Chappell also suffered the loss of a number of his senior managers. Mid-way through his period as director, David Biles had been seconded to work for the Royal Commission into Aboriginal Deaths in Custody, Peter Grabosky had taken leave of absence to work at the ANU, Dennis Challinger and Paul Wilson had resigned and Grant Wardlaw left in 1991 after fifteen years at the AIC—prior to his return as Acting AIC Director in April 1994.

In February 1994, the Keating Labor government conducted a *Review of Commonwealth Law Enforcement Arrangements* (Coad et al. 1994) that examined the nature of the Commonwealth's law enforcement responsibilities and interests. It recommended that the AIC should be subject

Plate 7.8 Duncan Chappell at the opening of the AICs building, 25 July 1990 (*Source* AIC Archives)

to an independent review of its role, clients, focus, priorities and structure. As we shall see (Chapter 14 below), one idea was to re-locate the Institute to the Australian National University—that was eventually rejected (John Braithwaite, Interview, 30 January 2021). This review was quickly undertaken over an eight-month period by the former Secretary to the Department of Administrative Services, Noel Tanzer AC, Des Hill, Assistant Director, Effectiveness Review and Strategic Planning, Victorian Department of Justice and Dr Grant Wardlaw (Tanzer et al. 1994). In his Interview (30 November 2020), Grant Wardlaw recalled how he had been blamed for the Review's recommendations concerning the AIC and their implementation—including removing half the staff over six months and beginning the process of exiting the Marcus Clarke Street building in order to meet the target of a $1.5 million reduction in expenditure. Wardlaw remained as Acting Director until Dr Adam Graycar commenced as the new director in November 1994. This was clearly one of the most difficult and turbulent periods in this Institute's history.

Adam Graycar's time as director over nine years was one of reform, rebuilding and stability for the organisation. There were, however, difficult financial constraints on the Institute and a poor industrial climate in the Canberra public service that created tensions with both staff and the CPSU.

Adam Graycar

Adam Graycar commenced his appointment as director of the AIC at the Institute's prominent offices in Marcus Clarke Street, Canberra City on 7 November 1994. Although he cannot recall reading the entire Tanzer Report, Adam began work rebuilding the Institute's policies and management processes, raising the intellectual calibre of its research outputs, enhancing its media and publications profile and working to improve stakeholder relations (Adam Graycar, Interview, 1 March 2021). Adam was ideally qualified to achieve these goals having had an academic career in public policy and related disciplines, as well as having had extensive experience in government administration. Immediately before being appointed to the AIC, he was Chief Executive Officer of the Office of Tertiary Education and Executive Director of the Department of Employment, Training and Further Education in South Australia, and prior to that South Australia's first Commissioner for the Ageing—an area that he maintained an interest in at the Institute with work on elder abuse. He also maintained an extensive set of relationships with organisations and individuals across the globe—that helped to enhance the Institute's standing in both academic and policy circles.

Adam decided to apply for the position at the AIC when his wife, Elizabeth Percival, was appointed as Executive Director of the Royal College of Nursing, Australia (RCNA) and they decided to move to Canberra from Adelaide together. This was the same motivation that had led John Braithwaite to come to the Institute in 1978 after his spouse, Valerie, had obtained a position at ANU. During Adam and Elizabeth's time in Canberra, the present author was appointed to write a history of the RCNA to mark its 50th anniversary (Smith 1999). Unaware that Elizabeth was Adam's spouse, the appointment was made without Adam's involvement, although he subsequently agreed to the author having a period of unpaid partial leave from his AIC duties. This work was undertaken remotely from the author's home in Melbourne and illustrates how Adam was able to accommodate the professional and personal needs of staff with flexibility and foresight. His many innovations at the Institute are recounted in other places throughout this book.

In 2003, Adam was offered the position as director of the Australian Institute of Family Studies (AIFS) in Melbourne with the support of the Minister, but unfortunately not that of Prime Minister John Howard. At approximately the same time, Adam was offered the position as head of the Cabinet Office in the Government of South Australia which he accepted and remained in that post until 2007. He then embarked on a number of senior academic roles first at Rutgers University in the US and then back in Australia at ANU, Flinders University and the University of Adelaide where he is now Professor of Public Policy and inaugural Director of the Stretton Institute. Adam received the Order of Australia Award in 2016 for significant service to tertiary education as an academic, to public administration through a range of leadership roles and to professional groups.

Toni Makkai

During Adam Graycar's term as director, he had appointed Dr Toni Makkai in 1997 as a Senior Research Analyst during a period of active recruitment of research staff—that included the present author. Like Adam Graycar and also John Braithwaite, Toni followed her spouse, Ian McAllister, who had taken up a position in Canberra—in her case coming from an academic post in the Department of Sociology at the University of Salford in England. Peter Grabosky, who had met Toni when she was undertaking post-doctoral research at the ANU with John Braithwaite on aged care and regulation, had suggested that she apply for the position at the AIC. Knowing that both Peter Grabosky and Adam Graycar were working at the AIC, she applied, successfully, for the position and commenced in late 1997 (Toni Makkai, Interview, 9 June 2022).

In 2001, Toni took over from Peter Grabosky as Director of Research and, when Adam resigned in September 2003, she was appointed Acting Director, and then in August 2004, made director, holding this role until May 2008. This was a period during which extensive staff recruitment occurred with overall numbers increasing substantially to 60 in 2008. It was also a period during which revenue was increased and a financial surplus was maintained during the years of stability under the Howard Coalition government—that included only three Ministerial changes.

Again, like Adam Graycar, Toni Makkai decided to leave as director when the Institute was functioning well and satisfying its stakeholders that included the new Rudd Labor government Minister of Home Affairs, Bob Debus. She commenced as full-time Dean of the College of Arts and Social Sciences at ANU in 2008. On her retirement in July 2015 to care for her mother, she continued in a number of advisory roles including the Ted Noffs Foundation Board of Directors, chairing the Griffith Criminology Institute's Industry and International Advisory Board and as a foundation Non-Executive Director of the Board of the Social Research Centre. In 2021, she was made a Member of the Order of Australia for significant service to tertiary education and to public administration.

In May 2008, the AICs Chief Financial Officer, Tony Marks, was appointed as Acting Director until Dr Adam Tomison took office as director in June 2009. This was the time during which the Institute had the highest number of staff—and an associated deficit for the year 2008–2009 of $599,607. It was also leading up to the period when the Institute experienced the most substantial governance changes ever—resulting from the legislative merger of the AIC and CRC and replacement of the Board and Council, respectively, with the CRAC from 1 July 2011 pursuant to the *Financial Framework Legislation Amendment Act 2010* (Cth).

Adam Tomison

Following this legislative change, Adam Tomison became Chief Executive Officer of the Institute on 1 July 2012 and remained in that role for his six-year term until Machinery of Government (MoG) changes occurred in July 2015. Chris Dawson was then appointed director of the AIC while retaining his position as CEO of the ACC. As we shall see in Chapter 14, this was another difficult and disruptive period in the Institute's history during which it faced the possibility of complete abolition or merger into a large government entity that would have unknown consequences. It also involved a substantial reduction in staff numbers to the lowest level in the Institute's history.

Following the merger of the AIC and CRC on 1 July 2011, the appointment of the AICs Director had to be made by the Commonwealth Attorney-General, rather than by the Governor-General, as required before that date. Pursuant to the amended section 16 of the *Criminology Research Act 1971* (Cth), the director of the Institute was given more extensive powers over the research and grant programs, subject to taking advice of the new CRAC and following any directions given by the Minister. Section 23 of the Act also empowered the director to engage staff under the *Public Service Act 1999* (Cth), to employ or engage staff for particular projects or, under section 24, to engage consultants.

Adam Tomison (Plate 7.9) was the most recent director with specific criminological research experience, having graduated with a Bachelor of Science with Honours in Psychology from Deakin University and a PhD from Monash University. He was, and remains, internationally recognised as an expert in the prevention of child abuse and family violence, the development of child protection and family support systems and first became well-known for his work developing the National Child Protection Clearinghouse, an internationally-recognised centre for excellence and the Australian Centre for the Study of Sexual Assault while at AIFS. He is a board member of the Canadian PNI member, the ICPC, and closely involved with various Australian and International child protection bodies.

From 2004 to 2008 Adam held various senior executive positions within the Northern Territory Department of Health and Families, including as director of NT Family and Children's Services (statutory child protection and family support services). In 2006–2007, he was the

Plate 7.9   Dr Adam Tomison, AIC Director 2009–2015 (*Source* AIC Annual Report 2011–2012, p. 2)

expert adviser (and Director of Policy and Research) for the 'Little Children are Sacred' NT Inquiry into the Protection of Aboriginal Children from Sexual Abuse (Donaldson 2016). As such, Adam combined both academic experience in criminology as well as extensive management experience in both Commonwealth and State and Territory crime and justice administration. Following the Machinery of Government changes at the Institute at the end of 2015, Adam Tomison was appointed Director-General of the Department of Attorney-General in Western Australia on 12 December 2016 replacing Pauline Bagdonavicius who was Acting Director-General following Cheryl Gwilliam's resignation—both of whom had chaired the CRAC. Since 1 July 2020, Adam Tomison has been Chair of the CRAC.

Directors Since 2015

As we shall see in Chapter 14, below, since July 2015, the Institute's Directors have been individuals heading-up the ACC and later the ACIC. Chris Dawson was appointed as AIC Director while also being CEO of the ACC between July 2015 and August 2018, when he left to become Commissioner of the Western Australia Police. Nicole Rose, former CEO of CrimTrac, who replaced Dawson as CEO of the ACIC, acted as AIC Director until Michael Phelan was appointed on 13 November 2017 (Plate 7.10).

Mike Phelan, who has qualifications in law, commerce and business administration, had an extensive career in law enforcement over 38 years, working initially on community policing, narcotics and serious fraud with the AFP and then as Director of the Australian High Tech Crime Centre—at the time of the AICs research collaboration with the

Plate 7.10   Michael Phelan, AIC Director 2017 to 2022 (*Source* AIC Archives)

centre. He later became Chief Police Officer for the ACT and then held senior appointments with the AFP becoming Deputy Commissioner in 2010. In 2008, he was awarded the Australian Police Medal and on 13 November 2022 retired from his positions with the ACIC and AIC.

These appointments of senior law enforcement bureaucrats take the management of the AIC back to its foundation days where criminal justice personnel played the primary roles. Importantly, however, the AIC has been well-served by having Dr Rick Brown as Deputy Director (Research) since the merger of the AIC and CRC on 1 July 2011 and as Deputy Director of the AIC since Dawson commenced as director. As noted in Chapter 10 below, Rick had extensive experience in criminological research working both for governments and as a consultant in the UK prior to coming to Australia in 2011. In his interview, he recalled how his work with the Police Research Group at the Home Office in the UK, provided him with experience and understanding of the needs of law enforcement relating to criminological, applied research. This permitted him to ensure that the AICs work, like that in the Home Office, would be attractive to police in that it demonstrated how crime prevention research could make a difference for law enforcement agencies (Rick Brown, Interview, 10 June 2022).

Staffing Numbers

As shown in Table 16.2, below, since its establishment, total AIC staff numbers increased gradually, peaking in 2008–2009 when 64 staff were employed, 39 of whom were academic research staff. Staffing numbers generally followed the fiscal fortunes of the Institute, as we have seen in Chapter 6 above, with a dramatic decline in the mid-1990s—leaving only eight research staff employed at 30 June 1997. The result of the partial merger with the ACC in 2015 also resulted in a substantial decline in numbers. By 30 June 2018, the Institute only had 20 staff including 14 academic researchers with the greatest losses being due to the transfer of most administrative staff to the ACIC. As is apparent from Fig. 7.1, the total number of academic research staff comprised approximately 40% of all staff (mean total staff per year 42; mean academic research

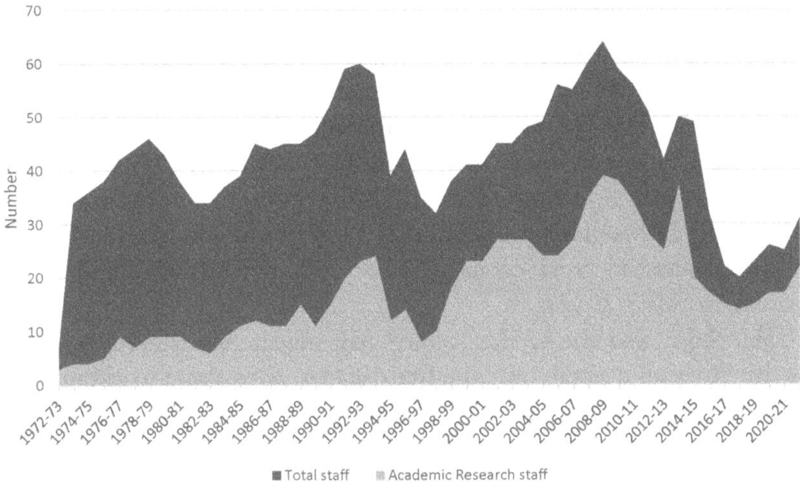

Fig. 7.1 Total AIC staff numbers and academic research staff, 1972–1973 to 2021–2022 (headcount at 30 June) (*Note* Numbers for total staff in 1974–1979 and academic research staff in 2005–2008 and 2009–2010 are estimates only due to the absence of data in these years (*Source* Derived from AIC Annual Reports 1973–2022, Canberra)

staff per year 17), with others having executive, administrative, financial, library and publishing functions.

Attracting qualified and experienced researchers to work at the Institute was often difficult, with many potential candidates being unable to move to Canberra from other cities, and some being unwilling to leave the 'freedom' of the academy for the confines of the public sector. Nonetheless, the Institute attracted and retained a number of highly qualified scholars, many of whom left to pursue Professorial roles in universities. The Institute has also been a training ground for younger criminologists with junior staff receiving practical training in data and policy analysis that equipped them for other positions in government, teaching or industry.

Table 16.2, below, presents information on the periods of employment of AICs staff in each financial year over the five decades. Data were obtained from the AICs Annual Reports and internal records where staff lists were not published in more recent Annual Reports. In the case of senior research staff, these are listed for individuals at Research Analyst level or higher, and names in bold are those who had PhDs at the time of leaving the AIC—some having begun and completed their research degrees during the period of their employment.

Of the 154 senior researchers listed, 62 (40%) had a PhD, with the highest proportion having doctorates in the period from the mid-1990s to the mid-2000s. This proportion is 11% points less than AIFS that, in 2022, reported 51% of its research and management staff having doctorates (AIFS 2022).

Table 16.2 also shows that senior AIC researchers stayed employed for five years on average over the five decades, with those working in the earlier decades tending to remain longer than those in more recent times. The present author had the longest period of employment of almost 25 years, followed by Dr Sat Mukherjee who remained for 23 years. It is also apparent that senior managers and Executives also stayed longer during the early years including Bill Miller, David Biles, Col Bevan and John Myrtle all being employed for more than 10 years each during the first three decades. Some administrative staff members also had lengthy periods of employment at the Institute including the longest-serving Personal Assistant to various Directors, Sylvia MacKellar, who began in 1987 and retired in September 2015—over 28 years in total (Plate 7.11).

Gender Issues

Table 16.2 also gives an indication of the gender of AIC staff at various levels of management and for senior research staff throughout the five decades. Of the 14 directors or acting directors, two were women, although Nicole Rose was only Acting Director for 3 months in 2017. Toni Makkai, however, was a researcher, manager then director for 11 years in all. All the AICs finance managers were men, apart from Yvette Whittaker who was the ACICs CFO since 2015 and performed this role also for the AIC. Two of the six directors of research were women, and two of the nine training, information and communications managers were women. In the case of the JV Barry Library, 90%

Plate 7.11 (l–r) Peter Grabosky, Sylvia MacKellar and Adam Graycar, c. 2008 (*Source* AIC Archives)

of library managers were women, while 62.3% of the senior research staff were women. This is only slightly higher than the overall proportion of APS staff who were women (60.2%) reported in the APSC *State of the Service Report* (2021). Considering current staffing in 2022, 77% of both AIC (research staff) and AIFS (research and management staff) were women.

Clear trends were present in the increasing proportion of women employed at the AIC over the five decades, which largely reflected the large increase in women graduating in criminology in Australia over this time. Col Bevan (2005, p. 332) noted that in the 1970s few women were employed at the Institute and few of them stayed very long— due to the chauvinism that was prevalent at the time. When Richard Harding arrived at the AIC, he also noted 'a paucity of female research staff' (Richard Harding, Interview, 18 November 2021). Peter Grabosky (Interview, 2 December 2020) recalled that 'most of the Board members of the Institute in those days were gentlemen in late-to middle age who really were not attuned to issues affecting women' and how Jocelynne Scutt's work on issues of sexual assault and domestic violence 'placed these issues on the agenda and helped to raise everybody's consciousness'. At 30 June 2022, 75% of the Institute's staff were women (AIC Annual Report 2022, p. 65) and major programs of research dealt with domestic and family violence, child abuse and sexual violence against women.

Arguably, the greatest change in the Institute's gender balance took place during Toni Makkai's directorship when she took the opportunity to make a number of senior appointments. These including Janet Smith as Library Manager in 2003, Judy Putt as Manager of Research Services in 2005 and Barbara Walsh as Manager of Information Services in 2007—each replacing men who had occupied these roles and resulting in the highest proportion of women occupying senior management positions in the history of the Institute. In her Interview (9 June 2022), Toni Makkai explained this as 'not being due to a formal quota strategy to increase the proportion of women as managers, but simply occurred because those appointed were most likely to do a terrific job, even if less experienced than others'. She went on to say: 'if you actually look at genuine quality and genuine potential, you're always going to end up with at least 50% of staff being female—those things are not distributed differently for men and women'. After she resigned as director, the Institute's senior management team reverted to its predominantly all-male composition as in previous years.

Voluntary Workers

As the Institute's budgets became tighter, and as government appropriation declined, directors sought out alternative ways in which to bolster the research capacity of the Institute. As early as 1975, for example, the Board considered ways in which to retain research staff following 'financial cuts on the research programme' (AIC Minutes, 3 February 1976, p. 3). One idea was to arrange secondments or periods of leave-of-absence to and from the Institute. One of the first examples of this was

Dr John Seymour's secondment to the Australian Law Reform Commission (ALRC) between 1979 and 1981. Seymour had been appointed as Senior Criminologist (Legal) at the end of 1976, having just completed a PhD at the University of Auckland on young offenders and having undergraduate degrees in law and arts from Auckland and a Diploma in Criminology from Cambridge (Plate 7.12). In his Interview (14 November 2022), John recalled meeting David Biles at the UN Crime Congress in Kyoto in 1970 who had suggested that he should apply for a position at the Institute in Canberra. When John began work at the AIC in 1976, he focussed on young offenders and child welfare law for two years until he was appointed a part-time Commissioner in charge of the ALRCs inquiry into child welfare law in 1979. It was agreed that he would retain his appointment with the AIC and be seconded to work full-time on the ALRCs reference—with the AIC paying his salary. He was happy to work on this reference until he secured an appointment as Senior Lecturer in Law at the ANU, commencing on 1 January 1982 (John Seymour, Interview, 14 November 2022).

The AIC also received secondees from other agencies. In 1986, for example, the AIC Board was informed that the ABS had agreed to outpost an ABS Officer to the Institute for a period of twelve months commencing on 1 January 1987 in order to assist in the production of a report similar to the US 'Report to the Nation on Crime and Justice'. 'This report was to be published in the Bicentennial year' (AIC Minutes, 12 June 1986, p. 5) and appeared in 1990 (Mukherjee et al. 1990). In 1992, director Duncan Chappell permitted Peter Grabosky to spend two years at the ANU working on regulatory compliance with Valerie and John Braithwaite (Peter Grabosky, Interview, 2 December 2020).

Following Peter Loof's resignation as Chairman of the AIC Board on 30 June 1991, Duncan Chappell as director sought the Board's approval to develop an Institute Fellow Program that 'would involve the appointment of a senior person, for a specific period, who would contribute his/ her particular knowledge and skills to an area or subject of special interest to the Institute' (AIC Minutes, 25 July 1991, p. 292). Peter Loof was the first Fellow appointed for a two-year term to undertake work

Plate 7.12   Dr John Seymour, Senior Criminologist (Legal) (c. 1976) (*Source* AIC Archives)

with the UN and was paid a modest honorarium as well as expenses involved in his UN activities. Initially, he accompanied the new AIC Board Chairman, Herman Woltring, to the next meeting of the UN in Vienna. Dr William Lucas, Director of Forensic Services in South Australia, was the second Fellow appointed to work on a national conference on sentencing and treatment of violent offenders in October 1991. At the next meeting of the Board in November 1991, the size of the honorarium was fixed at $200 per day for up to 10 working days, plus out-of-pocket expenses, subject to further extension beyond 10 days with the agreement of the Board. At this meeting, Dr Grant Wardlaw was also appointed as a Fellow (AIC Minutes, 28 November 1991, p. 1). Since then, a number of senior AIC staff who have left the Institute have been appointed as Fellows—including the present author to enable him to prepare this publication—albeit without any honorarium but with reimbursement of fieldwork expenses.

Another idea that was instituted during the directorship of Adam Graycar was to establish a network of Associates of the Institute. Adam explained this during his interview as being a group of people who could undertake unpaid work on projects that the Institute was unable to do, owing to resource constraints. On other occasions, Adam would invite academics to present a paper at an Institute conference that would then be submitted for publication in the *Trends and Issues* series. Adam concluded: 'we really did operate on a shoestring' (Adam Graycar, Interview, 1 March 2021).

Associates were given a free subscription to the *Trends and Issues* series, waiver of registration fees for the AICs National Outlook Conference, and for any AIC seminars in their city and access to the JV Barry Library. In return, they would be the Institute's point of liaison in their home city. In the first round of appointments, nine nominations were approved by the Board: Rod Broadhurst, Simon Bronitt, Riaz Hassan, Ross Homel, Ian O'Connor, Stephen Mugford, Rick Sarre, Kate Warner and Jon Bright. Two other nominations by Ian Freckelton and Peter Lewis were declined, although the Board agreed to accept re-nominations from them at a future date. Nominations were also able to be made from individuals in New Zealand, and all appointments were for an initial two-year period (AIC Minutes, 1 May 1996, pp. 4–5). Some of these Associates, such as Broadhurst and Sarre, continue to support the Institute's work through publications and speaking at events. By 2004, 20 individuals were Associates of the Institute, eight of whom were among the foundation group whose terms had been renewed (AIC Annual Report 2004, pp. 178–179). The practice of appointing Associates has since been discontinued.

Conclusions: Punching Above Its Weight

The title of this chapter reflects the often-cited phrase used to describe the output of an organisation as being well in excess of what might be expected given its size, budget and staffing. For example, in her Interview (29 March 2021), former Manager of the JV Barry Library, Jane Shelling, when asked how the Institute compared with other comparable agencies said:

> I think that we far exceed [other agencies] given the amount of money we have, I still can't believe how low our funding is, and how much we achieve with the amount of staff that we have, and it just shows that our people who are passionate about their work, do so well, get things right and deliver high-quality research so that we punch way above our weight than other organisations that are much better funded, much bigger organisations and places that are much more well-known.

As we shall see in Chapter 11, throughout the Institute's history, over one thousand research reports and papers have been published, in addition to work carried out in collaboration with University academics and industry analysts leading to numerous commercial books, criminology texts as well as journal articles and consultancy reports. This output by a small contingent of research staff means, however, that workload pressures are high—a factor that 'punching above one's weight' fails to recognise. Regular turnover of staff, although often motivated by opportunities for professional advancement and improved remuneration, can sometimes be due to over-work and dissatisfaction with the workplace. This has on occasions been demonstrated in the confidential AIC staff responses to the annual APS employee census (APSC 2021).

In order to quantify the output of Institute's research staff, the library catalogue was searched for the number of items recorded against individual staff members during the period of their work at the Institute. Although some publications by staff were released shortly after they left their research positions, this analysis provides an indication of the research output during the time of their actual employment. Only senior research staff and directors were included in the search and, as shall be shown in Chapter 11, the AICs catalogue records some 1662 publications over the AICs history in addition to various academic and commercial publications prepared by staff while employed at the Institute.

Table 7.1 shows the results for the 37 individuals who had more than 20 individual catalogue items during their time at the Institute, as sole or joint authors.

From this table, it is apparent that the current author had the highest number of items in the catalogue during the period of his employment, and the highest number of peer-reviewed publications (as determined by the catalogue search engine). This was, of course, due to the current author having the longest period of employment at the Institute as a researcher. In terms of items per year, Paul Wilson was the most productive both in terms of all item types (26 per year) as well as peer-reviewed publications (2.8 per year). Peter Grabosky ranked second in terms of all catalogue items (208) and items per year (12), and Jenny Cartwright (née Mouzos) had the second-highest rate of peer-reviewed publications per year (2.5 per year).

Table 7.1 also shows that some former Directors of the Institute and the current Deputy Director, Rick Brown, also ranked high on outputs, as did current and former Research Managers—partly due to Research Managers usually being co-authors of publications written jointly with the staff they supervised—noting that they invariably contributed substantially to research design, data collection and writing of these publications. Those staff who were responsible for crime monitoring projects, such as Vicki Dalton, Penny Jorna and Dr Samantha Bricknell, also had high levels of output, although fewer of these publications were peer-reviewed. It is also apparent that there were fewer peer-reviewed publications in the early years of the Institute than in later years—as is to be expected as formal peer review processes were only introduced with the commencement of the *Trends and Issues* series in 1986 followed by *Australian Studies in Crime Law and Justice* in 1989, the *Research and Public Policy* series in 1995 and the current *Research Report* series in 2016. In all, almost half of the 1662 AIC publications were peer-reviewed (789—47.5%).

Table 7.1   Publications recorded in the JV Barry Memorial Library Catalogue, 1975–2021 authors with more than 20 items

Name	Period	Years	Catalogue items	Items per year All	Peer-reviewed	Items per year Peer-reviewed
Russell Smith	1996–2020	24	228	10	58	2.4
Peter Grabosky	1983–2002	17	208	12	20	1.2
Paul Wilson	1986–1992	6	155	26	17	2.8
David Biles	1974–1994	20	154	8	2	0.1
Satyanshu Mukherjee	1977–2000	23	104	4	7	0.3
Bruce Swanton	1975–1995	20	93	5	5	0.3
Toni Makkai	1998–2008	10	88	9	12	1.2
Grant Wardlaw	1976–1994	18	73	4	1	0.1
Anthony Morgan	2006–2022	16	70	5	36	2.3
Jenny Cartwright / Mouzos	1999–2009	10	68	7	25	2.5
John Walker	1980–1995	15	64	4	12	0.8
Jason Payne	2001–2015	14	61	4	12	0.9
Ivan Potas	1975–1994	19	53	3	3	0.2
Samantha Bricknell	2006–2022	16	51	3	9	0.6
Adam Graycar	1994–2003	9	46	5	4	0.4
Peter Homel	2004–2014	10	43	4	6	0.6
Rick Brown	2011–2022	11	41	4	18	1.6
Matthew Willis	2004–2020	16	40	3	12	0.8
Judy Putt	1996–2010	7	40	6	6	0.9

Name	Period	Years	Catalogue items	Items per year All	Peer-reviewed	Items per year Peer-reviewed
Marianne James	1992–2008	16	37	2	10	0.6
Katie Willis	2001–2013	12	37	3	6	0.5
Kim-Kwang Raymond Choo	2006–2011	5	36	7	7	1.4
Hayley Boxall	2010–2022	12	34	3	18	1.5
Kelly Richards	2008–2014	6	31	5	9	1.5
Alexandra Gannoni	2011–2022	12	29	2	7	0.6
Dennis Challinger	1986–1989	3	28	9	0	0
Patricia Easteal	1991–1995	4	25	6	2	0.5
Vicki Dalton	1992–2002	10	25	3	10	1.0
Penny Jorna	2010–2019	9	25	3	7	0.8
Richard Harding	1984–1987	3	24	8	0	0
Jessica Anderson	2004–2014	10	23	2	5	0.5
Jane Mugford	1984–1998	14	22	2	0	0
Samantha Gray-Barry / Lyneham	2010–2022	12	22	2	12	1.0
Jocelynne Scutt	1976–1981	5	22	4	0	0
John Braithwaite	1978–1983	5	21	4	0	0
Col Bevan	1976–1986	10	21	2	0	0
Jacqueline Joudo-Larsen	2004–2012	8	21	3	4	0.5

In addition to these Institute outputs, some researchers, particularly those with established, or developing academic backgrounds, published a number of commercial books, often based on research undertaken during their time at the Institute. This was approved by directors (and a number of directors participated in this), on the understanding that contractual payments and royalties would be paid to the Institute if the work had been undertaken in work time (see discussion of retention of royalties in Chapter 5 above).

Institute Directors Harding, Graycar and Makkai published one or two commercial books each during their tenure while other senior staff published five or more books each as well as numerous journal articles, book chapters and reports. Toni Makkai, for example, published 27 articles and chapters in addition to her book *Regulating Health Care* in 2007. John Braithwaite was the earliest to engage in external publications, with four books and 25 refereed articles published between 1978 and 1983. The most prolific staff members who wrote externally were Peter Grabosky and the current author who collaborated on a number of projects including their three volumes on cybercrime for Federation Press and Cambridge, as well as eight other volumes published individually or with others for major international publishers Oxford, Elgar, Palgrave and others. The benefits to the Institute, apart from royalties, lay in the ability of these books to raise the profile of the Institute internationally, and their utility in attracting external funding for the Institute for new projects on these topics. The authors were also fêted with awards and received numerous invitations to speak at local and international conferences. In 2005, for example, the American Society of Criminology's Division of International Criminology gave its Distinguished Book Award to Smith et al. (2004) for *Cyber Criminals on Trial* published by Cambridge University Press. This raised the Institute's profile in the area of cybercrime research leading, in some measure, to the Institute receiving funding in excess of $3.5 million for research in this area over the ensuing years.

An additional performance measure that has been relied on since the advent of the Internet, has been the ability to count the number of times a given publication has been cited in the academic literature. Google Scholar provides a count of citations that includes not only commercially-published academic works, but also government publications—such as the AICs refereed series. Some examples of works written by AIC staff during their time with the AIC that received high citations include *Political Terrorism* (Wardlaw 1982—894 citations), *Women's Experiences of Male Violence* (Mouzos and Makkai 2004—591 citations), *Of Manners Gentle* (Grabosky and Braithwaite 1986—549 citations) and *Cyber Criminals on Trial* (Smith et al. 2004—251 citations).

Recent AIC Annual Reports also now include data on the citation of AIC publications as a measure of the reach of the Institute's research. In 2021–2022, for example, AIC research material published in that year was cited in 753 publications from over 50 countries, with 61% of citations being made in peer-reviewed journals, 16% in books, sections of books and reports and the remainder in government and other publications (AIC Annual Report 2022, p. 45).

Although the current work has explored many questions concerning the management and administration of the Institute, particularly through the contributions of its directors and senior managers, it is important to recognise the contribution of all staff, both as researchers as well as those in administrative roles, who facilitated the Institute's outputs and achievements. Many have not been identified personally in the current work, but their efforts throughout the five decades must be fully acknowledged as having contributed to the development of this unique public sector research entity. As a reminder of the many individuals who have contributed to the work of the Institute, Plate 7.13 shows the group of staff, former staff and supporters gathered for the Institute's 25th anniversary dinner on 25 November 1998. A much larger group will, hopefully, attend the 50th anniversary gathering in 2023.

These individuals are the engine that has driven the Institute throughout its history. As Research Manager, Dr Samantha Bricknell observed in her Interview (21 November 2022):

> I remember someone remarking on the work that the AIC contributes, compared to work prepared elsewhere, that the AICs work is recognised and is used. The fact that this has occurred over fifty years demonstrates that, to use a cliché, it really does punch above its weight.

Plate 7.13 AIC 25th Anniversary gathering, Hotel Kurrajong, Canberra, 25 November 1998 (*Source* AIC Archives)

References

Australian and New Zealand Society of Criminology (ANZSOC). 2017. Distinguished Criminologist Award 2016: Professor Duncan Chappell. *PacifiCrim* 14 (1): 8. https://anzsoc.org/files/pacificrim/PacifiCrim-14-Nov-2017.pdf. Accessed 24 July 2022.

Australian Institute of Criminology (AIC). 1973–2022. *Annual Reports.* Canberra: Australian Institute of Criminology.

Australian Institute of Criminology (AIC). 1974–1996. *Board of Management Minute Books.* Canberra: Australian Institute of Criminology.

Australian Institute of Family Studies (AIFS). 2022. *Our Researchers.* Canberra: AIFS. https://aifs.gov.au/research/profiles. Accessed 28 July 2022.

Australian Public Service Commission (APSC). 2021. *State of the Service Report 2020–21.* Canberra: APSC. https://www.apsc.gov.au/sites/default/files/2021-11/APSC-State-of-the-Service-Report-202021.pdf. Accessed 28 July 2022.

Berman, Margaret Dorothy (Peggy), and Kevin Childs. 1972. *Why Isn't She Dead!* Melbourne: Gold Star Publications.

Bevan, Colin Russell. 2005. *As the Walrus Said. The Time Has Come....* Canberra: Book Surge.

Chappell, Duncan. 2021. Some Reflections on the 50th Birthday of the Australian and New Zealand Journal of Criminology. In *The Changing Face of Criminology in Australia and New Zealand*, ed. Russell G. Smith, xiii–xvii. London: Sage.

Coad, William J., Prudence Ford, Malcolm Hazell, Peter Lamb, Norman Reaburn, and Adrian Whiddett. 1994. *Report of the Review of Commonwealth Law Enforcement Arrangements.* Canberra: Australian Government Publishing Service.

Criminology Research Council (CRC). 1974. *Annual Report 1973–74.* Canberra: Australian Institute of Criminology.

Donaldson, David. 2016. WA Names New Attorney General's DG, but DPC Appointments Still Waiting. *The Mandarin*, 24 November. https://www.the mandarin.com.au/72874-wa-names-new-attorney-generals-dg-but-dpc-app ointments-still-waiting/. Accessed 28 July 2022.

Fenwick, Jill. 2022. Notable Women of East Melbourne: Margaret (Peggy) Berman (1923–2002). *East Melbourne Historical Society*. https://emhs.org. au/biography/berman/margaret. Accessed 2 August 2022.

Finnane, Mark. 2004. Tributes: Norval Morris (1923–2004). *Current Issues in Criminal Justice* 15 (3): 267–271.

Garton, Stephen. 2007. Clifford, William (Bill) (1918–1986). In *Australian Dictionary of Biography*. Canberra: National Centre of Biography, Australian National University. https://adb.anu.edu.au/biography/clifford-william-bill-12328/text22147. Accessed 22 July 2022.

Grabosky, Peter N., and John Braithwaite. 1986. *Of Manners Gentle: Enforcement Strategies of Australian Business Regulatory Agencies.* Canberra: Oxford University Press.

Haigh, Gideon. 2008. *The Racket: How Abortion Law Became Legal in Australia.* Melbourne: Melbourne University Press.

Harding, Richard. 1983. 'An Ounce of Prevention …: Gun Control and Public Health in Australia. *Australian and New Zealand Journal of Criminology* 16 (1): 3–19.

Isles, Tim. 1979. Institute Chairman Retires. *AIC Reporter* 1 (1): 11.

Kaye, William. 1971. Report of the Board of Inquiry into Allegations of Corruption in the Police Force in Connection with Illegal Abortion Practices in the State of Victoria. No. 3-7343/71. Melbourne: Government Printer. https://www.parliament.vic.gov.au/papers/govpub/VPARL1 971-72No3.pdf. Accessed 1 August 2022.

Morris, Norval, and Gordon Hawkins. 1970. *The Honest Politician's Guide to Crime Control*. Chicago: The University of Chicago Press.

Mouzos, Jenny, and Toni Makkai. 2004. *Women's Experiences of Male Violence, Findings from the Australian Component of the International Violence Against Women Survey*. Research and Public Policy Series No. 56. Canberra: AIC.

Muirhead, James Henry. 1973. Some Thoughts at the Beginning, Current Comment. *Australian and New Zealand Journal of Criminology* 6 (2): 114–116.

Muirhead, James Henry. 1974. Memorandum from Judge J. H. Muirhead to Research Staff, National Archives of Australia D-P-13, M3548/37—Director's Appointment. Canberra: NAA.

Muirhead, James Henry. 1996. *A Brief Summing Up*. Northbridge: Access Press.

Mukherjee, Satyanshu K., Debbie Neuhaus, and John R. Walker. 1990. *Crime and Justice in Australia*. Canberra: Australian Institute of Criminology.

Murphy, Lionel. 1974. Debate on the Remuneration Tribunal's First Determination. Parliamentary Debates, Senate, 25 July, p. 512. Canberra: Government Printer.

Radzinowicz, Leon. 1973. *Report of Sir Leon Radzinowicz with Respect to the Australian Institute of Criminology*. Canberra: National Library of Australia (6093/72/4182).

Radzinowicz, Leon. 1999. *Adventures in Criminology*. London: Routledge.

Redo, Slawomir, M. 2012. *Blue Criminology: The Power of United Nations Ideas to Counter Crime Globally: A Monographic Study*. HEUNI Publication Series No. 72. Helsinki: HEUNI. https://heuni.fi/documents/47074104/0/Blue_Criminology_www_linked.pdf/0013989d-f932-25ab-ec52-5f21884da6d3/Blue_Criminology_www_linked.pdf?t=1610010139161. Accessed 13 May 2022.

Smith, Russell G. 1999. *In Pursuit of Nursing Excellence: A History of the Royal College of Nursing, Australia 1949–1999*. Melbourne: Oxford University Press.

Smith, Russell G., Peter N. Grabosky, and Gregor F. Urbas. 2004. *Cyber Criminals on Trial*. Cambridge: Cambridge University Press.

Tanzer, Noel, Des Hill, and Grant Wardlaw. 1994. *Review of the Australian Institute of Criminology: Report*. Canberra: Australian Institute of Criminology.

Wardlaw, Grant. 1982. *Political Terrorism: Theory, Tactics and Counter-Measures*. Cambridge: Cambridge University Press.

8

Seeking Suitable Accommodation

Introduction

This chapter explores the physical environment in which public sector criminological research is carried out. It begins by examining the geographical location of national research institutes, and, in the case of the AIC, considers the debate that arose over the choice of Canberra as its home base. Many consequences followed from this choice, including the difficulty of keeping in touch with state and territory interests, and how to attract and retain staff to work in the national capital—some of whom previously had established homes and employment in other jurisdictions that they were reluctant to leave. Having the Institute based in Canberra also led to increased travel costs for meetings and conferences, both for AIC staff and external parties attending AIC events. Nonetheless, Canberra is the seat of the Australian government and was a fitting place in which to house the national criminological research agency.

This chapter then explores the principles that underlie the choice and style of office accommodation required for a research institute. It examines the difficulties that government agencies, their Boards and

R. G. Smith, *Public Sector Criminological Research*, https://doi.org/10.1007/978-3-031-28356-7_8

Directors, faced in selecting office accommodation that was of an acceptable standard to satisfy the needs of the workforce, while not providing an ostentatious display of refinement and luxury that might lead to accusations that the government was wasting resources. It also examines the type of accommodation that was considered to be most suitable for workers who devote the bulk of their time to the relatively solitary academic pursuits of research, analysis and writing.

Using the AICs experience as illustrative of these challenges, this chapter charts the transition from the most modest of facilities provided to the AIC in 1973 to the most imposing in the 1990s, followed by a reversion back to more compact office space in the 2000s. Currently, we find AIC staff now working principally from home since the restrictions that began during the Coronavirus pandemic and only needing to gather for face-to-face meetings in the office when essential. This natural experiment of home-based work is analysed in terms of its potential for justifying future enduring changes to the AICs working environment.

The Debate Over Centralisation

One of the enduring challenges of a federal system of government is the determination of where the national capital should be located. Once a suitable city is chosen or built, the question then arises as to whether all government entities need to be based in this one central city. In countries as large as Australia, Canada and the US, for example, the choice of a capital city has been complex, with the solution being to construct a new city in a reasonably central place. In the US, Washington DC was established by the *Residence Act 1790* (Ch. 28, 1 Stat. 130), as the capital of the US following the American Revolution. In Canada, Ottawa was chosen by Queen Victoria as the capital city for the United Province of Canada in 1857, and confirmed on Confederation in 1867 (National Capital Commission 2021). In Australia, section 125 of the Australian Constitution provided for a capital to be established in New South Wales, no less than 100 miles from Sydney. Canberra was declared the national capital in 1913. Rivalries between large financial and population centres, as well as questions of security, transportation and trade made these choices difficult, often leaving those living in distant locations claiming to be left out of the picture and their importance and particular interests down-played.

A similarly difficult choice had to be made concerning the location of individual government entities. When a new entity was created, debates often became heated as to whether it should be based in the capital, or out-posted to the regions. As we shall see, these concerns were of greater importance in the pre-digital age when travel costs were high—particularly for those in distant locations that could require days of travel across multiple time zones. Selecting the national capital as the home for an institute of criminology, also carried with it the need to align both national and regional interests—despite the fact that most crime is perpetrated regionally, and dealt with by regional law enforcement, court and correctional agencies. The choice of Canberra as the AICs home location, ensured that Australian government interests were of principal importance in determining the AICs work program and funding. How, then, were these competing interests addressed?

In Australia, the *Criminology Research Act 1971* (Cth) commenced on 6 November 1972, and the inaugural meeting of the AICs Board of Management was held on 18 April 1973 in Canberra. At this meeting, the Acting Director, Judge James Muirhead QC, reported that he had begun a national survey of the states 'to locate areas of concern that may be common to the states, seek information as to particular problems and gain a better understanding of Australian needs in this field before examining or adopting overseas experience' (AIC Minutes, 18 April 1973, p. 2). This initial tour was designed to ensure that the AICs role would be inclusive of the states and territories, but it began a heated debate that continued throughout the Institute's life as to the correct balance between Commonwealth and state and territory interests. It also showed that the duties of AIC Directors and staff would inevitably require a good deal of travel, both within Australia, and internationally. Some directors, whom Richard Harding (1998) called 'travelling men', took up the challenge of international travel with enthusiasm, while others were more mindful of the need to stay at home, deal with daily duties in the office and conserve the budget. As Harding (1998, n.p.) observed in relation to the AICs first director, Bill Clifford:

> [He] spent a lot of time at the front end of Jumbos, when he was really
> needed in the tea room of the Information and Training Section or the
> production room of the Publications Section.

The inaugural meeting of the Board highlighted the need to obtain suitable accommodation for the Institute, with a suggestion that a new
building could be built, although this would take some years to be
accomplished. Those present discussed the accommodation provided for
overseas Institutes and asked Acting Director Muirhead to make further
inquiries—inevitably requiring additional travel (AIC Minutes, 18 April
1973, p. 3). It was later agreed that 'the Institute should be accommodated in Canberra in a building commensurate with its national identity
and to adequately meet the functions and attendant responsibilities with
which it is charged' (AIC Minutes, 28 June 1973, p. 23). In the short
term, a minimum space of 4000 square feet was needed, but in the
longer-term, a new building was suggested with administrative, training,
conference and library facilities as well as residential accommodation and
a canteen for up to 100 persons at a time. Such a building was estimated
to cost approximately $2 million (in 1973 prices). A location near the
ANU or in the northern Canberra suburb of Belconnen was thought to
be suitable.

Having the Institute based in Canberra, however, caused various
difficulties in terms of administration and staffing from the outset.
At the second Board meeting, fog in Canberra prevented the flight
of Board member, Mr L. K. Downs, Under-Secretary of the Department of the Attorney-General and Justice in New South Wales, from
landing in Canberra (AIC Minutes, 22 May 1973, p. 5)—a continual
cause of meeting apologies throughout Canberra's winters during the
ensuing years. The Board later considered the question of the payment of
accommodation and travel expenses for people attending seminars and
meetings in Canberra and agreed that such payments should be made
to encourage state participation—and to avoid absences due to poor
weather affecting flights (AIC Minutes, 28 June 1973, pp. 9, 21).

Apart from fog, the Canberra location also caused difficulties in
attracting and retaining new staff—a topic to be considered further
below. The first round of recruitment in April 1973 resulted in three

Senior Criminologists being appointed: Harold G. Weir, who was previously director (Education and Welfare) with the Australian Parliamentary Research Service in Canberra; David Biles, Senior Lecturer in the Criminology Department at the University of Melbourne and Mary Daunton-Fear, Senior Lecturer in Law at the University of Adelaide—the last two of whom were unable to take up their positions until January 1974 (AIC Annual Report 1973, p. 7).

As will be seen in the following chapters, the need to spread the Institute's influence beyond Canberra, to ensure that communication and liaison were encouraged throughout the country, to enable staff to be recruited easily and to minimise travel expenses, led to various solutions being proposed and tried. These included a proposal in February 1974 that a regional branch office be established in Albury—half way between Melbourne and Sydney—that staff be permitted to work remotely at other government offices in the states and territories, or from home, and that the Institute increase its presence regionally through the use of conferences and seminars or via electronic communications. Some of these ideas were tested and implemented by some directors, while others were avoided or opposed, as shall be seen below.

The Facilities Required by a Research Institute

Government agencies, like private sector organisations, have gone through various phases in their choice of office design throughout the preceding fifty years. Depending on the age of buildings in the area of choice, and any planning and heritage requirements that have to be complied with, modern buildings in twentieth-century capital cities such as Canberra have generally had uniform attributes on offer. Concrete and steel frames support external walls of glass windows, with tiled or carpeted floors and simple partitions internally that create either closed office spaces—often without natural lighting—or open-plan spaces with desks and shoulder-high walls. Desirable features such as offices with windows, air conditioning that actually works, external views across parks and doors that provide some measure of sound insulation are invariably allocated to staff based on seniority, salary levels and status. However, such attributes are not always available and suitable for the type of work carried out.

Gripenstraw and Saini (2020, n.p.) in their *Brief History of the Modern Office* review the transition of office design from 'packed rows of desks' through cubicles, once described as 'barren, rat-hole places', to offices designed to facilitate telecommuting and word processing using computers. Now, since the onset of COVID-19, remote working has increased enormously and given rise to policies and solutions for dealing with many employees who now work from home—generally formulated 'on the run' during the pandemic. In the case of legal practices, for example, remote working has required a complete redesign of the legal office working environment, with managers required to devise flexible arrangements that enable staff to have access to different types of work spaces tailored to the specific needs of the individual—be they at home or in an office (Clarke 2021).

What then, do criminologists need in terms of office accommodation to make their work comfortable, efficient, cost effective and relatively free from stress? Research work requires a level of quiet to aid concentration, ergonomically-designed desks and equipment, adequate storage space for paper and electronic files, availability of meeting rooms that permit privacy and space (especially in times of social distancing to minimise pandemic risks), and access to recreational areas for eating and relaxing—designed in such a way as not to disturb other workers. Sander's (2018) research into the effectiveness of open-plan offices found not only that they can compromise individual employees' ability to focus and concentrate on their work, but they actually impede effective communication between staff—one of their original aims. The work undertaken by criminologists is a good example of the need for workers to have a quiet environment in which to concentrate on planning research, analysing findings, reading materials and writing—all usually conducted online since the 1990s. Criminologists, both in universities and in government, of course, continue to participate in meetings, seminars, focus groups and conferences but these are often conducted infrequently and at specially-designed locations. Senior academics and managers need to meet with their colleagues, but not all of the time, and often only for very short periods. Most recently, audio-visual technologies enable workers to meet online without having to move from their desks. Many tasks undertaken in criminology, require careful concentration and uninterrupted periods of work that are difficult to achieve in open-plan workplaces. During the Coronavirus pandemic in 2020, when social distancing limited face-to-face interactions, productivity was found to increase as many people worked from home or other offices online.

The AIC, like many other businesses and government departments, followed the office designs dictated by architectural fashion, beginning with separate offices in the early 1970s, through open-plan offices designed for the typing pool, through office cubicles with minimal privacy, to the current approach that permits working from home if the facilities are suitable, with face-to-face meetings called and attended when necessary. Little thought was given to novel office designs that would be suitable for the specific tasks being undertaken at the AIC during its 50 years. Instead, new directors simply adapted existing layouts, or chose designs promoted by current architectural practice, generally driven by a desire to minimise cost. Throughout the AICs history, its office accommodation has generally changed as its financial circumstances and staffing numbers have fluctuated, leaving the Institute at the time of writing in the most modest accommodation it has had since the time of its original offices in Ethos House, in Canberra City.

The AICs Premises

Ethos House, Civic, Canberra City

Choosing a suitable building in which to house the AIC presented a number of challenges. In 1973, office accommodation in Canberra was relatively uniform, with the Parliamentary Triangle and the city centre (Civic) offering office spaces for the larger and more established departments, while smaller ones battled in the furnished or unfurnished corporate market-place for suitable facilities. The further away one went from Capital Hill, the lower the rentals were. As a result, the AICs initial home was located in an office block, Ethos House, at 28-36 Ainslie

Place, Civic that provided accommodation for the first six months, in somewhat cramped conditions (Plate 8.1). On 1 February 1973, Judge Muirhead started work at these offices with a small staff. The office accommodation in Civic was far from satisfactory, with the small number of staff being 'fragmented and working in crowded conditions' (AIC Annual Report 1973, p. 15).

At the inaugural meeting of the Institute's Board of Management held at the Attorney-General's Department in Canberra on the morning of 18 April 1973, various options for suitable accommodation were canvassed, noting that even if immediate approval were given to construct a new building, this would not be completed until the 1976–1977 year. The Board examined the types of accommodation provided to overseas institutes, such as UNAFEI in Tokyo that provided not only for offices for staff but also accommodation for those attending training activities (AIC Minutes, 18 April 1973, p. 3). In the short term, however, rented office space was the preferred option, with at least 4500 square feet of space, while in the longer-term, funding in the order of $2 million was sought for a permanent new building in Canberra (AIC Minutes, 28 June 1973, p. 9).

Plate 8.1 Ethos House, at 28-36 Ainslie Place, Civic, c. 2016 (*Source* Gareth Halverson [Civium, Canberra, c. 2016])

When Sir Leon Radzinowicz provided advice in September 1973 on the administration and progress of the AIC, he considered that adequate premises for the Institute in central Canberra should be provided as soon as possible. He wrote:

The location of the Institute somewhere in the periphery of Canberra would not do, nor would temporary buildings kept for too long and in the hope that something more important would come along be a satisfactory solution… if the real intention is to build up in Australia an institute of an exceptional stature, then much greater priority should be assigned to its building right now. (Radzinowicz 1973, p. 9)

It transpired, however, that this advice was ignored for many years to come. In February 1974, a proposal was advanced that the Institute's permanent home should be in Albury/Wodonga on the Murray River border between New South Wales and Victoria. This was approximately 300 kilometres from Melbourne, 350 kilometres from Canberra and almost 570 kilometres from Sydney. The Attorney-General was opposed to the idea and the Acting Director, Jim Muirhead considered that it 'would be a disaster' (Muirhead 1974). The Board quickly ruled out the suggestion, favouring Canberra because of its national identity, and the need for the Institute to be close to other Commonwealth departments, the National Library and the ANU. It was also seen as the most appropriate place for overseas delegates to visit. Importantly, Albury/Wodonga did not have the same level of communication facilities as Canberra and it might be difficult to attract staff—this last problem, also affected Canberra as a location, throughout its history (AIC Minutes, 25 February 1974, p. 3).

Colbee Court, Phillip

It subsequently transpired that funding to purchase a dedicated building for the Institute was not able to be obtained and so a temporary arrangement was undertaken to rent a building in one of Canberra's suburban, light-industrial locations at 10-16 Colbee Court, Phillip, about 10 kilometres from the city centre in what one of its early staff members,

Grant Wardlaw, described as 'a not very flash area of Canberra' but was, nonetheless 'a very pleasant place to work' (Grant Wardlaw, Interview, 30 November 2020). Considered by the director, Bill Clifford, to be a preferable choice to the alternative at the Tuggeranong lakeside, in the south of the ACT—about 25 kilometres from the city centre (Letter from Director Richard Harding to staff, 28 February 1990, AIC Archives)—the Institute moved into the two-level building in September 1973 (Plate 8.2). Each level provided two areas of 3400 square feet of office space each with the Research and Executive staff being located on the upper level and the Library, Training and Information Services and Publications staff located on the ground level along with seminar rooms. Storage was also available in a basement (AIC Annual Report 1974, p. 2).

The original Colbee Court building (at 10-16) was not without its problems, and these were compounded when the adjacent building at 18-20 was added to the lease in April 1975 (Plate 8.3). When the Institute eventually moved to new premises in July 1990, the director at the time, Richard Harding, reflecting on his time at Colbee Court, asked:

Plate 8.2 10-16 Colbee Court, Philip ACT (*Source* AIC Photo Archives)

Plate 8.3 Participants in Training Project No 3 Planning and Policy for Crime Control Personnel, 10 May 1974—10-16 Colbee Court, Philip ACT (*Source* AIC Annual Report 1974, p. 20)

Did the air-conditioning ever get fixed before it was time to go? Was the Institute ever sued for occupier's liability by people who tumbled down those extraordinary stairs? (Letter from Richard Harding to staff, 28 February 1990, AIC Archives)

In late 1984, it was noted that the premises 'in some ways fall short of the Institute's needs in relation to its functions' and that the plans to construct purpose-designed premises had not come to fruition 'due to various exigencies' (AIC Annual Report 1985, p. 8). In his Interview (30 January 2021), John Braithwaite explained that Bill Clifford had originally had 'an extremely grandiose plan' for a dedicated building for the Institute to be constructed on a site in the parliamentary triangle in Canberra with international convention facilities such as simultaneous translation capabilities for UN events. He continued efforts, unsuccessfully, to secure such a dedicated building for the Institute throughout his time as director, but the government was not persuaded. Instead, resources were allocated to improve the Colbee Court building: replacement of the antiquated PABX system, up-grading the air conditioning system, improving the audio-visual equipment and realigning partitioning—with the new materials being removable (AIC Annual Report 1985, p. 8).

In opening the 'more salubrious' rented premises in Civic on 25 July 1990, the then Minister for Justice and Consumer Affairs, Senator, The Hon. Michael Tate, referred to the need to move from Colbee Court taking on some urgency after the former Attorney-General, The Hon. Mr Justice Lionel Bowen QC, stumbled down the stairs. Minister Tate then recounted his own memories of Colbee Court:

I do recall the old building as … most people here would recall – what a rabbit warren it was. In fact, there were two buildings and if you wanted to go from one part to another you had to stumble down the steps in the middle of winter that could be in sleet or snow or whatever else might be assaulting the person as you tried to move from one part to another. I recall there was a pet shop directly over the road, a bulk produce store on one side, and just before the move there was a blue movie manufacturer somewhat adjacent. You could learn to scuba dive, frame pictures, hire videos, upgrade computers, do it yourself, eat Vietnamese, French or Malaysian, or for those on the Institute's lower rung of salaries of course, shop at St Vincent DePaul—all within a very, very short radius of those premises. But in fact of course, one knows that it was inhabited by various pigeons at various times; they used to get trapped in toilets and I'll say nothing about the odour that made their whereabouts obvious to all those who had to use them—in fact it was a very poor building indeed, and not only was it a great safety hazard, it must have had some impact (though you'd be searching in vain to find it) on the quality of the work done. It cannot have been a good environment for people to have to produce the work that was nevertheless being produced in the Institute. (Video file of the opening of the Institute building, 25 July 1990, AIC Archive)

Marcus Clarke Street, Civic

The move to new premises in 1990 was well-overdue, but not without controversy, as it was decided to rent a new state-of-the-art building in Canberra City that became a landmark in the national capital as the 'Criminology Building' (Plate 8.4). Even today, older taxi drivers may take you to Marcus Clarke Street if you ask to go to the 'Criminology Building' when visiting Canberra (despite the $30,000 a year branding having been removed in 1996). The new building was adjacent to a new Canberra hotel and was reputed to have been constructed as a Casino for the hotel guests—appropriate given the Institute's later research into problem gambling! In 1994, David Brown observed:

> The decision to move from its former modest premises in Woden to its current prized spot next to the Lakeside Hotel, at a rental cost of one-third of its budget allocation was financially irresponsible and provocative. For visitors to Canberra the words CRIMINOLOGY ringing the outside of what looks like a hotel by the lake invoke a sense of the surreal, one wonders if this is Christo at work and SOCIOLOGY, ANTHRO-POLGY, QUANTUM PHYSICS and so on, will suddenly appear writ large on other lakeside buildings. (Brown 1994, p. 127)

In 1973–1974, the annual cost of the Colbee Court building, including rental, alterations and services, was $46,255, rising to $297,830 in 1988–1989. For the new building in 1990–1991, these costs increased to $869,722 rising to $987,067 in 1994–1995 (AIC Annual Reports 1974, 1989, 1992, 1995). Although the new premises were far more stylish than previously, the review of the AICs operations in 1994 concluded that these costs were overly expensive for a small statutory authority. The Tanzer Review (1994, p. 8) found that:

> The AIC is paying excessively for a prestige location which is simply not necessary. In addition, there are items in the lease which are either excessive or unjustified. Principally, these are the lease payments for car parking (largely unrecovered from staff) and the naming rights to the building. Finally, the design of the building is such that, given the requirements for

Plate 8.4 Marcus Clarke Street, Canberra City, 1990 (*Source* AIC, Archives)

the layout of offices and working areas, there is significant unproductive space which nevertheless attracts a high rental charge.

The review undertook a financial assessment of the Institute's operations and included a predicted decrease in building rental expenses from $1,025,000 to $600,000 until the termination of the lease on 31 October 1999 (Tanzer et al. 1994, p. 44). With the likelihood of a large reduction in staff, there would be a good deal of unused office space, but early termination of the lease was estimated to incur a liability of approximately $5.5 million. The only solution was to sub-let the premises, but finding a suitable tenant was difficult, and the Institute was also required to pay for reinstatement of the building by removing the elaborate and expensive fixtures and fittings that the director had installed. Fortunately, the Commonwealth Director of Public Prosecutions, Michael Rozenes QC, was persuaded that the building was suitable for his department and so a sub-lease was arranged. Some regarded the building as a 'vanity project' for the AICs Director, although it did 'increase the profile of the Institute' considerably (Grant Wardlaw, Interview, 30 November 2020).

The result was that the AIC was left with a large financial burden relating to its premises for a number of years—a situation that was repeated in 2015 when the move to 4 National Circuit, Barton, took place following the partial merger with the ACC.

Leichhardt Street, Griffith

With the arrival of Adam Graycar as the Institute's new director in November 1994, the decision was made to move to new commercial premises at 74 Leichhardt Street, Griffith in December 1995—just 6 kilometres from the city centre (Plate 8.5). Rental costs were much more manageable at approximately $500,000 a year for the 1729 square metres of floor space on two levels. The building had previously housed the Griffith local library and had offices on the first level with library resources below. The Institute remained in this building until moving in with the ACC in 2015, leaving two years remaining in the, then current, lease until December 2017. The previous offices were left vacant until the lease expired, following which the building was demolished and replaced by residential apartments.

The new building was opened by the Attorney-General and Minister for Justice, the Honourable Daryl Williams AM QC MP on 24 July 1996 (AIC Annual Report 1997, p. 1). Prior to moving into the new premises, the offices were renovated and the library installed in the ground floor. Executive and research staff were located on the upper level in offices, with junior staff in open-plan cubicles. This arrangement was similar to that in Colbee Court, with working conditions somewhat cramped, and meeting spaces limited. Commencing in 1998–1999, the then director, Adam Graycar, undertook a program of refurbishment of the premises, installing a glass wall in each office to improve natural light and increasing the size of some offices. The Board room was also refurnished with an expensive table and bookshelves installed.

One major difficulty that had not been rectified during these renovations was that members of the public and other visitors entered through the front door into the office space without any security controls, apart from the need to pass by the Institute's long-standing receptionist, Kerry

Plate 8.5   74 Leichhardt Street, Griffith (*Source* AIC Archives)

Feldman, seated adjacent to the front door. This arrangement breached the Commonwealth government security policies and for this, and other reasons, another refurbishment of the office was undertaken in 2007. This major redesign of the building permitted visitors to enter public meeting rooms and conference facilities, but not have access to the remainder of the ground floor or first floor, including the library. The cost of the refurbishment works were shared with the owner of the building, but the overall expense was less than moving to larger and better premises in a different building. The official handover occurred on 22 February 2007 (AIC Annual Report 2008, p. 2).

The redesign of the AICs offices in 2007 provides an illustration of how competing interests led to a superficially modern design, but one that was difficult to live with in practice. Borrowing from Jeremy Bentham's Panopticon principles (Semple 1993), the AIC designed its first-floor office space with a central group of four enclosed offices for senior managers in the centre of the floor, looking out through glass windows to open-plan 'pods' of four desks in each, opposite each Manager that would permit surveillance of the activities of each workplace team. The AICs Director and deputy director had separate offices alongside one wall, again overlooking the junior staff—who were housed in pods with less space than more senior researchers (Plate 8.6).

The ground floor had meeting and conference rooms, administrative offices, the library and archival storage (Plate 8.7).

Although much more pleasant than some other 'rat-hole cubicles' in offices, this arrangement had a number of flaws. Junior researchers were required to work at relatively small desk spaces with minimal space for books and papers. They were also close to others without sound privacy. The offices for managers were of average size, but without shelving for books and papers and few filing cabinets were available. Their offices were also close to the kitchen and recreation area that meant that office doors had to remain closed for sound privacy. The placement of managers was intended to be adjacent to the open-plan area for the staff they supervised, and yet many research projects crossed management groups such that some staff could be located on the remote side of the floor. Meeting rooms and the library were located on the ground floor requiring research staff to navigate narrow stairs frequently and avoid other staff opening doors inwards at the top of stairwells. Generally, the space available for quiet discussion in groups was minimal, while an elaborate Board Room was expansive. The new design provided more open space than the original office-based design, but was less satisfactory for the research activities being undertaken.

National Circuit, Barton

As noted in Chapter 14, below, the partial merger of the AIC with the ACC in 2015 required a move to a new building designed for various Commonwealth entities, including the ACC and part of AGD. Located near to the AFP headquarters in Canberra, accommodation in a new office block of five upper levels and four levels of car-parking basements, was offered to the AIC in order for it to be close to the ACC (Plate 8.8). On 10 December 2015, AIC staff relocated to the ACCs building at

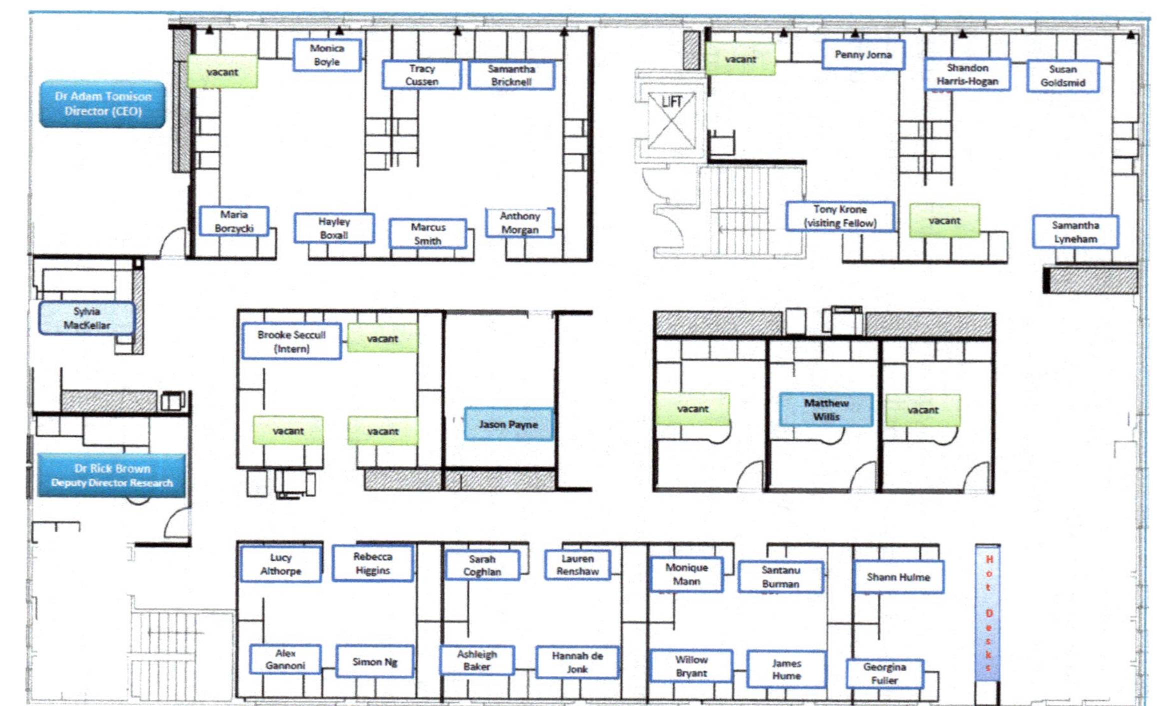

Plate 8.6   Office layout, 1st Floor, 74 Leichhardt Street, Griffith (*Source* AIC Archives)

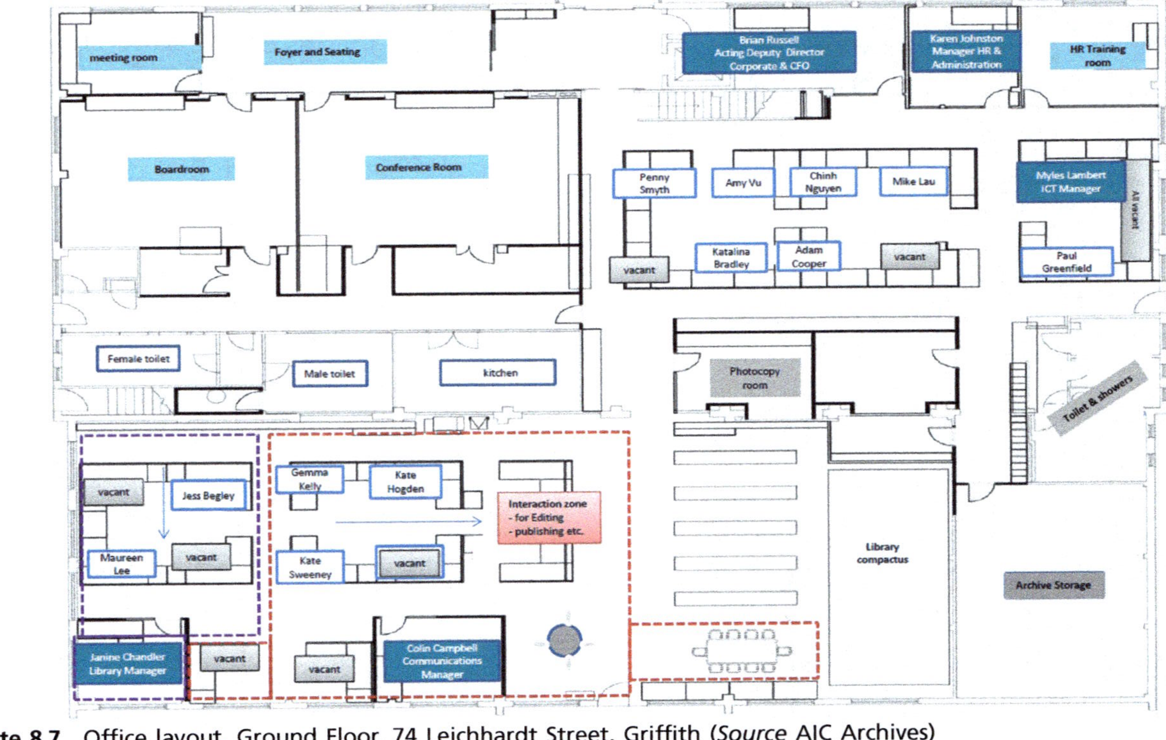

Plate 8.7   Office layout, Ground Floor, 74 Leichhardt Street, Griffith (*Source* AIC Archives)

Plate 8.8   4 National Circuit, Barton, November 2007 (*Source* AIC photograph, 2015)

4 National Circuit, Barton where a small section of the first level was provided for AIC staff and the JV Barry Library. This space was somewhat cramped and entirely open-plan, save for a small office for the AICs Deputy Director. The Chief Executive of the ACC—who was also designated as the Acting Director of the AIC—had an office on another floor of the building—located some distance away from the AICs new operational area.

The office arrangement was open-plan with small cubicles for research staff, regardless of seniority, and with some ACC staff also housed nearby, making the environment far from quiet. Although the desks provided were new and functional, the principal problem with this new arrangement was that AIC research staff were now employed by the ACC—while being seconded back to undertake work for the AIC—and were subject to the ACCs security and other policies.

In 2017, further reductions in AIC staff numbers and the need to permit freer access to the AICs library and offices, led to a move to the ground floor of the ACCs building—now the ACIC (see below). Again, an open-plan office space had to be designed and an expensive fit-out undertaken for desks, the library, a small meeting room, kitchen and sole office for the deputy director. The problems of lack of desk and storage space and noise coming from ACIC staff and contractors who shared part of the area, remained unresolved. In addition, members of the public still had to be escorted into the locked area through three secure, automatic and reinforced glass doors and were unable to visit without a pre-arranged time being agreed. Additional problems related to the mobile phone signals and wireless Internet reception being largely blocked by the concrete structure. Limited parking, at cost, was available and a pleasant, but expensive café, located within the building. When additional meeting rooms were required, these had to be booked at high hourly rates in a commercial conference centre located nearby on the ground floor. This added to the AICs already high cost-burden for sharing these offices and services.

Home-Based Work

In 2020, with government responses to the COVID-19 pandemic restricting contact between individuals, the AICs staff were required to work remotely from home in almost all cases. This left the ground floor office accommodation at 4 National Circuit, Barton, largely empty, with rental costs continuing to be incurred. Since 2021, as the majority of staff were vaccinated, some were able to return to the office, although many preferred to continue home-based work on most days of the week. At the time of writing, it appears that the location of staff will remain flexible for some time.

Comparisons Within and Beyond Australia

The various public sector crime and justice research bodies described in Chapter 2, above, have all been closely aligned with their administering Departments and, as such, have occupied premises in their buildings.

In New South Wales, when BOCSAR was established in 1969, it was provided office space in the Sydney office of the Department of Justice, now the Department of Communities and Justice, located on Level 1 of the Henry Deane Building, 20 Lee Street, Haymarket in Sydney, and close to Sydney's Central Station. Prime real estate in Sydney would be unaffordable for a small entity such as BOCSAR and sharing accommodation was essential. By 1972, BOCSAR had relocated to comfortable accommodation in the Goodsell Building in Chifley Square in Sydney, where it shared office space with the Attorney-General's Department. BOCSAR now has its office in the outer Sydney suburb of Parramatta.

Similar arrangements applied in South Australia where OCSAR-shared accommodation at the Attorney-General's Department since its establishment in 1978 and the newest bodies, the Victorian Crime Statistics Agency (CSA) has offices in the Department of Justice and Community Safety building at 121 Exhibition Street, Melbourne since it was established in 2014. The Western Australian Office of Crime Statistics and Research (WACSAR) shares part of the David Malcolm Justice Centre, in Barrack Street, Perth.

Commonwealth entities that undertook research relevant to crime and social policy were also housed in other Commonwealth buildings, although the AIHW that was established as a statutory authority in 1987 to report to the nation on the state of its health, had offices both in the Canberra suburb of Bruce and an office in Oxford Street in Darlinghurst, Sydney. AIFS, that was established in February 1980 within the portfolio of the Department of Social Services, is the other principal social policy research agency in the Commonwealth but has its office at Southbank, in central Melbourne.

Other criminological research bodies in Australia are generally based in universities and form part of relevant Departments of Law, such as at the University of Sydney's Institute of Criminology, or in Schools of Criminology, such as at Griffith University in Queensland.

Internationally, as has been noted above, members of the United Nations PNI, such as UNAFEI in Tokyo, HEUNI in Helsinki and UNICRI in Turin have purpose-built accommodation, while the crime research sections of government in the UK, are located in the central Home Office buildings in London and the NIJ in Washington DC.

UNICRI has a large campus on the River Po in Turin that provides both research and administration offices as well as economically-sized residential rooms for visiting delegates and students—visited by a number of AIC staff (Plate 8.9).

In Japan, UNAFEIs offices have been unique in that since its establishment in 1960, it has had its own complex of offices for administration, research and accommodation for those attending its substantial conference and training seminar programs. In 2020, it moved from its original building in Fuchu, to new premises in the International Justice Centre in Akishima, Tokyo (Plate 8.10). Again, the AIC has had close ties with UNAFEI and AIC staff have visited on a number of occasions as Expert Advisors.

The early directors of the AIC were clearly impressed with the idea of such premises and the provision of accommodation for training delegates and wanted a similar complex to be constructed in Canberra. Unfortunately, the Australian government's budget was unable to support this.

Plate 8.9 UNICRIs campus at Viale Maestri del Lavoro, Turin (*Source* Courtesy of the Director, UNICRI)

Plate 8.10   UNAFEIs current campus at Akishima, Tokyo (*Source* UNAFEI 2020, p. 3)

Thematic Conclusions

The present chapter has explored the types of accommodation needed for public sector criminological research and used the AICs experiences of office accommodation in Canberra as illustrative of the issues that arose in satisfying competing interests. A number of observations may be made about the nature of accommodation relevant to the five themes explored in the present work.

The first theme concerning differences between criminological research in the public sector and that in the academy, was largely unaffected by the location and nature of accommodation provided, although conventional offices provided for academic scholars are, arguably, preferable to open-plan public sector workplaces.

The choice of premises for the AIC in Canberra emphasised the perceived need for the AIC to focus on national concerns, rather than those affecting only the states and territories. As Richard Harding observed in his interview, it was easier for the heads of Commonwealth statutory authorities to 'be tuned into what was happening in Canberra' 'if they were based there' (Richard Harding, Interview, 18 November 2021). Being located close to the Commonwealth parliament, and central government agencies, has provided a constant reminder to the AICs executives that Commonwealth interests are paramount, and that federal offending should be its primary concern. The provision of somewhat minimal physical facilities, however, meant that some of the Institute's aims could not easily be satisfied—such as the original desire to have on-site accommodation for those attending training sessions and conferences. Instead, the Institute was required to devote a proportion of its budget to providing residential accommodation for the majority of delegates who travelled from the states and territories and from overseas. Even when more commodious premises were obtained in 1990, residential facilities were still not available.

The third theme that deals with the methods of research, is largely unaffected by the types of accommodation provided to the AIC during its history, although the recent heavy reliance on desk-based research and computing emphasised the need for fully-networked work spaces and quiet working conditions—that were not always available for

AIC research staff. Similarly, the fourth theme that concerns political and academic influences in the conduct of criminological research raises the possibility that having the Institute based in Canberra among politicians and public officials keen to see practical solutions to crime problems arising from the Institute's research, might limit the possibility of conducting theoretical, blue-skies and critical work whose practical applications might not be immediately obvious. In Australia, it has been the case that critical, left-realist, theoretical and sociological research has mainly been conducted in red-brick Universities in the states.

Finally, the ability of the Institute to conduct its research activities effectively was, and continues to be, heavily dependent on the level of government funding provided. Linked to the political complexion of the government in power, the Institute faced regular challenges in satisfying its performance indicators when budgets were severely restricted on a number of occasions. In opening the Institute on 16 October 1973, the then Attorney-General, Senator the Honourable Lionel Murphy QC, concluded his address by recalling comments that Sir Leon Radzinowicz made to the Attorney when they met in Sydney in July 1973:

> [Radzinowicz] expressed his high hopes for the success of the Institute and indicated its potentiality. He has the belief that this Institute could be a great Institute and make a valuable international contribution—but he sounded a warning and he said it was possible that if the Institute did not get the support of the Governments, if it did not enrol in its ranks the people who ought to be enrolled, if it did not act with vigour and understand the important contribution that it could make, well then it would not succeed and, if it did not succeed, all of those associated with it, those in the government, those in the various ways who are associated with it, would deserve the condemnation of the world. (Murphy 1973, pp. 12–13)

In addition, recent changes in the Institute's accommodation that is now shared with the ACIC has raised many difficult questions of the perceived extent and impact of the relationship between the Institute, as an independent statutory authority, and the ACIC an intelligence agency that worked with and for law enforcement. As will be shown below, this unintended consequence of the partial merger between the

AIC and ACIC, and the sharing of premises, has coloured the Institute's research focus and, arguably, detracted from its role as an independent government research body. As the effects of the Coronavirus pandemic become clearer, it may be that the reality of remote working from home will create an impression in the community that the Institute's research is, indeed, quite separate from the specific interests of law enforcement agencies. In his Interview (3 November 2022), Michael Phelan explained that although much research work can be conducted off-site, when work is undertaken using security classified resources, home-based work can become impossible. For example, displaying a classified dataset on an off-site computer, even if secured with appropriate encryption and end-point security, would require everyone who has access to that home-based location to have undergone security clearances to the level required of all ACIC staff.

Rick Brown also discussed the need for an agency such as the AIC to have an identifiable home base in an official office. While it may be feasible to have the library off-site with resources available on-call, and for staff to work from home, there is a need for a sense of community and visibility that having a physical office can provide.

> There's something about the importance of place, and a home, that's quite intangible. The fact that we have a space with a big logo on the wall and a big library is part of the identity of the AIC that I think you would lose if you went completely virtual. (Rick Brown, Interview, 4 November 2022)

References

Australian Institute of Criminology (AIC). 1973–1974. *Board of Management Minute Books*. Canberra: Australian Institute of Criminology.

Australian Institute of Criminology (AIC). 1973–2008. *Annual Reports*. Canberra: Australian Institute of Criminology.

Brown, David. 1994. Facing the Knife. *Alternative Law Journal* 19 (3): 125–128. http://www6.austlii.edu.au/cgi-bin/viewdoc/au/journals/AltLawJl/1994/59.html. Accessed 18 September 2020.

Clarke, Ann. 2021. Five Ways in Which the Legal Office Is Changing. *The Law Society*. https://communities.lawsociety.org.uk/coronavirus-managing-in-a-recession/five-ways-in-which-the-legal-office-is-changing/6001581. article?utm_source=professional_update&utm_medium=email&utm_cam paign=PU-01%2f15%2f2021&sc_camp=5C0FE0D28B474F6BA2EE3 74CB3EE601B. Accessed 16 January 2021.

Gripenstraw, K., and Anne Noyes Saini. 2020. A Brief History of the Modern Office. *Harvard Business Review*, 15 July. https://hbr.org/2020/07/a-brief-his tory-of-the-modern-office. Accessed 4 January 2021.

Harding, Richard. 1998. 'Richard Harding's Address to the Australian Institute of Criminology's Silver Jubilee Dinner', November 1998, Canberra, Video File. Canberra: AIC Archives.

Muirhead, James Henry. 1974. Memorandum from Judge J. H. Muirhead: Introduction and Development, National Archives of Australia D/A/1. Canberra: NAA.

Murphy, Lionel. 1973. Opening Ceremony Address. In *Proceedings of the First Residential Conference of the Australian Institute of Criminology: Australian Crime Prevention and Treatment. Research Resources and Needs: An Exercise in Co-ordination*, 16 October, vol. 1, 8–13. Canberra.

National Capital Commission (NCC). 2021. *A Capital in the Making*. Ottawa: NCC. http://www.canadascapital.gc.ca/bins/ncc_web_content_p age.asp?cid=16297-24515-24516-25146&lang=1. Accessed 4 January 2021.

Radzinowicz, Leon. 1973. *Report of Sir Leon Radzinowicz with Respect to the Australian Institute of Criminology*. Canberra: National Library of Australia (6093/72/4182).

Sander, Elizabeth. 2018. A New Study Should Be the Final Nail for Open-Plan Offices. *The Conversation*, 18 July. https://theconversation.com/a-new-study-should-be-the-final-nail-for-open-plan-offices-99756. Accessed 3 December 2022.

Semple, Janet. 1993. *Bentham's Prison: A Study of the Panopticon Penitentiary*. Oxford: Clarendon Press.

Tanzer, Noel, Des Hill, and Grant Wardlaw. 1994. *Review of the Australian Institute of Criminology: Report*. Canberra: Australian Institute of Criminology.

United Nations Asia and Far East Institute for the Prevention of Crime and the Treatment of Offenders (UNAFEI). 2020. *Brochure*. Tokyo: UNAFEI. https://www.unafei.or.jp/english/about/Brochure.html. Accessed 16 February 2021.

9

The Digital Takeover and the JV Barry Library

Establishment

For any research organisation, access to information is of critical importance. Each of the criminological research bodies established in Australia and elsewhere has either maintained its own specialist library, or has access to a collection in nearby institutions. From the outset, the AIC determined to build Australia's largest and most comprehensive collection of criminological books and periodicals for use, not only by Institute staff and other public sector officials, but also by academics, policymakers, students and members of the community throughout Australia, as well as in nearby Asia–Pacific countries. At the opening ceremony of the Institute's library at Colbee Court, in Canberra on 12 February 1974, Acting Director Judge Muirhead QC observed:

> The library … is the embryo of what will follow. It is, perhaps, primitive by modern standards in Canberra. Its shelves are few, its volumes are restricted, but it can already be termed … a working library…. It will grow to the finest criminological library in this part of the world. It will,

R. G. Smith, *Public Sector Criminological Research*, https://doi.org/10.1007/978-3-031-28356-7_9

of course, be the working centre, or the nub, of the Institute. (Muirhead, AIC Archives, Audio File, 12 February 1974)

Having seen the libraries present in PNI research institutes in other countries in the 1970s, the AICs early Board members and directors were keen to create a similar resource for Australia. In Japan, for example, UNAFEIs campus has always had an extensive library to serve the needs of its research staff and also students and delegates attending its training programs (Plate 9.1). Acting Director, Muirhead, and Board member, Peter Loof, in particular, were supportive of establishing such a library in Canberra along the lines of others they had seen during overseas travel.

In order to advance the establishment of a library, one of the first appointments to the staff of the Institute made by Judge Muirhead was that of a full-time librarian. Diana Solman took up the position and came

Plate 9.1 UNAFEIs current library at Akishima, Tokyo (*Source* UNAFEI [2020, p. 12])

with a Diploma of Education, a Bachelor of Arts and a Library Registration Certificate, having been recruited from Tasmania, where she was the only graduate teacher/librarian in that state at the time. However, somewhat lacking in experience of public sector libraries, it was anticipated that she would only stay for a short time to assist with the establishment of the library (Personal communication, John Myrtle, 27 January 2021). Judge Muirhead noted that 'she has no knowledge of foreign languages, no criminological training, is married, 28 years of age and has worked in libraries before' (Radzinowicz and Muirhead 1973, p. 27). Mrs Solman reported to another early recruit, Harold Weir, who held the position of Senior Criminologist and was in charge of the Information and Training Divisions. These various divisions of the Institute—the library, information services and training divisions—were required to work closely with each other—a relationship that created various tensions concerning staffing levels, funding and roles—as will be shown in this and the next chapter.

When the Institute was established, it was decided that the library would be named in honour of the late Sir John Barry, as the JV Barry Memorial Library—a fitting tribute to one of the principal promoters of the AIC and its library (AIC Annual Report, 1973). After the move to new premises in 1990, the library was known simply as the JV Barry Library. Early tasks involved establishing the collection and commencing a manual card catalogue, undertaken by the first permanent Librarian, Sylvia Blomfield (Plate 9.2), who was appointed by Judge Muirhead, in 1974. Sylvia came to the Institute with a Bachelor of Arts from the University of Sydney and a Diploma in Librarianship, having worked in the head office library of John Fairfax and Sons Pty Ltd for three years, and the Commonwealth Parliamentary Library for five years (Personal Communication, Sylvia Blomfield, 3 December 2022). One of her first tasks at the Institute was to develop a working collection for use by the AICs staff and the research community. She remained in the role until 1979.

From 1980, the Institute had eight Librarians-in-charge or Heads of Information Services: Mary Gosling (1980–1984), Gael Parr (Acting

Plate 9.2 Sylvia Blomfield, c. 1977 (*Source* AIC Archives)

1984), Nikki Riszko (1984–1986), John Myrtle (1986–2003), Janet Smith (2003–2010), Janine Chandler (2010–2013), Jane Shelling (2014–2021) and, since November 2021, Samantha Jackson. Interestingly, the timing of these appointments largely corresponded with changes in the Institute's Directors—perhaps reflecting the desire of new Directors to implement changes throughout the organisation upon their arrival.

Collection Development

As with other aspects of the Institute's development, the choice of what the library's collection should include raised important questions about the role of the Institute, who its principal stakeholders were and the level of funding that the library required. The Institute's early focus on legal research and its international focus led the library, initially, to favour the acquisition of legal texts, periodicals and law reports for use by legally-trained research staff, and books that would have wide usage in Australia and overseas. Judge Muirhead was clearly supportive of the need to establish a legal collection and Sylvia Blomfield worked closely with Mary Daunton-Fear, Senior Criminologist (Legal), who prepared acquisitions lists for Sylvia to use in developing the library's collection.

In July and August 1973, Judge Muirhead had extensive discussions with Sir Leon Radzinowicz who was visiting Australia at the invitation of the Commonwealth and New South Wales governments to advise on criminological research and policy development in Australia (Plate 9.3).

Radzinowicz's (1973) report to the Commonwealth of 17 September 1973 included two recommendations that related to the development of the Institute's library.

Radzinowicz argued that one of the major objectives of the Australian Institute should be to act as a centre for information relating to criminological thought, penal policy and the working of the administration of criminal justice. He believed that the Institute should 'acquire and continue to maintain a good selection of leading periodicals: major reports, proceedings of other scientific bodies and miscellaneous pamphlets' (Radzinowicz 1973, p. 7). Although he believed that this suggestion was generally supported by the acting director and the Institute's Board, he considered 'their thinking on the subject [was] much too modest' and that 'an initial capital in the region of $100,000 [$1m in 2022] would be required to lay the foundation of such a collection, with an annual regular expenditure to follow' (Radzinowicz 1973, p. 7). This might have been appropriate for the Cambridge Institute's library that had funding from the Wolfson Foundation and was one of the leading criminological libraries in the English-speaking world (see Radzinowicz 1988), but was clearly far in excess of the AICs meagre budget

Plate 9.3   Sir Leon Radzinowicz at his press conference at the Goodsell Building, Chifley Square, Sydney, 17 July 1973 (*Source* AIC Archives)

for the purchase of books and periodicals in the first year of its operation. Judge Muirhead reported to Radzinowicz during their third meeting on 2 August 1973:

> There is a fixed sum budget for the library every year of $9,000… This sum is for books and periodicals. I had an initial capital of $30,000 and I spent all but $2,000 of this–including wages, travelling, etc. (Radzinowicz 1973, p. 27)

By 30 June 1974, books worth $15,534 had been acquired, with $1,000 spent on library shelving and $723 on operating expenses (AIC Annual Report, 1974). It was not until 1994 that the operating expenses of the library reached over $100,000, shortly before major reductions in funding were imposed (AIC Annual Report, 1994). Over the first twelve years, the value of the collection increased substantially, although operating costs of the library remained relatively constant until 1984 (see Fig. 9.1).

During the early years of the library, the collection also grew following receipt of some major donations. In 1975, the book collection of Sir Eugene Gorman QC was donated by his son Dr Pierre Gorman, and a selection of books from the personal library of Sir John Barry was also added to the collection. John Myrtle, Librarian-in-charge from 1986 to 2003, recalled during his interview that 'while the AICs library collection could not hope to comprehensively cover research literature, over time the collection developed to be the most comprehensive library-based collection in the field of criminology and criminal justice in Australia' (John Myrtle, Interview, 3 December 2020). John Myrtle noted that Gael Parr, as Acquisitions Librarian and later Acting Librarian-in-charge in 1984, had responsibility for collection development and brought to

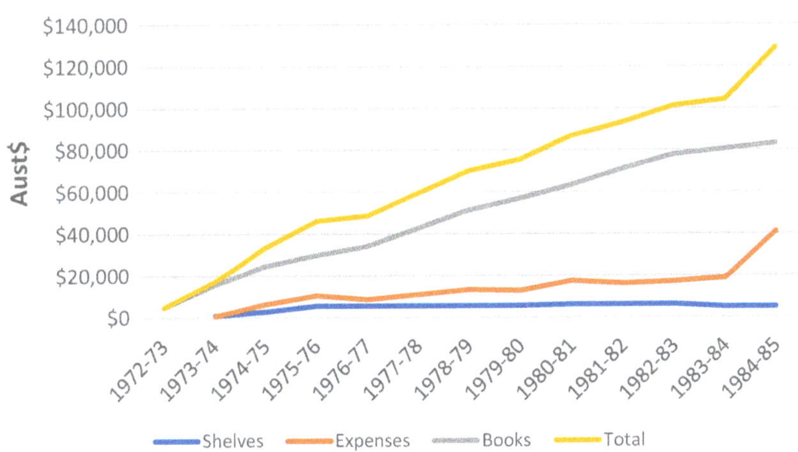

Fig. 9.1 JV Barry Memorial Library Finances, 1972 to 1985 (*Source* AIC Annual Reports, 1972–1973 to 1984–1985)

this position extensive experience at the State Library of New South Wales. 'Her systematic approach included negotiating several critically important publication exchange agreements with criminal justice agencies both in Australia and overseas, such as the exchange agreement with the National Institute of Justice in the United States that resulted in the acquisition of a considerable quantity of print and microfiche publications' (John Myrtle, Interview, 3 December 2020).

The focus of the collection also changed over time, with one principal change being the reduction, and eventual removal of almost all legal resources, including the handsome collection of law reports that once graced the walls of the Board Room prior to 2000. Those Institute researchers with legal qualifications, such as Mary Daunton-Fear, John Seymour, Ivan Potas, Arie Freiberg, Gregor Urbas, the present author and others, came to rely on inter-library loans from AGD and University libraries, until online legal resources became more widely available. In the 1980s and 1990s, Lorraine Weinman, Senior Principal Librarian in charge of the AGDs libraries, facilitated regular meetings of AGD portfolio librarians to promote the sharing of legal resources.

The choice of which resources to include in the collection was extremely complex and difficult with many competing demands made on the library's relatively modest acquisitions budget. The collections policy provided guidance on which items to include and these tended to focus on resources published in, or relevant to, Australia in preference to overseas material. In terms of crime types, the library always sought to obtain recently-published criminological works, and research that was relevant to contemporary crime problems. This meant, of course, that when a new crime type was no longer of current interest, pressure arose to cease collecting material on that topic. Examples of this include capital punishment, bushfire arson and public drunkenness. By failing to maintain the collection of current material on such topics, when they again became of importance, an updated collection had to be initiated—that invariably took time and resources. More enduring topics, such as homicide, Indigenous crime and justice, sexual offending and economic crime had to be maintained as current collections at all times. The related question then arises as to whether collections on ephemeral crime types should be kept at all (Jane Shelling, Interview, 29 March 2021). The answer invariably depended on the availability of resources.

The Size and Value of the Collection

Estimating the value of the collection over time is difficult with changes in accounting practices and counting rules concerning books, monographs and periodicals occurring regularly. In 1984, for example, accrual accounting was introduced and the value of books was the estimated non-written down value amounting to $80,399—at 30 June 1984. Thereafter, the practice of capitalising book value was discontinued apart from ad hoc valuations being conducted in some years. In August 1999, for example, the collection was valued at $1,115,915 which was similar to the valuation at 30 June 2013 of $1,138,966 (the fair value of books was $95,351) (AIC Annual Report, 2013).

Counting the number of books and serials in the collection was also problematic, particularly as the library increasingly had access to large numbers of digital volumes and journals as part of group subscriptions. At 30 June 1997, for example, the count of monographs was 23,747 and 1,454 serials. These numbers fluctuated over time, with some large changes taking place—such as the 20% reduction in holdings in 2008, and a further large reduction when the Institute moved to 4 National Circuit, Barton when much of the collection was scanned and hard copies destroyed. By 2021, the library held 31,070 monographs, 1,704 serials, 5,329 conference papers and 47,792 journal articles. Of the 31,070 books, only 11,411 were printed volumes actually on the shelves in 2021.

Networking

An important tool for improving access to criminological resources for the government was Sylvia Blomfield's initiative to establish a network of criminal justice libraries in Australia. The aim was to document each library's location, duration of operation, staff numbers, structure and the services they provided. She gathered information for the study by circulating a questionnaire to libraries throughout Australia that included questions on their criminological and criminal justice operations and holdings. A summary of the findings of the survey was compiled by Margaret McAleese, Law Librarian at ANU, who reported that many of the libraries surveyed were relatively new and poorly staffed (nearly half with only one staff member, unlike the 6.5 full-time-equivalent staffing present at the JV Barry Memorial Library at the time).

The first initiative in creating a network was to hold a seminar for criminal justice system librarians that took place on 25 and 26 March 1977 at the AIC in Colbee Court. Twenty-five attended representing police, correctional, court and university libraries as well as staff of the JV Barry Memorial Library. The aim was to improve the effectiveness of criminology libraries in different agencies, with particular attention directed to defining the role of criminology libraries, and the possibility of rationalising their services and collections through cooperative activities.

Three participants from Monash University contributed papers to the seminar. Monash University's Law Librarian, Ted Glasson, addressed the question of cooperation between Australian criminology libraries, while Arie Freiberg, an early recruit to the Institute as a Senior Research Officer, and at the time a Senior Tutor in law at Monash, examined the idea of creating a national clearinghouse of criminological information—that the Institute later developed in the form of its quarterly *Information Bulletin.* This was published initially from March 1974 to June 1982 and again from June 1984 to December 1986 in a new series following a lapse of two years due to inadequate staffing resources in the library. These Bulletins contained abstracts of recent publications, statistical reports, recent library accessions and indexes to the resources included.

Richard Fox, at the time a Reader in Law at Monash University, gave a keynote presentation outlining the need for coordination of criminology libraries throughout Australia as well as the need to address the 'lamentable condition of Australian prison libraries'. Delegates to the seminar subsequently resolved to develop uniform standards for

Australian prison libraries (Roberts 1987), although this took more than a decade to progress, eventually leading to the publication of the *Australian Prison Libraries: Minimum Standard Guidelines* (Australian Library and Information Association [ALIA] 1990, 2015). This was just one of many positive outcomes of the eight seminars conducted by the AIC for criminology librarians between 1977 and 1992. During discussions at these seminars, it became clear that the JV Barry Memorial Library would have a central role to play in coordinating the network of criminological libraries throughout Australia. One element of this would be to establish a union catalogue of monograph holdings and union list of serials accessible to all libraries in the network. The aim was for participants to provide free, reciprocal photo-copying of holdings for use by members of the network—an important initiative in the pre-digital age.

During the 1990s, the staff of the JV Barry Library continued to provide services to public sector criminology libraries and research institutes throughout Australia and internationally (see Chapter 13, below on relations with the United Nations Criminal Justice Information Network). The Institute's reputation spread widely as an established public sector criminological library that could provide advice and assistance to new and developing comparable bodies (Plate 9.4).

In 1990, for example, John Myrtle participated in reviews of the libraries of both the New South Wales Police Service and Queensland Police (John Myrtle, Interview, 3 December 2020). These advisory services often involved travel and occupied considerable time of the library staff. In her interview, Jane Shelling noted that such activities tended to be of benefit to the Institute where reciprocity occurs, and often it was the AIC that provided greater benefits to other entities than it received. Nonetheless, the AICs library has continued to provide these services, such as through its membership of the Australasian Libraries in Emergency and Security (ALIES), a network of Australian and New Zealand emergency management agencies (Jane Shelling, Interview, 29 March 2021).

Plate 9.4 Staff of the JV Barry Library in 1989 (left to right: Jean Cahill, Gael Parr, John Myrtle, Wendy Limbrick, Fran Ballard, Pamela Garfoot) (*Source* AIC Archives)

Digitisation

The period since the Institute was established has seen profound changes in the development of information and communications technologies that have had a major impact on the role and functioning of libraries. In addition to providing an extensive network in which information could be exchanged, developments in digitisation and the creation of the Internet have made it possible to house entire libraries in a laptop computer's drive, rather than by occupying expensive floor space in buildings. As Choo, Smith and McCusker (2007, p. 16) noted:

> The first computer occupied 70 cubic metres of floor space.... In the 1970s a megabyte of semiconductor memory cost approximately $550,000. In the 1990s it cost $4. Microprocessors in the 1990s were 100,000 times faster than their 1950s predecessors. Based on those rates of change, a desktop computer in 2020 will be as powerful as all the computers currently situated in Silicon Valley in the United States.

When the AIC was established in the 1970s, communications were conducted by post, landline telephones and facsimiles; networked computing was limited to the *Advanced Research Projects Agency Network* (ARPANET), mobile phones had just been invented and CDs were not yet available. Since then, society has seen the World Wide Web established in 1990, Wikipedia created in 2001, Wireless networking in 2005, and cloud services since 2008 (see Curran 2010; Smith 2010 for reviews of developments in digital technologies). Digitisation has effectively replaced conventional libraries and this has been reflected in the Institute's collection policies, office space required for books and serials, skill sets of librarians and the costs of providing access to resources and maintaining collections (see Cameron 2021 for a discussion of the impact of digitisation of libraries and archives). After fifty years, the Institute is approaching a time at which a physical collection of monographs and journals might not be necessary—with librarians simply providing expertise to help users navigate access to online collections. Susskind and Susskind (2017, p. 290) anticipate this position with the suggestion that technology will undertake the vast majority of routine tasks, leaving the more difficult tasks that entail moral deliberation for professionals to handle. The future criminology library is likely, therefore, to be staffed by a small number of skilled individuals who are able to deal with these difficult, non-routine tasks that library users may encounter.

The Introduction of Computerised Services

In December 1975, the AICs Board of Management supported the development of a national bibliography of criminological material that derived from the content of the AICs *Information Bulletins*. This would enable users to search for information on the manual card catalogue using subject classifications, and over time through the use of computer databases. During the first decade, the Institute sought to acquire the latest information technology, including microfilm readers and early data processors (Plate 9.5).

Plate 9.5 Library assistant, Anna Davie with Microfilm reader-printer, 1975 (*Source* AIC Annual Report, 1975, p. 4)

The Institute's first experimentation with computers took the form of the Australian Criminology Database, CINCH (Computerised Information from National Criminological Holdings). This was described at the inaugural seminar for librarians in the criminal justice system in March 1977 by Anatole Koneonewsky, AIC Senior Research Officer, who explained how CINCH was located on the CSIRONET mainframe computer developed by the Commonwealth Scientific and Industrial Research Organisation (CSIRO) in Canberra that provided limited access for AIC staff. The creation of CINCH involved research assistants searching a large number of journals and monographs for suitable criminological records, and library staff then providing subject headings under which the search results could be classified. Information was transferred to a computer that was located remotely from the Institute. AIC research staff could then undertake searches for the Institute's clients, and make the relevant items available from the JV Barry Memorial Library's holdings for reading.

In 1984, the Institute's Librarian, Nikki Riszko, negotiated for CINCH to be made available as part of AUSINET (the Australian

Information Network). At the time, AUSINET held a number of bibliographic or reference databases that had been developed by various research agencies including the Australian Council of Educational Research (ACER), AIFS and the AICs CINCH collection. The AIFS database was similar to CINCH in that it had been developed by a government research agency that had already made a significant investment in quality library services. The transfer to AUSINET entailed the conversion of data using IBMs Storage and Information Retrieval System (STAIRS) by contract indexers (Riszko 1985, see also Middleton 2006). Two members of the AICs library staff attended an AUSINET operator training course at the NLA to learn how to create and search the database. A portable computer terminal was then purchased and housed at the AICs library. In May 1985, access to CINCH became publicly available on AUSINET following a launch by Mr Justice Michael Kirby at the Lakeside Hotel (Plate 9.6) (AIC Annual Report 1985, pp. 41–44).

In 1986, the library's manual card catalogue was transferred to the National Library of Australia's Australian Bibliographic Network (ABN) on microfiche. Much-needed funding of $307,000 was then provided from the Commonwealth Confiscated Assets Fund to expand CINCH. The National Library also provided the OZLINE system that hosted CINCH from 1989, which also provided access to other reference databases (Plate 9.7). In 1990, the Institute was invited by RMIT in Melbourne to participate in an important CD-ROM publishing initiative called AUSTROM. This was a compilation of a number of popular library-based databases including the Australian Public Affairs Information Service (APAIS), the Australian Government Information Service (AGIS) managed by AGD and the AIFS database—all on the one CD-ROM. Revenue from AUSTROM subscriptions was distributed to database providers on the basis of the relative size of the databases included. As a result, for the first time, the CINCH database generated significant income from its indexing work. Also at this time, the database of the National Criminal Justice Research System was acquired by the JV Barry Library on CD-ROM. More recently, however, usage of CINCH has declined as most users are seeking online, full-text material rather than simply indexed material such as that available on CINCH. Although the financial returns from CINCH have declined, in June

Plate 9.6 Mr Justice Michael Kirby launching CINCH online, May 1985 (*Source* AIC Archives)

2021 it still held 63,000 records with the library contributing material at the rate of 80 records a month (Jane Shelling, Interview, 29 March 2021).

From March 1999, the Institute was involved in implementing the National Library's new Kinetica service, which replaced the ABN and Pamela Garfoot became a member of the Expert Advisory Group on Cataloguing providing recommendations on cataloguing workflow with the new system. Pamela left the Institute in 2000 to become Chief Librarian at the Department of Finance.

Plate 9.7   (l-r) Minister for Justice and Consumer Affairs, Michael Tate AO, inspecting CINCH on AUSINET using INMAGIC software, 31 July 1987, with Duncan Chappell and John Myrtle (*Source* AIC Archives)

Library Reviews and Their Consequences

During the first decade, usage of the services provided by the JV Barry Memorial Library continued to increase, despite a reduction in library staffing due to ceilings being imposed on the Institute's staff numbers. Without a reference librarian, the library was limited in the reference assistance it could provide to clients. By 1983, the library had only four staff including the Librarian-in-Charge, Mary Gosling, leading to the loss of various services including indexing journals and monographs for the Information Bulletins which ceased in June 1982; updating CINCH which was by then three years out of date, and updating the Union List of Criminology Periodicals that was also out of date. In a report of a review of the library dated 16 August 1982, Mary Gosling observed:

> The JV Barry Memorial Library has reached a critical stage in its history. Important Library services will have to be curtained if the staffing situation does not improve. These curtailments will have a long-term effect not only on the AIC staff but also on researchers throughout Australia. The board of Management is requested to give careful consideration to the future role of the JV Barry Memorial Library. (Gosling 1982, p. 7)

During 1983, the Institute's Board acted to remedy the decline in services provided by the library by asking the Acting Librarian-in-charge, Gael Parr, to appoint an Information Services Librarian to arrange for CINCH to be updated, reinstate the Information Bulletins and conduct the Fourth Seminar for criminology librarians.

In August 1984, during Richard Harding's first year as Director, a new Librarian-in-charge was appointed, Nikki Riszko, who had a Bachelor of Arts from the University of Otago in New Zealand and a Graduate Diploma in Librarianship from Canberra College of Advanced Education. By July 1985, the library had seven staff resulting in a large increase in its services. Orders for monographs worth $11,510 were placed, mainly at the request of AIC research staff. The library at the time held 12,747 monographs, 3,526 microfiche records and approximately 900 serials. Library loans increased by 35% between 1983–1984 and 1984–1985 mainly due to requests by AIC staff for inter-library loans. During 1985, after the public gained access to CINCH on AUSINET, the library's services continued to expand with online searches provided and 478 reference queries made by staff. A further 519 external queries were also answered. At the time, CINCH held 2,500 entries.

During 1986, funding for the library increased to $56,000 which provided for an Information Services Librarian, Acquisitions Librarian, Cataloguer, Loans Officer, Collections Maintenance Officer and Typist, in addition to John Myrtle as the new Librarian-in-charge. John Myrtle, like Diana Solman, had no background in criminology, having previously worked as a librarian for the Department of Aviation for five years. He did, however, have experience with bibliographic/research databases, and a keen interest and knowledge of government and public affairs that led to Dennis Challinger, the AICs Assistant Director (Information and Training), recruiting him for the position commencing in April 1986.

John Myrtle's time at the Institute saw many substantial developments take place in the management of the Institute's information resources. One which took on considerable importance was the creation of a website for the Institute which began in 1996 when John engaged a group of information technology students from the Australian National University to develop the website. The importance of the website and how it developed is examined further in the next chapter.

In 1994, a review was conducted into the nature of the Commonwealth's law enforcement responsibilities and interests, and one recommendation made was that the AIC should be subject to an independent review of its role, clients, focus, priorities and structure (Coad et al. 1994). The AICs review resulted in 80 recommendations being made including the following regarding the library (Tanzer et al. 1994, p. 22):

74. The Review recommends that the Library examine strategies to prioritise its tasks and clients in such a manner as to enable it to deal with the cataloguing backlog which currently exists. This may well involve foregoing some tasks or denying some forms of service or denying service to some current clients.

The Tanzer Review et al. (1994, p. 21) also recommended that 'the research function of the AIC be reorganised into three research program areas, namely crime analysis and policy, crime and violence control and prevention, and deaths in custody' and that these areas should be supported by the library and conference programs. John Myrtle and the staff of the library faced a difficult time in attempting to implement these recommendations given the large reduction in the Institute's appropriation. Of particular importance was the Tanzer Review's other recommendation to redesign the information technology program, by creating a new plan, new purchases of computers, the creation of an AIC data centre and 'a new client-centred focus for information technology services' (Tanzer et al. 1994, p. 21). The outcome for the library was, as John Myrtle recalled in his interview, difficult and confusing:

> Many of the staff were puzzled by the major recommendations of the review that recommended wholesale reductions in funding and staff levels. A number of experienced staff with good subject knowledge (including some from the library) were offered redundancies—it was a depressing and unnecessary experience. (John Myrtle, Interview, 3 December 2020)

The review also led to a change in the management structure of the Institute and the library with a senior bureaucrat taking on the role of oversight of the library, a task that, according to John Myrtle, 'he displayed little interest in' (John Myrtle, Interview, 3 December 2020). Following this manager's departure due to ill health, the Librarian-in-charge reported directly to the Institute's new director, Adam Graycar.

In addition to gradually increasing the online collection, that included electronic versions of the Institute's publications, the library staff undertook considerable work archiving the Institute's records, including the Institute's photograph collection that entailed identifying and labelling photographs and preserving the collection in accordance with appropriate archival storage policies. In 2001, the library staff drafted a strategic plan for the Library with the assistance of a consultant, Alison Ransome, University Librarian at Southern Cross University.

John Myrtle was also instrumental in commemorating the 100th anniversary of the birth of Sir John Barry with an afternoon symposium on Sir John's life held at the JV Barry Library on 13 June 2003 conducted in collaboration with ANZSOC. Speakers included Mark Finnane, Barry's biographer, Norval Morris who sent a recorded message from the University of Chicago, David Biles, Don Weatherburn and the author of the current volume as Chair of the event. The symposium was endorsed and supported by Sir John's widow, Lady Barry, and his three children John, Joan and Susie Barry. John Myrtle retired from the Institute in May 2003 and prior to his departure, at the 106th meeting of the Institute's Board of Management, his service of 17 years to the Institute was recognised with the presentation of a framed minute of appreciation.

Janet Smith commenced as Librarian-in-charge in May 2003, having previously worked at the NLA and then as Librarian-in-charge of the Commonwealth Department of the Environment. She then became

Foundation Director of a consultancy group, Infoscan, that developed and managed bibliographic and reference databases on behalf of government agencies. Janet moved to Washington DC with her family in 1995 having been appointed as Librarian-in-charge of Australia's embassy library in Washington. She returned to Australia in 1999 and was recruited to a senior systems librarian position with the Commonwealth's Parliamentary Library.

At the Institute, Janet sought to ensure that the library had a leading role to play in the provision of information services both for the Institute's research staff as well as the wider criminal justice community. She worked to enhance the Institute's online collection and created new resources such as the Indigenous Justice Clearinghouse in 2007 in collaboration with the Attorney-General's Department in New South Wales. Janet Smith retired in 2010 following a diagnosis of cancer, and died in Canberra on 24 January 2011 (Plate 9.8).

Plate 9.8   Janet Smith, Librarian-in-charge, 2005 (*Source* AIC Archives)

During Janet's time as Librarian-in-charge, the Board of Management asked for a review to be conducted of the JV Barry Library's operations and services. The terms of reference asked the reviewers to report on: the nature and volume of demand for the library's services, and how these can be met; information requirements of key stakeholders; potential improvements to processes, products, and services; challenges to the library; the unique capabilities of the library and how they can be developed; and how the library should manage the AIC's datasets (AIC Annual Report, 2008, p. 39).

The review report of February 2008, conducted by consultants Sherrey Quinn and Ian McCallum of Libraries Alive! (2008), contained a number of recommendations, concerning: the management of print and electronic collections; the development of a strategic plan; performance measurement and reporting; environmental scanning of and the changing ways of dealing with digital information; establishing a closer relationship with research staff; the need for continuing IT developments, particularly the implementation of Web 2.0; and the need for effective dataset management. This last recommendation regarding management of datasets raised a complex and difficult question, as the AIC was unable to provide staffing resources that were needed to manage the 200 or so databases held, but needed to provide access to the information when requested. The solution offered was to provide a general index of the datasets and consider aligning the collection with another data repository such as the Australian Social Science Data Archive. Over the ensuing years, as staff numbers declined, this question remained of ongoing concern.

Although it found strong support for the work of the library among AIC researchers and stakeholders, the Review recommended the need for improved performance measurement and reporting within an explicit strategic framework. With the abolition of the former Information Services section, a strategic plan was developed that focussed on the library's role and scope within the context of a more general strategic plan for the Communications and Information section of the Institute.

Shortly before leaving the Institute, the director at the time, Toni Makkai, provided feedback on a draft of the final report that she found to be in need of significant editing with many of its proposed recommendations unsupported by evidence. The director asked for additional evidence of the usage of the collection and the extent to which it duplicated resources available in other libraries or online. In its Final Report, the consultants sought to address these criticisms by advocating for a model that would achieve a balance between maintaining existing services using the print collection and expanding online services that would ensure that the library was cost-effective and did not duplicate services available elsewhere.

The Report did, however, provide some baseline data on the Library's collection and its ongoing cost. At the time of the review, it was estimated that the collection held 26,000 print and 1,300 online monographs and 1,900 journal titles with 3,767 full-text digital titles. In addition, the library had access to eight index-only databases including the 50,000 CINCH records. The library's estimated budget for 2007–2008 was $450,000—three-quarters of which related to employee costs. The total library cost was, accordingly, 6.2% of the Institute's total expenditure (Libraries Alive! 2008). At the time, the consultants concluded that:

> The JV Barry Library collection is a unique resource. Its content has been carefully selected, it comprehensively covers Australian criminology and it is a body of information on criminology and related subjects that is not replicated elsewhere in Australia or the world (Libraries Alive! 2008, p. 36)

Janine Chandler had been working in the library since 2005 and because of her knowledge of the collection and its management, she was appointed Manager of Information Resources in 2010 after Janet Smith retired. As such, she was responsible for continuing the task of implementing the recommendations of the 2008 review until she also retired from the Institute at the time of the relocation to the first floor of the ACICs building at 4 National Circuit, Barton in 2015 (Plate 9.9).

Plate 9.9 Library staff at 74 Leichhardt Street, August 2013 (left to right: Lepa Petrovic, Janine Chandler, Jessica Begley and Maureen Lee) (*Source*: *Incite*, August 2013, p. 25)

The Library's Move to 4 National Circuit

The subsequent decade was challenging for the JV Barry Library, with changes in managers, relocation to new premises in 2015 and 2017, reduction in the physical collection, large-scale digitisation of resources, the re-development of a new website and the need to satisfy, not only the AICs interests, but also those of the ACIC and the Department of Home Affairs. The decade also saw a substantial increase in the Institute's social media presence that required careful moderation, given the AICs close relationship with the ACIC that tended to adopt a low public profile. Despite this, the Institute managed to increase its social media presence, create a Blog and a YouTube channel, 'Criminology TV' and develop a virtual seminar program. In 2020, the library staff also had a major role to play in introducing the new website and supporting remote working for all the Institute's staff during the coronavirus pandemic, ensuring that they had access to the Institute's electronic resources.

Jane Shelling came to the Institute in 2014 as Manager of the JV Barry Library from her previous position with the Alcohol and Other Drugs Council of Australia (ADCA) where she managed the National Drug Sector Information Service. She was well-placed to manage the Institute's library because of her knowledge of social science research and the information needs associated with it. Jane retired from the Institute on 9 July 2021 and, after a somewhat lengthy recruitment process, Samantha Jackson was appointed as Library Manager on 29 November 2021.

One of Jane's first tasks was to establish clearly the library's place in relation to the larger Information and Communications Division managed by Colin Campbell. This required clear delineation of the duties associated with the library apart from the website, publication and conference administration. Jane Shelling noted in her interview that there was not a clear understanding of the roles of library manager and communications manager in terms of who the library was serving—be it the AICs staff or the public generally. Jane and before her John Myrtle were both opposed to offering an information service to everyone— particularly secondary school students and crime novelists—as there were insufficient staff at the Institute to manage the workload, and others in the community were, arguably, better suited to do this. She observed that other public sector bodies rarely provided such a service, and most recently, members of the public are referred on to public libraries for help (Jane Shelling, Interview, 29 March 2021). The level of assistance being sought by the public has also declined in recent times as the Internet has developed and users can now locate answers to many of their questions online themselves.

Since becoming more closely aligned with the ACIC, the library has experienced an increase in workload responding to information requests from each of these agencies, despite the small number of staff employed in the JV Barry Library, relative to the size of these much larger entities (Plate 9.10).

At the time of the relocation to the ACCs premises in 2015, and prompted by an earlier review of the Library's Collection Asset Recognition and Valuation Policy to meet the Australian Accounting Standard requirements that sought to set a clear policy on both the capitalisation and valuation of the Library collection, a full review of the collection

Plate 9.10 Library staff at 4 National Circuit, 11 June 2021 (left to right: Katy Norman, Senior Research Editor; Jane Shelling, former Library Manager; Megan Whittle, Reference Librarian; Samantha McCrossen, Library Technician. *Absent*: Yvette Maconachie, Systems Librarian) (*Source* AIC Archives, 11 June 2021)

was conducted. The aim of the review was to determine how best to rationalise the Library's collection to allow for more of the collection to become electronic; to reduce the physical footprint through the disposal of multiple copies of items; to correct errors in the system revealed through a change in library management system; and to match the items in the Library collection to the list held in the Financial Management System.

This review led to a substantial proportion of the collection being scanned and hard copies destroyed, along with duplicated items and multiple copies of the same item being located and also removed from the collection. In addition, serials available in other libraries or able to be accessed electronically were removed. In all, more than 8,000 items were removed from the collection in 2015, as shown in Table 9.1.

The digitisation of items in the collection took approximately 6 months in 2015 prior to the move to 4 National Circuit in Barton,

Table 9.1 Estimated disposals of the library's collection, 2015

Collection type	Number
Dispose of capitalised folios (Digitised and/or freely available)	3,000–4,000
Dispose of duplicate records	1,250–1,500
Dispose of AIC publications	400–500
Dispose of books now available free of charge	1,000–2,000
Dispose of 2 sets of special publication that are series articles	2
Total disposals	6,652–8,002

Source AIC Archives, 2015

costing some $35,200. This was undertaken with some urgency as only limited floor space was provided for the library by the ACC in the new premises. In all, over half a million pages from the physical library collection were digitised (AIC Annual Report 2015–2016, p. ix). Difficult decisions had to be made concerning the removal of various types of items in the collection. In the case of consultancy reports collected by the Institute that contained data and statistics collected by external bodies, it was decided that these would be retained, either in hard copy or scanned, in order to ensure ready access to these resources that often were removed from the original publisher's websites or collections. One example is the fraud victimisation survey reports published regularly by consultancy practices, such as KPMG, PricewaterhouseCoopers and others globally. The AICs library is often asked to provide copies of these to other researchers on Inter-library Loans (Jane Shelling, Interview, 29 March 2021).

During its time at the ACC/ACICs premises at 4 National Circuit, the JV Barry Library continued to provide a service to the Institute's research staff as well as responding to requests for information from other Commonwealth officers and overseas academics and researchers. Staff numbers continued to decline and by 2021, the bulk of the library's work was undertaken electronically. At the time of the relocation, the library also had to deal with the introduction of a new online, open-source catalogue, Koha, the revision of the website, installation of new computing hardware and software and recruitment and training of new staff. Jane Shelling managed to navigate these issues as best she could, and following the move, conducted a full stocktake of the collection, at the time comprising 11,287 titles. By March 2021, this had increased to 11,828 print books on the shelves with total library holdings in all formats numbering 95,566 items (CRAC Report, 23 March 2021).

As discussed below, a number of difficulties arose as a result of the proposed merger between the AIC and ACC in 2015. For the JV Barry Library, the primary problem concerned the classified nature of ACC/ACICs holdings. Jane Shelling noted in her interview:

> We draw a very big line between us and the ACIC in terms of their material, so we don't keep any of their material within our world; we only keep AIC material and make it very clear to them that all of our material is available to the public. (Jane Shelling, Interview, 29 March 2021)

Significance of the JV Barry Library

Since the JV Barry Library opened its doors in 1974, it has provided an invaluable service to policy-makers, government officials, scholars, students and members of the community throughout Australia and overseas. The library began with a modest collection of fewer than 5,000 volumes that has grown to a print and digital collection comprising almost 100,000 items valued at more than $1 million in 2022.

The five decades have, however, seen many challenges for the library with budget cuts affecting growth of the collection and reductions in staffing numbers, and changes in aims and functions leading to unreasonably large demands being placed on the library to deliver not only the conventional services of a library, but also a range of allied functions including publication of research, dissemination of information, fact-checking of research findings and provision of information and advice to users throughout Australia and overseas. This lack of focus made the task of librarians demanding and at times deeply unsatisfying as they sought to satisfy disparate demands on their time with often dwindling resources of time, money and personnel. Nonetheless, the library was an important part of the Institute with library staff comprising one-eighth of all the AICs personnel in December 2022. Because, at this time, the

Institute comprised predominantly research and library staff, this created a much closer and productive working relationship between the library and the researchers who made use of it, than previously.

The JV Barry Library was, however, loved by many and when the regular attempts were made to limit its functions, or abolish it entirely, strident criticism rose up, for example, teachers at one secondary school in Canberra, Stirling College (since 1997, Canberra College), on learning that Federal budget cuts would result in their students being unable to use the library wrote:

> The effect of this will be to deny our students a most valuable teaching resource. The library's resources are both wide-ranging and comprehensive and have provided excellent research material for legal studies students preparing essays and assignments.... The Institute of Criminology has gone out of its way to widen the understanding of legal-studies teachers in the area of criminology. This has been by way of holding seminars and providing a variety of resource material. This service has been most appreciated and the benefits have flowed directly to students through more effective teaching. (Brocklebank and Stepniak 1981, p. 2)

Internationally, the library has provided and continues to provide, an invaluable service in collecting and disseminating crime and justice statistics and information about Australia generally, for use by other governments and scholars. Pat Mayhew considered the JV Barry Library to be 'a truly exceptional resource. There was nothing like it in the Home Office, and I can't think of any other research centre in the public sector that would have had one as good' (Personal Communication, 21 November 2022). Again, when its removal was mooted, numerous requests to reconsider such a proposal were promptly sent to the relevant decision-makers, resulting in plans for abolition of the Institute and its library being cancelled. Examples of these came from a number of the UN PNI agencies as well as from individual government agencies and scholars in a range of countries. One example is a submission made by Michael Levi, Professor of Criminology, Cardiff University, who wrote in October 2016:

The JV Barry Library is a valuable national resource and needs to be maintained. In short, now more than ever, when there are so many 'online' and 'offline' challenges facing contemporary societies, we need research that both is and is perceived as independent and of international standard. If the quality and quantity of research drops, then this may not be noticed immediately, but it is part of the fabric of friction and scrutiny that in the medium and long run is much healthier for the agencies themselves as well as for the public interest in the polity. Australia has a fine tradition of empirical research in serious crime, and care should be taken that this is not imperilled by measures that are bureaucratically convenient but may have unintended negative side-effects. (Levi 2016, p. 1)

References

Australian Institute of Criminology (AIC). 1973–2016. *Annual Reports 1973–2016*. Canberra: Australian Institute of Criminology.

Australian Library and Information Association. 1990. *Australian Prison Libraries: Minimum Standard Guidelines*. Canberra: Australian Library and Information Association.

Australian Library and Information Association. 2015. *Minimum Standard Guidelines for Library Services to Prisoners*. Canberra: Australian Library and Information Association.

Brocklebank, Brian, and Dan Stepniak. 1981. Institute of Criminology. *Canberra Times*, 30 July, p. 2.

Cameron, Fiona R. 2021. *The Future of Digital Data, Heritage and Curation in a More-than-Human World*. Sydney: Routledge.

Choo, Kim-Kwang Raymond, Russell G. Smith, and Rob McCusker. 2007. *Future Directions in Technology-Enabled Crime: 2007–09*. Research and Public Policy Series No. 78. Canberra: Australian Institute of Criminology.

Coad, William J., Prudence Ford, Malcolm Hazell, Peter Lamb, Norman Reaburn, and Adrian Whiddett. 1994. *Report of the Review of Commonwealth Law Enforcement Arrangements*. Canberra: Australian Government Publishing Service.

Curran, James. 2010. Reinterpreting Internet History. In *Handbook of Internet Crime*, ed. Yvonne Jewkes and Majid Yar, 273–301. Cullompton: Willan Publishing.

Gosling, Mary E. 1982. *The J. V. Barry Memorial Library: A Review of Its Functions and Policy*. Unpublished Report, 16 August. Canberra: Australian Institute of Criminology.

Levi, Michael. 2016. *Submission to the Senate Legal and Constitutional Affairs Legislation Committee Inquiry into the Australian Crime Commission Amendment (Criminology Research) Bill 2016, No 25*. Canberra: Department of the Senate.

Libraries Alive! 2008. *Review of the JV Barry Library, Australian Institute of Criminology: Final Report*. Canberra: Libraries Alive!

Middleton, Michael. 2006. Scientific and Technological Information Services in Australia: II. Discipline Formation. *Information Management, Australian Academic & Research Libraries* 37 (3): 179–199. https://doi.org/10.1080/00048623.2006.10755336. Accessed 19 April 2021.

Radzinowicz, Leon. 1973. *Report of Sir Leon Radzinowicz with Respect to the Australian Institute of Criminology*. New York and Canberra: National Library of Australia (6093 / 72/4182).

Radzinowicz, Leon. 1988. *The Cambridge Institute of Criminology: Its Background and Scope*. London: HMSO.

Radzinowicz, Leon, and James Muirhead. 1973. Conversation between Sir Leon Radzinowicz and Judge Muirhead in *Proposed Visit to Australia of Sir Leon Radzinowicz: Fees and Allowances* (No 10 – 46-2-1(i)). Canberra: National Library of Australia.

Riszko, Nikki. 1985. *CINCH: Computerised Information from National Criminological Holdings*. In The Future Now: Changing Information Sources: Proceedings of the First Asian-Pacific Special and Law Librarians' Conference, Incorporating the 7th National Special Librarians' Conference and 2nd National Law Librarians' Conference, pp. 363–372, 1–6 September. Library Association of Australia and the Australian Law Librarians' Group, Sydney.

Roberts, Philip John. 1987. *Standards in Australian Prison Libraries: Report and Recommendations Submitted to the Library Association of Australia General Council*. North Quay: National Corrective Services Librarians' Group.

Smith, Russell G. 2010. The Development of Cybercrime. In *Crime Over Time: Temporal Perspectives on Crime and Punishment in Australia*, ed. Robyn Lincoln and Shirleene Robinson, 211–236. Newcastle upon Tyne: Cambridge Scholars Publishing.

Susskind, Richard, and Daniel Susskind. 2017. *The Future of the Professions.* Oxford: Oxford University Press.

Tanzer, Noel, Des Hill, and Grant Wardlaw. 1994. *Review of the Australian Institute of Criminology: Report.* Canberra: Australian Institute of Criminology.

United Nations Asia and Far East Institute for the Prevention of Crime and the Treatment of Offenders (UNAFEI). 2020. *Brochure.* Tokyo: UNAFEI. https://www.unafei.or.jp/english/about/Brochure.html Accessed 16 February 2021.

10

Focussing on Research

Introduction

Setting up a public sector criminological research institute entails not only acquiring suitable funding for premises, a library and staffing, but also a complex process of determining what the focus of the research should be and how that research should be undertaken. This includes questions concerning the selection of research topics (and determining by whom they are selected), what research methodologies should be employed, what ethical standards of research must be adhered to and how the needs of government and the community can best be satisfied. Even if the findings of research are unsupportive of current government policies, as long as the research is methodologically and theoretically sound and is presented in a clear, compelling and concise way, it is likely that the research undertaken will attract respect and be seen as creating a useful and reliable source of evidence that the government can trust and rely on.

This chapter assesses how the Institute fared with these challenges by considering its approach to developing and managing research projects,

R. G. Smith, *Public Sector Criminological Research*, https://doi.org/10.1007/978-3-031-28356-7_10

determining the subject-matter of research undertaken and the soundness of how information was collected, analysed and reported. Examples are provided of how the AICs directors sought to avoid politicised controversies in crime and justice while maintaining their duty as public officials to provide fearless, independent, high-quality research and advice to government. It considers which research was most sought-after by differing levels of government and the public and which time-series data collections endured while others ceased.

Criminologists working within the public sector were often faced with challenges concerning their roles and functions. Paul Wiles, who later became Director of Research at the Home Office in the UK, raised this question at the time the AIC was established:

> Those who work in such settings are constantly faced with the possibility that they may be torn between the competing demands placed upon them as a consequence of their dual allegiance. As researchers, their criteria, or relevance, appropriate methodology and success will be derived from their discipline; as civil servants, they must also take account of pragmatic politics in these matters and may well find it difficult to renounce, when necessary, the criteria which are operating within their parent institution. (Wiles 1976, p. 6)

The AICs former director, Duncan Chappell, also identified the difficulties the Institute's researchers faced in conducting research on crime and justice topics relevant to practitioners, noting that 'the academic approach has not found favour with some criminal justice agency personnel who believe that the Institute has failed to meet its original mandate to provide an applied research resource for people working in the field' (Chappell 1983, p. 21).

This chapter seeks to explore these questions by examining how research was conducted at the Institute, and particularly, by documenting the topics examined and the methodologies used to conduct research in a public sector environment. A number of relevant issues have, however, already been dealt with in other chapters—including how funding was sourced and allocated, and the levels of funding needed to conduct the types of research that were proposed; whether research should have a policy focus that examines practical criminal justice questions, or if theoretical, whether critical analysis was appropriate; what the relationship was between criminal justice training activities and educational initiatives; the library resources required to support research activities and where they should be located; and questions of how research findings are best able to be disseminated to stakeholders and the community.

Although consideration of some of these questions have arisen, and will arise, elsewhere in this volume, efforts have been made to avoid duplication of the observations made in other chapters. Instead, the present chapter explores the administrative and policy arrangements put in place to manage the AICs research activities, and the nature of the research conducted over the preceding five decades—both in terms of its subject-matter as well as its methodologies.

Managing the Research Enterprise

When the Institute was established, as we have seen, the enterprise was one of cooperative federalism. The interests of both the Commonwealth and the states (and later the territories) were meant to be given prominence in the types of research carried out—although striking the right balance was always a matter for discussion, debate and conflict. Should, for example, the Institute focus on cross-border human trafficking as opposed to family violence; or should it focus on money laundering as opposed to armed robbery? The Board of Management and the CRC were charged with ensuring that all competing interests were satisfied, with individual directors being responsible for implementing the chosen paths to follow. At the head of the governance structure lay the Minister's Office and the administering Department. Each of these levels of authority had to be consulted and satisfied with the type and amount of research that was conducted.

Although Ministers and their Departmental heads had differing levels of involvement in setting the research agenda, the Institute's Board and Council arguably had a greater role to play, particularly in satisfying local state and territory interests. When the Institute was established, there were few resources available to governments for the provision of information on the nature, extent and control of crime. In his interview, Grant Wardlaw, who later became one of the members of the Tanzer Review in 1984, referred to the changes that had taken place in public administration since the Institute had been established.

> The landscape had changed very dramatically over the period from the founding of the Institute until the Review in terms of... public administration and the provision of government services; who would deliver them–private versus government; the model for the Institute–how much should it be based on an academic model and how much it should be a government research bureau meeting more closely defined government priorities. That was a tension that ran through the whole of the history of the Institute. (Grant Wardlaw, Interview, 30 November 2020)

By the time of the Tanzer Review (1994), the academic criminological community had developed considerably, and questions arose as to the role of the federal government in providing a research function internally, as opposed simply to funding external academic research. When the Institute was established, however, both Acting Director Muirhead and Board Chair Mahony considered that the government was, indeed, best able to undertake a broad range of research to inform crime and justice policy.

Nonetheless, it was important for directors to be aware of the views of the existing government administration in setting research agendas. As governments changed, so did directors and board members—with the consequence that the research focus also changed. Director Richard Harding, for example, was closely aligned with the Hawke Labor government in 1984 and was willing to promote a research agenda that reflected the needs of the Labor government's policies. This included a focus on Aboriginal affairs, deaths in custody, domestic violence and crime statistics–among other topics. Harding recalled in his interview that the choice of research topics was largely left to himself to determine in consultation with colleagues:

> I didn't have to go and ask the Minister, can I do this, can I do that? When dealing with Ministers you can't be too indifferent to their reactions when you tell them what you're going to do....You can sometimes

give more status to what you're doing by saying that 'the Minister wants this to be done'. (Richard Harding, Interview, 18 November 2021)

Although acknowledging the role that Ministers had, Harding observed that the Board had more practical influence on the choice of topics than the Minister. Having a good relationship with the Chair of the Board was important. Harding, for example, worked very well with Peter Loof, and had regular meetings with him, and sought his assistance to 'square away his [Harding's] priorities with the state representatives on the Board'.

To share the administrative burden, directors, from the outset, appointed Assistant Directors to manage the various work units within the organisation. In the case of the research function, this was the Assistant Director (Research), later the Director of Research, and most recently the Deputy Director of the Institute, each of whom was responsible not only for research activities, but also management of publications, conferences and staffing. Six individuals have headed-up Research over the five decades, a third of whom were women–Toni Makkai from 2001 to 2003 and Judy Putt as Manager of Research Services from 2005 to 2010. The longest serving head of Research was Rick Brown (Plate 10.1) who was appointed to the Institute in 2011 by Director Adam Tomison and who, since the commencement of the relationship with the ACC/ACIC in 2015, has been the Deputy Director of the Institute which entails general management of all aspects of the organisation, in consultation with the ACICs Chief Executive Officer, who is also named as the Institute's formal director.

Rick Brown came to the Institute from the UK where he had been managing a research consultancy that focussed on a range of crime and justice topics. Prior to that he had worked at the Home Office in the UK from 1994 to 2001, initially in the Police Research Group that had been established in 1992 within the Policing Directorate of the Home Office. After the Crime Reduction Program was introduced, the Police Research Unit became the Policing and Reducing Crime Unit in 1998 that was eventually merged into the Research and Statistics Directorate (Rick Brown, Interview, 10 June 2022). Rick holds a PhD from LSE, a Master of Arts from the University of Westminster and a Bachelor of Arts (with Honours) degree from Hatfield Polytechnic. He is also a Visiting

Plate 10.1   Dr Rick Brown, Director Research 2011–2015, Deputy Director 2016-current (*Source* AIC Archives)

Fellow of the Policing and Criminal Justice Department at the University of Derby in the UK.

When the AICs director, Adam Tomison was looking for a Deputy Director of Research after Judy Putt had resigned in 2010, he asked Peter Homel, who was a Research Manager at the AIC, to see if Rick would be interested in the position. Peter had known Rick since they had met at the Home Office in 2000 when they both worked in the Policing and Reducing Crime Unit and persuaded Rick to apply for the position in Canberra. This would be a major career change for Rick as he had to disband his consultancy in the UK, and move his family to Australia–not without its difficulties (Rick Brown, Interview, 10 June 2022) as described in Chapter 8, above.

Rick's research experience covered not only quantitative and qualitative studies, but he had extensive experience is managing the sensitivities of working within a government administration, while also seeking to satisfy the interests of academic and community stakeholders. Rick, along with Adam Tomison, managed the difficult transition of the AIC from an independent statutory authority, to a public service entity, and then guided the Institute through the travails of the failed merger with the ACC in 2015–with its associated loss of accommodation, staff and budget–to its current position as a small but ever-expanding government research agency.

The parallels between Rick Brown's background and the Institute's first head of Research, David Biles, are notable. David Biles was born in England in 1932 and, like Rick, moved to Australia as a teenager (Rick arrived in his 40s). David first trained in education and after teaching in regional Victorian schools took up teaching roles in four Victorian prisons. He was then appointed a Lecturer in the Criminology Department at the University of Melbourne where he remained until he commenced at the AIC in 1974. David maintained his links with correctional administration throughout his time at the Institute, collecting and publishing corrections data and being intimately involved with the Asia and Pacific Conference of Correctional Administrators. Like Rick, he had continuing links with universities as well as with ANZSOC–including as President from 1980 to 1983–which honoured him with its Distinguished Criminologist Award in 2014, prior to his death in 2017. As such, David Biles was able effectively to integrate the interests of academics and policy-makers during his time as head of Research. An example of this was David's work with the Royal Commission into Aboriginal Deaths in Custody as Head of Research–on secondment from the AIC–which is still part of the Institute's work agenda, through the National Deaths in Custody Program, to this day (Plate 10.2).

When Richard Harding commenced as Director in 1984, he re-organised the Institute's administrative structure, creating a new position of Deputy Director to which David Biles was appointed–without even

Plate 10.2   David Biles, Assistant Director (Research) 1974–1984, Deputy Director 1984–1992, Acting Director 1987 (*Source* AIC Archives)

advertising the position. He did, however, advertise the new role of Assistant Director (Research) for which there were a number of highly qualified applicants including Clifford Shearing from the Centre of Criminology at the University of Toronto, and internal applicants, Peter Grabosky and Paul Wilson, among others. Harding appointed Paul Wilson who stayed in the position for five years until 1991 followed by Peter Grabosky who later became Deputy Director in 2001.

Toni Makkai (Plate 10.3), who began at the Institute in 1997 as a Senior Research Analyst, took over as Director of Research in 2001

Plate 10.3 Dr Toni Makkai, Director of Research 2001–2003, Acting Director 2003–2004, Director 2004–2008 (*Source* AIC Archives)

after Peter Grabosky vacated this position to take up a Chair in the Research School of Social Sciences at ANU. After Adam Graycar resigned as Director in September 2003, Toni Makkai became Acting Director, and then Director in August 2004.

In 2008, Toni resigned as Director to become Dean and Director of the College of Arts and Social Sciences at ANU. During Toni Makkai's directorship, no Deputy Director had been appointed and this role remained vacant until Rick Brown commenced in 2016. Since then, there has been no Director of Research, given the much smaller size of the Research workforce.

Each of the individuals who has headed-up Research at the Institute has shaped the role in various ways, and brought to bear their own perceptions of the policy focus, research methodologies and specific research topics for the Institute to pursue. David Biles, for example, actively promoted research into correctional administration; Paul Wilson had a keen interest in crimes of violence; Peter Grabosky had wide-ranging interests in co-production of crime prevention, cybercrime and white-collar crime; Toni Makkai actively pursued drug-related research; Judy Putt had interests in community policing, family violence and Indigenous justice; and Rick Brown continued his interest in the prevention of volume street crime. Most of these research interests focussed on state and territory criminal justice issues, but as Directors of Research, it was necessary for each person to become familiar with the full range of the Institute's federal as well as state and territory research concerns.

Selecting Topics for Research

The Institute's research focus was always somewhat eclectic, with some academic critics lamenting its positivist emphasis on the collection of data, while others in government criticising some of its work as being primarily of interest to the states and territories, rather than the Commonwealth. In reviewing the establishment of the Institute in 1979, Peter Loof (1979, p. 2) noted:

> From the outset an emphasis was placed on the need for applied research – the need for practical solutions to practical problems and the need to develop priorities for research designed to bring practical results in areas of greatest need.

Following this ukase did not, however, require researchers to ignore criminological theories—as some critics of the Institute have alleged (Carson and O'Malley 1989; Brown 1994)–as often the solutions to practical problems could be found through a sound understanding of applied theory.

When the Institute was established, the focus was clearly on sentencing and correctional issues. The first research projects approved by the Board were:

1. a survey of the problems of federal prisoners;
2. the effectiveness of short-term sentences in Australia;
3. fines, forfeiture, restitution and compensation sentences; and
4. the effectiveness of non-custodial sentences.

The Board estimated that researching these projects alone would cost 'in the order of $147,000 and take considerable time for completion' (AIC Board Minutes, 28 June 1973, p. 8). Apart from these topics, a further 10 proposals were deferred or declined by the Board including a number dealing with correctional topics, one on 'the incidence of migrant crime', another on 'the Aboriginal and officialdom—a gap to be bridged. How wide the gap—where the bridge?' and a further one on 'delinquency and the young Aboriginal'.

This early interest in Aboriginal criminal justice topics is noteworthy, particularly as the Institute did little work on these questions in its early years—an issue that Richard Harding sought to address (Richard Harding, Interview, 18 November 2021). He immediately appointed Kayleen Hazlehurst as a Senior Research Officer to work on this topic, and in 1985 Harding persuaded the Victorian Minister to authorise the Institute to study deaths in prison custody, that John Walker largely undertook. By March 1987, when the Royal Commission into Aboriginal Deaths in Custody commenced, the Institute had already amassed considerable research leading to David Biles being seconded as Research Director for the Royal Commission. Harding noted that this 'was a terrific thing to have done. Instead of floundering in the rear on a huge national issue, the Institute was able, indirectly perhaps, to take a role in this big issue' (Interview 18 November 2021). Research on Indigenous issues continued, sporadically, until it has been given greater emphasis with the creation of an Indigenous Justice Research Program with funding of $750,000 commencing in 2021 (AIC Minutes, 24 November 2021, p. 2). This supports other AIC research carried out with the National Indigenous Australians Agency and the Indigenous Justice Clearinghouse.

The process of selecting topics for research was, initially, and for many years, somewhat ad hoc. Directors and Boards made decisions to pursue topics that interested them or were topical. This, of course, provided no guarantee that interest in these selected topics would remain current. As Peter Grabosky noted in his interview (3 December 2020): 'Time marches on—what was a pressing issue three decades ago might not still be today—for example, public drunkenness and policing homosexuality'—both pressing issues in the 1960s and '70s. As new researchers were appointed, it was often left to them to choose their own topics. Grant Wardlaw, confirmed this during his Interview:

> When I arrived here, David [Biles] welcomed me on my first day and said 'here's your office, here's a pen and paper... there's a fantastic library downstairs, I suggest you go and sit down there and read your way through anything that's interesting for two months and then come back to me... and tell me what your research topics are going to be.' I said, is there anything that anyone's interested in, or wants to do, and he said 'no it's up to you to work that out'. So there was no direction or plan at all... By the time that Richard [Harding] had arrived, it was pretty much an imperative that this was not just a free-for-all where you do what you feel like. (Grant Wardlaw, Interview, 30 November 2020) (Plate 10.4)

John Seymour also referred to the lack of direction at the time he was employed at the Institute from 1976 to 1978.

> I was never aware of any research plan.... I can't ever remember sitting down and discussing what the Institute ought to be doing and making use of the multi-disciplinary people we had including psychologists, statisticians and lawyers. There was never any attempt to create an overall plan on any particular topic, and no real direction as to what we ought to do. (John Seymour, Interview, 14 November 2022)

At that time, the Board and Directors chose topics for the Training Division to address, and these tended to coincide, largely, with the topics examined by the research staff. In the early years, these, again, focussed on corrections and sentencing until Richard Harding expanded the focus to examine current criminological topics such as domestic violence and firearms. What was missing, however, was the creation of a link between the research that had been conducted and the use of the findings from that research in the Institute's training activities. As Grant Wardlaw noted

Plate 10.4 Dr Grant Wardlaw, Criminologist, 1976–1979, Acting Director, April–November 1994 (*Source* AIC Archives)

in his interview (30 November 2020), the Training Division was quite separate from the Research Division.

As noted above in Chapter 5, the Review of Commonwealth Functions conducted by the Fraser Coalition government in 1981 (the Razor Gang–see Fraser 1981) led the Management and Special Services Division of AGD to conduct a *Review of the Staff and Organisational Structure of the Australian Institute of Criminology* (McDonald and Moore 1981). This also involved the establishment on 18 September 1981 of a Working Committee of the AICs Board to examine the Institute's research priorities that reported on 27 November 1981 and led to the creation of a *Policy With Respect to Research Priorities* (AIC Minutes, 9 March 1982,

Annexure). The policy included two principal objectives of the Institute's research as being: to reduce the costs associated with crime or the operation of the criminal justice system; or to evaluate or improve the efficiency of the criminal justice system. The Board then enumerated seven guidelines upon which research topics should be selected that included: the need to cover all areas of criminology; that projects be related to the Institute's objectives; that areas of need be ascertained through the use of a Delphi process; that particular attention be given to research dealing with practical problems of administrators; that the need for evaluation be considered; the urgency of topics; the relationship of topics to other allied research; and the results of consultation with government agencies and experts (AIC Minutes, 9 March 1982, Annexure). This was one of the first occasions that the Board attempted to delineate ways in which the Institute's research agenda should be determined.

Over the next decade, however, the selection of topics continued to be ad hoc leading to the criticism provided in the Tanzer Review (1994), that 'the AIC has attempted to serve too many clients and stretched its resources too thinly' (p. 11). One consequence of this was that it 'engaged in research or gave advice in areas in which it possesses no demonstrable depth of expertise, thus laying itself open to charges of shallowness' (p. 11). The solution to this recommended by the Review was to establish specific research priorities as determined by the Minister in accordance with a revised mission statement:

> The primary purpose of the AIC is to assist Government to make informed decisions that will contribute to the promotion of justice and the prevention of crime. (Tanzer et al. 1994, p. 12)

In October 1993, Duncan Kerr, as Minister of Justice, wrote to the director advising a set of suggested research priorities. These were: the future of crime; the context of crime; sophisticated crime; policing; crime prevention; violence prevention; deaths in custody and drug issues (Tanzer et al. 1994, p. 13). In view of the highly reduced budget, the new director, Adam Graycar, sought to re-focus the research program to meet these priorities while taking into account Tanzer's (1994, p. 13) comment that 'it would not [be] possible comprehensively to address all of the listed projects even within the AICs existing resources'. It was, therefore, suggested that priorities could be assessed against six criteria including: impact, expertise, practicality, other agencies' work, if a Cabinet mandate and budget was present, and the AICs assessment of importance.

Over the next three decades, the Institute sought to identify priorities in consultation with stakeholders, particularly the Minister and the Board. Planning days with all staff present were held on occasions, but often these produced inconclusive research agendas that sometimes were not followed, or had to be revised to accommodate new topical issues or new areas of staffing expertise. Arguably, the most pronounced change occurred following the development of the closer relationship with the ACC/ACIC that has led to an enhanced focus on serious and organised crime and associated law enforcement issues. Ministerial influence has also dictated an increased emphasis on family violence and child sexual abuse in the most recent decade.

The Corporate Plan of the AIC (2022) for 2021–2022 included a Mission Statement as being 'to promote evidence-informed crime and justice policy and practice in Australia' (p. ii) with five research priorities specified: transnational and serious and organised crime; illicit drugs; economic crime; violence against women and children and Indigenous over-representation in the criminal justice system. In addition to undertaking projects on each of these research priorities, the AIC also administers a number of statistical collections on crime and justice— the National Homicide Monitoring Program, the National Deaths in Custody Program, the Fraud Against the Commonwealth census, the Identity Crime and Misuse Survey and, since 1 July 2021, the Australian Sexual Offences Statistical Collection (AIC 2022, p. 5). This latest collection will collate information about sexual violence from the perspective of both offenders and victims as well as looking at historical information about patterns of offending.

With the development of the *National Plan to Combat Cybercrime* (Australian Government 2022), the Institute developed a national cybercrime survey as a new monitoring program. With funding from the Proceeds of Crime Fund, the cybercrime survey will provide national prevalence and trend information not only on pure cybercrimes such as malware and ransomware attacks but also some forms of cyber-enabled crime such as consumer fraud and online harassment. This study will also include data on misuse of personal information (from the identity crime and misuse survey), the cost of cybercrime and will be innovative as it will seek to test intervention strategies that seek to prevent cyber-victimisation (Anthony Morgan, Interview, 17 November 2022). From 2023, the Institute will also manage the Human Trafficking and Modern Slavery National Minimum Dataset. 'Although not intended as a prevalence data collection, it will bring together data from key Commonwealth agencies as well as civil society organisations to understand human trafficking comprehensively' (Samantha Bricknell, Interview, 21 November 2022).

Dr Samantha Bricknell (Plate 10.5) has managed the Institute's monitoring programs since she commenced at the AIC in October 2006, having come to the AIC from AIHW. She graduated from the ANU with a PhD in anthropology and has specialised in the areas of homicide, deaths in custody, human trafficking and slavery, family and domestic violence, illicit firearms and environmental crime. Describing the AICs monitoring programs as an 'eclectic' group of programs (Samantha Bricknell, Interview, 21 November 2022), 'each of which have been born because there has been an external request for long-term monitoring–some of which have been around for thirty years or more and others with very short life-spans'.

In her Interview (21 November 2022), Samantha Bricknell noted that:

> some monitoring programs such as Homicide and Deaths in Custody have ebbed and flowed in terms of how much they have been used or recognised, but in the last five years, the importance of collating long-term data on these issues has really come to the fore. In the case of homicide monitoring, the AIC is being recognised as the one that should always provide the data, and develop indicator work around intimate partner and family homicides.

In March 2021, the AICs Director, Michael Phelan, submitted a proposal to the Advisory Council that the Drug Use Monitoring in Australia (DUMA) program cease to be administered by the AIC from

Plate 10.5 Dr Samantha Bricknell, AIC Research Manager, 2014–2022 (*Source* AIC Archives)

the end of 2021, with the intellectual property rights over the data collection being made available to the states and territories so that they could continue the data collection. This proposal was supported by the Commonwealth with its representative on the Council advising that 'the Commonwealth does not rely on DUMA and would support diverting funding to other AIC research' (AIC Minutes, 29 March 2021, pp. 2–3). Four Council members present were reluctant to see DUMA end and the director agreed to canvass the views of others. Of those who replied, all supported the continuation of DUMA—with Western Australia being the only one to offer actual funding. As a result, the director 'retired' DUMA from 31 December 2021 (AIC, Minutes, 30 July 2021, p. 4). Adam Tomison, who supported the continuation of DUMA by the AIC, commented during his interview (26 October 2022), 'I think this is a missed opportunity... DUMA triangulates nicely with other attempts to look at drug markets such as waste water analysis, and it should have been maintained'. Adam took up the challenge by ensuring that the Western Australian government was able to fund and continue DUMA in its own state.

The Institute's planned performance results for 2022–2023 include requirements to publish 28 peer-reviewed publications and a further 25 other publications in addition to conducting at least 10 Roundtables, workshops, seminars and other forums annually (Department of Home Affairs 2022, p. 149). In 2021–2022, these targets were met with peer-reviewed publication numbering 35–10 more than the target of 25 for the year (p. 148). With a budgeted research staff of 30 for 2022–2023, this would mean that, on average, each staff member would need to publish approximately two publications for the year. In previous years, when staff numbers were fewer than at present (such as in 2017–2018 when there were only 14 research staff), the publication output per person was much higher—as the performance targets have remained the same for many years.

Research Topics Examined

Over its 50-year history, the Institute has conducted research and policy analysis on an extensive range of criminological topics and published over 2,000 separate AIC reports or other works. These have included research on: monitoring trends in violent crimes such as homicide, firearms offences, sexual violence and human trafficking; investigating white-collar crime, fraud and crime involving new technologies; evaluating the effectiveness of crime control measures such as closed-circuit television, electronic monitoring of offenders, restorative justice, anti-money laundering controls and capital punishment; conducting assessments of boutique criminal justice topics including fisheries crime, farm crime, ATM robberies, cloud computing and carbon trading; and examining support for victims of both violent crimes and federal offences, and avenues to enhance the rehabilitation of offenders.

One measure of the range of research undertaken by the Institute is the scope of the material contained in its longest-running publication series *Trends and Issues in Crime and Criminal Justice*. These short policy-focussed papers were developed in 1986 as a concise summary of contemporary crime and justice topics in which new data or policy developments were canvassed. Papers were written in clear language and were of a modest length of around 4,000 words that politicians and policy advisers could easily digest. Academics also liked this type of publication that could easily form the basis of a new lecture or tutorial. For present purposes, the principal topic examined in each publication was identified and these were grouped into 23 categories to illustrate the range of topics covered. Of course, many papers dealt with multiple topics but an attempt was made to count the topic that corresponded most closely with the gist of the content of the work (Fig. 10.1).

The topics chosen for publication in the *Trends and Issues* series largely arose from research projects undertaken by the Institute and CRC grant recipients, while others arose from the research interests of individual staff members. The area of economic and business crime, which accounted for the highest percentage of publications, was driven not only by the availability of research funds in this area, but also by the research interests of a number of senior staff. Other specific topics, such as quantification of the costs of crime, were also able to be examined owing to suitably qualified staff being available. During some periods in the history of the Institute, a number of legally-qualified staff were employed which enabled research to be conducted into sentencing laws, evidentiary issues such as DNA evidence, money laundering and law reform generally.

During his time at the Institute, and later at the ALRC, John Seymour undertook research on child welfare law and young offenders that was eventually published as *Dealing with Young Offenders* (1988). In his interview (14 November 2022), Seymour compared the manner in which the topics for research were identified at the AIC with the process adopted by the ALRC. In the early years at the AIC, topics were selected based on the expertise and interest of researchers or the suggestions of the Board and director that was a largely uncoordinated approach without

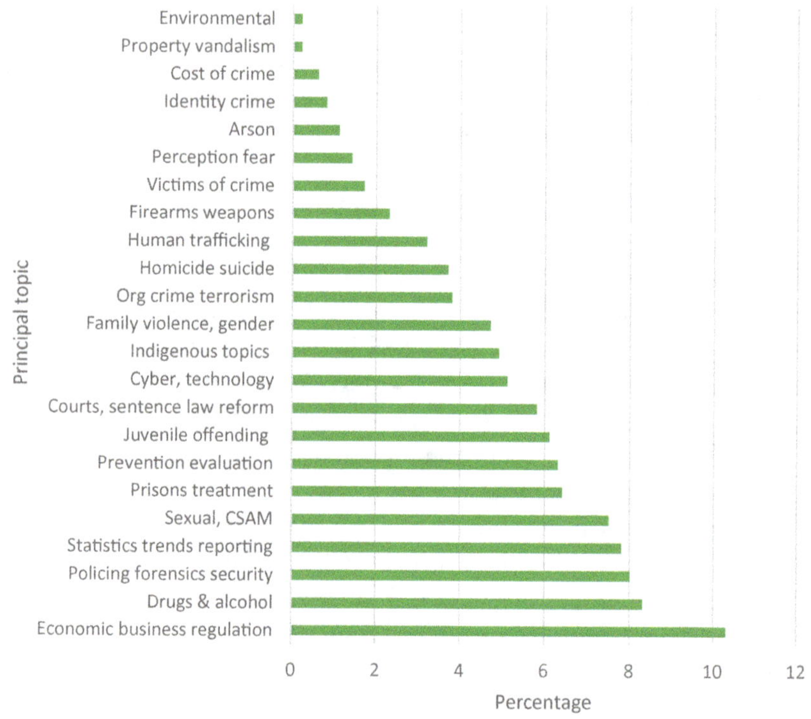

Fig. 10.1 Principal categories of research examined in *Trends and Issues* papers, 1986 to 2022 (percentage) (*Note* The full topic categories were: Economic, business, white collar crime & regulation; Drugs & alcohol research; Statistics, trends & reporting; Policing, forensics & security; Sexual offending, child abuse and child sexual abuse materials; Corrections & treatment of offenders; Prevention of crime & evaluation studies; Courts, sentencing, legal issues & law reform; Juvenile offending & responses; Cybercrime & technology; Family violence & gender research; Indigenous offending, victims & responses; Homicide & suicide research; Organised crime & terrorism; Trafficking people & commodities; Firearms & weapons; Victims of crime; Perceptions & fear of crime; Arson; Identity crime; Cost of crime; Property crime & vandalism; Crimes against the environment) (*Source* Derived from AIC Publications listing, http://www.aic.gov. au/publications/current%20series/tandi.html)

an overall research plan. At the ALRC, however, research was undertaken pursuant to a reference by the Attorney-General. This process that is adopted by statutory commissions of inquiry provided detailed terms of reference that limited the scope of the inquiry and how the reference should be addressed. For example, when John Seymour was seconded to the ALRCs Inquiry into *Child Welfare* in the ACT (ALRC 1981), he was given specific directions as to the scope of the work to be undertaken that would fulfil the terms of reference. Inquiries by the ALRC also included specific recommendation for reform as well as draft legislation. This was also the case with the ALRCs Inquiry into *Sentencing of Federal Offenders* (ALRC 1980) with Seymour being one of the Commissioners along with Duncan Chappell as Commissioner in Charge and Bill Clifford as a Consultant supported by a number of AIC researchers. John concluded by noting how the 'the rigour and clarity of role of the ALRC contrasted very sharply with the lack of direction and uncertainty as to role which prevailed at the AIC' (John Seymour, Interview, 14 November 2022). Of course, the AIC had a much smaller budget than the ALRC and was established as a criminological research institute rather than a statutory commission of inquiry. As such, it was expected to have greater flexibility in its selection of topics and processes.

The Institute's directors also used their own professional backgrounds to shape the research agendas of the Institute that included work on correctional management, art and antiquities theft, drug offences, crimes against older persons and child abuse and neglect. As staff and directors came and went, so the research topics dealt with changed. The various reviews conducted into the work of the Institute, particularly those in 1993–1994 (Coad et al. 1994; Tanzer et al. 1994), also sought to change the focus of research away from state and territory criminal justice concerns to those of the Commonwealth (see James and Sutton 1994 for a commentary of this). Of course, the bulk of crime is, constitutionally, a state and territory concern and, accordingly, state and territory interests always remained important.

To illustrate how topics changed throughout the fifty years, the number of *Trends and Issues* papers published in each decade were counted for each of the above crime type categories, with the results shown in Fig. 10.2.

From Fig. 10.2, it is apparent that some topics were more prevalent during the early years of the publication series, such as research relating to the criminal justice institutions of corrections and policing as well as serious violent crimes such as homicide and trends in crime

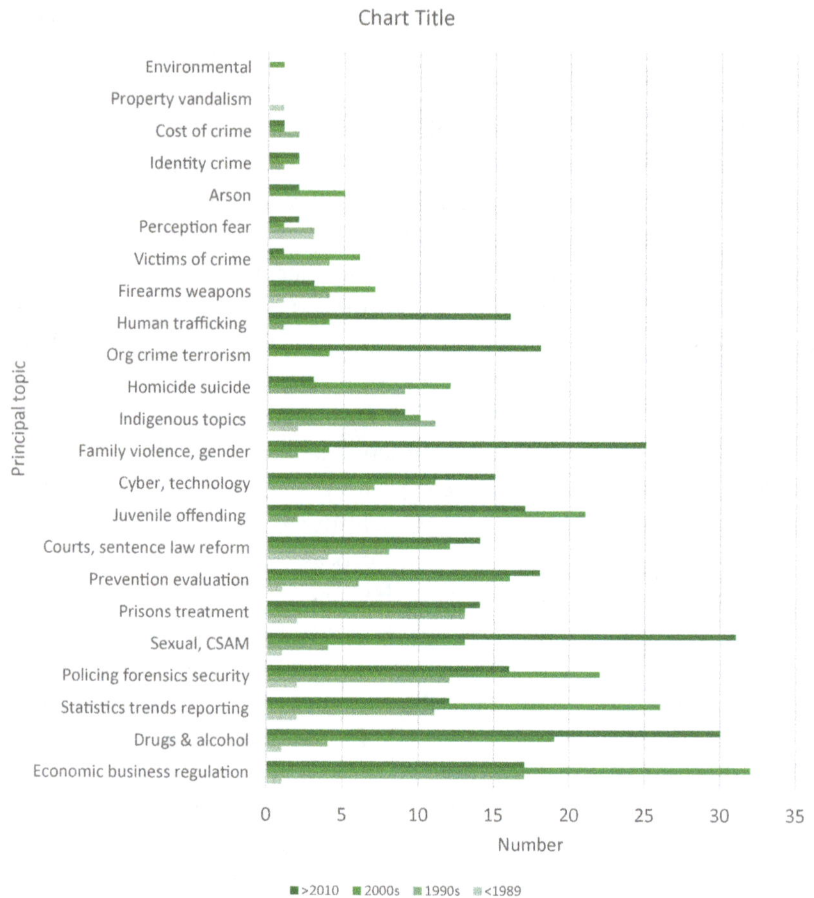

Fig. 10.2 Principal categories of research examined in *Trends and Issues* papers, by decade (number) (*Source* Derived from AIC Publications listing, http://www. aic.gov.au/publications/current%20series/tandi.html)

statistics. Since the 2000s, there has been an increase in publications on economic crime and cybercrime, while since the 2010s publications on drugs, organised crime, sexual offending and family violence have increased substantially. Although Director Adam Tomison was able to promote research on domestic violence and child abuse, he argued in his interview that now 'perhaps there is too much emphasis on that to the detriment of other areas – although these are key social issues and it's good that AIC is at the forefront of research knowledge yet again' (Adam Tomison, Interview, 26 October 2022).

As we have seen in Chapter 6, above, the topics chosen for *Trends and Issues* papers, differed a good deal from those present in research funded by the CRC with the principal differences arising from a higher proportion of CRC-funded projects relating to criminal justice institutional topics such as corrections, the courts and policing as well as juvenile justice research and crime trends. Indigenous justice topics were also more prevalent in CRC-funded research than in *Trends and Issues* papers.

One topic of research that has been notably absent from the Institute's publications has been crimes against the environment. Apart from a comprehensive review published by Bricknell (2010) and occasional papers on specific issues such as crime in the fisheries industry, farm crime and illegal logging, the area of environmental crime is likely to take on increased importance as the effects of climate change continue to affect society. The economic impact of environmental crime is also in need of further research in Australia and internationally (see Smith and Hickman 2022). As Samantha Bricknell observed in her interview (21 November 2022): 'it would be really neat for the AIC to innovate on that front because I'm not sure who else could do it'.

Research Methodologies

One of the enduring challenges that faced the Institute throughout its history was the choice between collecting new information and quantitative data, or simply providing analysis and interpretation of data collected by others—be they academics or other government research agencies. This raised complex questions as to the role of the organisation, the ability of its staff to conduct quantitative research, whether other bodies were better suited to undertake these tasks, and if the Institute was funded sufficiently well to enable it to collect and analyse large statistical collections.

Statistical Analysis

In the mid-1970s, graduates with an interest in criminal justice research tended to be trained in law or humanities or were practitioners with policing or correctional agencies. Few had any training in statistics, apart from those who had undertaken psychology degrees at University. The AICs first cohort of researchers included mainly lawyers and criminal justice practitioners who had little experience in quantitative research and crime statistics. The exceptions were Cedric Bullard, a sociologist, who began at the Institute in 1974 (Plate 10.6) and who took on responsibility for data collection and analysis, Satyanshu Mukherjee who began in 1977 and John Walker who started in 1980, the latter two having had formal training in quantitative research and experience with crime statistics.

Sat Mukherjee joined the AIC in 1977 and retired in 2000–the second-longest serving member of the research staff. Prior to coming to

Plate 10.6   Cedric Bullard, Principal Statistician, 1974–1978 (*Source* AIC Archives)

Australia, he worked at the UN Social Defence Institute in Rome having an impressive curriculum vitae including a Bachelor of Arts degree and a Master's degree in economics from Agra University in India, a postgraduate Diploma in Criminology at the Tata Institute of Social Science, a Master's degree in criminology from the University of Pennsylvania, a PhD in social work at the University of Delhi and a PhD in sociology at the University of Pennsylvania. At the AIC, Sat was instrumental in establishing and developing the Institute's crime datasets over two decades and represented the Institute throughout Australia and internationally including at UN Congresses on the Prevention of Crime and Treatment of Offenders (Plate 10.7).

Following Sat's death in August 2021, Richard Harding observed:

His book, *Crime Trends in Twentieth Century Australia*, published in 1981, was an enormous breakthrough for those of us working in the field of

Plate 10.7 (l-r) Director Bill Clifford and Dr Satyanshu Mukherjee just before they both attended the preparatory meeting for the 6th UN Congress in Ottawa in June 1978 (*Source* AIC Archives)

criminology. Before then, there were simply bits and pieces, differing by jurisdiction, confusing to interpret. My friend, the distinguished US criminologist Franklin Zimring, attended a conference with me (on gun control) at the AIC late in 1981, and he said that 'this is a $10 million dollar piece of work.' The point he was trying to make in the hearing of sceptical bureaucrats, is that good data is priceless. (Smith 2021, p. 20)

In 1980, Sat was joined at the Institute by John Walker who undertook a series of other quantitative studies over the following 15 years (Plate 10.8). In his interview, John admitted that he didn't know much about criminology at the time and had qualified in economics from LSE in London in 1969 before coming to Australia. John explained the circumstances in which he came to the Institute as follows.

While I was working in Canberra for the Department of Environment, Housing and Community Development, I was looking for new directions. The AIC had discovered that the guy who helped Sat Mukherjee with basic statistics and entered the data onto the CSIROs mainframe computer (then the biggest in the southern hemisphere, and extremely expensive to rent time on) was misusing the Institute's expensive computer access. On being asked to leave, he 'wiped' Sat's entire body of work from the CSIRO machine. Sat had been researching and writing his seminal work *Crime Trends in Twentieth Century Australia*, covering the period 1900 to 1976. The AIC then clearly needed a new 'computer guy with some data analysis skills', and a work colleague recommended me to his friend Sat Mukherjee. (John Walker, Interview, 30 November 2020)

Apart from Sat, David Biles and John, there were few researchers with in-depth data analysis skills at the AIC at that time, and after John recovered the missing data for Sat's publication (Mukherjee et al. 1981), he was asked to provide 'number crunching' for the other AIC researchers who often struggled with quantitative research. During a secondment to the Home Office in the UK in 1988, John worked with Pat Mayhew and other European colleagues on developing the ICVS–that Australia participated in between 1989 and 2004 (see Johnson 2005). Back in Australia, John also developed the early methodology for the AICs regular costs

Plate 10.8 John Walker BSc (Econ) (London), Criminologist, 1980–1995 (*Source* AIC Archives)

of crime assessments–that continue to this day. As John noted, '[i]t dawned on me the extent to which criminologists ignored the economics of crime, and economists ignored the criminal economy' (John Walker, Interview, 30 November 2020).

As we have seen in Chapter 3, above, having trained quantitative researchers and statisticians at the Institute raised the question as to whether or not it should go down the path of collecting crime statistics itself. This debate has remained current throughout the Institute's history, resulting in legislative changes, and approaches to quantitative research differing as new directors came and went. Generally, the Institute has sought to match its research methodologies to the needs of the topics being examined–although almost all research projects have had a statistical, quantitative research basis, with some using more sophisticated statistical analytic techniques than others. During Toni Makkai's directorship, the emphasis on using more advanced analytic techniques for research increased greatly, with Makkai arranging for the, then current, Statistical Package for the Social Sciences (SPSS) to be replaced by STATA that permitted users to generate their own command codes rather than relying on Graphic User Interfaces (GUIs) in SPSS. Although the sophistication of STATA for data entry and statistical analysis was much richer than with SPSS, staff were required to undergo substantial training to become proficient with STATA. It was also complicated and difficult to use for generating charts in publications, and files were unable to be kept on some network drives. For survey research, the Institute purchased licences for a number of different programs, each with their own challenges and each requiring training to be undertaken and software adapted to the needs of the AIC. Qualitative research also required the purchase of appropriate software licences and, again, staff needed advanced training.

After Toni Makkai left the Institute, researchers continued to use STATA and other software for data analysis such as 'R', although it was invariably difficult to recruit new staff with experience of using STATA–thus requiring them to undergo further training. Generally, there has been a small number of researchers with statistical skills, mostly coming from a background in psychology, with the remaining research staff either not requiring these skills for the non-quantitative work they did, or relying on others in the Institute to assist when needed. For some projects, data collection and analysis was outsourced to consultants with the relevant skills–if budgets allowed. The difficulty remains, particularly in times when research staffing numbers were low, that there were insufficient staff able to undertake this kind of work, leaving those skilled in statistical analysis, having an increased workload.

Forensic Research

Often, the discipline of criminology is confused or conflated with forensic science, with some criminology students undertaking courses in order to pursue careers in forensic science, forensic pathology or criminal profiling. Although the AIC has undertaken some research touching on forensic science, such as the legality and effectiveness of DNA evidence in criminal proceedings (Weiser Easteal and Easteal 1990; Smith and Mann 2015), the use of biometrics (Franks and Smith 2021) and cloud authentication and forensics (Choo and Slay 2016), generally directors and Boards have decided to leave forensic research to dedicated law enforcement agencies and coronial offices that specialise in these fields. In determining applications for funding provided by the CRC/CRG, it has generally been the policy that funding will not be provided for research that falls within the normal operational responsibilities of government departments, or institutions, or which is more appropriately funded by other research bodies. This invariably makes pure forensic work ineligible.

In the 2020s, however, following the partial merger with the ACC/ACIC, the Institute decided to create a Serious and Organised Crime Research Laboratory, headed by Anthony Morgan (Plate 10.9) to facilitate research on large datasets such as those maintained by law enforcement agencies and the ACC/ACIC.

In his interview (17 November 2022), Morgan described the rationale and aims of the laboratory:

> The idea of the branding of the Lab was to create a new capability within the AIC that was progressive and would focus on the analysis of big datasets and use machine learning in a new way. This arose partly because we now had access to data that we've never had before.

It transpired however, that for the kind of research that the Lab undertook, it was not necessary to acquire and make use of software and hardware that would be needed to analyse big data and linked datasets, as the research undertaken was not making use of extremely large volumes of data. The AICs Laboratory has, however, produced a number of publications that have made use of de-identified data that previously were unavailable for analysis. Examples include research on the prediction of high-harm offending among outlaw motor cycle gangs using machine learning (Cubitt and Morgan 2022) and a study of the criminal histories

Plate 10.9   Anthony Morgan, Research Manager, Serious and Organised Crime Research Laboratory, AIC (*Source* AIC Archives)

of a sample of 3,007 individuals affiliated with known organised crime groups using trajectory analysis (Morgan and Payne 2021).

Survey Research

Throughout its history, the AIC and the CRC undertook to conduct, or to fund, a wide variety of projects involving survey research. These included individual victimisation surveys such as those relating to cyber-scams or domestic violence, business victimisation surveys, such as those focussed on farm crime, surveys of professionals such as the legal and other sectors regulated by the Australian Transaction Reports and Analysis Centre (AUSTRAC) and surveys of government entities such as the Commonwealth fraud census. Some of these have been devised and administered by AIC staff in-house, while others have been developed by the AIC, administered by survey consultants who provide online panels of participants. Data analysis is the undertaken by AIC staff who add value to the findings by referring to the criminological literature. On other occasions, an entire survey has been undertaken by consultants–usually owing to the unavailability of staff and resources within the AIC, or the need for results to be gathered within a short time frame. One of the benefits of this approach noted by Research Manager, Anthony Morgan, in his interview (17 November 2022) is for survey research to be conducted with large samples much more quickly than would be the case if undertaken by central statistical agencies. The disadvantage is that online panels are usually less representative of the population than probability samples.

In addition to victimisation surveys, the AIC has undertaken a number of projects that have analysed administrative datasets such as coronial records for the homicide monitoring reports, or police or prosecution files relating to specific crime types such as fraud or sentencing outcomes. Most recently, the AIC has undertaken data analysis of digital records relevant to patterns of offending in areas such as online child abuse and access to child abuse materials–in one case involving access to international datasets.

Legal and Legislative Research

In the early years of the Institute's research, a number of staff were legally qualified and were able to undertake studies involving legal and legislative analysis. Most of this work entailed legal analysis of sentencing decisions, but more recent research has explored jurisprudence of cybercrime legislation and DNA evidence in criminal matters. In 1975, for example, the AIC had a dedicated Legal Affairs Section headed by Mary Daunton-Fear who was a member of the International Law Association and on the Executive of the ACPC. She was one of the first scholars in Australia to conduct extensive research into sentencing, beginning with a project to publish volumes documenting the sentencing jurisprudence in each of the Australian states. Her first book dealt with Western Australia (Daunton-Fear 1977) followed by South Australia (Daunton-Fear 1980). Others at the AIC in the 1970s who continued this line of research included David Biles, Ivan Potas, John Newton and Arie Freiberg. One AIC publication arose from a question by Lionel Murphy, then Attorney-General, to David Biles in 1975: 'what the meaning of life means'. This wasn't an existential inquiry but a request for research into the duration of life sentences actually served. David and Arie Frieberg took up the challenge and presented a 183 page report later in 1975 (Freiberg and Biles 1975). This prompt response to a Minister's passing request was obviously a credit to the authors as well as the Institute (Peter Grabosky, Interview, 3 December 2020). Mary Daunton-Fear and others continued to develop their interest in sentencing with further publications on specific sentencing dispositions and types of offenders, such as women, Aborigines, habitual criminals and others.

As the number of legally-trained AIC researchers declined, and as legal library subscriptions were cancelled, it was more likely that legal research would be undertaken by AGD–where a number of former AIC staff members were employed. On numerous occasions, however, AIC projects entailed the use of multiple methodologies in which empirical research was integrated with legal and policy analysis–often undertaken by teams of suitably qualified AIC personnel.

Green-Fields Research

One type of research that was infrequently undertaken was novel, exploratory research on new crime types, new theoretical approaches or new crime prevention approaches. Such studies were often difficult to sell to directors and Board members who needed to demonstrate a level of trust in the ability of the researchers to undertake such research that would be likely to yield cost-effective findings. On the few occasions, where this has occurred, the outcomes have, indeed, been worthwhile. Examples include John Braithwaite's research on white-collar crime, Jocelynne Scutt's work on violence against women, Peter Grabosky's co-production of crime control initiatives, John Walker's costs of crime analyses, Toni Makkai's DUMA research, Jerry Ratcliffe's research into geo-spatial crime mapping, Samantha Bricknell's environmental crime research and the studies of cybercrime and anti-money laundering conducted by Peter Grabosky and the present author. Current projects involving new methods to explore child sexual abuse, modern slavery and organised crime are also likely to produce valuable new methodologies and findings. Most of this work has been undertaken by AIC researchers in-house rather than by external academics funded by the CRC and AIC–often because of the difficulty of convincing Council members that funding such novel areas of research would be beneficial. Similar problems have arisen for researchers trying to persuade other funding bodies, such as the ARC, of the need to be adventurous in supporting green-fields research. On a number of occasions, novel and boutique research topics have been suggested by AIC researchers themselves mainly arising from personal interest or prior research undertaken prior to joining the Institute. The present author's work on medical misconduct, telemedicine, human tissue transplantation, Millennium crime risks, GST fraud and electronic voting were all novel topics that some directors and Boards supported while others took more persuasion.

Challenges in Conducting Research in the Public Sector

Conducting criminological research in the public sector raises a number of specific, idiosyncratic challenges that are less likely to be present in other academic environments or in private sector consultancies. The most contentious and difficult to resolve for the AIC have been in relation to how confidential government information is dealt with, how personal identifying information is handled and how human research ethics protocols are employed in government research.

Dealing with Confidential Information

Conducting research within government carries with it certain restrictions and obligations to ensure that confidential information is not released publicly. The AICs research reports and *Trends and Issues* papers not only undergo academic peer-reviewing, but also have to progress through a number of levels of official approval–largely to ensure that officials are not taken by surprise when the reports are released that may attract media attention. At the AIC, reports are checked by research line managers, copy editors, typesetters, the AICs (Deputy) Director, and in recent years the CEO of the ACIC, communications officers, Ministerial staffers and relevant Ministers. Each has an opportunity to provide suggestions for improvement of publications, and, in the experience of the present author, censorship of content has not occurred–although changes in expression and emphasis have been required as part of the editorial and publication process. In very recent years, following a period during which Ministerial approval was often subject to lengthy delays, a decision was made to present the Institute's publications to the Minister for noting (rather than approval as in the past) on the understanding that they would be released publicly after the expiration of 14 days. This was usually achieved by simply placing new reports on the Institute's website–unlike in earlier times when Ministers released reports in person, often accompanied by elaborate media conferences.

In the case of research that has made use of confidential, or security-classified data or information, the level of scrutiny given to reports has been much more intensive, both from within the AICs portfolio agencies but also from other departments that have funded or procured the research. Scrutiny of publications is undertaken not only to protect the identity of individual public officials, particularly intelligence officers, but also members of the public whose private information may be held by governments under confidentiality obligations imposed by privacy or individual departmental legislation. On other occasions, political interests may lead to research not being published in its original form, or its public release delayed to a more politically-palatable time–sometime years into the future. Such restrictions are not unique to government research, in Australia or internationally, with some University or private sector consultancy reports never being publicly released owing to the terms of funding contracts or conditions on how data were obtained.

Difficulties in having government research reports released are not unique to criminology, and during the coronavirus pandemic in 2020, much medical research that contained sensitivities in terms of government policy, sometimes lead to unnecessary restrictions being imposed on publication due to political advisers being overly risk-averse. This has happened to AIC research reports on a number of occasions, including instances in which, objectively, the findings being reported were innocuous–simply presenting information already available to the public. Some public officials believed that gathering information together in a single report, albeit coming from publicly-available sources, could create undue attention to the topic in question that otherwise might have been overlooked. The recent alignment of the AIC with the ACIC has, although the AIC continues to be an independent statutory authority, led to greater scrutiny being undertaken prior to the release of publications, as well as scrutiny of media contacts and reporting in social media. As will be examined below, there was a good deal of concern that the proposed merger between the AIC and the ACIC would result in the Institute's research becoming less available to the public. In a submission to the Senate Legal and Constitutional Affairs Legislation Committee on the Australian Crime Commission Amendment (Criminology Research) Bill 2016, former director, Adam Graycar, argued that:

> If [the AIC's] future outputs come through an intelligence agency there are two likely scenarios. One is that much of what is researched will not be publicly available as it will be stamped with a security classification. The second is that it might not be believed, as coming from an intelligence agency people might always question hidden agenda and transparency of methodology and data. In short, people are less likely to take the output seriously and give it credibility. Without credibility research is hollow. (Graycar 2016, n.p.)

After seven years of working closely with the ACIC, the Institute's research output has not been overly restricted–indeed, since October 2015, 295 AIC reports have been released on the AICs website. On the rare occasions where confidential or classified material has been used in the AICs research, the decision has been taken to release tandem reports—one including classified material that remains confidential, and another, excluding classified material, that is suitable for public release. The AIC has undertaken this strategy on a number of occasions, both before and after the MoG process in 2015. Although declassified reports can be of some use to the general public in demonstrating that research has, at least, been conducted on a particular topic, it is sometimes impossible for details of methodology or finely-grained data to be fully understood once reports have been sanitised. It is, of course, important for the names and identifying information regarding intelligence analysts, or informers to be withheld, but the risk arises that the process of redaction can lead to findings being difficult to understand if their contextual background is unable to be published. There is, in addition, the risk that governments can redact research reports unnecessarily extensively for political reasons. The Institute's recent association with the ACIC has, on the whole, avoided these problems although the risk remains that if research is published in sanitised form it may be harder to follow and difficult to replicate.

Freedom of Information and Privacy

The advent of Freedom of Information legislation in 1982 in Australia provided an opportunity for members of the public, and journalists in particular, to attempt to find out what government research has been conducted on sensitive topics that might not have been publicly released. The AIC is required to adhere to the obligations for disclosure of government documents under the *Freedom of Information Act 1982* (Cth), but it can refuse access to some documents, or parts of documents, that are exempt under the Act. Exempt documents may include those relating to national security, documents containing material obtained in confidence and Cabinet documents or other matters as set out in the legislation.

Since 1982, there have been occasional requests made for the release of documents under the Act and one or two documents released annually. Since 1 May 2011, the AIC has been required by Section 11C of the *Freedom of Information Act 1982* (Cth) to publish a disclosure log that lists information that has been released in response to a Freedom of Information access request. Prior to this, less data exist regarding requests made and information provided.

Requests for information have generally related to unpublished reports and drafts of reports, internal evaluations of projects, unpublished statistics, correspondence and peer reviewer reports on AIC publications. Data on the number of requests, as opposed to documents released, are not publicly available and information on the reasons for exempting access to documents is not available, other than the categories of exemption specified in the legislation such as documents relating to national security, documents containing material obtained in confidence and Cabinet documents or other exemptions set out in Part IV of the Act.

In order to obtain access to personal information collected by other agencies for research purposes, the AIC has also made use of the Public Interest Determination provisions of the *Privacy Act 1988* (Cth). In 2019, for example, the AIC obtained a Public Interest Determination to allow the AFP to disclose personal information regarding a homicide offender in the Australian Capital Territory for the purposes of the AICs National Homicide Monitoring Program (OAIC 2019). Earlier, in 2002, the Privacy Commissioner made a determination allowing disclosure, by the Commonwealth Director of Public Prosecutions (CDPP) of personal information to the AIC pertaining to cases of serious fraud, dishonesty and deception. This was obtained for the *Serious Fraud in Australia and New Zealand* research project undertaken by the AIC in collaboration with PricewaterhouseCoopers and published in 2003 (AIC/PwC 2003). The ability of the AIC to undertake these resource intensive, slow and difficult procedures to facilitate the gathering of data for research projects is a further indication of the ability of complex research to be undertaken within government that might be impossible for academic scholars to achieve.

Similarly difficult research designs have been used by AIC staff to conduct surveys of business entities. For example, in 2007, a survey of Australia's business sector was conducted for the *Australian Business Assessment of Computer User Security* study in order to quantify cases of cybercrime affecting this sector, the costs involved and response activities undertaken. To obtain a national sampling frame, access to the ABS Australian Business Register was sought requiring approval from the Australian Government Statistician, the Statistical Clearing House and Parliamentary Tabling–again a lengthy, costly and complex process designed to reduce 'survey burden' on the business sector caused by unnecessary government surveys of the sector. From a population of over 900,000, a sample of over 20,000 was developed with 4,000 fully interviewed. The results of this study were published by Richards (2009) and Challice (2009).

Another survey was conducted as part of the AICs research into anti-money laundering and counter-terrorism financing (AML/CTF) in 2009. Again, in order to obtain a national sampling frame, a determination under Section 121(3)(a) of the *Anti-Money Laundering and Counter Terrorism Financing Act 2006* (Cth) had to be obtained from AUSTRACs Chief Executive Officer to permit the disclosure to the AIC of AUSTRACs list of over 10,000 reporting entities enrolled with AUSTRAC. This was necessary so that the AIC could conduct the survey of all AML/CTF officers to obtain their views regarding the operation and effectiveness of the legislation. The findings of this were published by Walters et al. (2012). Again, these types of national research would be difficult, if not impossible, for researchers located outside government to undertake.

Ethics Protocols in Public Sector Research

Following the Second World War in which unethical human experimentation was undertaken in detention and concentration camps by the Nazis, the World Medical Assembly in 1964 adopted what came to be known as the Helsinki Declaration that set out principles and procedures for medical research. This also applied to social scientific research involving humans and became accepted for criminologists conducting research in universities. In Australia in October 1983, the National Health and Medical Research Council issued its *National Statement on Human Experimentation and Supplementary Notes* that were subsequently revised in November 1992 as *the National Statement on Ethical Conduct in Research Involving Humans* (NHMRC 1992). The current Statement released in July 2018 (NHMRC 2018) is currently undergoing revisions following public consultation that was completed in 2020 (NHMRC 2021).

In 1992, the Commonwealth Government determined to establish Human Research Ethics Committees (HREC) in a number of federal agencies including the AIHW, the ANU and the AIC, among others who were involved in the conduct on research involving human participants. For a social science research body, applying the principles designed for medical research presented a number of difficulties, particularly concerning obtaining consent from participants who are being covertly observed during observational studies and examining documentary and archival records from criminal justice agencies that contain personal information. Nonetheless, the AIC established its own HREC in 1993, registered this with the NHMRC (No. EC 00102) and gradually became compliant with the National Statement over time. Soon after the establishment of the AICs HREC, the AICs Director was advised that:

> [T]he composition of your ethics committee is not in accordance with NHMRC guidelines. You would need to add a medical graduate with research experience... However, I would note that the NHMRC guidelines are directed principally towards medical research and may not sufficiently accommodate the needs of institutions such as the AIC. (Letter from Linda R. Gowing to Duncan Chappell, 30 July 1993, AIC Archives)

Creating a HREC for a criminological research institute, although understandable within universities, was not always considered necessary or appropriate within government agencies generally—and also within private sector consultancies (that often conducted interviews and examined confidential datasets as part of what is essentially social scientific research). At this time, research conducted by law enforcement and correctional agencies rarely had HREC oversight, and it was not until the mid-2000s in Australia that criminal justice agencies started to become compliant with the National Statement. Victoria Police, for example, set up its own HREC in 2005 under the chairmanship of the current author. Other police and intelligence agencies, however, continued to gather information from 'assets' in much more invasive ways and, although they were required to comply with extensive statutory obligations before doing so, they did not perceive their tasks as involving 'research' that would require Ethics Committee approval. Other government entities and consultancies in the private sector simply relied on their own professional standards when engaging in activities that clearly amounted to human research, such as conducting surveys and interviews.

The first Chair of the AICs HREC was Dr Valerie Braithwaite (Plate 10.10), now Emeritus Professor at the Regulatory Institutions Network (RegNet) at ANU. In 1993, she was Director of the Centre for Tax System Integrity, and from 2006 to 2008 Head of RegNet in the Research School of Pacific and Asian Studies. Her disciplinary background in psychology was invaluable in dealing with the ethical challenges presented by criminological research within government. Meetings at the time were held three times a year with an initial membership of seven representing each of the required qualifications dictated by the NHMRC. On occasions, it was difficult to recruit members, particularly clergy, sometimes making the committee non-compliant, but as the AIC only rarely obtained NHMRC funding, this was tolerated. During the early years of the 2000s, the Committee dealt with relatively small numbers of applications, and few were rejected, although methodologies were sometimes subject to revision. Over time, as the numbers of applications increased, it became difficult to have all matters dealt with promptly, although in some cases urgent applications were dealt with out-of-session.

Between 1992 and 2022, the AICs HREC dealt with over 300 applications, in addition to considering some requests for exemption and advice on whether applications were necessary. As the number of HRECs has increased across the criminal justice sector, AIC researchers have been required in recent times to apply to multiple HRECs from multiple states and territories and multiple agencies. The NHMRCs protocols for avoiding duplication of processes have not, however, always been successful in reducing unnecessary or multiple approvals.

Plate 10.10 Dr Valerie Braithwaite, AIC, HREC Chair (*Source* Valerie Braithwaite)

Some of the more difficult applications related to research involving children or people in dependent relationships, people involved in illegal activities who might be asked to make admissions of having committed criminal offences, Aboriginal and Torres Strait Islanders and people whose primary language was not English, and most recently, since the relationship with the ACIC commenced, questions of conducting research on classified intelligence. Difficult questions also arose when researchers sought to interview offenders and victims of crime. In 1993, for example, the research methodology adopted in a study of marital violence in migrant communities had to be changed by removing interviews with offenders and changing the sampling protocols for victims of domestic violence to ensure that free consent was present and confidentiality maintained (AIC Archives, correspondence 8 July 1993). These difficulties arose continually with research on these topics throughout the AICs history. Valerie Braithwaite's appointment as Chair of the AICs

Committee was seen as a way to moderate some of the excessive zeal of some Ethics Committees that was inappropriate for the social sciences. As John Braithwaite argued (Interview, 30 January 2021), both Valerie and I worried 'about the over-reach of the Ethics Committee in ways that were going to kill-off criminological research so that no-one would ever do a victim survey or a self-report delinquency survey again'.

Thematic Conclusions

The five themes identified in Chapter 1 have particular relevance to the conduct of criminological research in organisations such as the AIC. The first theme concerned the differences that arose between criminological research conducted in the public sector generally and that carried out by academic criminologists based in higher educational institutions. The research topics addressed by the AIC included a higher proportion dealing with criminal justice entities than those undertaken by academic criminologists, and AIC research was able to address a number of boutique crime types that many academics had initially ignored–including money laundering, human slavery, bushfire arson and cybercrime.

The second theme concerned the focus of the AICs research on Commonwealth as opposed to state and territory interests. In terms of the research undertaken, the Institute achieved a reasonable balance between these two sometimes opposing interests, although in the most recent decade, there has been an increased emphasis on research focussing on the Commonwealth rather than the states and territories, largely due to the partial merger with the ACIC. Recent research has also examined more transnational crime questions that have greater relevance to the Commonwealth than to the states and territories.

The third theme dealt with the methods of research used in the public sector as opposed to those employed in the private sector and in the academy. The AICs research, particularly in its early years, included more descriptive statistical content than University-based research that focussed more often on theoretical critiques and, in the case of quantitative research, often undertook more sophisticated statistical data analysis.

The fourth theme related to the extent to which critical, left-realist or sociological approaches were adopted. The AIC clearly had to tread a fine line between undertaking research that provided objective evidence that might be critical of government policies and research that supported the views of serving governments. Although the Institute's publications often included discussion of policy implications of the research findings, there was rarely any strident criticism of government policies expressed–and on the occasions where this did occur, repercussions were swift. The Institute's research was, however, often discussed frankly with departmental staff in confidential meetings where policy criticism could be presented without fear of publicity. Some topics were, however, avoided by the Institute owing to their political sensitivities, allowing academics and consultants to provide the necessary input.

The final theme that focussed on the financing of public sector criminological research showed some obvious differences between the work of the AIC and that conducted in universities. Generally, the AIC was unable to seek research funding from conventional sources, such as the ARC, but instead had greater opportunities than universities to obtain funding from other government departments–particularly the Commonwealth. Often, however, the amount of departmental funding was modest and timelines far shorter than for academic research, thus requiring research methods to be less elaborate and with a shorter duration than academic criminologists might expect. In seeking research funding from within government, however, the AIC was often not required to undertake the extensive application procedures that funding bodies such as the ARC require, instead sometimes obtaining funding on the basis of concise and unrefereed submissions. Another advantage of seeking internal government funding was that the AIC was often able to secure further, ongoing funding to enable longitudinal data collections to be undertaken without having to repeat detailed justifications for further research on each occasion.

References

Australian Government. 2022. *National Plan to Combat Cybercrime.* Canberra: Department of Home Affairs. https://www.homeaffairs.gov.au/criminal-justice/files/national-plan-combat-cybercrime-2022.pdf. Accessed 16 November 2022.

Australian Institute of Criminology and PricewaterhouseCoopers (AIC/PwC). 2003. *Serious Fraud in Australia and New Zealand.* Research and Public Policy Series, No. 48. Canberra: Australian Institute of Criminology/ PricewaterhouseCoopers.

Australian Institute of Criminology (AIC). 2022. *Corporate Plan 2021–22.* Canberra: Australian Institute of Criminology. https://www.aic.gov.au/sites/default/files/2021-07/aic_corporate_plan_2021-22.pdf. Accessed 8 February 2022.

Australian Law Reform Commission (ALRC). 1980. *Sentencing of Federal Offenders.* Report No. 15. Canberra: AGPS.

Australian Law Reform Commission (ALRC). 1981. *Child Welfare.* Report No. 18. Canberra: AGPS.

Bricknell, Samantha. 2010. *Environmental Crime in Australia.* Research and Public Policy Series, No. 109. Canberra: Australian Institute of Criminology.

Brown, David. 1994. Facing the Knife. *Alternative Law Journal* 19 (3): 125–128. http://www6.austlii.edu.au/cgi-bin/viewdoc/au/journals/AltLawJl/1994/59.html. Accessed 18 September 2020.

Carson, Kit, and Pat O'Malley. 1989. The Institutional Foundations of Contemporary Australian Criminology. *Australian and New Zealand Journal of Sociology* 25 (3): 333–355.

Challice, Graham. 2009. *The Australian Business Assessment of Computer User Security (ABACUS) Survey: Methodology Report.* Technical and Background Paper, No. 32. Canberra: Australian Institute of Criminology. https://www.aic.gov.au/publications/tbp/tbp32.

Chappell, Duncan. 1983. Australia. In *International Handbook of Contemporary Developments in Criminology: Europe, Africa, the Middle East and Asia,* ed. Elliott Johnson. London: Greenwood Press.

Choo, Kim-Kwang Raymond, and Jill Slay. 2016. *Cloud Authentication and Forensics.* National Drug Law Enforcement Research Fund (NDLERF) Monograph No. 69. Canberra: Australian Institute of Criminology.

Coad, William J., Prudence Ford, Malcolm Hazell, Peter Lamb, Norman Reaburn, and Adrian Whiddett. 1994. *Report of the Review of Commonwealth Law Enforcement Arrangements*. Canberra: Australian Government Publishing Service.

Cubitt, Timothy, and Anthony Morgan. 2022. *Predicting High-Harm Offending Using Machine Learning: An Application to Outlaw Motorcycle Gangs*. Trends and Issues in Crime and Criminal Justice, No 646. Canberra: Australian Institute of Criminology.

Daunton-Fear, Mary. 1977. *Sentencing in Western Australia*. St Lucia: University of Queensland Press in association with the AIC.

Daunton-Fear, Mary. 1980. *Sentencing in South Australia*. Sydney: Law Book Co. Ltd. in association with the AIC.

Department of Home Affairs. 2022. *Portfolio Budget Statements: Australian Institute of Criminology 2022–23*. Canberra: Department of Home Affairs.

Franks, Christie, and Russell G. Smith. 2021. *Changing Perceptions of Biometric Technologies*. Research Report No. 20. Canberra: Australian Institute of Criminology.

Fraser, Malcolm. 1981. Ministerial Statement on the Review of Commonwealth Functions, *Parliamentary Debates*. House of Representatives, 30 April, p. 1838.

Freiberg, Arie, and David Biles. 1975. *The Meaning of 'Life': A Study of Life Sentences in Australia*. Canberra: Australian Institute of Criminology. https://www.aic.gov.au/publications/archive/archive-129. Accessed 26 May 2022.

Graycar, Adam. 2016. *Submission to the Senate Legal and Constitutional Affairs Legislation Committee on the Australian Crime Commission Amendment (Criminology Research) Bill 2016*. Canberra: Parliament House.

James, Steve, and Adam Sutton. 1994. Criminology and Crime Control in Australia. *Australian and New Zealand Journal of Criminology* 27 (3): 299–308.

Johnson, Holly. 2005. Crime Victimisation in Australia: Key Findings of the 2004 International Crime Victimisation Survey. *Trends and Issues in Crime and Criminal Justice* no. 298. Canberra: Australian Institute of Criminology.

Loof, Peter R. 1979. *Establishment of the Australian Institute of Criminology and the Criminology Research Council: Proposals, Criteria and Negotiations Associated with the Establishment of the Institute and the Council*. Canberra: Attorney-General's Department.

McDonald, D. I., and C. Moore. 1981. *Review of the Staff and Organisational Structure of the Australian Institute of Criminology*. Management and Special

Services Division. Canberra: Attorney-General's Department (Referred to in AIC, Minutes, 14 December 1981, p. 4).

Morgan, Anthony, and Jason Payne. 2021. *Organised Crime and Criminal Careers: Findings from an Australian Sample*. Trends and Issues in Crime and Criminal Justice, No. 637. Canberra: Australian Institute of Criminology.

Mukherjee, Satyanshu K., Evelyn N. Jacobsen, John R. Walker, and Robert W. Fitzgerald. 1981. *Crime Trends in Twentieth Century Australia*. North Sydney: George Allen and Unwin Australia.

National Health and Medical Research Council (NHMRC). 1992. *National Statement on Ethical Conduct in Research Involving Humans*. Canberra: NHMRC.

National Health and Medical Research Council (NHMRC). 2018. *National Statement on Ethical Conduct in Human Research*. Canberra: NHMRC.

National Health and Medical Research Council (NHMRC). 2021. *Public Consultation on National Statement Content*. Canberra: NHMRC. https://www.nhmrc.gov.au/research-policy/ethics/national-statement-ethical-conduct-human-research. Accessed 26 June 2021.

Office of the Australian Information Commissioner (OAIC). 2019. *Privacy (Disclosure of Homicide Data) Public Interest Determination 2019*. https://www.legislation.gov.au/Details/F2019L00322. Accessed 4 July 2021.

Richards, Kelly. 2009. *The Australian Business Assessment of Computer User Security: A National Survey*. Research and Public Policy Series, No. 102. Canberra: Australian Institute of Criminology. https://www.aic.gov.au/publications/rpp/rpp102.

Seymour, John. 1988. *Dealing with Young Offenders*. Sydney: Law Book Company Ltd.

Smith, Marcus, and Monique Mann. 2015. *Recent Developments in DNA Evidence*. Trends and Issues in Crime and Criminal Justice, No. 506. Canberra: Australian Institute of Criminology.

Smith, Russell G. 2021. Obituary: Dr Satyanshu Kumar Mukherjee. *PacifiCrim: ANZSOC Newsletter* 18 (2): 19–20.

Smith, Russell G., and Amelia Hickman. 2022. *Estimating the Costs of Serious and Organised Crime in Australia 2020–21. Statistical Report*. Canberra: Australian Institute of Criminology. https://www.aic.gov.au/publications/sr/sr. Accessed 1 May 2022.

Tanzer, Noel, Des Hill, and Grant Wardlaw. 1994. *Review of the Australian Institute of Criminology: Report*. Canberra: Australian Institute of Criminology.

Walters, Julie, Russell G. Smith, Brent Davis, Kim-Kwang Raymond Choo, and Hannah Chadwick. 2012. *The Anti-Money Laundering and Counter-Terrorism Financing Regime in Australia: Perceptions of Regulated Businesses in Australia*. Research and Public Policy Series, No. 117. Canberra: Australian Institute of Criminology.

Weiser Easteal, Patricia, and Simon Easteal. 1990. *The Forensic Use of DNA Profiling*. Trends and Issues in Crime and Criminal Justice, No. 26. Canberra: Australian Institute of Criminology.

Wiles, Paul. 1976. *The Sociology of Crime and Delinquency in Britain*, vol. 2. Oxford: Martin Robertson.

11

Publish or Perish: The Challenges of Disseminating Research

Introduction

Effective dissemination of research is an essential function of public sector criminological research organisations. Although the collection, analysis and reporting of information lies at the heart of public sector research, its communication to policy-makers, academics, stakeholders and members of the community, both locally and internationally, is critical to ensure that research is visible and that government resourcing is justified. The ways in which, and extent to which, research is disseminated provide principal indicators against which governments are able to measure the performance of publicly-funded entities.

In the case of the AIC, its founding legislation, the *Criminology Research Act* 1971 (Cth), provided in Sect. 6 that the functions of the Institute were, among others:

...

(b) to communicate to the Commonwealth and the States the results of research conducted by the Institute;

© The Author(s), under exclusive license to Springer Nature Switzerland AG 2023
R. G. Smith, *Public Sector Criminological Research*,
https://doi.org/10.1007/978-3-031-28356-7_11

(c) to conduct such seminars and courses of training or instruction for persons engaged, or to be engaged, in criminological research or in work related to the prevention or correction of criminal behaviour as are approved by the Board;

...

(h) to publish such material resulting from or connected with the performance of its functions as is approved by the Board.

Following amendments to this Act in 1986, 2010 and 2018, these functions were varied to require the Institute:

(a) to promote justice and reduce crime by:

(i) conducting criminological research; and

(ii) communicating the results of that research to the Commonwealth, the States, the Australian Capital Territory, the Northern Territory and the community;

and, in addition, in a new Sect. 6A(1), by permitting the Minister to request the Institute:

...

(b) to conduct seminars or courses of training or instruction in a matter specified by the Minister, being seminars or courses of training or instruction for persons engaged, or to be engaged, in criminological research or in work related to the prevention or correction of criminal behaviour.

These changes principally altered the source of, or approval required for, communication activities carried out by the Institute. Following these changes, it was for the Minister to determine which seminars or courses of training or instruction should be undertaken, that previously would have been for the director to decide. In addition, the revised provisions did not require the Board to approve publication activities that simply formed part of a general communication function. The functions of the current CRAC do, however, allow the Council to advise the director in relation to setting 'the priorities for communicating the results of... research' (s. 33). This represents an important means by which the interests of states and territories can be accommodated.

In 2022, the Institute's Strategic Direction Statement provided that:

> The [AIC] undertakes and communicates evidence-based crime and justice research to inform policy and practice through: monitoring trends in crime and the criminal justice system; building knowledge of offending and victimisation; identifying emerging or changed criminal activity; and building an evidence base for an effective criminal justice system and crime prevention. (Department of Home Affairs 2022, p. 147)

The statement goes on to state that:

> The AIC provides access to information for the AICs broad range of stakeholders. Through its publication program, the AICs website, social media, library and information services, and annual series of national conferences and roundtables, the AIC disseminates research findings and information about the nature and extent of crime, emerging trends, and effective responses to promote justice and reduce crime. (Department of Home Affairs 2022, p. 148)

Various performance measures are used to determine the extent to which the Institute's principal outcome measure– 'informed crime and justice policy and practice in Australia by undertaking, funding and disseminating policy-relevant research of national significance'–has been achieved. For the budgeted year 2022–23, these were: peer reviewing procedures for the required 28 publications each year, a further 25 non-peer-reviewed publications, 2 qualitative case studies and at least 10 roundtables, workshops, seminars or other forums each year (Department of Home Affairs 2022, p. 149). Achievement of these targets is, therefore, heavily dependent on dissemination of the AICs research products. Failure to meet targets is treated seriously and can potentially result in reductions in appropriation being made.

Dissemination of Research Findings

The dissemination of research findings has been the source of tension and conflict throughout the Institute's history with Ministers, heads of agencies and their advisers all being acutely conscious of the perceived damage that the presentation of information could have where it is seen to contradict government policies. The Institute's Directors have been careful to ensure that Ministers and agency heads are fully briefed on the Institute's research before it is made public, particularly where the findings might not accord with current government policies. On occasions, Ministerial advisers and departmental communications staff have presented the results of research in ways that are favourable to the government politically–sometimes verging on distortion of actual research findings. Methods such as citing trends using the raw number of reported crimes rather than rates of recorded offences per 100,000 of the population have been used to make findings more palatable polit-ically. Similarly, reporting the raw cost of crime rather than the cost as a proportion of GDP can influence media headlines considerably. Unless, Institute staff are available, authorised and willing to comment publicly on their actual research findings, the public can be, and have been, misled.

There are various ways in which research can be disseminated within government, and the AIC has, throughout its history, undertaken each of these with differing levels of success. The most obvious means of letting governments know what criminological research has been carried out is through the preparation of reports that are provided to stakeholders within relevant public sector entities, particularly those entities that have commissioned and paid for research to be undertaken. As noted above, relationships with Ministers and heads of portfolio agencies are critical, and failure to heed their desires and interests can lead to serious finan-cial and administrative consequences. On occasions, research that went against government policies faced a difficult process prior to its release in public–sometimes being released 'ten at a time around Christmas' when media scrutiny was likely to be low (Adam Tomison, Interview, 26 October 2022). Directors had to maintain a keen understanding of the attitudes held by Ministers concerning media publicity and the dissemination of research findings. Throughout its history, the AIC has had Ministerial supporters of research and a willingness for research findings to be presented publicly, while others have been afraid of research appearing in the media and the associated questions that could be asked of what the government should be doing about the topics canvassed.

In addition to liaising with Ministers and Departmental officials, the Institute has, since its inception, had close involvement with other stakeholders. This has often involved conducting roundtable discussions, both before research projects have been undertaken, to ensure that the focus of the study will be relevant and useful, and also after research has been finalised to report back to stakeholders on the outcomes of the research. In recent years, the requirement to conduct at least ten roundtables, workshops, seminars or other forums is now one of the Institute's principal outcome measures—and has, invariably, been met.

Most roundtables have taken place at the Institute's premises, although some have taken the form of 'road-shows' in which research staff have travelled around the country, and even overseas, doing tailored presentations to targeted audiences. During 2009, for example, as part of the AICs research into anti-money laundering, five roundtables were conducted with separate groups of industry stakeholders from the unregulated sectors to assess their views as to the desirability, or otherwise, of further legislative regulation of these sectors (see Walters et al. 2013). On occasions, roundtables have been conducted for internal government officials only or have been limited to individuals with specified security classification levels on topics such as organised crime, tax fraud and financing of terrorism. Generally, however, the Institute has been keen to ensure that it maintains openness with the community, both to understand what members of the public have to say, and to let the public know what research has been conducted and what the outcomes of the research were.

The more general role of dissemination of research through the preparation of and attendance at conferences and other events is examined in the next chapter which also provides and examination of the Institute's original mandate over criminological training activities.

Publications

The primary way in which the Institute's research has been disseminated has been through the production and release of written publications. The original functions of the Institute included a specific role 'to publish such material resulting from or connected with the performance of its functions as is approved by the Board' (s. 6(h) *Criminology Research Act 1971* (Cth)). In 1986, this power was transferred to the director who was empowered to publish material taking into account the advice of the Board (see now, s. 16(h) which provides that advice of the Advisory Council should be taken into account). The publication of research originally only required the *approval* of the director, not the Minister or the Advisory Council. This helped to ensure that research that could be critical of governments, could be published, providing the director agreed. During his interview, John Walker recalled that in the 1980s, Institute staff had similar levels of freedom to publish research as University academics: 'we simply had to provide the relevant Minister with advance copies of our reports! We were able to respond regularly to requests for interviews in the media, with no constraints on what we said' (John Walker, Interview, 30 November 2020). Of course, as noted above, the publication of reports that were critical of the government could, and did, alienate the Institute from the government of the day.

Although the Institute was, and remains, a government entity and not an academic institution, it has sought to follow the usual codes of conduct for academic research applicable to the social sciences. As noted in Chapter 10, above, since 1992, the AIC has maintained a HREC and has undertaken peer review of its principal publications–although not its statistical reports and bulletins–which is, perhaps, an anomaly in its quality-control processes. The Institute has sought to follow academic standards for reporting, referencing and authorship of publications as set out in the *Australian Code for the Responsible Conduct of Research* (NHMRC, ARC and Universities Australia 2018). Although other public sector research institutes, such as AIHW, have extensive internal review processes for publications, in addition to drafts being sent to external data providers and stakeholders for feedback, formal academic blind peer review processes are not undertaken. The AIC is, therefore, unusual in using blind peer review for its major publications with the advantage being that any publications that adhere to these principles have enhanced scientific merit can be used in academic debate about social scientific research and are acceptable for peer-reviewed academic publication. Such publications can also be used by Institute staff to bolster their curricula vitae that add to their suitability for academic appointment after leaving the Institute (see Chapter 7, above).

The Institute has approached these tasks by employing staff with responsibility for managing publications, editing manuscripts, typesetting and design, arranging for printing and distribution and, in recent years, uploading to the website. The Institute, and the director's role in publishing, can be undertaken either in-house or externally, and debates have continued over the fifty years as to whether an internal Publication Division is the most efficient and cost-effective way in which to publish research.

As early as November 1974, David Biles reported that a Memorandum of Agreement had been drawn up between the Institute and the University of Queensland Press to enable the proceedings of some Institute events to be published in book form (AIC Minutes, 13 November 1974, p. 2). The first such publication was a book by Mary Daunton-Fear on *Sentencing in Western Australia* (1977), followed by John Braithwaite's *Prisons, Education and Work* (1980). Discussions by the Board continued as to how best to facilitate publication of the Institute's research findings with the use of in-house publication being preferred instead of using the Government printing service that was overly slow due to an ever-increasing workload.

In March 1982, however, Prime Minister Malcolm Fraser called for the publications section of the Institute to be 'amalgamated or let out to commercial enterprise' (AIC Minutes, 9 March 1982, p. 6). Director, William Clifford, responded to this during a Board meeting by arguing:

[In] criminology in Australia there was no other concern undertaking production for the universities of material for higher level studies or keeping them abreast of modern developments. The publications section was therefore an educational facility . . . that could not be left to the vagaries of other publishing bodies. Any such diversion would prove more expensive and far more inefficient. (AIC Minutes, 9 March 1982, p. 6)

Compared with commercial publishers, the Institute's in-house approach enabled major reports to be published in book form much more quickly than would be the case if conventional academic publishers were engaged, making the Institute flexible and responsive to the needs of government. Former Librarian, Jane Shelling, affirmed this view during her interview: 'contracting out publications could be cost effective, but commercial publication would take too long and cost too much' (Jane Shelling, Interview, 23 March 2021).

Cost considerations, however, meant that the Institute needed to maintain a number of full-time staff to manage the ever-increasing workload. At various times, the Institute employed a permanent manager of publications, an editor, typesetter and designer. Typing of publications was first undertaken in-house by Anna Davie, while John Widdicombe used an off-set printing machine for printing during his 20-year term at the Institute that ended in October 1994–due to the economies introduced following the Tanzer review (1994) (Plate 11.1).

The final copies were then sent to the Canberra Times office for binding (Dennis Challinger, Interview, 18 February 2022). In the 1980s, printing was contracted-out until print-on-demand became available for the few current publications that had to be produced in physical form. As the workload in publications increased, short-term contractors were used to assist with editing and typesetting–sometimes creating problems due to their lack of familiarity with the subject-matter and AIC style. In addition, as former Director Richard Harding noted during his interview, 'actually, most of these outsourcing things end up costing more' (Richard Harding, Interview, 18 November 2021).

Another issue that arose on occasions was the potential for legal liability arising from the content of Institute publications to occur. Director Richard Harding recalled encountering this on his arrival at the Institute in 1984: 'the first week I was there, I was getting unpleasant lawyers' letters about John Braithwaite's book about corporate crime in the pharmaceutical industry threatening to sue the Institute' (Richard Harding, Interview, 18 November 2021). Such correspondence

Plate 11.1 (l-r) Lorraine Smith and John Widdicombe in the Publications Program (*Source* AIC Archives)

was invariably sent to the Australian Government's insurer for advice and settlement if required. In the case of the pharmaceutical industry, no action was taken. These issues again highlight the difficulties that arose where researchers were undertaking work in a government-funded, quasi-academic agency.

The Range of Institute Publications

During the 50 years, the Institute produced 42 different series of publications falling into six primary categories. In all, 2,147 separate AIC reports or other works were published—43 each year, on average—in addition to an extensive range of other scholarly works published as commercial monographs or in academics journals. The main categories of publications were:

Corporate publications, such as *Annual Reports*, and various iterations of newsletters such as the *Reporter* and *Criminology Today*;
Information reports that included the early *Information Bulletins*, and the more recent *Crime Facts Info* sheets;
Events reports, such as reports of training events, conferences and seminars;
Statistical reports such as *Facts and Figures, Monitoring, Statistical Reports and Bulletins and Technical and Background Papers*;
Research reports, that included the Institute's principal refereed publications *Trends and Issues in Crime and Criminal Justice* and *Research Reports*, as well as the major monograph series *Australian Studies in Law, Crime and Justice*, as well as various special publications and applied research reports;
Finally, the Institute published various **subject-specific reports** dealing with topics such as corrections, indigenous justice issues, crime prevention, violence, arson, illicit drugs, cybercrime and transnational crime. These often arose out of specifically-commissioned research such as the *Violence in Australia* series and *High-tech Crime Briefs*, or for specific stakeholder groups such as the Correctional Administrators and the National Drug Law Enforcement Research Fund (NDLERF)–these often ceasing once funding was discontinued.

In order to understand the longevity of each of the Institute's series of publications, the number of publications in each of the 42 series were plotted against 5-year time periods, marking their introduction and cessation–apart from the six current series that remain in 2022 (shaded in green in Fig. 11.1). From Fig. 11.1, it is apparent that the various publications series have varied considerably in their longevity extending from some that had only two parts (*Aborigines and Criminal Justice*, and *Violence Prevention Today*) to others that were published every year (the *Annual Reports*) or regularly over long periods of time (*Trends and Issues in Crime and Criminal Justice*, that began in 1986 and includes 659 papers to the end of 2022).

It is also apparent that each of the Institute's Directors took the opportunity during their period of office to introduce new publication series and to cancel existing ones–thus making their mark on the organisation. Bill Clifford introduced nine new series, reflecting his role

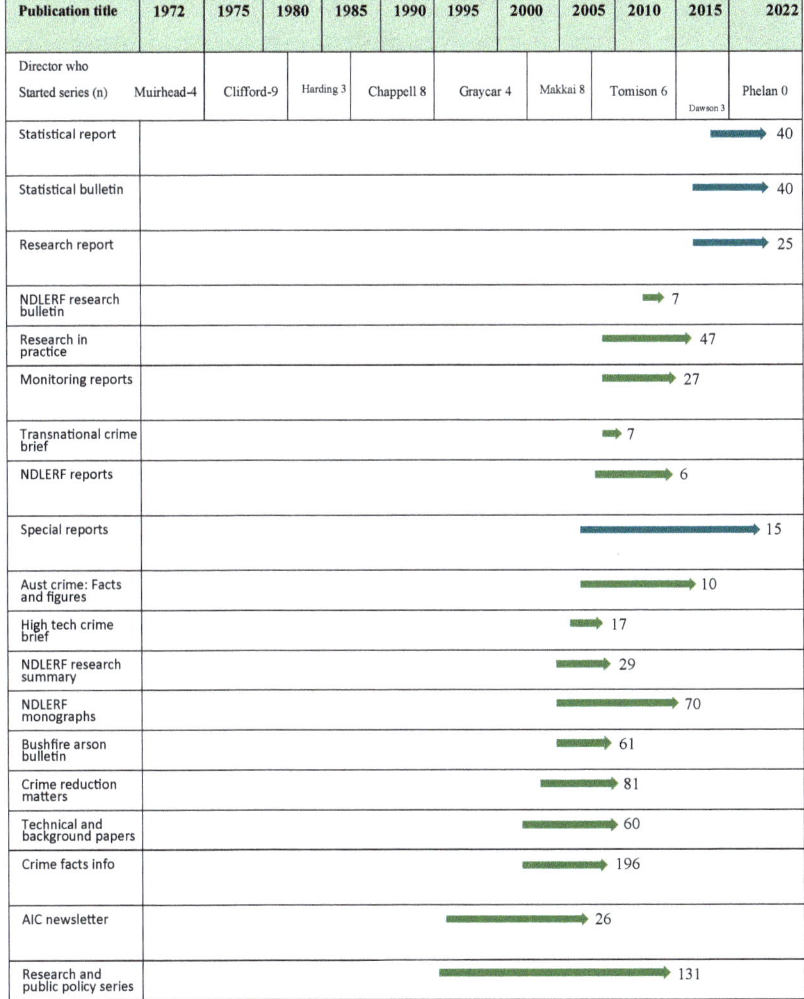

Fig. 11.1 Flow chart of AIC publications, 1972–2022

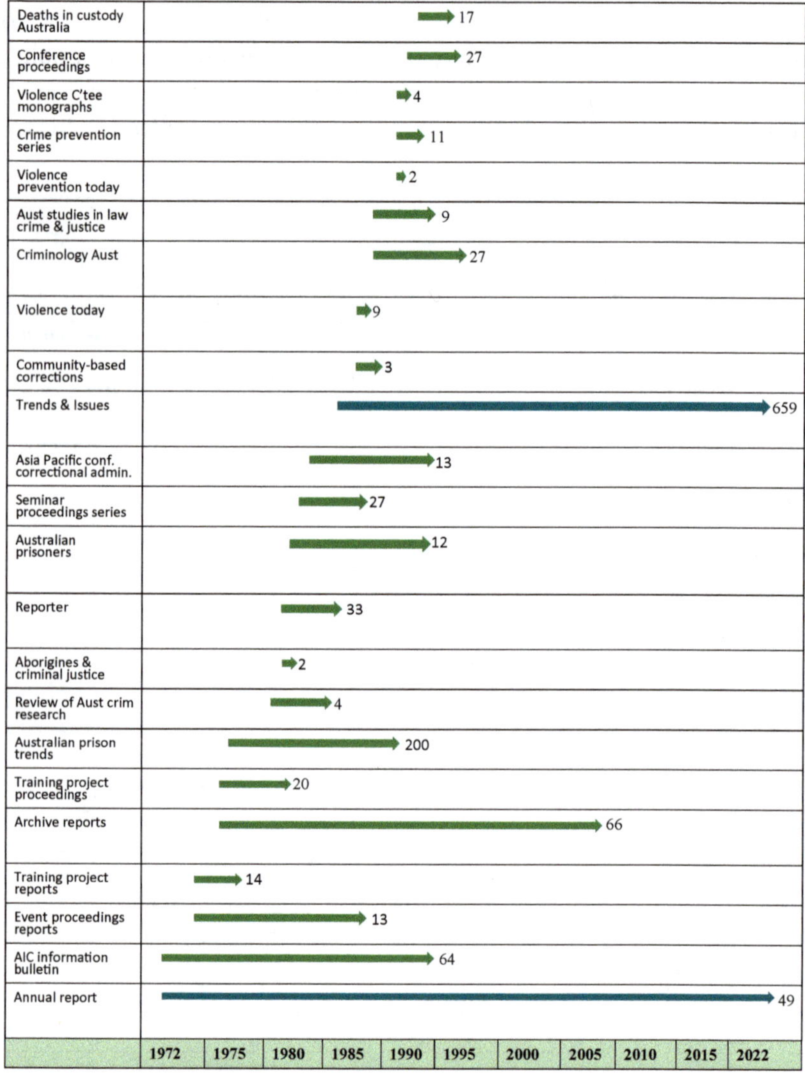

Fig. 11.1   (continued)

as the foundation permanent director, while Duncan Chappell introduced another eight series and terminated twelve others while in office. Adam Graycar (Interview, 1 March 2021) tried not to proliferate the number of series of publications, focussing on only two refereed series: *Trends and Issues* and *Research and Public Policy Papers* while terminating eight others. Adam Tomison introduced four new series and ceased thirteen others. This process of developing new series and removing others was time-consuming, costly and confusing to the readership and stakeholders.

The one series that was an enduring success was *Trends and Issues in Crime and Criminal Justice* commenced by Richard Harding in 1986 who explained its introduction during his interview:

[Paul Wilson and I decided that] if something is worth talking about then you could actually say something worth saying in four sides of paper . . . that's accessible to busy practitioners and it's meaningful to scholars. (Richard Harding, Interview, 18 November 2021)

Subsequent directors kept the series although tinkered with its presentation by changing colour schemes, paper quality, type fonts, layout in columns, and, importantly, length. Harding originally decreed that these papers would be 4,000 words in total and designed to fit into four multi-column pages that could be folded and printed on a single sheet of paper. This was later extended to six pages (from No 8 in 1987), but still able to fit into a single folded sheet.

In December 2016, following the advent of smart phones, it became necessary to remove columns to make reading on mobile devices easier. From paper No 512, that dealt with 'Digital forensics in the cloud era' (Martini et al. 2016), Rick Brown, as General Editor of the series, adopted a new colour scheme of teal and black, removed columns and permitted papers to occupy up to 20 pages and around 10,000 words. The number of papers published each year has also increased substantially with 29 papers being released in 2021 and 27 in 2022. This is a substantial output in this series alone for a staff of 18 researchers in 2022.

It should be noted, however, that authors of the AICs publications were not only research staff, but also academics who had to produce papers following the completion of AIC-funded research projects, and a number of external authors who submitted manuscripts for publication in the AICs various series. On the whole, however, the majority of publications were written by at least one AIC staff member, often in collaboration with external authors.

The production of large numbers of in-house publications has, however, been difficult, particularly in times where staffing numbers were capped. Having one editor and one designer in recent years slowed production greatly, as did the decision by previous directors to require authors to write, design and typeset their own publications using Word software–that was singularly unsuitable for the task. Arranging tables and charts in three columns was near impossible and made more difficult as peer review and editors' corrections had to be addressed sequentially as well. It was remarkable that the production targets could be achieved to the extent they were.

Online Dissemination and the Website

The Institute launched its website in June 1996. Initially, the website was the responsibility of the communications manager, but within twelve months responsibility was transferred to the staff of the J V Barry Library. When it was created, the website aimed to promote the AIC's work and corporate objectives, and in due course, full-text publications, statistics, directories, the library's catalogue and material on special subjects were all made available on the website. Prior to 2020, the website contained not only material generated by Institute staff, but also non-AIC resources and publications there were relevant to the topics being researched. In 2019, however, the website was refreshed and all non-AIC content was removed. This made the website considerably smaller in terms of size and detracted from the original aim of the Institute as a 'one stop shop' for all criminological research. Users seeking material on specific questions were no longer able to search the Institute's website to find both AIC and non-AIC content, being now required to search on the websites of other research agencies or use general search engines to locate non-AIC reports and articles.

During 1996–97, the staff of the JV Barry Library were involved in the early stages of development of websites for both the Institute and the CRC. Initially, this work was undertaken by casual staff, usually from the senior years of Information Technology and Engineering studies at ANU. These students enthusiastically embraced the opportunity to learn about the work of a government agency and to share in the development of an important information resource. Two notable contributors were a sister and brother team, Jacqui and Peter Levan, who commenced as part-time website officers and, after graduation, developed to be a two-person website management team at the Institute.

In March 1998, an online catalogue of the JV Barry Library was made available internally within the Institute. The Library system used was *FIRST*, developed in Melbourne by Optimus Prime Pty Ltd with the Institute's Deputy Librarian, Pamela Garfoot, having responsibility for the installation of the system. Using contract cataloguers, significant progress was made in eliminating cataloguing backlogs in anticipation of the Library 'going live' with the new online catalogue. 'Pamela Garfoot's leadership in planning and organising the implementation of the new system, and in supervising contract cataloguers, was critical for modernising library services for the Institute. Later, her professionalism and leadership in this and other tasks was recognised with her appointment as Chief Librarian for the Department of Finance' (John Myrtle, Interview, 3 December 2020).

The online catalogue of the JV Barry Library became available on the Institute's website in July 1998 and from March 1999, the Institute was involved in implementing the National Library's new Kinetica service, which replaced the ABN. Pamela Garfoot was a member of the Expert Advisory Group on Cataloguing that provided recommendations on cataloguing workflow using the new system. Using the experience gained in creating the AICs website, staff subsequently developed and launched websites for two other organisations: the National Police Ethnic Advisory Bureau (NPEAB), later re-named the Australasian Police Multicultural Advisory Bureau (APMAB); and the Asian Pacific Conference of Correctional Administrators (APCCA)—the latter of which was transferred from the Institute to the Singapore Prison Service in the latter half of 2002 (John Myrtle, Interview, 3 December 2020).

Throughout 1999 and 2000, the Library's staff continued to develop the Institute's website as a 'text-rich' source of criminological information. At this time, all issues of the Institute's publication, *Trends and Issues in Crime and Criminal Justice*, and a number of special subject sections were added. In August 1999, the Library's collection was valued at more than \$1.1 m (see Chapter 9 above).

Although the Institute continued to make a significant cataloguing contribution to the National Library's Kinetica service, because the Library's catalogue was now available online, fewer items were included on the local system. In 2001, staff of the Library carried out work to organise the Institute's photographic collection that entailed identifying and labelling photographs and preserving the collection in accordance with appropriate archival storage practices. The Institute also developed a website for the Campbell Collaboration Crime and Justice Coordinating Group (on the assessment and dissemination of evidence-based social science interventions). The Group's new website was launched in May 2001, and the Institute continued hosting it until 2005 (John Myrtle, Interview, 3 December 2020).

During 2001–02, the Library staff drafted a strategic plan to guide Library and website work over the next three years. Alison Ransome, University Librarian at Southern Cross University, was engaged as a consultant for the planning process. One of the outcomes of this was the creation of a number of subject-specific email alert services for Institute staff and selected external clients that continues to the present day.

Throughout its history, the Institute has sought to publish crime statistics and other data relevant to selected crime and justice topics. These were originally published in hard-copy form such as the early collections dealing with Australian prison trends, Australian prisoners and community-based corrections. The AIC's Principal Criminologist, Dr Satyanshu Mukherjee, was largely responsible for publishing this material, as Mark Finnane recalled in a recent obituary of Sat:

His direction of the data collections that were subsequently published (one of them in the Bicentennial History working volumes, the other by the AIC) was far-sighted indeed and remains unique. . . . So too his monograph on *Crime Trends in the Twentieth Century*—again unequalled for its reach and ambition, still the only such work for Australia. He had real vision and imagination for the kind of social science that would help us better understand this country. (Smith 2021, p. 20)

During Toni Makkai's tenure as director in 2005, a new statistical series was published, *Australian Crime Facts and Figures*, that lasted until Chris Dawson's time as director in 2016, when a new suite of statistical publications was offered including the Monitoring Reports, Statistical Bulletins and Statistical Reports. An attempt was also made to use web-based software to display statistical information on the Institute's website in such a way that users could manipulate data displays and select the variables they were most interested in. Datasets on *Crime Statistics Australia* relating to drug use, homicide, deaths in custody and identity crime and misuse were made available, but staffing resources delayed the inclusion of further collections. In 2020, new software, FLOURISH, enhanced the collections that were displayed, but as Jane Shelling, the Library Manager responsible for the website recalled prior to her retirement, 'Crime Statistics Australia has had a rocky time' (Jane Shelling, Interview, 23 March 2021).

Website and social media usage are important performance indicators for most government and business entities in recent years, and the managers of the JV Barry Library have compiled a variety of usage statistics for all Board meetings. In 2021–22, for example, the Annual Report noted that the AIC had 23,379 Facebook followers, 9,889 twitter followers, 4,664 email subscribers and 2,108 Criminology TV (the AICs YouTube channel) subscribers (AIC, Annual Report, 2022 at p. 5). The AICs website contained 1,832 AIC publications and 374 AIC video files on Criminology TV in 2022. The Library's Criminology Database, CINCH held over 64,000 records in 2021–22, and the monthly Crime and justice Alert service had 4,675 subscribers (AIC, Annual Report, 2022 at p. 43). In February 2021, the AIC also commenced CrimPod, a Podcast hosted by Spotify (https://open.spotify.com/show/5Mk4fb09e oUXTGj5NyY4Ag). The first five sessions were posted by 2022 and lasted for between 20 and 30 minutes each. They are presented by Rick Brown, the AIC's current Deputy Director, and provide a concise summary of some of the Institute's latest research findings.

Media Relations

Prior to the age of social media and online communications, print and visual media had an important role to play in dissemination of the Institute's research. However, as noted above, relations with the media could be fraught, particularly when research staff were willing to speak on topics that had political sensitivities. The AICs Criminologist, Dr Jocelynne Scutt, discovered this in the early 1980s when she appeared regularly in the media discussing rape law reform, as we have seen. Often public officials are reluctant to have a media profile, instead preferring to let government research reports speak for themselves, while others, such as academics and social commentators, are happy to speak publicly about their research and respond to difficult questions that journalists might ask. In the case of criminological research, the topics examined often attract extensive media attention, such as sexual assault, Indigenous deaths in custody, victims of crime, sentencing and trends and costs of crime. Some Institute staff were quite willing to 'beard the lion' and establish prominent media profiles—that occasionally created tensions with Boards and Ministers. During one of the earliest Board meetings, Acting Director Muirhead 'stressed that care should be taken when talking to the media' citing an instance in which 'a taped commentary done for the ABC was "edited" in such a manner as to provide a misleading impression'. On that occasion, the Chairman of the Board, Peter Loof, 'regarded this form of tape cutting as serious' and suggested that 'the matter should be taken up with the General Manager of the ABC' (AIC Board Minutes, 25 February 1974, p. 35).

Some Institute staff who had regular and willing contact with the media included Arie Freiberg, Jocelynne Scutt, Suzanne Hatty, Patricia Easteal and Paul Wilson–largely because their topics of research had high levels of public interest–particularly, sentencing and rape law reform. Peter Grabosky and the present author also gave regular media interviews on their cybercrime research in the 2000s. In the case of Dr Suzanne Hatty (AIC Senior Research Officer, 1984–87–Plate 11.2) and Dr Paul Wilson (Assistant Director AIC, 1986–91), the investigation by police of criminality alleged against each of them attracted considerable public interest in the years after they had left the Institute. It has been suggested that the research conducted by both Hatty and Wilson while at the AIC that was critical of the police, led to investigations into alleged criminal activity by each of them, relating to separate matters, that might otherwise have been dealt with as official warnings (Guilliatt 2004). In the event, Hatty's romantic involvement with a former prisoner led to her being charged and pleading guilty to perverting the course of justice with no conviction recorded by the New South Wales District Court in December 2001 (Guilliatt 2004) (Plate 11.2).

Paul Wilson's critical appraisal of the police began in the late 1960s when he was teaching psychology at the ANU. He published a book

Plate 11.2 Suzanne Hatty, Senior Research Officer, 1984–87 (*Source* AIC Archives)

with Duncan Chappell on attitudes of the public to the police (Chappell and Wilson 1969) that 'showed that large numbers of police lied, fabricated evidence in court, beat people unnecessarily, and framed innocent people' (Wilson 1990, p. 4). At a subsequent conference, the authors received 'a series of savage comments [with] Australia's senior police attacking our youth, our inexperience, our "obvious left-wing bias", and the fact that, as our survey sample did not contain any police officers or their relatives, we were intellectually incompetent' (Wilson 1990, p. 5). Years later, Paul Wilson again had contact with the police, on this occasion being convicted, after pleading not guilty, to four historical charges of indecent treatment of a child under the age of 12 relating to sexual acts he was alleged to have committed at his Brisbane home in the 1970s. He was sentenced in the Brisbane District Court in November 2016 to 18 months' imprisonment, suspended after six months (Kos 2016, n.p.).

Having a high media profile was seen as promoting the interests of a government research organisation by some, but considered undesirable and risky by others. In an Editorial written in the *Australian and New Zealand Journal of Criminology* in 1983 to mark the commencement of Richard Harding's term as the AICs Director, it was observed:

> Harding's outspokenness, his involvement in, and penchant for, public debate on important criminological issues, and the flourish and cogency with which he presses his point of view, have consistently attracted media attention and made him a well-known public figure on a national level – quite a rare thing in Australia for a person who operates from a scholarly and academic base, and a distinct advantage, one would suspect, for the Director of a national crime body. (Sallmann 1983, p. 193)

Adam Graycar, later noted, however, 'being in the media is important as long as you don't do it in a sensationalist way' (Interview, 1 March 2021).

In 1980, for example, the AICs Board discussed ways in which the Institute's media profile could be enhanced including by disseminating a weekly program of Institute work that might be of interest to the media, and 'using the womens' journals, television shows, newspapers, conferences, circulars to politicians–anything that might ensure wider dissemination' (AIC Minutes, 15 December 1980, p. 1). At the next Board meeting, Peter Loof, the Chairman of the Board, suggested that:

> important as publicity was, it could be overdone. Publicity could at times be counter productive and care needed to be exercised to balance publicity needs with the Institute's own objectives, such as programs that sought to become more responsive to the needs of State and Commonwealth Departments. (AIC Minutes, 3 March 1981, p. 1)

In order to guard against the potential negative aspects of media reporting, in 1987 the Institute engaged a professional journalist, Geraldine Badham, to assist the AICs head of publications, and former journalist, the late Jack Sandry (Plate 11.3), in developing close relations with the media. Topics for media interviews were raised with the Director by Jack Sandry and decisions made about who should do the interview.

These roles later developed into positions of Public Affairs Officers and Communications Managers. Having trained journalists and communications professionals, such as Garry Raffaele, Barbara Walsh, Scott Kelleher and Colin Campbell, facilitated the development of contacts with journalists who specialised in crime and justice reporting and enabled staff training to be undertaken to ensure that researchers were able to respond professionally to journalists' questions. On occasions, external media consultants were engaged to provide training for research staff on how to present research to print, radio and television audiences.

When Adam Graycar commenced as director in 1994, he recalled that 'there was a culture where individuals would find themselves on the radio saying outrageous things that would get a headline but they were not always research based' (Adam Graycar, Interview, 1 March 2021). To prevent this, he ensured that senior staff who had a media profile were trained in how to respond to media requests and interviews, so that the Institute's reputation would not be damaged.

An example of how media promotion of the Institute came close to disaster occurred in November 1985, shortly after Richard Harding had commenced as director. When Col Bevan was on leave, just before he retired as Head of Training, the Institute had undertaken to hold a *National Conference on Domestic Violence*. This was the second AIC

Plate 11.3 Jack Sandry (28 June 1936—19 August 2022) (*Source* AIC Archives)

conference to address this topic, the first, entitled *Violence in the Family*, was conducted by the Institute from 26 to 30 November 1979 and attended by 60 people from across Australia. The proceedings were published in an edited volume by Jocelynne Scutt (1980) who had organised the event in collaboration with the Commonwealth Department of Social Security.

The 1985 national conference was arranged by Jane Mugford, Principal Programs Officer, working with Col Bevan, and in his autobiography Col recalled that 'it had attracted much attention around Australia. All the women's organisations in particular had already indicated their determination to attend and to make quite a noise' (Bevan 2005, p. 368).

In Col's absence, Jack Sandry, whom Dennis Challinger (Interview, 18 February 2022) described as 'a knockabout sort of chap; an old-time reporter', had prepared 'a large, brilliantly-coloured poster advertising the coming seminar' (Plate 11.4). 'Dominating the design was a large depiction of Punch and Judy in action' (Bevan 2005, p. 371).

Plate 11.4 Proposed domestic violence conference poster, November 1985 (*Source* AIC Archives)

Although the poster would certainly have attracted attention, it was an unfortunate reflection of the trivialisation of family violence, and reinforcement of historical attitudes to such crimes portrayed as street entertainments. When Col returned to the Institute he rightly demanded that the poster not be used despite its $10,000 printing costs. Director, Richard Harding, agreed. The five-day conference, attended by over 300 participants, was highly successful in raising awareness of domestic violence and the proceedings were later published in the Institute's Seminar Proceedings Series by Suzanne Hatty (1986). Both these conferences were early precursors to the AICs continuing research on violence against women and children that, in 2021–22, was identified as one of the Institute's research priorities (AIC, Corporate Plan 2021–22, p. 5).

As will be discussed in Chapter 14 below, the partial merger with the ACC in 2015 led to most of the Institute's corporate and administrative staff being transferred to the ACC (and later the ACIC) including communications personnel. The AICs media activities were then managed by the ACICs communications division that was much more risk-averse in allowing research staff to speak directly with journalists, tending to prefer that interviews be conducted by the Minister or director only–particularly high-profile, televised interviews. In the 1980s and 1990s, the Institute's Public Affairs Officers would set up interviews with individual researchers and journalists, sometimes amounting to ten or more radio, newspaper or television interviews following the release of a single publication. This relative freedom to speak with the media was also seen at the Home Office in the UK in the 1970s where, as Mike Hough (2018) recalled when interviewed in 2018:

> When I started working at the Home Office in the 70s, we quite regularly briefed journalists on what we did and had open communication channels with key Home Affairs journalists as a matter of course. . . The big change was in the early 90s when the then conservative administration took a tight grip of publication.

In Australia in 1988–89, over 400 mentions of the Institute or Institute personnel were made in major metropolitan dailies and it was estimated that Institute personnel were interviewed approximately 1,200 times during the year (AIC, Annual Report 1989, p. 4). By 2007–08, only 53 media interviews were conducted (AIC, Annual Report 2008, p. 30) and in 2021–22 only 16 media interviews were undertaken, arising out of 93 media enquiries (AIC, Annual Report 2021–22, p. 35)–noting of course that online media, including social media, now occupy most of the Institute's current dissemination activities. Of course, even online journalism requires contact with researchers. Some researchers were more than happy to speak with the media, although, as Grant Wardlaw noted in his Interview, some such as David Biles were willing to speak on any topic that journalists advanced. Paul Wilson, in particular, became 'a lightning rod for criticism' because of his willingness to provide his own personal opinions rather than keeping to research findings (Grant Wardlaw, Interview, 30 November 2020) (Plate 11.5).

Plate 11.5 Dennis Challinger (2nd from left) and Paul Wilson (3rd from left) during a media shoot, c. 1987 (*Source* Dennis Challinger)

Currently, such high-profile interviews with researchers are rare. In her interview, Jane Shelling noted this problem, commenting: 'in terms of dissemination, there is a disconnect because ACIC don't necessarily want to be promoted, whereas the AIC does want to be promoted' (Jane Shelling, Interview, 23 March 2021).

The Future of Communications

Over the five decades, there have been differing ways in which governments have exercised control over the work of the Institute and how its research is disseminated. Legislative changes have reflected an increased move towards greater control being exercised by the Institute's Minister, with a somewhat reduced influence exercised by states and territories. The most recent alignment of the Institute with the ACIC has resulted in the Institute's media profile being more closely controlled than in the past although social media is used much more than in the past to disseminate research reports. The dissemination of research still must undergo various levels of approval from not only the ACICs communications staff, but also the Chief Executive and the Minister. This goes against the original aims of the Institute being independent of government and able to offer frank and unfettered advice to policy-makers and to the community generally.

The increased control over the Institute's external activities has also meant that those individuals within the criminological community who have views opposed to those of criminal justice agencies, have shown a reluctance to attend and speak out at Institute events. This had led to the Institute's research agenda being closely aligned with government interests with the risk that critical perspectives receive less prominence that they did in the past. As outlined above, the Institute once again finds itself wedged between 'a rock and a hard place'.

The most likely trend for the future in terms of dissemination of research is for communication over online platforms to increase. Coming out of the Coronavirus pandemic will see large-scale public events reduce in prevalence, being replaced by virtual meetings and webinars. The advantages of these are many, not only in protecting public health, but also in facilitating meetings across the globe by allowing those in different time zones to participate in different ways, and for the events to be available on-demand. Participation can also be more effectively moderated, with individuals being able to present their opinions in various ways during live events–not solely as presenters. Archiving of information also becomes less costly and more available in the form of electronic records–as long as protection of data from interference or degradation is ensured.

The loss of paper publications and large-scale face-to-face events, will, however, result in the loss of an income stream, and consideration will need to be given to having online payment systems and pay-walls for access to online events and digital information. Whether the public sector will be willing to endorse such an approach remains to be seen.

In sum, the Institute has clearly provided the community with access to substantial amounts of information, analysis and ideas for reform of the criminal justice system. The output of publications, conferences, media and social media has been remarkable given the relatively small budget the Institute has managed with and the comparatively small number of staff involved. This has, however, been achieved by relying more and more on individual researchers to do more work with fewer support staff and to take on additional roles that previously would be been undertaken by separate divisions of the organisation. For example, the 'typing pool' gave way to researchers producing manuscripts themselves, which although saving costs for the agency and increasing output, has increased the workload of research staff. The digital age has clearly changed the nature of the research activity of criminologists and made dissemination possible on a much wider scale. Arguably, this has resulted in an excess of research reports being produced on any given topic—some of greater value than others. How long such a transition to individually-based dissemination can continue remains to be seen.

References

Australian Institute of Criminology (AIC). 2022. *Corporate Plan 2021–22.* Canberra: Australian Institute of Criminology. https://www.aic.gov.au/sites/default/files/2021-07/aic_corporate_plan_2021-22.pdf Accessed: 8 February 2022.

Australian Institute of Criminology (AIC). 1989–2022. *Annual Report 1989–2022.* Canberra: Australian Institute of Criminology.

Bevan, Colin Russell. 2005. *As the Walrus Said. The Time Has Come . . .* Canberra: Book Surge.

Braithwaite, John. 1980. *Prisons, Education and Work: Towards a National Employment Strategy for Prisoners.* St. Lucia: University of Queensland Press in association with the AIC.

Chappell, Duncan and Paul R. Wilson. 1969. *The Police and the Public in Australia and New Zealand.* St Lucia: University of Queensland Press.

Daunton-Fear, Mary. 1977. *Sentencing in Western Australia.* St Lucia: University of Queensland Press in association with the AIC.

Department of Home Affairs. 2022. Portfolio Budget Statements: Australian Institute of Criminology 2022–23. Canberra: Department of Home Affairs.

Guilliatt, Richard. 2004. The Feminist and the Murderer: A Postmodern Love Story. *Sydney Morning Herald, Good Weekend*, 7 August.

Hatty, Suzanne, ed. 1986. National Conference on Domestic Violence. Seminar Proceedings Series no. 12. Canberra: Australian Institute of Criminology. https://www.aic.gov.au/publications/sps/sps12

Hough, Mike. 2018. Interviewed by Ben Bradford at European Society of Criminology Meeting, Sarajevo, Bosnia and Herzegovina, 10 September 2018. https://www.youtube.com/watch?v=_DLTlrqt_OA&t=7s Accessed 10 March 2022.

Kos, Andrew. 2016. Paul Wilson Sentencing: Attitudes Toward Child Sex Offending 'Different in 1970s', Defence Lawyer Says, *ABC News*, 24 November. https://www.abc.net.au/news/2016-11-24/queensland-criminologist-paul-wilson-sentence-child-sex-offences/8053398 Accessed 6 January 2022.

Martini, Ben, Quang Do and Kim-Kwang Raymond Choo. 2016. Digital Forensics in the Cloud Era: The Decline of Passwords and the Need for Legal Reform. *Trends and Issues in Crime and Criminal Justice* no. 512. Canberra: Australian Institute of Criminology.

National Health and Medical Research Council, Australian Research Council and Universities Australia. 2018. *Australian Code for the Responsible Conduct of Research*. Canberra: NHMRC.

Sallmann, Peter. 1983. Editorial: A New Hand on the Tiller at the Australian Institute of Criminology. *Australian and New Zealand Journal of Criminology* 16 (4): 193–195.

Scutt, Jocelynne A, ed. 1980. *Violence in the Family: A Collection of Conference Papers. Event proceedings and reports* no. 11. Canberra: Australian Institute of Criminology. https://www.aic.gov.au/publications/epr/epr-11

Smith, Russell G. 2021. Obituary: Dr Satyanshu Kumar Mukherjee, *Pacifi-Crim: ANZSOC Newsletter*, 18 (2): 19–20.

Tanzer, Noel, Des, Hill and Grant Wardlaw. 1994. *Review of the Australian Institute of Criminology: Report*. Canberra: Australian Institute of Criminology.

Walters, Julie, Hannah Chadwick, Kim-Kwang Raymond Choo and Russell G Smith. 2013. Industry Perspectives on Money Laundering and Financing of Terrorism Risks in Non-Financial Sector Businesses and Professions. *Research and Public Policy Series* no. 122–2. Canberra: Australian Institute of Criminology.

Wilson, Paul. 1990. *A Life of Crime*. Newham: Scribe Publications.

12

Training, Education, Conferences and Awards

Introduction: Training or Educating?

When public institutions are established, the formulation of their aims, roles and focus is heavily dependent on the views of those who conceptualised and developed the proposals for their creation and how they should be implemented. In the case of criminology, the need for research institutions was originally identified principally by criminal justice practitioners—from law enforcement, the courts and correctional agencies—in collaboration with politicians and public officials. In addition to acquiring basic information on the nature and extent of criminality, research was needed to understand how practitioners handled both offenders and victims of crime, how their daily work could be improved and how crime could best be prevented. Armed with the findings of empirical research, those who created institutes of criminology believed that the role of research institutions should include the presentation of information to assist practitioners in their daily work.

When the proposals for the AIC were being developed, 'it was originally envisaged that the Institute would conduct seminars and training courses designed to keep police, prison and parole officers and others

R. G. Smith, *Public Sector Criminological Research*, https://doi.org/10.1007/978-3-031-28356-7_12

up to date with modern techniques and developments in their respective callings' (AIC, Minutes, 3 March 1981, p. 2 citing the report by McClemens and Morris). The aim was to professionalise these services through the use of training programs for those 'in the higher echelons of the various services' (p. 2). This idea was subsequently reflected in the *Criminology Research Act 1971* (Cth) that specified the Institute's functions as including: 'to conduct such seminars and courses of training or instruction for persons engaged, or to be engaged, in criminological research or in work related to the prevention or correction of criminal behaviour as are approved by the Board' (s. 6(c)). During the second-reading speech on the Bill, the Attorney-General, the Hon. Tom Hughes QC, in discussing the proposed functions of the AIC, stated these objectives, noting, in particular, 'the need to provide training facilities for those in the South-East Asia area', drawing on the experience of other organisations such as UNAFEI in Japan (House of Representatives, Hansard, 24 February 1971, p. 572).

This role for the Institute was, arguably, not fully developed, leading to a number of difficult problems emerging in terms of scope and implementation during its early years of operation. One question that had not been considered was the relationship between training activities that the Institute could provide on a national basis, and the training offered by criminal justice agencies in the states (and later territories). John Seymour, raised this in his interview (14 November 2022), questioning what the training role of the Institute was during the 1970s: 'was it there to run seminars, and if so, what could the Institute, being a Commonwealth body, contribute to the seminars already provided by state agencies?'.

Another difficulty was the determination of the extent to which the Institute was meant to provide 'training' programs as opposed to 'educational' activities. On the one hand, those who developed the idea of the Institute, such as Sir John Barry, saw the need for police and prison officers to receive practical, skills-based training that would assist in their daily work. It was thought that this could be achieved through the provision of seminars and workshops for practitioners, along the lines of those carried out at UNAFEI—potentially, including residential facilities—which the proponents of the AIC had inspected during visits in the 1960s and early 1970s at other PNI institutes. Over time, however, as the Institute attracted academic scholars to its staff, the emphasis changed to a more educational focus that included the development of concept-based, theoretical instruction that could be used to explain and prevent criminal conduct. By populating the Institute with University-qualified academics, the work of the Institute began to resemble that of a tertiary educational institution—albeit without the presence of students. Although formal undergraduate and post-graduate teaching was never undertaken, the provision of seminars, roundtables and conferences was seen as an effective way in which to disseminate the Institute's research findings—and, potentially, to generate some additional income (Plate 12.1).

The Institute's Board and Directors occasionally differed in their opinions about whether the Institute should be seen as a training organisation or as a provider of academic learning, and the extent to which this should be a fee-for-service activity. Both Judge Muirhead and Bill Clifford took the view that the Institute should have a formal Training

Plate 12.1 John Myrtle (left) and Dennis Challinger addressing a public sector training group at Colbee Court, August 1987 (*Source* Dennis Challinger)

and Information Division and, from the outset, this delivered a regular and intensive program of training activities—free of charge to those who attended. The first of these, corresponding with the opening of the Institute on 16 October 1973, was a residential conference on the theme 'Australian crime prevention and treatment: Research resources and needs–An exercise in coordination'. The conference was held at the Hotel Canberra (adjacent to the Institute's subsequent premises) with fifty-seven attending—including six visiting experts and consultants including Mr Minoru Shikita, Deputy Director of UNAFEI in Japan—the first to sign the Institute's Visitors' Book on 16 October 1973. Interestingly, during this inaugural training conference, 'special mention was made of the growth of organised crime in Australia and the need for research into the role of strategic intelligence in combating organised crime' (AIC, Annual Report, 1974, p. 13). Coming full-circle, in 2022, one of the Institute's priority themes for research was also organised crime that is now conducted by the Institute's Serious and Organised Crime Research Laboratory that works closely with the ACIC making use of its strategic intelligence (AIC, Annual Report, 2020–21, p. 2). After 50 years, a solution to this crime problem remains elusive, despite the extensive research and discussion of the problem that has been undertaken by those at the AIC, the ACIC and elsewhere.

In the 1970s, when the Institute was established, there were few opportunities for practitioners and academics to learn about, and to discuss, the latest developments in criminological thought. Exceptions to this were the public seminar program conducted at the Sydney Institute of Criminology (Hawkins 1990, p. 15) and the lectures and seminars provided by the University of Melbourne's Criminology Department (Freiberg 2001). These public seminars were directed at both criminal justice practitioners and academics, students and interested citizens. As Hawkins noted, 'the object of the seminars is not to instruct or indoctrinate, but to provide a forum for discussion and the free expression of opinion' (Hawkins 1990, p. 15). As we shall see, there were differing views as to whether or not the Institute's seminar and training programs satisfied these aims.

Training

During the first decade of the Institute's existence, the Training and Information Division was managed, first by Harold Weir and then by Colin Bevan, whom Richard Harding described in his Interview as 'old style, hands-on, correctional people' (Richard Harding, Interview, 18 November 2021). Col Bevan, as he preferred to be known, came to the Institute from Queensland where he had had experience, initially as a teacher and then as the Chief Probation and Parole Office for the state. In 1974, David Biles recruited Col for the new position of Assistant Director (Training) at the AIC (Plate 12.2).

At the time, Col had been the Queensland representative, and later Vice-President, of the Australian Crime Prevention, Correction and After-care Council. He was well known to the Council's President, Mr Justice John McClemens, who was then Chief Judge at Common Law of the Supreme Court of New South Wales—'a large and kind-hearted man.. with a roaring voice and somewhat intimidating manner' (D'Apice 2000, n.p.) (Plate 12.3). McClemens considered Col an appropriate

Plate 12.2 Colin Bevan OAM, Assistant Director (Training) (*Source* AIC Archives)

Plate 12.3   (l-r) The Hon. Mr Justice Lionel Murphy QC, The Hon. Judge James Muirhead QC and the Hon Mr Justice J. H. McClemens at the official opening of the J V Barry Memorial Library, 12 February 1974 (*Source* AIC, Annual Report, 1974, p. 6)

candidate for the new role at the Institute, sharing his interest in crime prevention and the rehabilitation of prisoners (Bevan 2005).

Col Bevan commenced at the Institute in September 1975 and, as John Myrtle recalled:

Col introduced a gradual but definite change to the objectives of the Institute's training division, directing its energies to the needs of practitioners in the criminal justice and related professional fields. By the time he retired in November 1985 he had organised over 100 conferences and seminars for the Institute. On Australia Day 2016 Col was awarded a Medal of the Order of Australia 'for service to crime prevention education, and to the community.' Col Bevan died on 30 April 2016 at the age of 95. (Myrtle 2016, n.p.)

When he arrived at the Institute, Col was enthusiastic and looked forward to the challenges of the new position he had taken on. The Institute, at the time, was well resourced, and he had a staff of six reporting to him in the Training Division—some more competent than others as he recalled in his autobiography: 'the two senior men, although pleasant to work with and generally efficient and industrious could not put together a succession of grammatical sentences' (Bevan 2005, pp. 328–9). Col's dissatisfaction with his colleagues extended to the director as well, criticising Bill Clifford for 'always being away on some overseas trip or other'. He also had a scathing opinion of academics and the Research Division whom he considered to be largely self-interested: 'I was awake to the pathetically transparent little tricks played by academics to engineer overseas invitations for themselves at some future date' (Bevan 2005, pp. 332–3). He continued: 'the Institute was merely a stepping stone to their advancement in academia. It also provided them with a perfect opportunity to follow their own interests in an unsupervised, non-demanding, non-accountable-to-anybody atmosphere' (p. 298). Despite this, Col remained at the Institute for ten years and in his revealing memoirs recalls 'travelling first-class all over Australia' and enjoying the kudos of attending international conferences—like those attended by individuals he so despised in the Institute's Research Division (Plate 12.4).

After the first decade of conducting training programs, staffing and budgetary constraints led to the Training and Information Division facing difficulties. When Richard Harding took office as director in 1984, Col Bevan was nearing retirement and, in 1986 after he had left the Institute to return to Queensland, Harding appointed Dennis Challinger as Assistant Director of Training. Challinger came to the Institute from the Melbourne Criminology Department where he was Chairman of the Department with qualifications in mathematics from Monash University, a Master of Arts from the University of Melbourne and a Master of Philosophy in Criminology from Cambridge University. Richard Harding's view of training was that it was designed 'to bring top level people in to alert others to the leading-edge issues, not just a current practitioner-practice component' (Richard Harding, Interview, 18 November 2021). Both Harding and Challinger 'agreed

Plate 12.4   Col Bevan speaking at UNAFEI in Fuchu, Tokyo in 1979 (*Source* Bevan 2005, p. 361)

that training was a misnomer' and that the 'notion of training and getting a certificate of completion didn't gel' (Dennis Challinger, Interview, 18 February 2022). As such, the emphasis shifted from practical training sessions to the provision of academically-focussed conferences with Challinger specifically attempting to involve the researchers in the conference program, unlike Bevan who was happy to keep them well away from training activities. In his interview, Dennis Challinger explained the benefits of involving researchers in conferences as follows:

My view, originally–later dashed–was that conferences would involve the researchers, so if we had a researcher working on a particular topic which generally they had chosen for themselves, we could bring together people who were working in the area where that topic was central to their work, with people from other disciplines–it would enhance the work of the researcher, give the researcher a chance to bounce their ideas off a group of people... all sounding off each other–and sometimes that would work but over time there was less enthusiasm from researchers to be subject to this sort of helpful oversight. (Dennis Challinger, Interview, 18 February 2022)

In his Interview (30 January 2021), John Braithwaite provided an example of the benefits of integrating the Institute's research work into the training program:

> The Training Division facilitated a very practical linkage between the research that I did on [prisons, education and work], by shaping how the project would be run and facilitating the authorities' willingness to cooperate on the project and let me in to all the major prisons in the country to talk to their prison industry people, and then in a follow-up they committed to implementing many of the recommendations that came out of the research–all negotiated through the Training Division (see Braithwaite's (1984) Research Note published in the *Australian and New Zealand Journal of Criminology* that gave a rather bleak conclusion as to the benefits of applied criminological research).

Challinger, who had a background in mathematics, had previously taught quantitative criminological research methods at the University of Melbourne—including to the present author—in the Diploma of Criminology program in the 1970s and 1980s. At the Institute, he expanded the training and conference program to include business-oriented crime prevention—that he later used when he held management positions at both Telecom and Coles Myer in their retail crime prevention teams. In his interview, Dennis Challinger (Plate 12.5) recalled building up a network of retailers in meetings to explore strategies for preventing retail crime (Interview, 18 February 2022):

> The Institute provided a neutral ground for such a meeting... I got the major retailers to kick in money, we established an organisation outside the Institute called the National Retail Crime Prevention Council. We hired an Executive Officer and paid him a salary and had conferences once a year.

These led to a number of publications by the Institute (e.g. Challinger 1988; Gearson and Wilson 1992) that cemented ties with others interested in situational crime prevention internationally—including Ron Clarke and Pat Mayhew, both of whom visited the Institute a number of times from the UK Home Office. In the case of Pat Mayhew, she stayed

Plate 12.5 Dennis Challinger, Assistant Director, Training and Information, c. 1986 (*Source* AIC Archives)

at the AIC throughout 2002 and worked on a variety of projects as a Consultant, including the AICs cost of crime research (Mayhew 2003).

Although Challinger continued to conduct training activities for the Institute's stakeholders, he took the view that 'the Institute was a government instrumentality that was out to do useful things for society at large' rather than simply to raise income (Dennis Challinger, Interview,

18 February 2022). This failed to accord with the views of Chappell and Wilson, and led to Dennis becoming disenchanted with the path the Institute was taking. The move to Marcus Clarke Street with its 'outrageous rent' provided another example of what he regarded as government resources being wasted. Finally, when in 1989 a decision was made to move one of his training staff members, Jane Mugford, 'upstairs' to help with the contract research, without consulting Dennis, he decided to leave the Institute to enter the business world as an 'applied criminologist'—a novel concept and term at the time.

Conferences

By 1992, three of the Institute's principal staff members, Dennis Challinger, Col Bevan and David Biles had left, and with Duncan Chappell becoming director, the practitioner-focussed training activities had been replaced by an academic, educational emphasis, demonstrated in the conference program with Julia Vernon taking this on as Conference Manager in 1990 (Plate 12.6).

This was supported by Paul Wilson and later Peter Grabosky as Assistant Directors of Research, who expanded the academic output of the Institute into the 1990s. Both became Professors when they left the Institute, Wilson at Bond University (Plate 12.7) and Grabosky at the ANU.

The Institute's conference program was designed more to disseminate its own research and to raise the profile of the Institute, than to produce income. Over time, apart from a small number of select conferences, the Institute limited its conference involvement to providing sponsorship of academic conferences, such as those conducted for ANZSOC each year, and permitting staff to present their research at conferences managed by other organisations, both within Australia and internationally as a means of disseminating Institute research findings, and promoting the work of the Institute. For commercial conferences dealing with business crime-control topics, such as fraud prevention and cybercrime, speakers' fees and travel expenses were often paid to the Institute, sometimes in excess of $1,000 per event, that helped to off-set costs. Since 2000, however, as

Plate 12.6   Julia Vernon, Conference Manager, c. 1990 (*Source* AIC Archives)

the conference market tightened, speakers' fees were almost never paid to the Institute.

Presenting the result of one's research to peers and members of the community is one of the primary, and often more desirable, duties of scholars. Apart from the kudos of being invited to address international

Plate 12.7 Paul Wilson, Assistant Director, Research 1986–1991 (*Source* AIC Archives)

gatherings in often ancient and attractive locations, conference presentations provided an environment in which detailed and often critical feedback could be provided to the authors of reports, in addition to establishing networks of relationships that sometimes led to offers of further research or employment being made. Public officials, however, had to tread carefully when undertaking such activities as they could be criticised for having spent public moneys on extravagant travel for predominantly personal gain and self-promotion. The problem for directors was that the AIC was seen as the first place to go for those seeking expert speakers on criminology in Australia and there was a constant temptation to accept these desirable offers. In his interview, Richard Harding explained the problem as follows:

> The thing about these high status statutory officers is that opportunities come to them. As an academic I got used to the necessity for looking for opportunities to create them rather than to wait to be a passive recipient. By contrast, now on account of my position rather than my expertise, I began to be invited to conferences, policy meetings and so on. (Richard Harding, Interview 18 November 2021)

Both directors and senior research staff were, accordingly, faced with regular opportunities to speak at meetings and conferences throughout Australia and internationally, that could have occupied their entire working life, had all the invitations been accepted. A great deal of restraint was needed to limit acceptance of such invitations to those that were most likely to benefit the organisation directly. During some periods, the Institute acted as the Secretariat for annual conferences or was one of the organising institutions, carrying with it an expectation that the AIC would be represented every year. For large-scale, international events, directors were obliged to attend in person, although over time, this was delegated to senior research managers.

In the case of AIC-branded conferences and seminars, the Institute was occasionally criticised for having provided government funding to mount events that provided opportunities for other public officials and academics to present their work. Although these events often generated income for the Institute, on many occasions the net economic profit from the event was minimal—although there were clear benefits in terms of raising the Institute's public profile. As Adam Graycar, observed, 'You don't hold conferences to make money. You hold them to show your wares, to build networks, to show that you're in the business and that you're a credible player' (Interview, 1 March 2021).

In 1986, the director, Richard Harding and Dennis Challinger decided to hold a conference on the topic of the Jury. This was held at Colbee Court from 20 to 22 May 1986 with 23 speakers and a further 28 delegates attending that included members of the judiciary, legal practitioners, academics, policy-makers and AIC staff. The publicity that the event attracted was enhanced greatly by the fact that the former Attorney-General and Justice of the High Court, The Hon. Mr Justice Lionel Murphy QC, a great supporter of the Institute, had just been acquitted in April 1986 of changes of attempting to pervert the course of justice. Although suffering from colon cancer, Murphy agreed to deliver the opening address at the event, commencing with:

> I have been a life-long believer in the value of trial by jury. Recent events have confirmed my belief. Trial by jury should be maintained and extended as far as possible. (Challinger 1986, p. 13)

Although Murphy's address dealt with the jurisprudence surrounding Sect. 80 of the Australian Constitution that requires Commonwealth indictable offences to be tried by juries, the media interest in the topic was more to do with the recent events surrounding Murphy himself (Plate 12.8).

Shortly after the Institute's jury conference, Lionel Murphy died on 21 October 1986 at his home in Canberra. The following year, the former AIC Research Criminologist, Dr Jocelynne Scutt, who had also been an admiring Associate to Justice Murphy, edited a volume of commentaries on the Judge's life by eleven prominent Australians (Scutt 1987).

Collaborating with organisations to host conferences was not limited to academic bodies such as ANZSOC (as we have seen in Chapter 5, above), as the Institute used its extensive global networks to assist many public and private sector bodies in organising public events. For example, between 13 and 15 January 2003, the seventh meeting of the World Criminal Justice Library Network was organised by the Institute in association with the Australian Federal Police and held in Canberra at Burgmann College, ANU. The meeting attracted a number of overseas delegates, including two sponsored by the Institute from the University of the South Pacific and the Papua New Guinea Department of Justice

Plate 12.8   The Hon. Mr Justice Lionel Murphy QC (*Source* AIC Archives)

and Attorney-General (Plate 12.9). As will be shown in this chapter, below, the Institute also had a leading role to play in many events conducted by the UNODC as we shall see in Chapter 13, below. Such activities were seen, originally, as the core business of the Institute.

In his report to the Commonwealth regarding the establishment of the AIC, written in New York on 17 September 1973, Sir Leon Radzinowicz (1973, p. 7) argued that 'the Institute should carry out seminars and round-table conferences' as part of its regular activity, 'as long as there were not too many' in the first two years of its existence and on condition that they 'explore new topics and new approaches' rather than 'following traditional lines'. He went on to observe:

> Those who are invited should be recruited not only from official circles but people who hold controversial and indeed unorthodox views should be asked to participate and make their views known and discussed. (Radzinowicz, 1973, p. 7)

Plate 12.9   (l-r) Farapo Opa, Principal Librarian, PNG Department of Justice and Attorney-General with John Myrtle, January 2003 (*Source* AIC Newsletter, no. 19, 2003, p. 3)

Over its history, the AIC has, indeed, had delegates attending conferences who expressed some unorthodox views, occasionally leading to criticism from governments of the day. Examples include those involved in decarceration, drug law reform, support for victims of sexual and family violence, dealing with deaths in custody and reparation for Indigenous Australians and gun control. Advocates of these and other causes have sometimes shared platforms at AIC events with those the subject of criticism—occasionally leaving both sides somewhat uncomfortable. The Institute's position has generally been that it is best to facilitate free and open discussion, regardless of any backlash—although some directors were less willing to take such risks than others.

The choice of topics for AIC conferences generally followed the work program. Projects funded externally often included resources that enabled the Institute to conduct a conference or seminar either near the start of a new project to develop research questions to be addressed, or after the completion of a project as a means of disseminating the research findings. On a number of occasions, Institute staff with special interests were able to organise and present conferences on these topics, such as the present author's conference on *Health Care, Crime and Regulatory Control* in July 1997 (later published as Smith 1998) and *Crime in the Professions* in February 2000 (Smith 2002). Each Director of the Institute also developed conferences dealing with topics of personal research interest—that reflected the Institute's research at the time. Examples include Richard Harding's work on corrections and gun control, Duncan Chappell's work on art and antiquities crime, Adam Graycar's work on crime and older persons and Toni Makkai's work on illicit drugs.

Radzinowicz (1973, p. 8) also recommended having specific funding provided to enable the Director and the Director of Research to travel overseas to attend and present papers at congresses and events. Radzinowicz, himself, did not relish flying, as Jim Muirhead (1996, p. 99) observed while waiting for take-off at Melbourne's Tullamarine airport when Sir Leon 'persistently requested a glass of champagne... and refused to fasten his seatbelt'. Funding for travel was often available for AIC staff, but was regularly subject to criticism during difficult financial times. The Tanzer Review (1994), for example, was critical of the Institute's conference program and offered the following suggestions for better management:

> The Review recommends that the AIC conference program be much more closely aligned to the ongoing research program and certainly to the AICs agreed priority list. In devising conferences the program will rely much more heavily on the expertise of AIC research staff. In addition, the conferences program should seek to use a wider range of vehicles (seminars, briefings, etc.) for its information dissemination activities. All such activities should be driven by a clearly stated set of objectives and anticipated outcomes, including the need for each conference to cover its full costs, including assigned overheads. (Tanzer et al. 1994, p. 21)

In addition, Sir Leon had earlier expressed a note of caution for future Directors:

> As a general rule the Director of the Institute should refrain from making broad public statements on problems of crime and the administration of criminal justice, and on other related topics. He should confine himself to making statements, if necessary, that are directly connected with the work of the Institute, its reports, its seminars, and in fact to whatever has been done or is being done by the Institute as a whole. (Radzinowicz 1973, p. 8)

This advice has been adhered to by some directors more than others, although in recent years they have tended to limit public comments to overly brief, factual remarks only, leaving policy concerns for the Minister's Office alone to address. This has sometimes meant that the Institute, with its staff of highly qualified researchers, felt unable to provide frank advice on questions of crime prevention and control—a situation that is frustrating for the researchers in question, but also for the media and public who have sought genuine, and informed discussion of current policy questions.

Despite this, the AICs conferences provided an efficient means of disseminating research findings to government stakeholders, academics and those in the private sector. Quantifying the costs and benefits of AIC staff participating in external conferences and events is more difficult. Costs include staff time to seek permission to attend events, prepare presentations and actually travel to conference locations and participate in the activities. Benefits include meeting the AICs performance targets of disseminating work, professional development for staff, networking with other public officials and academics, and publicising the Institute's work locally and internationally. To make this quantification process accountable, directors and staff often gave detailed written reports following conferences and presented staff training seminars on their return. These, however, tended to fluctuate over time with accountability being less apparent publicly in recent times than in the past.

Since the onset of the global Coronavirus pandemic in 2020, AIC conferences and events were often conducted virtually, or in some cases, hybrid conferences were conducted with some face-to-face participation at the same time as live, online presentations. In 2020–21, all conference activity was cancelled and the Australian Crime and Violence Prevention Awards (ACVPA) ceremony was not held. This resumed as a face-to-face meeting once again during a conference organised by the AIC from 31 October to 2 November 2022. During the pandemics, supplier expenses further reduced in comparison with budget due to minimal travel and training undertaken (AIC, Annual Report 2021, p. 86). The savings in terms of travel costs and staff time have been considerable, although often AIC staff based in Canberra have been required to appear online in virtual conferences based in Europe or the US in the middle of the night!

Awards

In the academic community, it is *de rigueur* for associations to present awards each year to recognise individuals who have achieved excellence in their current research, teaching or administrative work. In the various criminological societies internationally, including ANZSOC, an ever-increasing list of awards and prizes is given for outstanding publications and activities by different classes of members including life-time achievement awards and fellowships. In addition, law enforcement agencies have a tradition of providing a wide range of awards and medals to their members in recognition of particular achievements and activities.

Following these traditions, in 1992, during Duncan Chappell's period as director and when Peter Grabosky was Director of Research, the Australian Heads of Government Violence Prevention Award was established to recognise and reward good practice in the prevention or reduction of violence and other types of crime in Australia. The idea for the Award came during a period of increased awareness of the problem of violence in the Australian community that arose following two mass firearms killings in Melbourne in August and December 1987 and a mass shooting incident in Sydney's Strathfield shopping mall in Sydney in August 1991. The Melbourne incidents led to the establishment of the National Committee on Violence in October 1988 to examine the nature and extent of violence in the community, and to develop strategies to prevent violence from occurring and to support victims and treat offenders. Duncan Chappell promoted the AIC to be appointed as Secretariat for the Committee with Peter Grabosky as the Research Director and other Institute members as research staff and assistants. It produced a wide range of publications, including the major monograph *Violence: Directions for Australia* (National Committee on Violence 1990). In his interview (30 January 2021), John Braithwaite saw the benefit of this work as being 'to work through a policy agenda so that as soon as the massacre at Port Arthur occurred in 1996, the policy work had been done' and the government had a range of solutions immediately available to use—including the firearm buy-back that was announced twelve days after the incident (see Mukherjee 1997). Braithwaite believed that this was, arguably, 'the highest impact thing that the Institute did in terms of changing Australia for the better' (Interview, 30 January 2021).

The Strathfield massacre in New South Wales led to the deaths of seven people and injury of six others. Using some of Peter Grabosky's ideas of 'regulation by reward' (subsequently published in 1995), it was decided to create a Violence Prevention Award worth up to $100,000 in late 1991. The award was designed to encourage communities to become more involved in violence prevention and to assist local governments in identifying and developing practical projects that would reduce violence in the community. The AIC was appointed to administer the Award under the direction of a Selection Board chaired by the AICs Director. Projects are judged according to their cost-effectiveness, success in preventing or reducing violence, extent to which they are community-based, their capacity to be developed elsewhere and, importantly, the extent to which they had been subjected to rigorous evaluation. Although the last criterion was originally recommended by Peter Grabosky, over time evidence of successful evaluation was less apparent among awardees.

The inaugural award was given in 1992 by Prime Minister Keating with three outstanding projects selected out of 184 nominations. The Julalikari Night Patrol in the Northern Territory, which dealt with violence associated with alcohol consumption among aborigines, received $40,000; the West End Forum in Victoria, which addressed the problem of violence in and around licensed premises, received $20,000 and the Kids' Help Line, now operating in five Australian States, to provide counselling to children received $20,000. Ten other projects were commended for their work in the areas of family violence, adolescents at risk, community action, justice institutions, preventive behaviour strategies, public violence, and violence and entertainment—each received $1,000 (AIC 1993; Keating 1993).

The award was later extended to include crime prevention initiatives, other than those solely relating to violence, and continues to be administered by the AIC. Award recipients are presented with a plaque by the AICs Director in the presence of the responsible Minister at Parliament House in Canberra. Between 1992 and 2022, 1,101 crime prevention initiatives have been recognised in the Awards scheme.

The Future of Training, Education, Conferences and Awards

Over the preceding fifty years, the Institute has produced and participated in a substantial number of meetings, training activities, public events and conferences. Most directors welcomed the opportunity to present the Institute's research and to network with stakeholders both in Australia and overseas in this way. This sometimes led to criticism over the costs involved and the time spent away from the office, but, on balance, the benefits outweighed these limitations, with the publicity obtained enabling the Institute to develop and maintain its reputation for undertaking and delivering trustworthy research of a high standard. The extent of participation in public events was substantial each year with senior staff each presenting more than a dozen papers every year—some considerably more in particular years.

Although participation in conferences and meetings satisfied the Institute's academic, educational remit, it was of a different nature to the training activities that the Institute was originally established to deliver. On his resignation as Director of the Institute in September 2003, Adam Graycar identified the need for the Institute to improve its training activities as one of the tasks he was unable fully to succeed in achieving:

> Our legislation gives the AIC training and research functions, and while we have performed well in the latter, we need more time to set up our training structures and adapt the feedback we get. The materials we have in our training are top quality and it always takes longer than expected to make a new function financially self-supporting, but we'll get there before too long. (Graycar 2003, p. 2) (Plate 12.10).

Over the twenty years since then, the Institute has continued to focus more on conducting and publishing research than delivering training programs, and, most recently, has largely relegated its training functions to reliance on virtual workshops, podcasts and social media. As the effects of the Coronavirus abate, the Institute will continue to deliver face-to-face events and participate more freely in local and international conferences. It is to be expected, however, that online and hybrid events become more prevalent in appropriate circumstances not only to minimise costs but also to save time and avoid environmental harms caused by extensive travel. As is the case with the Institute's other functions, the direction to be taken in delivery of training and educational activities remains uncertain and is subject to the vagaries of politics,

Plate 12.10   Dr Adam Graycar on his departure from the AIC in September 2003 (*Source* AIC Archives)

funding and the personal preferences of future directors and Advisory Council members.

References

Australian Institute of Criminology (AIC). 1993. *The Australian Violence Prevention Award 1992.* Canberra: Australian Institute of Criminology.

Australian Institute of Criminology (AIC). 1974–2021. Annual Report 1974–2021. Canberra: Australian Institute of Criminology.

Bevan, Colin Russell. 2005. *As the Walrus Said. The Time Has Come . . .* Canberra: Book Surge.

Braithwaite, John. 1984. Research Note: Education and Work: One Step Forward. Two Steps Back, *Australian and New Zealand Journal of Criminology* 17 (1): 49–57.

Challinger, Dennis. 1988. *Stop Stealing From Our Shops: Retail Theft in Australia.* Canberra: National Retail Crime Prevention Council.

Challinger, Dennis, ed. 1986. The Jury. *Seminar Proceedings*, no. 11. Canberra: Australian Institute of Criminology. https://www.aic.gov.au/sites/default/files/2021-04/aic-seminar-proceedings-11.pdf. Accessed 25 February 2022.

D'Apice, Richard J. W. 2000. *McClemens, John Henry (1905–1975)*. Australian Dictionary of Biography, vol 15, Melbourne: Melbourne University Press. https://adb.anu.edu.au/biography/mcclemens-john-henry-10912 Accessed: 6 February 2022.

Freiberg, Arie. 2001. *Department of Criminology, 1951–2001*. Melbourne: Department of Criminology, University of Melbourne.

Gearson, Susan, and Wilson, Paul R. 1992. *Preventing Retail Crime*. Canberra: Australian Institute of Criminology.

Grabosky, Peter N. 1995. Regulation by Reward: On the Use of Incentives as Regulatory Instruments. *Law and Policy* 17 (3): 256–281.

Graycar, Adam. 2003. Parting Words on Work that Matters. *AIC Newsletter*, no. 20, pp. 1–2. https://www.aic.gov.au/sites/default/files/2020-07/newsletter20.pdf Accessed 6 January 2022.

House of Representatives. 1971. Hansard, 27th Parliament, 24 February, p. 572, http://historichansard.net/hofreps/1971/19710224_reps_27_hor71/ Accessed 6 December 2022.

Hawkins, Gordon. 1990. Present at the Creation: The Inception and Development of the Institute of Criminology. *Current Issues in Crime and Criminal Justice*, 2 (1): 9–17. http://www.austlii.edu.au/au/journals/CICrimJust/1990/15.pdf. Accessed 3 February 2022.

Keating, Paul. 1993. Statement by the Prime Minister The Hon. P. J. Keating MP: Violence Prevention Awards. 26 February. https://pmtranscripts.pmc.gov.au/sites/default/files/original/00008831.pdf Accessed: 4 May 2022.

Mayhew, Patricia. 2003. Counting the Costs of Crime in Australia. *Trends & Issues in Crime and Criminal Justice*, no. 247, Canberra: Australian Institute of Criminology.

Muirhead, James Henry. 1996. *A Brief Summing Up*. Northbridge: Access Press.

Mukherjee, Satyanshu. 1997. Firearm-Related Violence in Australia. *Trends and Issues in Crime and Criminal Justice*, no. 70, Canberra: Australian Institute of Criminology.

Myrtle, John. 2016. Obituary: Colin Russell Bevan OAM 1921–2016, An Interesting and Varied Life in Australian Criminology. *PacifiCrim* 13 (2): 4.

National Committee on Violence. 1990. *Violence: Directions for Australia*, Canberra: AIC.

Radzinowicz, Leon. 1973. *Report of Sir Leon Radzinowicz with Respect to the Australian Institute of Criminology*, New York. Canberra: National Library of Australia (6093/72/4182).

Scutt, Jocelynne A., ed. 1987. *Lionel Murphy: A Radical Judge*. An Appraisal by Eleven Prominent Australians Melbourne: McCulloch Publishing Ltd.

Smith, Russell G, ed. 1998. *Health Care*. Crime and Regulatory Control, Sydney: Hawkins Press.

Smith, Russell G, ed. 2002. *Crime in the Professions*. Aldershot: Ashgate Publishing Limited.

Tanzer, Noel, Des Hill, and Grant Wardlaw. 1994. *Review of the Australian Institute of Criminology: Report*. Canberra: Australian Institute of Criminology.

13

International Relations

Introduction

As we have seen in Chapter 2, a number of initiatives were undertaken, internationally, to establish institutes and centres with a focus on crime and justice research. Most have been located within government agencies or universities, although a number have been privately-funded think tanks or business consultancies—such as the Max Planck Institute for the Study of Crime, Security and Law, in Germany and the RAND Corporation in the United States that includes a Justice Policy Program. Those who promoted the establishment of the AIC believed that it was important for there to be regular exchange of research, ideas and information that would inform not only those working in Australia of developments in criminal justice policy taking place in other countries, but also to share research undertaken by Australian scholars with those in comparable institutes and universities overseas. To facilitate this, Sir Leon Radzinowicz (1973, p. 8), in his Report to the Commonwealth on the establishment of the AIC, suggested:

© The Author(s), under exclusive license to Springer Nature
Switzerland AG 2023
R. G. Smith, *Public Sector Criminological Research*,
https://doi.org/10.1007/978-3-031-28356-7_13

> Funds should be provided to enable the Director of the Institute and the Director of Research to undertake journeys abroad in order to acquaint themselves with the workings of the leading criminological circles abroad. This item of expenditure should be a regular item of the Institute's budget.

In the pre-digital age of the 1970s, sharing of research invariably required individuals to travel to meetings and conferences internationally. As we have seen in Chapter 5, this entailed the allocation of both time and money to finance such travel—that attracted some criticism, particularly if travel expenditure was deemed to be excessive, or included luxury items such as first-class flights, fine-dining or accommodation in expensive hotels (see Tanzer et al. 1994). Even simply attending meetings in desirable tourist destinations could give rise to questions—despite the actual facilities enjoyed by AIC staff at some of these locations being far from luxurious.

In more recent times, with the advent of video conferencing, and, in particular, following the onset of the coronavirus pandemic, it has become possible for international liaison to be undertaken without the need for face-to-face meetings—although these are still necessary in certain circumstances, such as where levels of computer security may be in question, where individuals need to examine physical records in archives, where working relationships need to be established between heads of agencies or where confidential or highly personal or classified questions need to be discussed and resolution strategies negotiated (see the comprehensive review of the arguments for and against video conferencing for UN purposes by Joutsen 2022a).

The question that often arose was whether a public sector criminological research institute should primarily be inward-looking, focussing on the crime and justice questions arising within its own jurisdiction, or should be outward-looking, seeking evidence and answers to policy questions from other countries that could be applied or adapted to local conditions. This dilemma was particularly relevant to countries with few resources devoted to criminological research, such that there was a need to rely heavily on work carried out in more well-resourced countries. In the 1970s, Australia provided an example of this, and it was considered entirely justifiable, and desirable, for international liaison to be carried out regularly and in person.

In the Institute's original legislation, its functions were stated generally without specific reference to engaging in international activities (s. 6, *Criminology Research Act 1971* (Cth)). In 1986, however, a new function was added by the *Criminology Research Amendment Act 1986* (Cth) that specifically enabled the Institute 'to collaborate, in and outside Australia, with governments, institutions and authorities, and with bodies and persons, in relation to research, or the training of persons, in or in connection with the administration of criminal justice' (s. 6(hc)). These provisions have been retained in the current legislation although these functions are now given to the director (s. 16(k)). As such, the legislation places beyond question, the ability of the director to engage in international collaborative work.

The question has also arisen as to whether an agency such as the AIC should be able to speak to national questions of crime and justice policy and research on behalf of the entire country. Examples of this could include participating in international data collection exercises, such as the ICVS (van Kesteren et al. 2014), representing Australia's position on international criminal justice policy questions that have called for empirical research—such as the deterrent effects of capital punishment—or presenting research to inform decision-making regarding the development and acceptance of normative instruments such as UN Conventions. Clearly, some aspects of these discussions would be appropriate for staff from Departments of Foreign Affairs or the Attorney-General to address, but there have been many instances in which criminologists need to present and explain research findings themselves to international policy audiences. In the future, the use of video conferencing might help to facilitate the involvement of actual researchers (see Joutsen 2022a).

Further, the need for international liaison arises where comparative research work is undertaken by local researchers, or by others who wish to include their own country as a comparator. Having a network of established contacts enables researchers to know when such studies are being developed so that relevant countries can be represented in the research aims and methodologies, or the findings able to inform domestic policy. An example of this was when director Adam Graycar met with colleagues from the US through the UNODCs network and agreed to join the International Arrestee Drug Abuse Monitoring (I-ADAM) program that originally had contributors in seven countries: Chile, England, Malaysia, Netherlands, Scotland, South Africa and Taiwan (Taylor 2002). This led to Australia's own Drug Use Monitoring (DUMA) program being established, in respect of which Adam Graycar observed: 'without the international connections we would not have had DUMA' (Adam Graycar, Interview, 1 March 2021). International liaison also facilitated gaining access to confidential data held by government agencies that required the negotiation of access agreements and adherence to security policies. On a number of occasions in the past, the AIC has been involved in such studies, both as the principal researcher and as a collaborating partner.

Coming from a public sector environment, the task of establishing trust and security is sometimes easier than might be case for a university-based partner, or one from the private sector research community. An example of this occurred with the comparative study of sentencing cyber criminals undertaken by the AIC in the early 2000s that entailed collaboration between numerous public sector agencies in the US, the UK and Australia. Confidential Roundtable discussions were conducted in Washington, London and Canberra where public officials were able to share their experiences of investigating and prosecuting cyber criminals (Smith et al. 2004). Other studies have employed a comparative methodology in which representatives of numerous countries globally have been asked to contribute chapters to books edited by AIC staff (e.g. Graycar and Smith 2011; Smith et al. 2015).

As we shall see, the AICs Board, directors and staff have sought to achieve a reasonable balance in responding to these demands by ensuring that Australian policy-makers are aware of research conducted in other countries and that Australian interests are represented on the global stage but without neglecting local policy concerns or devoting too many resources to international pursuits. On occasions, the balance has shifted too far in one direction or the other, requiring correction by new directors or Boards. On the whole, however, the Institute has managed to satisfy both international and local interests reasonably well.

Relations with the United Nations

The development of the United Nations Criminal Justice Program since 1945 has been analysed and reviewed in the collection of essays by M. Cherif Bassiouni (1995) and also by Slawomir Redo's (2012) authoritative and extensive publication, *Blue Criminology*. In the latter volume, Redo, formerly Senior Expert in Crime Prevention at the UNODC in Vienna between 1981 and 2011, explained the relationship between criminological thought and the criminal justice policies and practices adopted by the UNODC. The work of the UN in studying, for example, transnational organised crime and drug crime, is, arguably, the foremost example of public sector criminology on a global scale and it is appropriate, therefore, to examine the AICs involvement in these activities over the preceding five decades.

The idea of establishing a criminological research institute in Australia was developed during discussions that took place at the first four UN Crime Congresses by members of the Australian delegations. These included Mr Justice John Barry, accompanied by Dr Norval Morris and Harold Vagg at the inaugural Crime Congress in Geneva in 1955 (Plate 13.1), Justices Barry and McClemens at the 2nd Crime Congress in London in 1960, Justice McClemens, accompanied by Norval Morris, three correctional officials from New South Wales, the First Secretary of the Stockholm Embassy and Dr Allen Bartholomew from Victoria at the 3rd Crime Congress in Stockholm in 1965, and John Maddison, Minister of Justice in New South Wales, Peter Loof, Norval Morris, five officials from correctional agencies and Gerald Harding from the Tokyo Embassy at the 4th Congress in Kyoto in 1970.

At breaks and side events during these lengthy proceedings, the principal players in the move to establish the AIC, Barry, McClemens, Morris and Loof, were able to refine their plans and secure the influence of some of the leaders in criminology. Although Barry appreciated the need for Australia to be represented at such international events, he was less than impressed with the operation at the first Crime Congress in Geneva, observing that '[t]he phoniness of the UN, the substantial incompetence of its secretariats, and the rootlessness of an international organization were strikingly brought home to me' (cited by Finnane 2006, p. 415).

Plate 13.1 Australian delegation at the 1st United Nations Crime Congress, Assembly Hall, Palais des Nations, Geneva, 1955. (front row r-l) Associate Professor Norval Morris, Mr Justice JV Barry, Harold Vagg, Deputy Comptroller of Prisons, New South Wales (*Source* Barry Family Archives, c/- Susy and John Barry)

Nonetheless, the scale of these congresses, the need for multi-lingual translations and the logistics of organising the events securely and efficiently cannot be discounted—particularly given the level of resourcing available in some locations.

Once established, the AIC was a regular participant in sessions of the UN Crime Committee, and, after 1991, the United Nations Commission on Crime Prevention and Criminal Justice. The AIC was also represented at some of the quinquennial congresses on the Prevention of Crime and the Treatment of Offenders (since 2005 known as the United Nations Congress on Crime Prevention and Criminal Justice) held in different countries since 1955. The most recent, 14th Crime Congress held in Kyoto in March 2021, was a hybrid conference with about 280 participants on-site and the vast majority, over 5,200, attending virtually—from 152 Member States, 114 non-governmental organisations, 37 intergovernmental organisations and 600 individual experts (Joutsen 2022a, p. 13). The Australian delegation of 21 members was led by the Hon. Peter Dutton MP, at the time Minister for Home Affairs, and included Dr Rick Brown representing the AIC as part of the PNI.

Once established, the AICs Director, Bill Clifford, set to work organising the Australian participation in the 5th Crime Congress held in Geneva in 1975 in the form of a delegation of 37 members headed by the Commonwealth Attorney-General, Kep Enderby. This was a substantial undertaking with Australia having the largest delegation of all participating nations. The Australian delegation included five of the seven AIC Board members, including the Chairman Frank Mahony and Deputy Chairman Peter Loof, as well as Bill Clifford and David Biles. Many international scholars were also present including Leon Radzinowicz from Cambridge, Ron Clarke from the UK Home Office and John Robson, former Secretary of Justice in New Zealand and inaugural Director of the Institute of Criminology at Victoria University, Wellington (Deckert 2021). In anticipation of the 5th Crime Congress, Bill Clifford had organised a Regional Preparatory meeting for Australian and South Pacific delegates, held at the AIC in January 1975. He had also visited UNAFEI in Tokyo and met John Robson in Wellington to prepare for the Congress in September 1975. Robson had also attended the second UN Crime Congress held in London in 1960 and made other visits to prisons in England, Denmark, Sweden and the United States in that connection over a period of three months. He recalled (Robson 1971, p. 198):

The overseas trip proved to be a most stimulating experience. The New Zealand taxpayers are pretty cynical on the subject of civil servants who travel overseas, but I hope they got value for money in my case. It was at the London Congress that I first met the late Sir John Barry, although we had been in correspondence for some time before then. He contributed substantially to what I gained from the trip.

Bill Clifford was also involved in substantial planning for the 1980 Crime Congress that Australia had offered to host, and its offer accepted by the UN in 1975 (see Clifford 1979 for the background to this, including his estimate that the Congress would cost between $3 million and $5 million to host in Sydney). Despite his extensive preliminary work, in 1979 the Fraser Coalition government decided to withdraw its offer of hosting the Congress (Redo 2012, p. 157). David Biles and Duncan Chappell (1995, p. 235) believed that this was due to 'security issues as well as escalating costs' and may have led to Australia's and the AICs reputations being tarnished. This Crime Congress was eventually held in Caracas, Venezuela—with the AIC represented only by Peter Loof and Frank Mahony from the Board, as well as the AICs Director. The Institute did, however, organise a special research session for the Congress at which Bill Clifford presented a paper (AIC Annual Report 1981, p. 2).

After Clifford retired from the AIC in 1983, and following discussion as to the utility of the AIC participating in further Crime Congresses, the AICs involvement became more limited, with representation being generally limited to directors and occasionally Board members or senior AIC managers such as Peter Grabosky who accompanied Adam Graycar at the 10th UN Crime Congress held in Vienna in 2000, and Research Manager, Peter Homel, who attended in 1995 and 2015. On other occasions, the Australian delegations were composed mainly of representatives of the Departments of Attorney-General, Foreign Affairs and, in 2021, Home Affairs. The last Congress to have a large Australian delegation, which numbered 25, occurred in 1985 in Milan with the AIC represented by Richard Harding, David Biles and Board Member for South Australia, Adam Sutton. Reflecting on the value of attending congresses, Richard Harding (1986, n.p.) observed:

> If one judges such a Congress in terms of its short-term operational impact, then it can hardly be disputed that it is not really cost-effective. … [Nonetheless] the Australian delegation contributed more than its share to the Congress deliberations. We sponsored three resolutions (Organised Crime, the Beijing Rules, and the Code of Conduct for Law Enforcement Officials), and co-sponsored four others. Our delegates were

prominent behind-the-scenes, as well as up-front. We knew what was going on, and could contribute to it because we had been thoroughly briefed.

Arguably, the greatest benefit of congresses was their delivery of normative criminal justice standards that individual Nation States could incorporate into their domestic laws. The *Standard Minimum Rules for the Treatment of Prisoners*, for example, that were adopted at the first Congress in 1955 and approved by the Economic and Social Council in 1957 were substantially reflected in the *Minimum Standard Guidelines for Corrections in Australia and New Zealand* (Conference of Ministers of Corrections 1987). The AICs research fed into the development of such initiatives that were then used to raise the profile of new areas of policy analysis for future implementation.

Crime Prevention and Criminal Justice Programme Network (PNI)

The idea of integrating research institutes into the UN Criminal Justice Programme was first mooted in 1954 and was formalised with the establishment of UNAFEI in Tokyo in 1962, followed by the UNICRI in Rome in 1968. Only UNICRI is a formal UN entity, with UNAFEI, the AIC and remaining institutes being, in most cases, affiliated with the UN in Memoranda of Association. Matti Joutsen, former Director of HEUNI, described four waves during which the research institutes joined the PNI (Redo 2012, p. 120). These are shown in Table 13.1.

After joining the Program Network, the Institutes, apart from UNICRI that was a UN entity, began a process leading to recognition by the UN, resulting in becoming formally affiliated with the UN in most instances. In the case of the AIC, this process began on 7 July 1988 when the AICs Director, Duncan Chappell, and Peter Loof, as Chairman of the Board, executed a Memorandum of Understanding (MOU) with the United Nations Crime Prevention and Criminal Justice Branch that set out the rights and obligations of the arrangement. The MOU was signed on behalf of the UN by Mrs (later Dame) Margaret Anstee,

Table 13.1 Waves of introducing PNI members

Wave	Year established*	Acronym (Type)	City (in 2022)	Full name
	1997	UNODC	Vienna Austria	United Nations Office on Drugs and Crime (PNI Secretariat)
1st	1962	UNAFEI (RI)	Tokyo Japan	Asia and Far East Institute for the Prevention of Crime and the Treatment of Offenders
	1968	UNICRI (IRI)	Turin Italy	United Nations Interregional Crime and Justice Research Institutes
	1975	ILANUD (RI)	San José Costa Rica	Latin American Institute for the Prevention of Crime and the Treatment of Offenders
	1981	HEUNI (RI-Aff)	Helsinki Finland	European Institute for Crime Prevention and Control, affiliated with the United Nations
	1987	UNAFRI (RI)	Kampala Uganda	African Regional Institute for the Prevention of Crime and the Treatment of Offenders
2nd	1972	AIC (NI)	Canberra Australia	Australian Institute of Criminology
	1972	NAUSS (RI)	Riyadh Saudi Arabia	Naif Arab University for Security Sciences
	1972	SII (SI)	Siracusa Italy	The Siracusa International Institute for Criminal Justice and Human Rights
	1991	ISPAC (SI)	Milan Italy	International Scientific and Professional Advisory Council of the United Nations Crime Prevention and Criminal Justice Programme
	1991	ICCLRCJP (SI)	Vancouver Canada	International Centre for Criminal Law Reform and Criminal Justice Policy
	1994	ICPC (SI)	Montreal Canada	International Centre for the Prevention of Crime

(continued)

Table 13.1 (continued)

Wave	Year established*	Acronym (Type)	City (in 2022)	Full name
3rd	1968	NIJ (NI)	Washington USA	National Institute of Justice (formerly National Institute of Law Enforcement and Criminal Justice)
	1984	RWI (SI)	Lund Sweden	Raoul Wallenberg Institute of Human Rights and Humanitarian Law
	1989	KICJ (NI)	Seoul South Korea	Korean Institute of Criminology and Justice (formerly Korean Institute of Criminology)
	1991	ISS (SI)	Pretoria South Africa	Institute for Security Studies (formerly Institute for Defence Policy)
4th	2003	BASEL (SI)	Basel Switzerland	Basel Institute on Governance - International Center for Asset Recovery
	2005	CCLS (NI)	Beijing PR China	College for Criminal Law Science, Beijing Normal University
	2011	TIJ (NI)	Bangkok Thailand	Thailand Institute of Justice

Note Years refer to establishment of the entities not their joining the PNI Abbreviations: IRI—Interregional Institute; RI—Regional Institute; Aff—Affiliated with the UN; SI—Specialised Institutes with an international mandate; NI—National Level Institutes; *Source* Derived from Redo (2012, p. 120), Viljanen and Joutsen (2012) and Joutsen (2022b)

Director-General of the UN Office in Vienna and Head of the Centre for Social Development and Humanitarian Affairs (AIC Annual Report 1988, pp. 2–3). In essence, these duties were to collaborate in research, participate in events, provide advice and access to experts and to assist in the conduct of UN activities. All work was to be resourced locally, without UN support but the Institute could, in return, publicise its affiliated status (Biles and Chappell 1995, pp. 235–6). In Australia, examples of this included the display of the UN flag on the AICs building and acknowledgement of its affiliated status on its letterhead and publications. At the opening of the AICs building on 25 July 1990, Director Duncan Chappell, after recalling his predecessor Bill Clifford's death in

1986, observed, 'Bill would have been especially pleased to see the UN flag flying outside this new building–he always retained a deep interest in and commitment to the international aspects of the Institute's work' (Chappell 1990, n.p.) (Plate 13.2).

The Institute then went through a formal affiliation process, details of which are set out in Resolution 1994/23 of the United Nations Economic and Social Council (United Nations 1995). Slawomir Redo (2012, p. 119) commented on the delay in achieving affiliated status by observing: 'this painstakingly long process of institutionalization of international criminology in Australia is an indicator of "blue blood" coagulation'. Once affiliated, Duncan Chappell also arranged for the Institute's new status to be printed on all official documents (Plate 13.3).

The AICs association with the UN not only provided some reflected glory, but also proved to be an effective way in which to showcase the

Plate 13.2   United Nations flag at AICs building in 1990 (*Source* AIC Archives)

8 July 1993

Professor Duncan Chappell
Director
Australian Institute of Criminology
GPO Box 2944
CANBERRA ACT 2601

Dear Duncan

Plate 13.3 AIC Letterhead, July 1993 (*Source* AIC Archives)

Institute's research on the global stage. At the opening of the Institute's new building in 1990, for example, the Minister for Justice and Consumer Affairs, Senator the Hon. Michael Tate (1990, n.p.) emphasised this:

> What is so remarkable and pleasing to note in the short history of the AIC is the fact that not only does it have a very deserved eminence within this nation but it has an international reputation which has been won, I don't say easily, but because of the very evident quality of the work, the members, the directors of the Institute, it has achieved very readily shall I say an eminence internationally which is certainly something which I've become conscious of as I move around on the very occasional overseas trip that the Prime Minister allows (mirth in audience).

Over time, however, questions arose as to the value of the Institute's relationship with the UN, the benefits of 'occasional trips' and whether the PNI was fulfilling its mandate. In his Interview (30 November 2020), John Walker recounted his views about why the Australian government's attitudes to UN work changed:

In the early years, the government wanted the AIC to be seen as a world leader in criminology, so the international activities were fully justifiable. Collaboration, particularly with the UNODC and UNICRI, produced some exciting research. Sadly, the winds of change during the Howard years, were not recognised, and the government's view that the AIC did too much international travelling probably contributed to the savage budget cuts of 1994.

Following the move to new premises in 1996, the UN flag no longer adorned the Institute's building. Viljanen and Joutsen (2012) described the objectives of the PNI as being to provide the UNODCs Secretariat with a regional perspective on various issues and to augment the limited capacity that the Secretariat had for technical assistance requested by the Member States. One of the principal problems with the concept of the Network was the lack of coordination of the activities of the individual PNI members. Because each was answerable to its own Government and Boards of Management, the focus was principally on undertaking their own research without contributing to a program of work that would enrich the UNODC and the Commission. Matti Joutsen noted this in September 1993 (cited by Viljanen and Joutsen 2012, p. 7):

> The Commission should pay much more attention to what the institutes are doing. As it stands now … the coordination appears to be largely limited to half-hearted listening while the institute representatives review their record of accomplishments over the preceding year … A further difficulty is that the activities reported to the Commission are almost inevitably in the past tense: they are records of what has been done, not what is planned…. The regrettable conclusion from the foregoing is that the Commission does not carry out its specific mandate of coordinating the work of the institutes. Worse, most members of the Commission do not seem to be aware of the work that the Institutes are doing, and thus of how the PNI could contribute to the UN programme.

Slawomir Redo (2012, p. 121) encapsulated the problem for PNI members such as the AIC well:

The other institutes must remain mindful of their original mandate, which for example in the case of the national institutes in Australia, South Africa, South Korea and the United States is understandably focused on national priorities in crime and justice. Quite simply, their management structure may not allow the institutes to carry out UN-related activities, unless these at the same time contribute to the basic mission of the institute in question.

In recent times, however, the Institutes have engaged in various activities that have been truly cooperative and of benefit to the work of the UNODC. Some examples of work that the AIC has participated in are illustrative of the benefits that have arisen. Of particular importance has been the support work undertaken by the Institutes in connection with forthcoming Crime Commissions and Crime Congresses, including the organisation and attendance at preparatory meetings, workshops, ancillary meetings and side events at congresses and sessions of the Commission (Joutsen 2022b). AIC staff have assisted in these activities, particularly those that have been based on current topics of research the Institute had been doing. In January 1975, for example, Australia hosted the Regional Preparatory Meeting for the 5th UN Crime Congress to be held in Geneva in September 1975 at which an Australian delegation of 37 members included Frank Mahony, Peter Loof, Bill Clifford and David Biles representing the AIC.

In more recent times, the Institute's work on cybercrime has become increasingly relevant to the concerns of the UNODC and PNI. In May 2018, for example, the PNI members coordinated a Workshop on the theme of the 27th session of the Commission entitled 'Criminal justice responses to prevent and counter cybercrime in all its forms, including through the strengthening of cooperation at the national and international levels'. The Workshop focussed on two central themes: policing economic cybercrime and legislative harmonisation and procedural reform across borders. Dr Rick Brown acted as Moderator with presentations by Professor Michael Levi of Cardiff University and Professor Jonathan Clough of Monash University, followed by discussion by panels of experts from among PNI members (Plate 13.4).

Plate 13.4 PNI Cybercrime Workshop, United Nations Commission on Crime Prevention and Criminal Justice, Vienna, 14 May 2018. [(l-r) The Author and Dr Rick Brown, AIC Deputy Director] (*Source* AIC Archives)

In May 2022, the AIC also moderated a PNI Workshop entitled 'Improving criminal justice responses to Internet-related crimes against children' at the annual session of the UN Crime Commission. This workshop was held at the Vienna International Centre with presentations by researchers from the AIC, HEUNI, UNICRI, the Karolinska Institutet in Stockholm, the UNODCs Global Programme to End Violence Against Children and academic researchers from the University of Adelaide and San Jose State University in the United States. The Workshop was made available to all Commission delegates online.

In addition to work carried out in conjunction with sessions of the Commission and at UN Crime Congresses, the AIC undertook a variety of other research activities for or on behalf of the UNODC. In March 1989, for example, the JV Barry Memorial Library became a full member of the United Nations Criminal Justice Information Network (UNCJIN) that sought to promote the exchange of criminological information internationally. This Network was the brainchild of Professors Ron Clarke and Graeme Newman in the US who promoted the idea to the UN Crime Prevention and Criminal Justice Branch and the PNI members.

In April 1991, Clarke and Newman convened a meeting at Rutgers University to create another network, the World Criminal Justice Library Network (WCJLN) that would 'bring together librarians and information specialists in the field of criminology' (Myrtle and Schultze 2011, p. 505). The AIC actively participated in these Networks and attended meetings in different host nations such as the large, three-day, international 7th meeting of the WCJLN in Canberra from 13 to 15 January 2003. The foundation libraries in the Network were the Radzinowicz Library in Cambridge, the German National Criminology Library in Tuebingen, the National Criminal Justice Reference Service of the NIJ in Washington, the Rutgers Criminal Justice Library and the JV Barry Library. Since its establishment, the Network has continued to grow and, as Adam Graycar recalled in his interview (1 March 2021), 'the Institute's international connections developed through the UNODC were important for the librarians who exchanged a huge amount of material, particularly between the three world-class libraries at Cambridge, Rutgers and the AIC'.

In April 1989, John Myrtle, the AICs Librarian-in-charge, travelled to Finland to advise HEUNI on the development of its computer-based library system, and in February 1992, he travelled to Kampala, Uganda, to advise UNAFRI on the establishment of a computerised library information system using a small computer donated by the AIC for this purpose (Biles and Chappell 1995, p. 236).

Armed with this growing expertise, in September 1990, John Myrtle attended the Eighth UN Crime Congress in Havana, Cuba, to speak about the UNCJIN network, and in April 1991, he presented a keynote address at the first World Criminal Justice Library Conference at Rutgers University. Two years later, in June 1993, he then presented a paper at the second conference in Siracusa, Italy. This work on computerisation of criminal justice information systems is examined in the HEUNI publication by Scherpenzeel (1992) that included the report of the first UN Workshop on Computerization of Criminal Justice Information held at the Eighth UN Crime Congress. In more recent times, however, with the increase in electronic resources, and since 2020 with the reduction in global travel and more restricted budgets, the AICs participation in international conferences and UNCJIN and WCJLN events has declined.

More recently, the PNI members have developed the International Criminal Justice Knowledge Centre (2022) as an electronic resource to share the extensive research outputs and expertise of the member institutes. Its aim is to respond to requests for information in relation to criminal justice issues, by referring users to the resources of PNI member institutes as well as organisations with expertise in specific topics. It has online links to partner agencies that have knowledge on specific criminal justice topics, as well as a calendar of criminal justice events, database of institutes and organisations and extensive publications database. The Centre is coordinated by the SII and supported by PNI members, including the AIC.

The AICs research staff have also undertaken a wide range of international activities on behalf of the UNODC and PNI. In 2001, for example, work was undertaken on the Global Programme Against Trafficking in Human Beings, organised by the UNODC that included preparation of comprehensive questionnaire materials for use in the United Nation's Global Programme and involved attendance at planning missions in the Philippines. In 2002, the AIC was asked to prepare a publication that described Australia's response to transnational organised crime. The resulting report, *The Worldwide Fight Against Transnational Organised Crime: Australia,* that was later published (AIC 2004), formed part of a global compilation undertaken by other PNI members for the UNODC. In October 2003, the present author participated as a Visiting Expert at a Brainstorming Session on 'Measures to Combat Economic Crime Including Money Laundering' conducted by UNAFEI in Tokyo, in preparation for a Workshop held at the 11th Crime Congress in Bangkok in 2005.

The AIC has also undertaken specific research projects with international reach. In 1989, 1992, 2000 and 2004, the AIC managed the Australian component of the ICVS with the 2004 component involving interviews with 7,000 Australians about their experience and perceptions of crime and the criminal justice system. John Walker was the initial point of contact at the AIC and visited Jan van Dijk at the Netherlands Ministry of Justice while he was seconded to the UK Home Office to discuss the Australian component of the survey. The study also presented information on risk factors associated with victimisation, unreported crime and fear of crime that has been used to inform future crime prevention and reduction activities (Walker et al. 1990). The 2004 study was undertaken by Dr Holly Johnson, AIC Visiting Research Fellow from Statistics Canada (Johnson 2005).

More recently, in 2018, the AIC managed a program of research for the UNODCs Sharing Electronic Resources and Laws on Crime (SHERLOC) by compiling summary case notes on organised economic criminal cases in Australia and Asia–Pacific countries. These were undertaken to support the work of the UNODC in making the jurisprudence from Australia and the region more widely available using the SHERLOC portal. Other recent projects have related to research on human trafficking, online child abuse, identity crime and cybercrime with findings shared at Workshops and meetings held in conjunction with commissions and congresses.

International Stakeholders

International Conferences and Meetings

Each year, staff of the Institute have attended or participated in a wide range of conferences and meetings. These have fallen into a number of categories including events to which the Institute or specific staff members have been invited to attend to present papers, chair sessions or act as rapporteurs. Institute staff have also submitted applications to present papers at conferences—usually those in respect of which staff members are members of professional associations, such as ANZSOC. Other opportunities have arisen where the Institute has been formally involved in organising conferences and has had a long-standing involvement in the particular society or organisation promoting the event.

One of the earliest examples of this was the creation of the Asian and Pacific Conference of Correctional Administrators in 1979 by the Director, Bill Clifford and Mr Tom Garner, Commissioner of Prisons in Hong Kong. This fulfilled a number of the Institute's original aims including the conduct of training programs for criminal justice personnel and engagement with practitioners in the Asia–Pacific region. The participants agreed to the Institute organising the conference largely because it was seen as independent and trustworthy—'it was an event which brought great kudos to the Institute, especially in the local region' (Dennis Challinger, Interview, 18 February 2022). The first conference was held in Hong Kong from 25 to 29 February 1980 with 27 representatives from 11 countries (Clifford, Kay and Isles 1980). It was originally created to facilitate preparation for the Sixth UN Crime Congress that was one of Bill Clifford's principal interests, particularly relating to human rights and obligations internationally. The proceedings of these conferences provide examples of the early attempts to draw together information on how differing countries in the region approached questions of criminal justice and the role of corrections. Thirteen conferences were held until the final one, again in Hong Kong, in November 1993, with 58 delegates attending (Biles and Harding 1994).

The financial year 1986–87 was a particularly active year for international liaison at the Institute with seven Institute staff visiting ten separate countries on official business. This level of international liaison was not unique, but illustrates the level of interest in international affairs—recalling that a proportion of travel costs were recovered from those who arranged the visits rather than the AIC. Between 10 April and 3 May 2001, director Adam Graycar undertook a gruelling series of international meetings that are documented in a 23-page report that summarised meeting with more than 50 individuals in Europe and North America. Multiple meetings in each location, or before or following the main activity, were also arranged to maximise the benefit to the government, but such travel created some disquiet within the Institute and the Department.

In relation to international conferences, the Tanzer Review of the AIC recommended that 'international activities will be at a significantly lower level than in recent years unless they are externally financed on a full cost recovery basis' (Tanzer et al. 1994, pp. 22–23). Because the AIC had acted as Secretariat for the Correctional Administrators, it was expected that the AICs Director and other senior delegates would attend (Plate 13.5). On each occasion, travel costs were incurred, although the

Plate 13.5 Richard Harding (at the right) at the opening of the Asian and Pacific Conference of Correctional Administrators, Kuala Lumpur, 14 September 1987 (*Source* Dennis Challinger)

host city paid for actual venue expenses. When the conference came to Australia in September 1988, costs were shared between Sydney and Melbourne, with a number of private sector correctional companies providing additional sponsorship. Nonetheless, participation in these conferences attracted some criticism—particularly when they took place in Pacific Island resorts such as in Tonga and Fiji.

In 1992–93, the Institute spent over $200,000 in respect of travelling allowances and expenses (AIC Annual Report 1993, p. 84). This was the most expended in one year since the Institute began. From 18 October 1992 to June 1993, the director, Duncan Chappell was in South Africa chairing the Commonwealth Observer Mission to South Africa at the request of the Commonwealth Secretary General. A number of other international activities took place with senior research staff attending United Nations and PNI meetings in Rome, Vienna and the UAE and other conferences in Indonesia and the United States.

The benefits of international liaison were, however, many as researchers were able to discover the latest information from both public and private sector organisations, develop relationships for future collaborative research projects and present the results of AIC research that informed other comparable bodies. One example of this was the Institute's involvement in the annual International Symposium on Economic Crime held at Jesus College, Cambridge. Owing to the subject-matter expertise of the present author, and others, the AIC was invited to become one of the organising institutions by providing speakers on more than a dozen occasions over the 40 years during which the Symposium has been conducted. As the Institute developed expertise in economic crimes such as money laundering, transaction fraud, identity crime and online consumer scams, attending the symposium provided an effective means of professional education for staff as well as allowing the Institute to showcase its research and to establish relationships among the 2,000 or so delegates who attended each year from over 100 countries.

Many diverse views have been expressed about the costs and benefits of engaging in international events and activities—some of which are quantifiable, while others are intangible. In his interview, former director, Adam Tomison, emphasised the international reputation the AIC has acquired from its research, and the support it has provided for other PNI members and organisations in developing their expertise and growing the sector. The AICs staff also benefited from learning from scholars and policy-makers in other countries and were able to contribute to the body of global criminological research (Adam Tomison, Interview, 26 October 2022). However, involvement in international activities came at a cost. In connection with the 13th UN Crime Congress held in Doha in April 2015 at which the AIC coordinated a workshop entitled 'Public Contribution to Crime Prevention and Raising Awareness of Criminal Justice–Experiences and Lessons Learned', Tomison observed:

> Huge amounts of work went into that.… It was not a good use of our time in the sense of the amount of time it took to get it all going. It was, however, incredibly well-received and seen as a benchmark for that Congress and so I was very proud of what we did. It was probably not the

best use of our time but it was an important part of supporting the crime and justice community. (Adam Tomison, Interview, 26 October 2022).

Associating with experts from other countries could, however, yield important benefits. Attending the Cambridge Symposium on Economic Crime enabled the present author to keep on top of global developments in the regulation of financial transactions that was used to inform the AICs AML/CTF research program. Peter Grabosky also recalled that 'much of what I learned about cybercrime was imparted at preparatory meetings for UN Congresses. This was subsequently shared widely through publications and presentations after returning to Australia' (Personal Communication 26 October 2022). The Director of the AIC in 2022, Michael Phelan, in his interview (3 November 2022) was highly supportive of the AICs international activities. This was reflected in his support for the AIC to undertake research for the Five Eyes law enforcement agencies that arose out of a meeting in Sydney in 2022. The Five Eyes agencies from the US, UK, Canada, New Zealand and Australia (see Kerbaj 2022) were able to commission the AIC to undertake this work quickly owing to the close relationship that now exists between the AIC and ACIC.

International Visiting Fellows

Another way in which the Institute developed and improved its international ties was to support overseas visitors spending time in Canberra, on some occasions at their own expense, and sometimes with partial support from the Institute. A wide range of policy specialists and academics visited the Institute, some staying for short periods in conjunction with attendance at conferences in Australia or Asia, while others stayed for a month or more working on specific projects, giving seminars and workshops, meeting officials from other departments and helping AIC staff with their research. Some of the AICs notable International Research Fellows have included Professor John Hudzik from Michigan State University who examined fiscal management for law enforcement funded by a Fulbright Senior Scholarship between 9 March and 21 April 1987;

Professor Gloria Laycock OBE, who had established the UK Home Office Police Research Group, spent four months at the AIC in 2001; Pat Mayhew OBE, also from the UK Home Office, visited the AIC in 2002–03 and worked on a variety of projects including the Institute's cost of crime research; Dr Holly Johnson, Visiting Research Fellow from Statistics Canada, who worked on the ICVS between March 2003 and June 2005; Professor Paul Ekblom, from the London Research Centre for Design Against Crime, who was a Visiting Research Fellow in November to December 2008 and gave a number of presentations on crime prevention and the role of design against crime and Professor Michael Levi, from Cardiff University, who was a Visiting Research Fellow in April 2009, worked on a publication dealing with fraud vulnerabilities and the global financial crisis. These were in addition to many eminent overseas scholars and practitioners who often visited to present papers at seminars, workshops and conferences.

The Future of International Relations

Public sector criminological research is epitomised internationally by the work of the UN Crime Prevention and Criminal Justice Program, and it was appropriate, therefore, that there be close involvement between this Program and those who sought to establish a government-funded research institute in Australia. The work of the UN on crime prevention and criminal justice was developed partly in response to the problems that arose during and after the Second World War, by seeking to coordinate research efforts in Nation States and global regions that dealt with both domestic crime problems that occurred on a global scale and cross-border, transnational crimes such as those involving illicit drugs, human trafficking, sea piracy and more recently organised economic crime and cybercrime (see Blaustein et al. 2022). In the early 1970s, few criminology departments in Australia, and the region, had an interest in these crime types and how they were dealt with globally—apart from the isolated but novel efforts of those such as Stanley Johnston in the Melbourne Department of Criminology who introduced the subject United Nations Criminal Law in 1978, which examined the jurisdiction and procedures of the UN in relation to crime and criminal justice—that the present author was able to undertake in 1981 (Smith 2018). As Richard Fox, former Chairman of the AIC Board, observed in his Interview (15 February 2022), 'Stan's concept of globalisation was way ahead of its time'. Developments in globalisation and computerisation have made 'Blue Criminology' a growing and increasingly important discipline, as Redo (2012) explained—but few resources were directed to undertaking research in these areas. The creation of the AIC, along with the other PNI member institutes, was, accordingly, an important and timely development. It should also be recalled that in recent years the UNODC, itself, has developed a much more extensive research capability and has not needed to rely on PNI members to undertake the research needed for UN activities. The role and importance of the PNI have, accordingly changed, undergoing what Rick Brown called 'an identity crisis'. Membership of the PNI now seems to provide more of a network for the benefit of the PNI members themselves as they share their research and contribute to group activities, than for the UN itself (Rick Brown, 4 November 2022). Efforts are, however, needed to ensure that the work of the PNI is supported into the future, as emphasised by Redo (2012, p. 215):

> There are important differences and similarities between international academic and practical perspectives in responding to crime. United Nations criminological thought has a far greater outreach than academic criminology, since it has a greater transformative power than the latter has, and rests on partly different methodological principles. … But there is also a common criminological thread in both pursuits. This is the need to counteract crime in the name of sustained development of a society and individual–so ably envisioned for the whole world by Gandhi.

Blaustein et al. (2022) explore this idea further in their work on the relationship between sustainable development and crime control. It has, however, been difficult to sustain government interest in funding such pursuits, especially during the pre-digital age, when overseas travel was a necessity to attend meetings and liaise with researchers in other countries. As we have seen, the need to undertake criminological research dealing with international crime problems was often seen as a pursuit that could be dispensed with in difficult financial times. State and territory interests in Australia also favoured the examination and development of solutions to their local crime problems in preference to considering international crime concerns.

Currently, however, the development of the internet, globalised illicit markets and the free movement of people, goods and services across borders have led to a growing concern with transnational crimes that has provided a clear justification for public sector criminological research to be supported, if not expanded, internationally. To meet these needs, the types of research undertaken by UN PNI members need to be supported and enhanced, with additional emphasis being placed on encouraging young criminologists to work in these areas. As we shall see below, this will require support from both universities, in giving priority to global crime concerns, as well as governments in providing research funding for criminological research in these areas. This will require a substantial overhaul of priorities away from research on local, street and domestic crime types to the crimes of the twenty-first century—such as cybercrime, environmental crime, transnational economic crime and border-related illegality—that are now costing economies considerably more than conventional crime (Smith and Hickman 2022). Public sector criminological research institutes, such as the AIC, are well placed to develop research in these areas that the current generation of criminology graduates tends to devalue. It is, therefore, important for governments to support international research that, in times of electronic communications, is now much easier and less costly to carry out.

References

Australian Institute of Criminology (AIC). 1981–1993. Annual Report 1981–1993. Canberra: Australian Institute of Criminology.

Australian Institute of Criminology (AIC). 2004. The Worldwide Fight Against Transnational Organised Crime: Australia, *Technical and Background Paper No. 9*, Canberra: Australian Institute of Criminology.

Bassiouni, M. Cherif, ed. 1995. *The Contributions of Specialized Institutes and Non-Governmental Organizations to the United Nations Criminal Justice Program, 233–238.* The Hague: Martinus Nijhoff Publishers.

Biles, David and Duncan Chappell. 1995. AIC: The International Role of the Australian Institute of Criminology, in Bassiouni, M. Cherif (ed.), The Contributions of Specialized Institutes and Non-Governmental Organizations to the United Nations Criminal Justice Program, 233–238, The Hague: Martinus Nijhoff Publishers.

Biles, David and Richard Harding. 1994. *Corrections in Asia and the Pacific: Record of the Thirteenth Asian and Pacific Conference of Correctional Administrators, Hong Kong, November 1993.* Asian and Pacific Conference of Correctional Administrators no. 13. Canberra: Australian Institute of Criminology. Blaustein, Chodor and Pino 2022.

Blaustein, Jarrett, Tom Chodor and Nathan W. Pino. 2022. *Unraveling the Crime-Development Nexus,* Lanham: Rowmkan and Littlefield.

Chappell, Duncan. 1990. Address at the Opening of the Australian Institute of Criminology's Marcus Clarke Street Building, AIC Archives, Video File, 25 July, Canberra.

Clifford, William. 1979. Director's Digest. *Australian Institute of Criminology Reporter* 1 (1): 3–5.

Clifford, William, Peter Kay and Tim Isles. 1980. *Corrections in Asia and the Pacific: Proceedings of the First Asian and Pacific Conference of Correctional Administrators, Hong Kong, 25–29 February 1980.* Asian and Pacific conference of correctional administrators no. 1. Canberra: Australian Institute of Criminology. https://www.aic.gov.au/publications/apcca/apcca1 Accessed 28 February 2022.

Conference of Ministers of Corrections. 1987. *Minimum Standard Guidelines for Corrections in Australia and New Zealand,* Melbourne: Conference of Ministers of Corrections.

Deckert, Antje. 2021. Battles and Legacies: Reviewing Robson's 1971 Article on Penal Policy in Aotearoa. In *The Changing Face of Criminology in Australia and New Zealand,* ed. Russell G. Smith, 163–175. London: Sage Publications Ltd.

Finnane, Mark. 2006. The ABC of Criminology: Anita Muhl. *JV Barry, Norval Morris and the Making of a Discipline in Australia, British Journal of Criminology* 46 (3): 399–422.

Graycar, Adam, and Russell G. Smith, eds. 2011. *Handbook of Global Research and Practice in Corruption.* Cheltenham: Edward Elgar Publishing Ltd.

Harding, Richard. 1986. The UN and Crime Prevention. *AIC Reporter* 6 (6): 3–4.

International Criminal Justice Knowledge Centre. 2022. http://justiceknowl edgecenter.org/ Accessed 27 October 2022.

Johnson, Holly. 2005. Crime Victimisation in Australia: Key Findings of the 2004 International Crime Victimisation Survey. *Trends and Issues in Crime and Criminal Justice* no. 298. Canberra: Australian Institute of Criminology.

Joutsen, Matti. 2022a. Staying Connected: The impact of the Covid-19 pandemic on United Nations Crime Programme meetings, Conference room paper submitted by the Permanent Mission of Finland to the thirty-first session of the United Nations Commission on Crime Prevention and Criminal Justice, E/CN.15/2022a/CRP.5, Vienna: UNODC.

Joutsen, Matti. 2022b. The PNI in a (Very Large) Nutshell, *PNI Newsletter*, Issue 01: 13–16. https://knowledge.tijthailand.org/en/publication/detail/ pni-newsletter-issue-1spring-2022b Accessed 19 August 2022b.

Kerbaj, Richard. 2022. *The Secret History of the Five Eyes: The Untold Story of the International Spy Network*. London: John Blake Publishing.

Myrtle, John, and Phyllis A. Schultze. 2011. World Criminal Justice Library Network. In *International Crime and Justice*, ed. Mangai Natarajan, 504–511. New York: Cambridge University Press.

Radzinowicz, Leon. 1973. *Report of Sir Leon Radzinowicz with Respect to the Australian Institute of Criminology*, New York. Canberra: National Library of Australia (6093 / 72/4182).

Redo, Slawomir M. 2012. *Blue Criminology: The Power of United Nations Ideas to Counter Crime Globally: A Monographic Study*, HEUNI Publication Series No. 72, Helsinki: HEUNI. https://heuni.fi/documents/47074104/0/ Blue_Criminology_www_linked.pdf/0013989d-f932-25ab-ec52-5f21884da 6d3/Blue_Criminology_www_linked.pdf?t=1610010139161 Accessed 13 May 2022.

Robson, John L. 1971. Penal Policy in New Zealand. *Australian and New Zealand Journal of Criminology* 4 (4): 195–206.

Scherpenzeel, Richard. 1992. *Computerization of Criminal Justice Information Systems*, HEUNI Publication Series No. 19, The Hague: The Netherlands

Smith, Russell G. 2018. Stanley William Johnston: A Personal Reflection, *PacifiCrim: ANZSOC Newsletter*, 15 (2): 17–18.

Smith, Russell G., Raymond C-C, Cheung, and Laurie Y-C, Lau, eds. 2015. *Cybercrime Risks and Responses: Eastern and Western Perspectives*. Houndmills: Palgrave Macmillan.

Smith, Russell G., Peter N. Grabosky, and Gregor F. Urbas. 2004. *Cyber Criminals on Trial*. Cambridge: Cambridge University Press.

Smith, Russell G. and Hickman, Amelia. 2022. Estimating the Costs of Serious and Organised Crime in Australia 2020–21. *Statistical Report*, no. 38, Canberra: Australian Institute of Criminology. https://www.aic.gov.au/pub lications/sr/sr38 Accessed 1 May 2022.

Tanzer, Noel, Des Hill and Grant Wardlaw. 1994. *Review of the Australian Institute of Criminology: Report*. Canberra: Australian Institute of Criminology.

Taylor, Bruce (ed.). 2002. *I-ADAM in Eight Countries: Approaches and Challenges*, Washington: Office of Justice Programs. http://www.ncjrs.gov/pdffil es1/nij/189768.pdf Accessed 31 August 2022.

United Nations. 1995. *Criteria and Procedures for the Affiliation with the United Nations of Institutes or Centres and the Establishment of United Nations Subregional Institutes in the Field of Crime Prevention and Criminal Justice*, 43rd Plenary Meeting of the Economic and Social Council, Resolution 1994/ 23, Official Records Supplement No. 1, 25 July 1994, New York: United Nations.

van Kesteren, John, Jan van Dijk, and Patricia Mayhew. 2014. The International Crime Victims Surveys: A Retrospective, *International Journal of Victimology*, 20 (1): 49–69.

Viljanen, Terhi, and Matti Joutsen. 2012. The Identity, Role and the Profile of the PNI: Some Questions that Need to be Asked—And Some Suggestions for Answers, Unpublished internal document for PNI members, 10 April, Canberra: AIC Archives.

Walker, John, Paul Wilson and Duncan Chappell. 1990. A Comparison of Crime in Australia and Other Countries, *Trends and Issues in Crime and Criminal Justice* no. 23, Canberra: Australian Institute of Criminology. https://www.aic.gov.au/publications/tandi/tandi23 Accessed 31 August 2022.

14

Merging Priorities

Introduction

When the AIC was established, the *Criminology Research Act 1972* (Cth) provided for the Institute to be a statutory authority of the Commonwealth with a Board of Management composed of three members appointed by the Commonwealth Attorney-General and three members representing the states. The advice of Sir Leon Radzinowicz (1965) on the creation of the Institute was, following the model of the Cambridge Institute, that the AIC should be independent of government and, accordingly, able to conduct research and provide advice free from party-political considerations. This was particularly important where crime statistics were being gathered or used for research purposes as the presentation of official crime data often led to government policies being challenged or criticised. Paul Wilson (1990), former Assistant Director, Research, for example, cited the case in the 1970s of officers of New South Wales Police deliberately underestimating the incidence of corruption and crime in the state to increase its clear-up rate—thus making the agency appear more efficient than it actually was. This was disclosed by a member of the Force, detective Sergeant Philip Arantz, who revealed the

R. G. Smith, *Public Sector Criminological Research*,
https://doi.org/10.1007/978-3-031-28356-7_14

correct data, leading to 'a public outcry. Arantz was promptly declared to be mentally unstable, and was quickly retired from the Force' (Wilson 1990, p. 137, and see Arantz 1993). Having an independent data collection agency would, arguably, have made disclosure of correct crime statistics less problematic. In her submission to the Senate inquiry into the AIC-ACC merger in 2016, former Director Toni Makkai (2016, p. 2), raised the problematic nature of crime statistics:

> Controversy over crime statistics and research is the norm and the ACIC will find itself dealing with contentious issues that are marginal to its core business. BOCSAR was given the job to produce independent crime statistics in New South Wales because of controversy over the statistics being produced by the police; similarly Victoria has created a new independent agency because of the controversy over its crime statistics; and the National Crime Authority (NCA) found itself in conflict with the government when it sought to enter the public debate on drugs and crime with a view contrary to the government's stated policy position. The NCA was closed and a new agency created.

The criterion of independence has been used more recently to support the establishment of other criminological research agencies including the ICCLR&CJP in Vancouver and the Crime Statistics Agency in Victoria, to mention just two. When the concept of the AIC was first being debated, one of the essential requirements requested by the states was that the Institute should *not* be set up within an existing Commonwealth department, but that it should be an independent Commonwealth instrumentality created by Commonwealth legislation (see Chapter 3, above).

Over time, as the Institute began publishing research that could be seen to be critical of government policies and practices, some individuals within the Departments responsible for the Institute began to question whether its work was sufficiently relevant and useful to justify the occasional political harm caused by its research findings. In this regard we can recall the observation of Geis (1994, p. 282) that 'the AIC provides a quintessential illustration of a government agency structurally and functionally caught between a rock and a hard place' (see Chapter 2 above).

More, importantly, the question arose as to whether a financial benefit could be obtained by either abolishing the Institute or passing some, or all, of its functions to other agencies. It was argued, for example, that some of the AICs functions should be moved to the ABS or AGD or that the Institute should be incorporated within a larger department in order to avoid the duplication of costs associated with providing office accommodation and corporate services. Such changes would, however, entail additional financial burdens on the agencies that took on the Institute's functions, in addition to the costs associated with dissolving the Institute such as staff redundancy payments and the costs of terminating leases for buildings and software. Loss of personnel would also entail loss of skills and experience that existing staff had acquired during their time with the Institute, lead to a decline in workplace morale and result in the resignation or termination of numerous staff. These staffing issues were raised by the CPSUs (2016) submission to the Senate Legal and Constitutional Affairs Legislation Committee's Inquiry into the Australian Crime Commission Amendment (Criminology Research) Bill 2016, noting the loss of 21 full-time equivalent positions at the AIC between July 2015 and October 2016. Many of these losses affected corporate and administrative staff rather than research staff and although some found positions with the ACIC, others experienced more profound career disruptions.

In addition, simply removing the Institute, or transferring its functions to another agency, would not solve the crime problems of the Commonwealth or the states and territories. Rather than reducing criticism of governments, such changes could be a source of new avenues of criticism.

Overseas Examples

The resolution of these issues, that continued to resonate throughout the Institute's history, were not unique to the AIC, and were faced by other public sector criminological research bodies in Australia and overseas. In the UK (Mayhew 2016), the US and the EU (Tonry 2010), governments sought to restrict or silence the work of such institutes using a variety of strategies. Gloria Laycock (2016, p. 3), in her submission opposing the merger of the AIC with the ACC in 2016, noted:

> The Home Office Research Unit (HORU), in which I worked for many years, was periodically threatened by incoming governments with no interest in independent research. The legislation which established HORU made it very difficult for any government to interfere with the existence or independence of the organisation. I think this was for the good of the British people and contributed to the greater understanding of crime and to the reductions which we have enjoyed in recent decades.

In his interview, John Walker (30 November 2020) recalled having been seconded from the AIC to the UK HORU in 1987. This was during a period when the government began outsourcing its research to University-based academics rather than relying on internal research staff—resulting in 'the Unit being scattered to the winds'. Walker's view of the AICs situation was that a merger with the ACC would primarily be of benefit to that entity:

> I think the most obvious effects of the ACIC/AIC alignment have been to broaden the range of the ACICs expertise, which is an important and positive outcome, but to hide the AIC from public view, which is, in my view, a bad result for the AIC and the broader criminological community. It would be tragic if the AIC became less visible—you don't want a research institute behind bars (John Walker, Interview, 30 November 2020).

Proposed Merger with AGD 1982

Proposals to dissolve or merge the AIC arose on a number of occasions throughout its fifty-year history. In 1982, for example, following a Functional Review of the AIC that arose from the 'Razor Gang' report (McDonald and Moore 1981; Cope 1981), the AICs Director, Bill Clifford, sought to oppose moves within AGD to amalgamate the AICs financial and personnel functions into the Department. The AICs Board agreed that such amalgamation would 'reduce the Institute to an adjunct of that Department' (AIC Board, Minutes, 8 June 1982, p. 6). Clifford continued his opposition to the reforms and was eventually successful in having the proposal withdrawn. In 1990, the Labor Government Minister for Justice and Consumer Affairs, Senator the Hon. Michael Tate, recalled this in his address at the opening of the Institute's new building on 25 July 1990:

> Only four years ago I recall there was a very real threat to the Institute–would it be drawn into, amalgamated into, absorbed into the Attorney-General's Department. Decisions were made then to give it a run to see whether in fact it could justify itself, and I can say without any hesitation that it certainly has achieved that eminence which ensures that it continued that autonomy–and when I say autonomy, the mere fact that it has worked so well with the Police Ministers Council, the Attorney-General's Committee, the Ministers for Corrections, shows that it's not an Ivory Tower autonomy. In fact there has been a tremendous contribution to the formulation of policy in all those areas of concern to those Ministerial Councils. (Minister for Justice and Consumer Affairs Senator The Hon. Michael Tate, audio file of the opening of the Institute 25 July 1990, AIC Archive)

Intelligence Agency Reviews 1974–2017

The idea of merging the AIC with a Commonwealth intelligence agency first arose following a lengthy history of reviews and reforms regarding such agencies (see Office of National Intelligence 2022). These included the first Hope Royal Commission that took place in 1974 shortly after the AIC was established, leading to the creation of the Office of National Assessments in 1978. This was followed by a second Hope Royal Commission in 1984, the Flood Inquiry in 2004, the Independent Review of the Intelligence Community in 2011 and the Independent Intelligence Review in 2017. These inquiries established and confirmed the differentiation between foreign and security intelligence, intelligence and law enforcement, intelligence collection and assessment and intelligence assessment and policy formulation (Department of Prime Minister and Cabinet 2017, p. 6). The question of the relationship between intelligence activities and academic research was only considered peripherally, although the 2017 Review noted that 'the ACICs investigative, research and information delivery functions in relation to current and emerging crime threats and criminal justice issues is also interacting more intensively with related intelligence areas' (Department of Prime Minister and Cabinet 2017, p. 48). The 2017 Review also argued that:

> There have been some important initiatives by agencies to enhance appropriate and productive exchanges on science and technology issues with publicly funded research agencies, academia and industry within Australia. Such outreach is useful and highly desirable, but in our view Australian intelligence interests generally would benefit significantly if this engagement was more systematic and better co-ordinated. (Department of Prime Minister and Cabinet 2017, pp. 80–81)

This led to the creation of a National Intelligence Community Innovation Fund and Hub whose aim was to operationalise research outcomes and to integrate the work of government, industry and academia with the intelligence community. The question of merging a law enforcement intelligence agency, such as the ACIC, with a research body, such as the AIC, was not, however, canvassed in the 2017 or earlier reviews, and the AIC was not mentioned in any of these reports.

Grant Wardlaw, former Director of the Office of Strategic Crime Assessments (OSCA) and the Australian Bureau of Criminal Intelligence (ABCI)—agencies that were themselves merged to become the National Crime Authority (NCA) and then the ACC—considered the merger of the AIC and the ACC 'a terrible idea'. He observed further that 'making financial savings by putting everything to do with crime together was inherently nonsensical' (Interview, 30 November 2020).

> There are good reasons to have close links between the ACC and the AIC and CrimTrac but there is a problem of the ACC being so large that it swamps the views and culture of the AIC. There are intelligence organisations that do things that look like research but they're not research

organisations. … One example is the problem of using classified information by an academic organisation that publishes and has a public profile (Grant Wardlaw, Interview, 30 November 2020).

This concern that the culture of the AIC and ACC were irreconcilably different was emphasised in many of the submissions made to the Senate Legal and Constitutional Affairs Legislation Committee's (2016) Inquiry into the Australian Crime Commission Amendment (Criminology Research) Bill in 2016. Former Director, Duncan Chappell (2016, p. 1), for example, submitted that 'the fundamental aims and ethos of both agencies are radically different'.

Governance Reviews, 2003–2011

In November 2002, the Howard Coalition government commissioned a review of the corporate governance of statutory authorities with a view to improving performance and the relationships between office holders and responsible Ministers. The Review was undertaken by John Uhrig AO and reported on 27 June 2003. The Report (Uhrig 2003) raised concerns regarding the role of Boards of Management as well as the legislative basis for authorities and how they should report to Ministers. Underlying the review was the debate over the need for, and independence of statutory authorities. It also reinforced the idea of clear Ministerial expectations of statutory authorities and open lines of communication between departments and authorities. Richard Fox, at the time Chair of the AIC Board, outlined the rationale for the review during his Interview (15 July 2022):

John Howard had the idea that there should be Ministerial direction of statutory authorities rather than by a Board of Management which could go off on a frolick of its own and could out-vote the Minister. … Howard was shrinking the power of representatives on any entity and giving the Minister absolute authority to veto decisions. … If you did research and it was not palatable, it wouldn't see the light of day–or you'd better just amend it slightly if you wouldn't mind otherwise your contract will not be renewed.

Over time, the recommendations of the Uhrig Review were examined by AGD specifically in relation to the AIC-CRC and in 2006, Allan Behm, a former Diplomat and at the time Strategic Advisor to the Board of Booz Allen Hamilton, was appointed by the Coalition Minister for Justice and Customs, Chris Ellison, to undertake a review of the *Criminology Research Act 1971* (Cth). Allan Behm had previously been the Commonwealth representative on the AIC Board and the focus of his review was on the governance and accountability arrangements of the AIC and CRC. Issues that were examined included the question of Commonwealth, state and territory involvement, governance issues, the CEOs role, accountability to the Minister, representation on and the role of the Advisory Council / Board and the grants program (AIC Board Minutes, 22 November 2006, p. 5). This, once again, raised the possibility of the absorption of the AIC-CRC into AGD. Following the change of government on 3 December 2007, however, the new Labor Minister for Home Affairs, Bob Debus, was able to be persuaded that absorption was not appropriate but that amending the *Criminology Research Act 1971* (Cth) to merge the CRC with the AIC and to regulate the merged body under the *Financial Management and Accountability Act 1997* (Cth) would be preferable in order to preserve the Institute's independence and to safeguard the interests of the states and territories in the Institute's work.

This proposal was developed further during Adam Tomison's tenure as Director. Tomison commenced at the AIC in June 2009 shortly after Brendan O'Connor had been appointed as the Labor Minister for Home Affairs. At the time, the Institute had 'fallen out of favour with the government as it was considered to be insufficiently focussed on Commonwealth interests and that some of the work being done was not providing value for money' (Adam Tomison, Interview, 26 October 2022). As such, Tomison was given twelve months to change the Institute, failing which, in all likelihood, it would be closed down. This was a major challenge for the new director, particularly at that time with the highest number of staff in the Institute's history and a substantial budget cut looming. He saw the solution as being to bring in more contract revenue and to reduce staffing as much as was possible—while still maintaining a viable and effective workforce. During Adam's time as Director, contract research increased from 20% of the budget in 2009 to 40% in 2015. A decision was also made to reduce the size of the DUMA program from nine to five collection sites. The states whose sites were to be retired were offered the opportunity to take them over or to share the costs of maintaining them with the AIC—but none took up the offer. The result was that the cost of this program decreased considerably.

After further discussion between the Department, the AICs Board, the Director and the Chair of the CRC, the *Financial Framework Legislation Amendment Act 2010* (Cth) was enacted with effect from 1 July 2011 to merge the CRC with the AIC and to create the CRAC. Although this resulted in only a small reduction in annual appropriation, it began a period during which the AICs deficit increased each year until a surplus was again achieved in 2017–18 (see Fig. 5.2, above). The AIC had, however, survived another attempt to remove its independence. In his interview (26 October 2022), Director, Adam Tomison, considered that 'the key concern I had about the legislative change was whether we would lose state and territory engagement that would make us more vulnerable to Commonwealth action if they were not happy with us'. In the event, the principal changes that took place were to alter the composition of the Advisory Council by no longer having an academic criminologist as its Chair, and for some heads of justice agencies to delegate their duties on the Council to subordinates.

Skehill Review of Small and Medium Agencies in the Attorney-General's Portfolio 2012

The next threat to the AICs independence came later in 2011 from the AGDs *Strategic Review of Small and Medium Agencies in the Attorney-General's Portfolio* conducted for the Minister for Finance and Deregulation at the request of Cabinet. The aim of this review was to assess various small and medium-sized agencies against the Expenditure Review Principles of appropriateness, effectiveness, efficiency, integration, performance assessment and strategic alignment, and to advise on how to enhance value for money for the government by considering, *inter alia*, the potential for use of shared services and administrative arrangements for the 13 agencies concerned. These small and medium entities included the law enforcement agencies within the portfolio, ACLEI, AUSTRAC and CrimTrac, as well as the AIC—despite the fact that the AIC was not an operational law enforcement agency. Stephen Skehill (2012), a former Australian Government Solicitor, former Secretary of AGD and Special Counsel with the legal practice, Mallesons Stephen Jaques, led the Review and reported in January 2012.

Applying the Expenditure Review Principles, it was decided to retain these bodies as separate independent agencies, noting that CrimTrac would be subject to further review. With respect to the AIC, it was concluded that the then current corporate services arrangements were acceptable, but that once the Attorney-General's corporate services business offering was made available, the AIC, along with the other agencies, should decide whether to take up those arrangements (Skehill 2012, p. 120). In the event, the AIC decided to remain unchanged.

The arguments canvassed in the Review included the question of the need for the AIC to be independent of the AGD, as well as the adequacy of the AIC providing its own corporate services in terms of cost-effectiveness. In relation to independence, the review Report argued for maintaining the AICs independence on two grounds: first, to ensure that the government had access to the best advice that may come, not only from within the public service, but also from external community sources; and secondly, to ensure participation by stakeholders, particularly from state and territory police—explained as follows:

> Vital stakeholders (state and territory police and justice agencies) are only induced to participate and provide an essential contribution (access to criminal justice data and policing operations which are the foundation of much of the AIC's research) because of the AIC's independence. Jurisdictions have made it clear that they would cease to support the AIC and no longer provide the same access to data if the agency was no longer independent and was only a part of the Attorney-General's Department.(Skehill 2012, p. 116)

This argument is of relevance to the subsequent attempt to merge the AIC with the ACC that created concerns over perceptions that the AIC would no longer be considered as an independent research body. The other argument that the Skehill Review (2012, p. 117) considered related to the fact that the AICs jurisdiction extended beyond Commonwealth criminal matters to wider concerns over all forms of crime prevention and criminal justice reform—in the states and territories, nationally and internationally—that would exceed the AGDs jurisdiction.

Finally, the Review considered that the AICs corporate support arrangements were relatively cost-effective and that there would likely be no saving or any appreciable increase in effectiveness or efficiency in requiring changes to be made (p. 119). This finding also contradicted the position subsequently imposed on the AIC that it be required to enter into a shared services agreement with the ACC/ACIC.

National Commission of Audit 2013–14

Not long later, in 2013–14, further attention was paid to the AICs independent status in the *Report of the National Commission of Audit* (Shepherd et al. 2014). In October 2013, one of the first activities of the Abbott Coalition government was to establish a National Commission of Audit to identify areas of waste and duplication in Commonwealth government expenditure. Its aim was to review the state of the government's finances and to advise on steps to ensure Australia's long-term fiscal strategy was responsible and sustainable. In the First Phase Report, sixty-four recommendations were made—some of which entailed giving the private sector an increased role so that services could, hopefully, be delivered more efficiently.

In the year ended 30 June 2013, the Commonwealth Government recorded an underlying cash deficit of $18.8 billion, or 1.2% of GDP, with the projected deficit for 2013–14 of $47.0 billion or 3.0% of GDP. To improve this position, the National Commission of Audit was asked to make recommendations that would secure a surplus of one percent of GDP by 2023–24 with net debt declining to around 5% of GDP (Shepherd et al. 2014, p. xv). It should be recalled that in 2012–13, the AICs Commonwealth appropriation amounted to 0.00035% of GDP

($5.3 million), only a small fraction of the target set by the Commission (see Fig. 5.3, above). Nonetheless, the AICs roles in conducting and funding research were examined for potential for savings by avoiding duplication, increasing alignment with government policies and through consolidation if required.

The Commission's Report identified the presence of a number of separate national criminal law enforcement, intelligence and information agencies that included the ACC, AUSTRAC, CrimTrac and the AIC. The possible range of recommendations available to reduce expenditure and to rationalise agencies were: to abolish, not to abolish, to merge, to consolidate, to privatise or to review with a view to merging, abolishing or transferring agencies.

In order to improve efficiency, the Commission recommended that CrimTrac should be merged with the ACC (which subsequently took place), AUSTRAC's position should be further reviewed and consideration should be given to relocating the AIC to a university (Shepherd et al. 2014, p. 208–recommendation 50). As we have already seen, universities such as the ANU were not willing to take on the AIC given its specific focus, cost and the ability, or inability, of its staff to undertake university-level teaching and research. Instead, the possibility of merger with the ACC was subsequently pursued.

Proposed Merger with a University

As already noted in previous chapters, the location of a criminological research institute within a University environment was contemplated, and adopted, in various jurisdictions and countries since the 1960s, giving rise to the possibility that an Australian institute could also be housed in a University department. Over time, however, the approach taken was to create applied, policy-focussed criminological entities within the public service, and have academic-focussed research undertaken in Universities. After 40 years of adopting this model, the idea of relocating the AIC to a University created many fundamental challenges.

Removing the AIC from the public sector while enhancing its independence and facilitating its ability to provide frank and fearless advice that might be critical of government policy positions, meant that its researchers would no longer be privy to the internal workings of government, and less able to make use of classified material when conducting research (Michael Phelan, Interview, 3 November 2022). Some argued that working in a University would enhance the Institute's security and longevity—although as we have seen in the case of the closure of the Berkeley School of Criminology in California in 1976 (Koehler 2015), being located in a University was no guarantee of financial and official support. Others have argued that the AICs staff would not be suitably trained as academic teachers and scholars—although, as Adam Graycar observed in his interview (1 March 2021), 'the Institute had more PhDs than any criminology department in an Australian university at the time', and that many AIC researchers obtained senior academic positions after leaving the AIC. Finally, there were the perceptions that public sector, 'administrative criminologists', would not have the ability to engage in theoretical analysis and sociological commentary needed for University scholarship, that was certainly the case with some AIC researchers but by no means all. John Braithwaite, Andrew Hopkins, Peter Grabosky, Arie Freiberg, Grant Wardlaw, John Seymour, John Walker and Jocelynne Scutt, as well as most of the former AICs Directors, performed more than satisfactorily in both roles.

Probably the principal impediment to transferring the AIC to a University, once it had an established history and position, was that University administrations were unconvinced of the benefits, both financial as well as reputational, for such a move. This was the view taken in 1994 when the idea of transferring the Institute to the ANU was considered. In his interview, John Braithwaite (30 January 2021) recalled how Bill Coad and Grant Wardlaw had offered to move the Institute to ANU for John to take on. At the time, however, ANU was not all that interested largely due to the financial burden it would have created for the University, although Braithwaite thought that 'the merging of the AIC library with the ANU law library did, however, make a kind of economic sense to the university'. Some years later, as Toni Makkai noted in her Interview, the creation of the National Security College and the Strategic and Defence Studies Centre at the ANU in 1966 was a successful example of a public sector body working well in a University environment. This enabled students to be appropriately trained for policy work in government in an accredited way. However, Makkai cautioned that 'it is necessary to have a director who is acceptable to the Commonwealth, who also understands how Universities work and you've got to have a sympathetic Vice-Chancellor' (Toni Makkai, Interview, 9 June 2022). In her submission to the Senate Inquiry into the AIC-ACC merger in 2016, Makkai (2016, p. 5) argued that 'there are risks to [co-location with a university] unless there is an effective contractual arrangement with strong high level board oversight coupled with a mandated review process'. In the event, the idea of moving the AIC to a University was never pursued, although close ties were maintained between the AIC and many tertiary institutions.

AIC-ACC Proposed Merger 2015–16

Background

With the preceding history in mind, the Abbott Coalition government continued its efforts to rationalise the AIC in some way, seemingly motivated by the need to reduce expenditure, but also to accord with its policy initiatives of amalgamating smaller government entities within larger ones and bringing all of the Commonwealth crime-related agencies together. Director Adam Tomison also recalled in his interview (26 October 2022) that he later became aware that one specific AIC publication, *Same-sex Intimate Partner Homicide in Australia* (Gannoni and Cussen 2014), had alienated 'some within a particular part of government', adding fuel to the desire to proceed with the merger. The government was also motivated by its *Smaller Government Reform Agenda* announced in the 2014–15 Federal Budget that sought to reduce the number of government entities and promote efficiency of government through improvements in interoperability of related functions. At the time, consideration was also given to merging the AIHW with the ABS to consolidate social data collection in the one larger agency. This, however, did not proceed (Samantha Bricknell, Interview, 21 November 2022).

After the idea of relocating the AIC to a university was rejected, discussions continued between Minister of Justice, Michael Keenan, the AICs Director, Adam Tomison, Iain Anderson, First Assistant Secretary of the Criminal Justice Division of AGD, Katherine Jones, Deputy Secretary National Security, Criminal Justice and Emergency Management at AGD and the then CEO of the ACC, Chris Dawson, who had commenced in that role in April 2014. Dawson was intent on continuing the so-called 'Fusion Capability' of the ACC that sought to 'fuse multiple sources of intelligence' (ACC Annual Report 2014, p. 14) and expand it to include CrimTrac's datasets and the AICs so-called 'research capability'.

When Adam Tomison heard of the proposal to bring the AIC into the ACC, he and Deputy Director of Research, Rick Brown, developed a proposal that would enable research and intelligence to be shared, but without the necessity to relocate the AIC within the ACC. They also sought to engage with the Advisory Council members and the academic community through ANZSOC to lobby AGD to withdraw the proposed plan—but without success (Adam Tomison, Interview, 26 October 2022). Adam's concern was that a full merger of the AIC and the ACC would result in the AIC being smothered by the much larger agency—at the time, the ACC had over 600 core staff, and grew to over 700 following its merger with CrimTrac. By contrast, the AIC had 50 staff, 37 of whom were academic staff (6% of the ACCs staff at 30 June 2014). Adam Tomison's term as Director was also nearing its end on 12 July 2015 with his subsequent position as Director-General of the Western Australian Department of the Attorney-General commencing in November 2016. His successor as AIC Director (and CEO of the ACIC), Chris Dawson, also left these positions in August 2017, moving to Perth where he became Commissioner of the Western Australia Police Force, and then from on 15 July 2022, Governor of Western Australia.

At the meeting of the CRAC on Friday 13 March 2015, the focus of the meeting was on the merger proposal with Chris Dawson attending the meeting to explain the current state of play. Prior to the meeting, Iain Anderson, the Commonwealth's representative on the Advisory Council, had visited or phoned each jurisdiction to explain the proposal, and the outcome of the discussion was that the Council members identified a number of critical issues to be addressed and concluded that the preferred way forward was for the AIC to remain as an agency with some statutory powers reporting to the CEO of the ACC, but not to become a division of the ACC. The main issues identified by the Council members were: preservation of the AICs name and brand; maintenance of an independent and objective AIC research function; allowing fee-for-service work including future work for state and territory jurisdictions and key stakeholders; maintenance of the CRG grants process and the ability of the Advisory Council to shape it; continuation of the Advisory Council's role and the creation of a transition plan for the AIC Director's position (AIC Minutes, 13 March 2015, p. 6).

By April 2015, public speculation had arisen that the merger of the ACC and AIC would be included in the 2015 federal budget, although this did not occur (Neilson 2015; Greene 2015). Instead, the Coalition government undertook the peremptory step of initiating a MoG procedure that involved the transfer of the AICs staff to employment with the ACC, the appointment of Chris Dawson as the AICs Interim Director following the end of Adam Tomison's term as Director on 12 July 2015 (Keenan 2015a) and the secondment of the research staff to continue working for the AIC until legislative changes could be enacted. The reason for the secondment was that the ACCs legislation did not allow for its staff (including the new AICs staff) to undertake criminological research. An attempt was also made at this time to create a new Branch of the ACC entitled the Crime and Justice Research Centre, until it was realised that this title was already being used by criminologists working at the Queensland University of Technology. The addition of the word 'National' preceding the title was thought to solve the problem, but it transpired that the name was never used in practice. These developments were all indicative of the haste and lack of planning and consultation that had gone into the MoG and proposed merger (see the submission by Civil Liberties Australia (2016) to the Senate Inquiry into the proposed merger).

These changes were then considered at the meeting of the Law Crime and Community Safety Council meeting on 22 May 2015 and in a meeting of the State and Territory Attorneys-General, but the Commonwealth position remained that the AIC would cease to exist and its functions would be transferred to the ACC, with the ACCs CEO acting as the AICs Director until the legislation could be amended. As such, most of the Advisory Council's concerns were not addressed, and a number of other concerns raised by stakeholders were still to be resolved. These included the question of how to protect the AICs datasets to ensure that they would not be used for intelligence purposes by the ACIC, how the CRG program would operate under ACIC control, what should be the composition of the new Advisory Council to ensure that it was not dominated by Commonwealth and law enforcement interests and the effect of the merger on AIC staffing (AIC, Minutes 20 November 2015).

Legislative Changes

In order to achieve the proposed merger of the ACC and the AIC, the *Criminology Research Act 1971* (Cth) had to be repealed and the *Australian Crime Commission Act 2002* (Cth) had to be amended in various ways to enable the ACCs staff (including former AIC staff) to undertake criminological research and to give effect to a number of associated administrative changes. The initial Bill dealing with these changes, was the Australian Crime Commission Amendment (Criminology Research) Bill 2015 (Cth) that was introduced into the 44th Parliament on 15 October 2015, passed by the House of Representatives, and, following debate, referred to the Senate Legal and Constitutional Affairs Legislation Committee on 19 November 2015. The Committee recommended by a majority vote on 26 November 2015 that the Bill be passed, with dissenting views expressed by Australian Labor Party Senators, who recommended that further consideration be given to the concerns raised by stakeholders, and Australian Greens Senators, who recommended that the Bill be rejected in its entirety. In the event, the Bill lapsed on prorogation of Parliament.

The proceedings relating to the 2015 Bill were undertaken quickly with the Senate Committee's Report having only two days of public hearings with six witnesses attending including only two academic criminologists, Professors Janet Ransley and Rick Sarre. The remaining witnesses from the AIC, ACC and AGD were all largely supportive of the Bill and the merger. Only three written submissions were made, one, jointly by the AGD, ACC and AIC (2015), one from the ACPC and another from Civil Liberties Australia (2016). Only the evidence from the AGD, ACC and AIC was supportive of the Bill. The AIC was unable to make a separate submission regarding the Bill, but was required to accord with the views expressed by the AGD and ACC.

Following the merger of the ACC and CrimTrac, the newly-titled ACIC commenced operations on 1 July 2016, by which time the ACICs CEO, Chris Dawson, had been appointed Interim Director of the AIC pursuant to a MoG process that transferred all the AICs staff to employment with the ACIC, and involved the physical relocation of the AIC to the shared accommodation with the ACC at 4 National Circuit (see Chapter 8, above). Prior to the reintroduction of the Bill, various alterations were made to the Bill's Explanatory Memorandum (but not to the Bill itself) that sought to address the concerns raised about the 2015 Bill. The new Bill was not, however amended with the changes reflected in the Explanatory Memorandum being non-legislative and advisory only—including the important proposal that the CRAC would be non-legislated and advisory only. As indicated below, the joint submission of the AGD, ACIC and AIC (2016) to the Bill provided a very limited response to the concerns raised, essentially requiring the community to trust that the ACIC would respect the Institute's independence and functions without any legislated authority.

On 14 September 2016, the Australian Crime Commission Amendment (Criminology Research) Bill 2016 (Cth) was introduced into the House of Representatives, was passed and introduced into the Senate on 10 November 2016 following an inquiry by the Senate Legal and Constitutional Affairs Legislation Committee. The Senate Committee's inquiry into the 2016 Bill had no public hearings but received 25 written submissions from academic criminologists across Australia and internationally, and one joint submission from the AGD, ACIC and AIC that, like the previous one, was supportive of the Bill. All the remaining submissions were opposed to the Bill and the merger.

Although the Senate Committee recommended passing the 2016 Bill by a majority, both the ALP and the Australian Greens' Senators offered dissenting reports both rejecting the Bill. The ALP Senators concluded that 'the proposed merger is unnecessary, and would lead to the degradation of valuable independent criminological research' while the Greens Senators concluded that:

> Should this Bill pass there is a significant risk that broad ranging criminological research that focusses on understanding the causes of crime, and recommending crime prevention strategies, will take second place to the law enforcement needs of the ACC and that the government's stated aim of providing Australian law enforcement agencies with central access to criminological research could have been achieved by administrative changes which would not require merging the AIC into the ACC. (Senate Legal and Constitutional Affairs Committee 2016, pp. 21, 23)

The evidence provided to these Committees cogently argued against the merger on a number of grounds that the government largely failed to address. These related to: the removal of functional and financial independence of the AIC from the ACIC; the likely change of emphasis in its research focus to Commonwealth and law enforcement concerns to the potential exclusion of state and territory concerns; the loss of the Institute's statutory advisoLLry body that would become non-legislated and less powerful; the difficulty in publicly disclosing research and interacting with the public due to the security requirements of the ACIC; the restricted access to the AICs library and the AICs premises by those without a security clearance; the loss of current AIC staff due to the disruption resulting from the proposed merger; the removal of the independent position of the AICs Director; the transfer of staff and services to the ACIC through the MoG process prior to the legislation passing and, finally, the overall lack of need to abolish the AIC when most of the research needs of the ACIC could be provided by alternative means. As the Bills Digest concluded: 'the merger does mean the loss of an independent criminology research organisation in Australia that, importantly, has a national focus. There is potential for the merger to impact on the AICs current research role' (Neilsen 2015, p. 7). The Bills Digest continued by raising a number of questions (at p. 7):

> A final question for the Parliament might be: does the Bill ensure that the priorities of the AIC will not be lost or subsumed in the merger as was suggested in discussions at Estimates earlier this year? Is there also a potential for a conflict of interest to arise, such as when the AIC is conducting research that requires critiquing the ACC priorities and operations?

After the second Senate Committee Report was tabled, the 2016 Bill was returned to the House without legislative priority eventually leading to the Government electing not to proceed with the legislation at all and to maintain the *status quo*. Since then, the AIC has had to respond to many challenges in order to maintain its position, hanging in an uncertain space between independence and integration with the larger agency. More difficult to resolve have been the myriad concerns relating to financing, staffing, facilities and reputation arising from the failed merger.

Remaining Concerns

During the debates and in evidence to the Senate Committee, various arguments were raised as to the potential benefits associated with merging the AIC with the ACC/ACIC. The stated objective of the government was to enable the ACIC to make use of the research expertise of the AIC by allowing AIC researchers to have access to the law enforcement intelligence holdings belonging to the Commission. This, it was argued, would enrich the AICs research by enabling it to integrate its public-source data with classified material, but also to provide the ACICs intelligence analysts with access to the AICs data sources. The difficulties that this posed were, however, considerable and irreconcilable, as both the ACICs intelligence holdings and the AICs research data were governed by their own legislative and ethical controls that would make sharing between the two difficult and problematic. The primary concern related to the fact that each agency collected its information for specific purposes (intelligence gathering or criminological research) and the subjects of those activities (criminals or research participants) provided information on the basis that it would not be used for unstated, ulterior purposes. Owing to the level of secrecy surrounding the operations of the ACIC, members of the public would simply be unaware of how any of their information provided to the AIC for research purposes would be used, or potentially misused.

The secondary aim of the proposed merger, that the government denied was a factor (Keenan 2015b), was to minimise costs for the government, by relocating the AICs corporate administration and enabling the ACIC to provide this for both entities. In times of government shared services agreements, this could easily have been achieved without the need to merge entire agencies. The financial cost of dissolving one of the agencies in terms of removing or relocating staff, selling assets and cancelling contractual arrangements was also found to be extensive, and exceeded the potential cost savings resulting from the merger arising from the removal of the Director's remuneration package. As Gloria Laycock (2016, p. 2) argued in her submission to the Committee:

> Mergers are necessarily time consuming, costly and disruptive. I would suggest that prior to making any such changes the Committee would wish to reassure itself that the research capability of the criminal intelligence agency could not be boosted through some other less costly and disruptive mechanism.

There were, in addition, many indirect risks of such a merger that were identified during the parliamentary debates and Senate Inquiries and which eventually occurred. As a result, the government finally reached the conclusion that the merger and the proposed legislative amendments should not proceed. These conclusions were able to be achieved through the efforts, not only of the minority opposition views in parliament, but also due to the national and international opposition to the idea that became apparent during the Senate Committee's deliberations. The result has been not entirely satisfactory with the merger remaining incomplete and the negative aspects of the MoG process continuing to create difficulties for the AIC.

Post-Merger Existence of the AIC

Unlike some public sector criminological research institutes that have succumbed to threats to their existence from government reform policies, the AIC, through a mixture of deft management and good fortune, has been able to survive as an independent statutory authority, although with far fewer staff, less control over its corporate services and a tarnished reputation among some stakeholders. It has, however, continued to conduct and publish research, liaise with Commonwealth, state, territory and international stakeholders and has undertaken some collaborative research with the ACIC and other entities within its portfolio, and beyond. Some of the specific challenges that have been encountered in navigating the merger and MoG processes, and how they have been resolved, are as follows.

Independence

Following the changes undertaken during the MoG process and the partial merger, the AIC has maintained its legislative independence as a statutory government entity, but has experienced a number of administrative changes that have led to a closer alignment with Commonwealth law enforcement and intelligence activities. Although the ALP was eventually opposed to the merger, since its election to government, there has been no indication of a desire to de-merger or alter the changes imposed on the AIC in 2015–16. There have, however, been other non-legislative changes that have affected the AIC. Following the change in government on 23 May 2022, the Institute was moved from the Home Affairs Portfolio to that of Attorney-General on 1 July 2022. This reinstated its position within the Attorney-General's Portfolio of 50 years ago when the Institute's legislation was first proclaimed on 6 November 1972.

During the debate surrounding the proposed merger, the question of removal of the AICs Director was one of the important aspects of loss of independence that was raised. The result of the MoG process was that the CEO of the ACIC became the AICs Director, with a deputy director being responsible for delivering the research functions of the AIC. Like the former ACC CEO, Chris Dawson, the subsequent CEO of the ACIC, Michael Phelan, employed his extensive experience of law enforcement administration to manage the affairs of the AIC but was heavily reliant on the criminological expertise of Deputy Director, Rick Brown, and the experience of the Justice administrators on the Advisory Council, to set the AICs research agenda and to monitor the Institute's publication and outreach activities. The time available to these CEO-Directors has, however, been limited as the workload of running the much larger agency was, and continues to be, extremely demanding. Michael Phelan in his Interview (3 November 2022) estimated that between five and ten percent of his time was devoted to AIC matters. Arguably, it is unnecessary to have an AIC Director who also has to act as CEO of the ACIC, when the responsibilities of managing the AIC could effectively be undertaken by a single experienced criminologist—as in the past. Both the AICs director and deputy director in 2022 believed that the AICs independence has, in fact, been retained and that the corporate services functions do not detract from the AICs ability to carry out its research functions independently of the larger organisation. Mike Phelan commented during his interview (3 November 2022), 'whilst the administration of the AIC is looked after by the ACIC, by and large, the vast majority of people see it as an independent agency'. Rick Brown, in his Interview (4 November 2022) after noting the AICs maintenance of a large research output of publications under its own brand, concluded that, externally, 'it looks like the AIC is an agency that's pretty vibrant'.

Administration

Following the MoG process, the Institute's physical independence declined due to its move to share office space in the ACICs building at 4 National Circuit in Canberra, and the employment of Institute staff by the ACIC—with the somewhat artificial secondment of AIC researchers to work for the AIC entity when undertaking research. When the merger was first proposed, AIC staff were invited to participate in a closed information workshop held at the Australian Institute of Police Management (AIPM) campus in the Sydney beach-side suburb of Manly from 4 to 6 November 2015. Both ACC and AIC staff attended this meeting and debated the many practical aspects of the proposed merger with presentations by ACC senior executives as well as Grant Wardlaw, academic Wendy O'Brien, ANZSOC President Rick Sarre and Warwick Jones, Executive Director of the AIPM (Plate 14.1). The workshop was, arguably, more effective in identifying the differences between research and intelligence functions, than in determining how they could work effectively together. The practical aspects of working together were developed slowly over then ensuing seven years—and continue to evolve.

Perhaps the consequence of the partial merger and MoG process with the greatest harm to the Institute, was the loss of two-thirds of its staff who either resigned their positions or were transferred to other roles with the ACIC. In the case of the AICs research staff, on 30 June 2014 there were 37 employed by the AIC—by 30 June 2018 there were only 14 employed by the ACIC—reduction of 62%. This led to personal disruption for those affected as well as costs to the organisation and the need

Plate 14.1   ACC-AIC Workshop, Manly 4–6 November 2015. [(l-r) Warwick Jones, Executive Director AIPM, Judy Lind, Executive Director ACC, Chris Dawson, CEO ACC and Rick Brown, Deputy Director AIC] (*Source* AIC Archives)

for substantial retraining in mastering the ACICs policies and procedures—particularly those relating to information security. The need to develop effective ways in which AIC and ACIC information and data could be shared securely presented difficulties and costly challenges, not all of which were able to be effectively implemented. The ACC, and later the ACIC, attempted to ensure that those staff who remained employed had their remuneration levels maintained, but a number suffered indirect losses through the move—such as, for example, having to pay parking fees in the more expensive location of the ACCs new premises, as well as child care costs and travel expenses to the new location.

The MoG process also led to the implementation of a shared-services agreement being entered into between the AIC and the ACC. In return for a substantial annual fee ($1.6 million in 2021–22–AIC, Annual Report, 2022, p. 87), the AIC was provided with accommodation in the new building, information and technology services, financial, legal, human resources and security services, communications, publications and media services and the services provided by the ACICs CEO as Director of the AIC. Some former AIC administrative staff had taken on roles in these areas and were able to make use of their prior experience when working on AIC-related functions, while other activities were taken on by ACIC staff who were unfamiliar with the AICs work, staff and activities. The cost of engaging the ACIC to undertake these services was offset by the savings represented by the former AIC Director's salary package over the forward years.

Owing to the size and budget of the ACC, however, and the relatively insignificant size and cost of maintaining the AIC, some of the services provided to the AIC were subject to delays, misunderstandings and errors during the early years following the change. In addition, many of the ACCs security procedures, although appropriate for a national policing intelligence agency, were oppressive and unnecessary for a small research organisation that interacted closely with the public. Psychological risk-profiling during recruitment and random drug and alcohol testing are examples that had little relevance for academic researchers but were obligatory for all ACIC personnel—including former AIC staff.

Of greater importance was the reluctance, or inability, of the ACCs communications division to assist the AICs staff in interacting freely and openly with the media following release of publications. As noted in previous chapters, the AIC was an outward-facing agency in which its research and publications were intended for wide, public dissemination. The ACC, however, was reluctant to publicise its work and only rarely released de-classified intelligence reports for public consumption. This created an ongoing source of tension among the personnel in the two organisations concerning their relationships with the media. AIC researchers were used to speaking with journalists with whom they had an ongoing relationship; but following the MoG, contacts and invitations were screened and many interviews were declined, abandoned or restricted to senior executives to undertake.

Research

In the absence of legislative change, the Criminology Research Advisory Council continued as a legislated entity with five different Chairs between 2013 and 2022, the most recent of whom was former Director, Dr Adam Tomison, in his role as Director-General of the Department of Justice in Western Australia. The principal challenge for the Council was to ensure that state and territory interests were taken into account in setting the strategic research priorities of the AIC. In his Interview (4 November 2022), Deputy Director Rick Brown observed that the outcome of the merger was that:

> It sent a signal to all of us that, prior to the merger, we were not necessarily doing what was expected of us. ... This led to a change in the work we did, such as reducing consultancy work which was largely about supporting states and territories through evaluation work–which was, to a degree, at odds with our Commonwealth position.

Since 2015, there has been an increased emphasis on serious and organised crime, illicit drugs, economic crime and cybercrime—all promoted by the Commonwealth—while the AICs recent research on sexual offending, family and domestic violence and Indigenous over-representation in the criminal justice system have all continued to reflect state and territory interests. One change that demonstrates the willingness of the AICs Director to shape the research program, was his decision to terminate the DUMA program—one of the Institute's hallmark data collection studies that had attracted international praise. Although the DUMA data are of use not only for the states and territories, but also for the Commonwealth, it represented a degree of duplication and competition with the ACICs own illicit drug intelligence work—the National Wastewater Drug Monitoring Program, 2016 to 2021, the Illicit Drug Data Report, 2002 to 2020 as well as its Methylamphetamine Supply Reduction Report in 2019.

The AIC has continued its outreach activities of hosting workshops, seminars and conferences, although these have been subject to stricter financial controls than previously as the fiscal climate has changed following the pandemic. The AICs close relationship with ANZSOC—that included providing secretarial support on a cost-recovery basis, and financially supporting the Society's conferences—gradually declined with the AIC developing its own, public sector-focussed conference instead, and terminating the position of ANZSOC Secretary in 2022. Interestingly, after years of debate as to the propriety and benefits of the AIC being part of the UN PNI network, work in this area has taken on new importance—presumably owing to the current crime types being focussed on by the Network and the UN emphasising transnational organised crime, cybercrime, corruption, human trafficking and child sexual abuse—all topics relevant to the Commonwealth's focus.

Conclusions

Throughout the preceding five decades, the Institute has survived many attempts to change or limit its focus and activities, to merge it with other larger organisations, or to withdraw its funding, repeal its legislation and cease its operations entirely. The current Labor administration, at the time of writing, has given no indication of seeking to alter the *status quo* that sees the Institute sharing accommodation and corporate services with the ACIC, while having its staff continuing to work as secondees under the *Criminology Research Act 1971* (Cth) but remaining as public servants employed by the ACIC within the Attorney-General's Portfolio. The current, or future governments might, however, seek to make changes to these arrangements.

Despite the continuation of the current situation, the many tensions identified during the process of the proposed merger with the ACC/ACIC, failed legislative reforms and MoG changes, continue to create challenges for the Institute in satisfying its role as Australia's national research and knowledge centre on crime and justice that seeks to promote justice and reduce crime by undertaking and communicating evidence-based research to inform policy and practice. The director and deputy director of the Institute have a difficult and challenging path to follow with competing demands placed on them by governments, other public and private sector organisations, the diverse academic criminological community, international stakeholders who depend on the Institute's research to understand the crime and justice landscape in Australia and members of the public who want the crime problem solved in the most cost-effective and timely way. As we shall see in the final chapter, there is abundant evidence of the value of the research undertaken by the AIC since it was established, but the question that remains unresolved is whether future governments will be willing to allow the Institute to continue producing research on the socially and politically sensitive topics of crime and criminal justice, or decide to impose restrictions that limit its potential to be critical of government policy.

The future may also see a solution to the tensions that currently exist in the AICs relationship with the ACIC as its provider of accommodation, corporate services and as an employer of its staff. The completion of the proposed merger of 2015–16 is one possibility; the reversion to the Institute's pre-merger / MoG position is another. Whether governments are willing to undertake the legislative, administrative, personnel and financial changes needed to give effect to such changes remains to be seen, but the direction for the future is likely to depend, heavily, on the way in which the Institute performs in delivering research of value to the government and the community in the months and years ahead.

References

Arantz, Philip. 1993. *A Collusion of Powers*, Dunedoo, New South Wales.

Attorney-General's Department (AGD), Australian Criminal Intelligence Commission (ACIC) and Australian Institute of Criminology (AIC). 2016. *Submission to the Senate Legal and Constitutional Affairs Legislation Committee Inquiry into the Australian Crime Commission Amendment (Criminology Research) Bill 2016*, No 20, 28 October 2016, Canberra: Department of the Senate.

Attorney-General's Department (AGD), Australian Criminal Intelligence Commission (ACIC) and Australian Institute of Criminology (AIC). 2015. *Submission to the Senate Legal and Constitutional Affairs Legislation Committee Inquiry into the Australian Crime Commission Amendment (Criminology Research) Bill 2015*, November 2015, Canberra: Department of the Senate.

Australian Crime Commission (ACC). 2014. *Annual Report 2013–14.* Canberra: Australian Crime Commission.

Australian Institute of Criminology (AIC). 2022. *Annual Report 2021–2022.* Canberra: Australian Institute of Criminology.

Chappell, Duncan. 2016. *Submission to the Senate Legal and Constitutional Affairs Legislation Committee Inquiry into the Australian Crime Commission Amendment (Criminology Research) Bill 2016*, No 16, 27 October 2016, Canberra: Department of the Senate.

Civil Liberties Australia. 2016. *Submission to the Senate Legal and Constitutional Affairs Legislation Committee Inquiry into the Australian Crime Commission Amendment (Criminology Research) Bill 2016*, No 14, 27 October 2016, Canberra: Department of the Senate.

Community and Public Sector Union (CPSU). 2016. *Submission to the Senate Legal and Constitutional Affairs Legislation Committee Inquiry into the Australian Crime Commission Amendment (Criminology Research) Bill 2016*, No 19, 28 October 2016, Canberra: Department of the Senate.

Cope, R.L. 1981. Commonwealth Official Publications and the Razor Gang: Some Thoughts. *The Australian Library Journal* 30 (3): 73.

Department of the Prime Minister and Cabinet (PM&C). 2017. *Independent Intelligence Review*, Canberra: PM&C. https://pmc.gov.au/sites/def ault/files/publications/2017-Independent-Intelligence-Review.pdfAccessed 7 September 2022.

Gannoni, Alexandra, and Tracy Cussen. 2014. Same-sex Intimate Partner Homicide in Australia, *Trends and Issues in Crime and Criminal Justice* no. 469, Canberra: Australian Institute of Criminology.

Geis, Gilbert. 1994. 'This Sort of Thing Isn't Helpful:' The Dilemmas of the Australian Institute of Criminology. *Australian and New Zealand Journal of Criminology* 27 (3): 282–298.

Greene, Andrew. 2015. Budget 2015: Crime Commission Tipped to Merge with Australian Institute of Criminology in Budget Shake-up, *ABC News*, 27 April. https://www.abc.net.au/news/2015-04-27/crime-agencies-tipped-to-merge-in-budget-shake-up/6423132 Accessed 12 September 2022.

Keenan, Michael. 2015a. Interim Director for the Australian Institute of Criminology, *Minister for Justice Media Release,* 13 July. https://parlinfo.aph.gov.au/parlInfo/download/media/pressrel/3949251/upload_binary/3949251.pdf;fileType=application%2Fpdf#search=%22media/pressrel/3949251%22 Accessed 12 September 2022.

Keenan, Michael. 2015b. New Crime and Justice Research Centre, *Minister for Justice Media Release,* 25 September. https://parlinfo.aph.gov.au/parlInfo/download/media/pressrel/4096188/upload_binary/4096188.pdf;fileType=application%2Fpdf#search=%22media/pressrel/4096188%22 Accessed 22 September 2022.

Koehler, Johann. 2015. Development and Fracture of a Discipline: Legacies of the School of Criminology At Berkeley. *Criminology* 53 (4): 513–544.

Laycock, Gloria. 2016. *Submission to the Senate Legal and Constitutional Affairs Legislation Committee Inquiry into the Australian Crime Commission Amendment (Criminology Research) Bill 2016*, No 1, 23 October, Canberra: Department of the Senate.

Makkai, Toni. 2016. *Submission to the Senate Legal and Constitutional Affairs Legislation Committee Inquiry into the Australian Crime Commission Amendment (Criminology Research) Bill 2016*, No 21, 28 October 2016, Canberra: Department of the Senate.

Mayhew, Patricia. 2016. In Defence of Administrative Criminology. *Crime Science* 5 (7): 1–10.

McDonald, D. I., and C. Moore. 1981. *Review of the Staff and Organisational Structure of the Australian Institute of Criminology*, Management and Special Services Division, Canberra: Attorney-General's Department (Referred to in AIC, Minutes, 14 December 1981, p. 4).

Neilson, Mary Anne. 2016. Bills Digest: Australian Crime Commission Amendment (Criminology Research) Bill 2015, Parliamentary Library Bills Digest, No. 17, 2016–17. Canberra: Parliament of

Australia. https://parlinfo.aph.gov.au/parlInfo/download/legislation/billsdgs/4859010/upload_binary/4859010.pdf Accessed 10 September 2022.

Office of National Intelligence (ONI). 2022. The National Intelligence Community: Where It All Began. Canberra: ONI. https://www.oni.gov.au/where-it-all-began-aic Accessed 7 September 2022.

Radzinowicz, Leon. 1965. *The Need for Criminology and a Proposal for an Institute of Criminology*. London: Heineman.

Senate Legal and Constitutional Affairs Committee. 2016. *Australian Crime Commission Amendment (Criminology Research) Bill 2016*, Canberra: Department of the Senate.

Shepherd, Tony, Peter Boxall, Tony Cole, Robert Fisher and Amanda Vanstone. 2014. *Towards Responsible Government: The Report of the National Commission of Audit: Phase One*, Canberra: National Commission of Audit. https://web.archive.org.au/awa/20140501135754mp_/http://pandora.nla.gov.au/pan/143632/20140502-0001/www.ncoa.gov.au/report/docs/phase_one_report.pdf. Accessed 3 August 2022.

Skehill, Stephen. 2012. *Strategic Review of Small and Medium Agencies in the Attorney-General's Portfolio: Report to the Australian Government*, Canberra: Department of Finance and Deregulation.

Tate, Michael. 1990. Address at the Opening of the Australian Institute of Criminology's Marcus Clarke Street Building, AIC Archives, Video File, 25 July, Canberra.

Tonry, Michael. 2010. 'Public Criminology' and Evidence-based Policy. *Criminology and Public Policy* 9 (4): 783–797.

Uhrig, John. 2003. *Review of the Corporate Governance of Statutory Authorities and Office Holders*, Parliamentary Paper No. 352, Canberra: Commonwealth of Australia. https://nla.gov.au/nla.obj-922761191/view?partId=nla.obj-924650826#page/n135/mode/1up Accessed 3 August 2022.

Wilson, Paul. 1990. *A Life of Crime*. Newham: Scribe Publications.

15

Conclusions

Introduction

Regardless of the precise location of workplaces for public sector criminologists, whether in dedicated research institutes, intelligence agencies or policy departments, there is much work they can do to inform both government policy-making and the community as to the nature, extent and solutions to contemporary crime problems. The model previously adopted by the AIC generally worked well, straddling academic research and government policy-making, while maintaining adherence to principles of independent ethical research and allowing completed studies to be made publicly available.

Central to determining the future of organisations such as the AIC, is the need to clarify the aims and scope of their remit having regard to the funding that governments are willing to provide. This issue was identified shortly after the Institute began its work when Sir Leon Radzinowicz visited Canberra to assess the operation of the fledgling organisation. He noted in his report of 17 September 1973: '... in all frankness, I cannot say that I regard the Institute yet as a truly going concern. In addition, several problems touching upon its direction and organisation still

R. G. Smith, *Public Sector Criminological Research*,
https://doi.org/10.1007/978-3-031-28356-7_15

require careful rethinking and possible reshaping' (Radzinowicz 1973, p. 3).

When the AIC was established fifty years ago, its proponents had ambitious plans for its scope and jurisdiction, that entailed equally demanding requirements for funding. Some argued that the AIC should have a wide remit to serve both government and the community in undertaking research, providing information and publications and disseminating its research through the use of local and international conferences and meetings. The original idea was for the AIC to be Australia's source of research and information on crime and justice for the global audience, coordinated through the UNODCs PNI and other international consortia of academics and policy-makers. Thus, anyone in Australia or other countries needing statistics, research, publications or policy-relevant information on crime and justice in and affecting Australia, would be able to obtain these from the AIC. This idea, in the pre-globalised world, formed part of wider agendas to bring together interested parties from all nations to solve current and emerging crime problems. The UN PNI was considered to be an appropriate means of achieving these objectives. As globalisation developed, and as transnational crime problems increased in importance—particularly those involving organised crime—the need for such a body grew in importance and urgency.

With these ideas underpinning the negotiation of the AICs role and jurisdiction, an entity was created that required substantial resourcing, a highly trained workforce, an efficient and well-resourced library and access to government networks on a global scale. Unfortunately, from the outset, such resourcing was not provided, leaving the Institute with a near-impossible set of demands to fulfil, with uncertain funding, a largely transient staff and an ever-changing political environment that had conflicting views on the need, and desirability of having one of its entities providing independent research evidence that was often critical of government criminal justice policies. The result has been that the Institute has been under-resourced throughout its life and although 'punching above its weight' in terms of research output—largely achieved through reliance on staff who were willing to go beyond the call of duty to satisfy sometimes unreasonable demands on their time—it has faced regular attempts to reduce its budget without corresponding reductions in expectations. One example is the Minister's expectations and performance indicators that, in recent times, have remained much the same in terms of output—despite the annual reductions in appropriation as a percentage of GDP, and the associated decline in research staff. It is a tribute to those staff who have survived the recent, partial merger and MoG process, that the performance measures have been satisfied and, in some cases, exceeded.

During each of the many inquiries and reviews into the AICs activities, recommendations were made to alter its focus, limit its staffing allocation, reduce its overheads and change its affiliations—all without addressing the obvious problem that the AIC was being asked to undertake too many functions without adequate financial backing. As a result, the AIC had to seek funding from alternative sources, to confine the scope of its research by avoiding long-term, costly projects and to limit external, international activities, conference programs and pro-bono work for community organisations. The 18 research staff in 2022 reflects the same headcount in the early 1990s—despite the research demands having increased dramatically.

If public sector criminological research is valued by governments, particularly the Commonwealth government, then consideration needs to be given to defining the proper roles and jurisdiction of the Institute, based on the level of funding that the government wishes to allocate. Simply maintaining a micro-entity, housed within a larger department, but nonetheless being required to undertake all the criminological research demanded by the government, is a policy bound to fail. Instead, the functions of the Institute could be limited to those deemed most urgently needed by the nation, and resourcing allocated of a sufficient level to enable such work to be undertaken to an acceptable standard of quality and timeliness. Richard Harding in his Interview (18 November 2021) noted the importance of having a criminological research institute: 'its very creation is an affirmation of taking these important socio-political issues very seriously and trying to achieve some kind of best practice through research'.

It is clear from the above discussion that criminological research conducted by independent entities within government has many advantages over work outsourced to academic and consulting sectors, both in terms of efficiency, cost-effectiveness and timeliness, but governments need to be willing to set reasonable boundaries on expectations and provide realistic funding to enable such work to be undertaken. If appropriate changes are made, then the future of public sector criminological research should be bright.

Some Achievements

At the risk of engaging in Frank Zimring's (1984, p. ix) cardinal sin of 'institutional boosterism', it is, nonetheless, appropriate to recall some of the novel and worthwhile research activities that the AIC has undertaken and the reputation it enjoys internationally. The following examples have been distilled from the recollections of the individuals interviewed for the current study, supplemented by the achievements identified in submissions made to the Senate Legal and Constitutional Affairs Committees (2015, 2016) when the Institute was under threat of absorption by the ACC/ACIC. These observations from across Australia and internationally, demonstrate the utility and productivity that the Institute's staff have provided. In addition there are some observations by former Institute staff, no longer alive, who undertook evaluative studies on the Institute's research. In 1987, for example, David Biles, conducted a review of projects funded by the Criminology Research Council, and concluded:

> Evidence supplied by the researchers showed that well over one-third of the completed projects clearly had had either a direct or indirect impact on criminal justice practice or policy. In addition, most other projects had either been cited in court cases or had been used by practitioners. Furthermore, in a significant number of cases it could be shown that Council-funded projects had been influential in promoting legislative changes. (Criminology Research Council 1987, p. 4)

When asked to identify the Institute's top achievements, Adam Graycar (Interview 1 March 2021) focussed on its publications, such as the *Trends and Issues* series, that communicated effectively with stakeholders, its library that was one of the best in the world, its conferences and its pathbreaking research undertaken by credible and qualified staff. Put simply, Graycar argued that 'it led the way and set new agendas on topics that others had ignored'. The generation of reliable evidence to support policy objectives was identified by most Interviewees as the Institute's primary achievement. John Walker (Interview, 30 November 2020) was more guarded in his conclusions:

> In the current 'anti-expert' political climate in Australia, as in much of the western world, evidence-based research is routinely ignored wherever inconvenient or counter to the political leadership. . . We might hope that, at last, some genuine political interest may now emerge for properly researched solutions to crime, rather than the simplistic 'tough on crime' that we have endured for four decades. I will not be holding my breath, though!

John Walker (Interview 30 November 2020) also thought that 'the AIC acted as a focus for criminological research, encouraging the study of criminology in universities and helping to introduce criminology to policing and to research units in departments of justice'. The Institute has employed well over 1000 researchers over its five decades, some staying for 20 years or more while others stayed for shorter periods to acquire criminological research skills and experience that they could then use in other workplaces. As shown in the staff timeline (Table 16.2), senior research staff remained at the Institute for five years on average which was long enough to enable them to develop expertise in specific methodologies and topics of research.

Although the short-time frames adopted by the Senate Legal and Constitutional Affairs Legislation Committees in 2015 and 2016 for receipt of submissions from the public precluded extensive responses from being submitted, those who were able to respond were uniform in their support for the Institute's work, its benefit to Australia and internationally and the need for its independent status to be preserved. The Australian Crime Prevention Council (2016, pp. 2–3), for example, specifically emphasised its importance for the Asia–Pacific region:

> The work of the AIC has been recognised worldwide for many years, including by the United Nations. It has proved to be an effective bridge builder with other countries to organise and muster resources in the fight against crime. . . . The AIC is highly respected in all of these jurisdictions and the diminution of its independence, research, publications, overseas assistance and conference organizing functions would have an adverse effect on Australia's criminal justice influence and role in the region.

The criminological community also joined forces to ensure that the Committee members were made fully aware of the potential negative implications of loss of independence and the potential for loss of academic research integrity if the merger took place. Four highly respected international criminologists—including two with expertise in serious and organised crime—made submissions to the Committee cautioning against the proposed changes and confirming the Institute's recognised international reputation. Professor Michael Levi (2016, pp. 1–2), of Cardiff University, noted the importance of ensuring that research remains independent:

> Australia has a fine tradition of empirical research in serious crime, and care should be taken that this is not imperilled by measures that are bureaucratically convenient but may have unintended negative side-effects. . . . In an increasingly hostile anti-authority mood around the world, the need to show research independence is particularly significant. Research on the public is much better when seen to come from a research body and not from the government or worse from an intelligence agency itself, as these contaminate both the responses and people's perceptions of the validity of the findings.

The renowned public sector criminologist, Pat Mayhew (2016, pp. 1–2), who had extensive experience dealing with challenges of research in the

UK Home Office, identified a number of ways in which the Institute's research would be harmed by the merger. These included restricting its ability to gather information and constraining the nature and content of research publications. She also feared that access to the Institute's library would be restricted if housed within an intelligence agency.

Professor Gloria Laycock (2016, p. 2) also noted that 'the AIC is a significant presence in the international criminological research community. Staff of the AIC represent Australia with enormous credit as the only independent research voice which addresses issues across the whole of Australia'. Professor Ernesto, Savona (2016, p. 1), Professor of Criminology and Director of Transcrime in Milan, and former President of the European Society of Criminology, was the first to respond to the 2016 Committee's Inquiry, making clear the value the Institute had for the international community:

> Over the years, the Australian Institute of Criminology's research has been of great significance and used by organisations in Europe regularly. It has also played an important role as one of the United Nations Office on Drugs and Crime research bodies. . . . Since the Australian Institute of Criminology was established, it has provided important, rigorous criminological research that has assisted organisations throughout the world. Its administrative model has, I believe, worked extremely well, and I personally believe that it should be permitted to operate as it was originally established – as a separate, independent research organization, rather than being aligned with a government intelligence agency that would inevitably change its focus, make data collection difficult and potentially unethical, and restrict the public dissemination of its research.

These assessments were supported by similar sentiments expressed by 20 Australian respondents, as indicated above (Chapter 14). These views clearly contributed to the government's decision *not* to proceed with the legislation—by which time some of the elements of the merger had already occurred.

Some Disappointments, But Other Achievements

To balance these glowing accounts, it is also appropriate to document some of the occasions on which the Institute failed in its objectives or omitted to undertake work that, on reflection, would have been beneficial—perhaps more so than some of the activities that it actually undertook. Of course, negative research findings that fail to support a given hypothesis, can be of considerable value—despite the views of some academic journal editors who have been known to screen them out during publication processes (Fielding 1996). What is of less value, and what a government could perceive as being a poor return on investment, are instances in which research was undertaken that was clearly not needed by the government or the community, poorly conceived or undertaken, or research that duplicated previous studies simply for the opportunity to increase publication outputs. Fortunately, there have been few examples of these in the Institute's history.

What was particularly disappointing, was the tendency for the Institute's research to be overly reactive rather than predictive of future crime problems or policy areas in which evidence was needed as new social, economic and political issues arose. Australia, like other countries, had regular exposure to criminal justice concerns that would inevitably be repeated, or adapted to new conditions. Examples have included bushfire arson, fraud arising from natural disaster support payments, cases involving serial murder and sexual violence, criminal negligence arising from industrial accidents or environmental pollution, major cybercrime attacks and financial failures, incarceration and deaths in custody of First Nations peoples and offending by serious offenders while on parole. In each of these areas, there is a need for research evidence that discloses trends in offending and victimisation and identifies criminal justice responses that have addressed or failed to address the issues in the past.

Some of the Institute's statistical monitoring collections have been essential in providing such evidence although some long-term data collections lost their value due to early cessation (e.g. armed robbery, firearms, DUMA) while others changed their orientation or methods making changes difficult to track over time. Where such crime problems arise, governments and the community invariably look to public sector research bodies for evidence to document the harms involved and the extent of change from similar events in the past. On occasions, all the Institute could do was to present the partial evidence from a discontinued data collection, and start work collecting new data. Where datasets have been maintained over long periods, such as the Deaths in Custody and the Homicide collections, this has provided timely evidence that has been used in connection with ongoing policy debates—such as Black Lives Matter (Fiona Dowsley, Interview, 8 December 2020). On occasions, however, the Institute has been reluctant to extend such datasets to document new topics of concern—such as deaths in Immigration Detention Centres where raw statistics are now published by the Department of Home Affairs (2022) but exclude the many variables examined in the AICs *Deaths in Custody* collection. As Research Manager, Anthony Morgan, concluded in his interview (17 November 2022):

> The National Homicide and Deaths in Custody Monitoring Programs are absolutely critical. They remain the single source of truth—there are no other collections that offer the depth of coverage, as demonstrated by the fact that they are always cited in news and parliament and elsewhere.

Despite this, as Dr Samantha Bricknell noted in her interview (21 November 2022), 'the disappointment is whether people actually know that the collections are out there, and if the people who should know that the collections are there, make use of them. We need to consider how to give better prominence to these collections so that when our Minister, or state and territory equivalents, or the UN need this information, then they know it's there'.

The prediction of the occurrence, or recurrence of contemporary crime problems is one of the necessary duties of Boards and Directors, and on a number of occasions, they have clearly been missing-in-action. Grant Wardlaw (Interview 30 November 2020) argued that 'the real value of the Institute in collecting datasets is coming up with the ideas and getting them started in the first place... It's the effort that's required to conceptualise the need and how you're going to go about it and the negotiations on who is going to keep it going'.

One clear example of the Institute's innovation was the research undertaken for the National Committee on Violence, chaired by Duncan Chappell, that was established in 1988 as a joint initiative of the Commonwealth, states and Northern Territory governments. The AIC provided the Secretariat for the Committee with Peter Grabosky as Research Director and other AIC staff responsible for administration and publishing. The Committee provided a national review of the state of violence in Australia and offered an extensive range of solutions that governments have drawn on over many years. A wide range of publications appeared between 1988 and 1990 including a series *Violence Today* that provided reviews of specific types of violence, a series of three major monographs, a four-day national conference and a 285 page report *Violence: Directions for Australia* (National Committee on Violence 1990). In his Interview (30 January 2021), John Braithwaite concluded that 'one of the best things that the Institute did was the National Committee on Violence work. I think that's a very under-estimated contribution of the Institute of Criminology'.

One area of disappointment has been the inability of public sector criminological research to have led to a reduction in the incidence and cost of many crime types that have serious impacts on the community. Examples abound, and include the substantial investment in researching illicit drug activity, sexual violence, child abuse, consumer fraud and organised crime that have continued to increase in prevalence and harm, despite the efforts of the Institute, the academic community and law enforcement alike. As Mike Hough (2014, p. 220) recalled, 'the evidence was clear that changes at the margin in policing volume or policing style achieve at best only a very marginal impact on crime'. In some cases, this has not been the fault of the criminological research community that has produced evidence-based crime reduction policies that simply have been ignored by governments, or poorly implemented in practice. In other cases, however, criminological research has been beneficial in alerting governments to measures that will not succeed, or in being responsible for supporting initiatives that will succeed. On balance, however, it seems that policies based on good research too often are ignored, or not implemented due to spurious fiscal arguments. In this context, the Institute's attempts to quantify the cost of crime, commencing with John Walker's 'gravity model' (1992), have provided governments with a means of conducting cost–benefit analyses of crime reduction initiatives—on the few occasions where these have occurred.

Over the five decades, the government and the Institute's executive have been unable to resolve the mutually antagonistic purposes of the organisation being on the one hand to undertake and publish academically sound criminological research, and, on the other hand, to train, inform and assist criminal justice personnel in their daily work in law enforcement, the courts and correctional agencies and those working in non-government crime prevention activities. The AIC, like other PNI entities, was established with the latter roles as the primary functions of the organisations, but over time these have waned in importance or been transferred to agencies created to service the training needs of specific sectors. Only some PNI bodies have continued their original training function, while others, including the AIC, have gradually removed this from its formal roles. As a result, the place of criminal justice training remains unclear, and in some jurisdictions, is inadequately supported. The resolution of this remains for further discussion among governments in the years ahead.

As shown in Chapter 12, the Institute has been highly successful in generating substantial quantities of criminological research, but the challenge remains as to how this body of work can best be used, not only to support policy development and legislation, but also to inform criminal justice personnel in how best to address the challenges of their daily work. More important has been the criticism levelled at the Institute, particularly with respect to its first few decades, that its research program was poorly planned and coordinated. Recalling his experience at the Institute in the mid-1970s, John Seymour observed: 'I was never really comfortable at the Institute. It was aimless and it didn't quite know what it was doing and why it was doing it' (John Seymour, Interview, 14 November 2022).

Thematic Conclusions

What, then, can we conclude from the current study in response to the thematic questions identified in the Introductory chapter?

Public Sector Versus Academic Criminology

The first theme concerned the differences that arose between criminological research conducted in the public sector generally and that carried out by academic criminologists based in higher educational institutions. When the AIC was established, and in common with other contemporary public sector research institutes, there was a heavy focus on the conduct of research that would be of benefit to correctional and justice agencies and their staff. The research often had a legal and legislative focus, particularly concerning sentencing law and practice and the correctional outcomes associated with sanctions. As such, offender behaviour was a primary focus with some studies designed to evaluate the effectiveness of specific sentences—including capital punishment. Other research was undertaken on crime prevention with a focus on program evaluation, while numerous studies considered victim-related questions—but often with a focus on their experiences in the criminal courts—such as initiatives to assist victims of sexual assault. These topics of research were chosen not only because of the professional backgrounds of Board members and directors, but due to many of the Institute's staff having had legal training. The Institute's early directors were also closely aligned with the criminal justice work of the UN, particularly in connection with crime prevention and corrections. Bill Clifford's initial interest in crime prevention internationally began an enduring body of research on crime prevention and the evaluation of crime reduction programs that have included specific publications devoted to crime prevention in the 1980s and continue into the 2020s with the successful Australian Crime and Violence Prevention Awards Program.

These interests were different from those of many academic criminologists whose research often focussed on juvenile justice issues and conventional street crime. There was also interest from medical and psychiatric professionals in a number of crime and justice questions. Over time, the Institute's interests broadened wider than many academic criminologists, partially due to changes in training of staff, but also due to the more prominent need to satisfy Ministerial and Departmental interests. The Institute was, for example, able to develop expertise in white collar, economic, organised and cybercrime that few academics pursued. This gave the Institute an advantage in being able to expand its expertise to benefit its principal stakeholders. In her interview (21 November 2022), Samantha Bricknell, emphasised the importance of the Institute's 'ability to build collaborative bridges with a broad group of players' that was evident in the research in these areas. The tension remained, however, that conventional criminological research focused on street crime and volume crime that was of primary interest to the states and territories. This had to be accommodated within the Institute's broader research agenda, along with those more boutique topics that the Commonwealth favoured. The Institute was also well-placed to pursue its international research agenda with crime surveys that included Australia as a target nation.

A clear finding of the current study is that the research agenda undertaken by the Institute was to a large extent dependent on the subject-matter expertise of its own research staff, Directors of Research and the directors themselves. This was due to the need to have qualified staff readily available to start work on new projects who had prior knowledge of the topics in question. Where this was present, research could be undertaken quickly and efficiently; without it, recruitment and training had to be undertaken that delayed starting new work. Peter Grabosky in his Interview (2 December 2020) cited examples of research undertaken by staff with specialist expertise including Jocelynne Scutt's work on sexual violence and domestic violence in the early 1980s, John Braithwaite and Andrew Hopkins' work on white collar and corporate crime in the late 1970s, Bill Clifford's international work on human rights and crime prevention during his time as Director, David Biles's work on corrections, Sat Mukherjee's studies of crime trends and sentencing and the AICs comprehensive work on violence in Australia, economic crime and cybercrime—all indicative of the Institute's novel and policy-relevant research. Grabosky remarked about some of the Institute's datasets: 'their longevity is testimony to their worth'.

Simply having had many famous researchers on the payroll, did not, of itself, make the Institute famous. As the late Professor Harold Ford (1973, p. 173) noted in his witty comments on the centenary of the Melbourne Law School: 'before taking credit for their careers it is worth noting the explanation of Leslie Stephen, the philosopher, that when some great English school is said to have produced a famous man, the word "produced" means "failed to extinguish"'.

Commonwealth Versus State and Territory Interests

Related to the first theme is the debate that has occurred, particularly in Australia, over the focus of the AICs research activities and whether they should relate primarily to crime types and criminal justice policy questions that affect the Commonwealth of Australia, national questions more generally or provincial crime concerns that affect the Australian states and territories. The questions arising from this theme, that have arisen because of Australia's federal constitutional system, have been pervasive throughout the Institute's history, often arising due to economic factors, and also due to the establishment of criminological research institutes mainly by national, as opposed to provincial, legislatures.

In Australia, the principal location of such controversies was in connection with the funding of criminological research. The AICs legislation created the CRC as a funding entity with resources provided, proportionally by the eight states and territories matched exactly by the Commonwealth. This, of course, meant that the Commonwealth sought to ensure that its interests were given an appropriate weighting. The states and territories argued, however, that constitutionally, crime was predominantly within their jurisdictional remit. This led to ongoing debate on the topics for research and allocation of funding between Commonwealth and state/territory interests. Having to satisfy multiple jurisdictions also meant that the AIC and grants program invariably had to undertake nationally-relevant studies that were difficult to negotiate, costly to undertake and slow to complete. Where the AIC felt unable to maintain nationally-relevant projects, such as we have seen in the case of DUMA in 2022, it was up to the states and territories to take them on as best as they could—often leading to the destruction of national datasets.

This debate was not only evident in Australia, but also internationally. Speaking on the occasion of the 60th anniversary of the establishment of UNAFEI in Tokyo on 21 October 2022, the former Director of HEUNI, Professor Matti Joutsen (2022), outlined the transition that had taken place in the focus of the UNODCs work away from correctional research and domestic crime concerns—evergreen topics—to transnational organised crime and terrorism in the years after 1990. The AIC followed this transition and since the 1990s has taken on an increasingly heavy emphasis on these global crime topics. This has tended to satisfy the Commonwealth's research agenda, but created ongoing concern that state and territory domestic crime concerns were receiving less attention. In his Interview (4 November 2022), AIC Deputy Director, Rick Brown, noted the move in research emphasis away from the states and territories to the Commonwealth since the partial merger with the ACC in 2015—'we're not now doing work on the functioning of criminal justice systems in the way we once did, largely because that's not the sort of work that Commonwealth policy makers are asking us to do'. He also argued that the current role of the AIC has changed now that the academic criminological community has expanded and that numerous state and territory bodies have taken on research functions that the AIC once undertook.

In recent years the AIC as well as UNAFEI and the other PNI members, have been required to consider throughout their histories how to satisfy these mutually conflicting agendas of conducting research on domestic, conventional criminal justice topics, or venturing into the global interests of organised crime and cybercrime that occupy the twenty-first century. There has also been a desire to undertake international comparative criminological research that the Institute has only undertaken on a few occasions—principally due to the cost of such work, but also because of the necessity for the Institute to show that its research was primary relevant to Australia rather than other countries. This fallacy is clearly apparent when one considers the benefits of comparative studies for alerting governments to reform agendas that have been successful overseas that could be applied domestically. The AICs international cybercrime research is a case in point (Smith et al. 2004).

Quantitative Versus Qualitative Approaches

The third theme dealt with the methods of research conducted in the public sector as opposed to those employed in the private sector and in the academy. The focus here was on the extent to which quantitative methods were employed, particularly the creation and use of time-series datasets, rather than qualitative, theoretical, sociological, legal or historical methodologies and approaches (see Hough's 2014, p. 221 assessment of the validity of Jock Young's attack on 'datasaurs' and other quantitative researchers). Following the conventional path of administrative criminology in the public sector, the AIC began its life collecting official crime statistics from criminal justice agencies—particularly prisons and community correctional bodies. With the few available staff, it was all that the Institute could do to undertake the collection itself, leading to criticism that sophisticated data analysis had been omitted and rigorous integration with the previous literature had been left out of reports. This was remedied over time where resources permitted, but the Institute has regularly been responsible for publishing largely descriptive, data-heavy reports, with only minimal commentary and policy analysis. Of course, the Institute was also charged with undertaking research in respect of novel crime types, such as money laundering, transnational crime and cybercrime, where there was minimal academic commentary available and the existing crime statistics were either non-existent or unsuitable for rigorous analysis, leaving the Institute to begin the research by presenting largely descriptive work. Focussing on the crime types of the twenty-first century also meant that qualitative research was difficult or impossible, with subjects located overseas or simply being unknown or unable to be contacted. As such, public sector criminological research in recent times has been far more difficult to undertake than research on conventional street and volume crime types. Nonetheless, the AIC has always been prepared to venture into new fields of research and, as Fiona Dowsley commented in her Interview (8 December 2020): 'it's always been comforting to have the AIC there as a national resource. We just know that the things that come from the AIC you can rely on, you can trust and it's a great way into any topic'.

Government-Friendly Versus Critical Approaches

Some public sector criminological research has been criticised because it has been uncritical of government policies and constrained by political considerations. Caught, as ever, 'between a rock and a hard place' the Institute's research had to be aware of the political ramifications of its publication, and willing to face the financial consequences if the research findings embarrassed a sitting government. On a number of occasions, this was resolved simply by deciding not to conduct research on the topic in question. In the early years of the AICs history when the Minister had greater levels of control over research priorities, the choice of topics was often focused on uncontroversial areas. The difficulty that faced the Institute was, however, that the research that governments needed for policy development was often in areas of party-political debate—such as Indigenous disadvantage, border control, corruption and public sector fraud. Current Advisory Council member, Fiona Dowsley, observed in her Interview (8 December 2020), the AIC 'needs to work in an independent, truth-to-power, frank and fearless kind of way, but this will require a certain force of will from the people leading the organisation to ensure that independence remains and the work is still respected'. On a number of occasions, the Institute undertook research for agencies on the understanding that the findings would never be made public, but used for internal policy purposes only. Such occasions were, however, relatively rare with the vast majority of the AICs research becoming publicly available.

The areas in which the Institute and other public sector research bodies have rarely ventured, however, have related to research and commentary of a critical, left-realist or sociological nature. An example of this, is the general reluctance of the AIC to deal with Southern, as opposed to Northern criminological perspectives (Carrington et al. 2018) that would be relevant to Indigenous disadvantage and the effects of colonisation, or the increasing use of imprisonment as a sanction or the failure to consider decriminalisation of controlled drugs. Instead, the Institute has opted to present evidence to document the extent and nature of the crime problems in question, and leave the development of policy responses to governments. Adam Tomison described the importance of the Institute's role in this regard as follows:

> What we were offering, and I think the Institute still does, is to ascertain what are the implications of this research and how can we use it in government in terms of preventing social ills and reducing crime (Adam Tomison, Interview, 26 October 2022).

Value for Money

The final theme evident in the current research was on the financing of criminological research and how the topics, methods, timelines and outputs of public sector criminological research bodies have differed from research conducted in the private sector and by academics. When the Institute was established, those responsible for designing its operational structure, such as Peter Loof, Frank Mahony, Nigel Bowen and Sir Leon Radzinowicz, emphasised the need for the Institute to be adequately funded. Dennis Challinger (Interview 18 February 2022), recalled that Peter Loof, in particular, 'was a very thoughtful man. He had a soft spot for the Institute and wanted it to succeed'. Over time, however, the Institute's appropriation was rarely adequate for the work it was required to perform and, as we have seen, as a percentage of GDP, its funding has declined overall throughout the five decades—although some of the decline was due to reduced staffing numbers. Despite this, the Institute's level of research output has continued to expand, even when staff numbers declined and physical resources became limited. Former librarian, Jane Shelling observed in her Interview (29 March 2021): 'I think that we are quite unique in that we're able to present something from within the government that provides more value for money than a lot of the other private companies could do–and even some of the academic institutions'.

Of greater importance has been the fact that the Institute has managed to avoid annihilation during the continual attempts by governments to reduce its funding, impose ceilings on staffing numbers, move it to smaller premises and merge it with larger agencies. Unlike comparable bodies in other countries, the Institute's directors and senior managers, supported by Board members and community stakeholders, have been able to demonstrate the worth of the organisation's research and justified its return-on-investment to both government and opposition parties. This success has been achieved through the use of various approaches—maintaining close ties with Ministers and their advisers, having supportive Board members, being able to demonstrate the value of research to governments, garnering the support of international partners and showing how the Institute's research has been used by those in a diverse range of government agencies, businesses, community organisations and individuals—all of whom need reliable evidence of the nature and extent of current crime problems, and the most effective ways in which they can be controlled. In the words of Richard Harding (Interview, 18 November 2021): '[The AIC] has succeeded as much as it has been permitted to succeed, as much as political agendas and jealousies and resentments and opportunism in other quarters allow it to succeed'. Grant Wardlaw (Interview 30 November 2020) was more positive: 'It was a bold and very positive initiative when it was first proposed, and all organisations—particularly where a lot of the time it appears to be contested ground—are going to have difficulties. If you look at the total output of the Institute over the years it's made a substantial contribution'.

In his address on 30 June 2011 at a dinner to mark the AIC becoming regulated under the *Financial Management and Accountability Act 1997* (Cth) that merged the functions of the AIC with the CRC, Professor Richard Fox (2011, p. 5) offered the following advice:

Beware, the Institute will never be able to escape the tension of a potentially fickle relationship with the media, with sources of funding and with government when undertaking policy-oriented research. Its defence is to assert its integrity in the quality, balance and independence of its research and its willingness to fight to maintain the environment in which it can undertake its work and widely disseminate its findings.

A Future for Public Sector Criminological Research?

The future is likely to see no diminution in the need for independent, methodologically-robust and informed criminological research by and for governments but the question remains as to who is best able to produce this in a timely and cost-efficient way? On the one hand, University academics could continue to undertake consultancies that seek to satisfy the needs of government. They would, however, not have access to classified and other material that government-based researchers can make use of, and some academic work, although important in developing theoretical conceptions of the causes of crime, might not satisfy current policy needs in a more applied sense. There is also the difficulty of attracting University scholars to the crime research interests of the Commonwealth government that tend to focus on concerns other than conventional street and volume crime types (Smith 2017, p. 48).

Alternatively, governments could look to private sector consultants to undertake the work required, although often the criminological skill-base within this sector is lacking, and costs tend to be much higher than for similar work undertaken in-house. Another approach is to continue to rely on criminologists employed within government agencies, but to ensure that their work remains independent of political and financial constraints and is able to be undertaken using realistic time frames and staffing levels. It remains to be seen which balance of these approaches will be adopted by future Australian and overseas governments and how effective the chosen approach will be in producing and disseminating the required crime and justice research needed for the remainder of the twenty-first century (Smith 2017, p. 48). Finally, we may see hybrid models develop in which academic criminologists take on positions within government, but seeking to provide independent advice. An example of this in the UK was the appointment on 1 October 2022 of Emeritus Professor Lawrence Sherman as Chief Scientific Officer at the Metropolitan Police (2022). Sherman's research career began in 1971 in New York and included work in Australia on restorative justice with Dr Heather Strang and subsequently as Wolfson Professor of Criminology at Cambridge University, thus providing sufficient evidence of objectivity to ensure that independent advice is given to the police.

Although the work of the Institute and other public sector criminological research bodies cannot be said to have provided a solution to crime in Australia and elsewhere, this research has provided information that has raised the profile of specific crime problems with governments and the community and shown how they could be avoided, or minimised in the future. Research will never be a panacea to all the government's criminal justice concerns, as Gordon Hawkins (1990, p. 17) observed when writing for the 30th anniversary of the foundation of the Sydney Institute of Criminology:

> It would be foolish to pretend that the Institute has by its efforts produced any substantial diminution in the squalor, inefficiency and inequity which continue to characterise the administration of justice in New South Wales. The most that can be said is that it has drawn attention to some of those ills, made specific suggestions for amelioration, and contributed to knowledge of the facts which is an essential precondition of effective reformative action.

The AIC can make similar claims to its achievements that have identified many criminal justice concerns experienced by the Commonwealth and the states and territories. It has provided a substantial evidence-base that has informed policy and legislative reform not only throughout Australia, but internationally—and will, with good management and appropriate funding, continue to do so in the years ahead.

References

Australian Crime Prevention Council. 2016. *Submission to the Senate Legal and Constitutional Affairs Legislation Committee Inquiry into the Australian Crime Commission Amendment (Criminology Research) Bill 2016*, No. 15, 28 October 2016. Canberra: Department of the Senate.

Carrington, Kerry, Russell Hogg, John Scott, and Máximo. Sozzo. 2018. *Southern Criminology*. London: Routledge.

Criminology Research Council (CRC). 1973–2010. *Annual Reports*. Canberra: Australian Institute of Criminology.

Department of Home Affairs. 2022. *Immigration Detention and Community Statistics Summary*. Canberra: Department of Home Affairs. https://www.homeaffairs.gov.au/research-and-stats/files/immigration-detention-statistics-30-june-2022.pdf. Accessed 10 November 2022.

Fielding, Nigel. 1996. Bias in Criminological Research. *The Journal of Forensic Psychiatry* 7 (1): 5–14.

Ford, Harold A. J. 1973. The Centenary of the Faculty of Law 1873–1873. *Melbourne University Law Review* 9 (2): 171–174.

Fox, Richard G. 2011. *Unpublished Address at the Dinner to Mark the Cessation of the AICs Board and CRC*, 30 June. Canberra: Archives of Richard Fox.

Hawkins, Gordon. 1990. Present at the Creation: The Inception and Development of the Institute of Criminology. *Current Issues in Crime and Criminal Justice* 2 (1): 9–17. http://www.austlii.edu.au/au/journals/CICrimJust/1990/15.pdf. Accessed 3 February 2022.

Hough, Mike. 2014. Confessions of a Recovering 'Administrative Criminologist': Jock Young, Quantitative Research and Policy Research. *Crime Media Culture* 10 (3): 215–226.

Joutsen, Matti. 2022. Creating Inclusive Societies: The Reduction of Reoffending in the Context of the UN Crime Programme. In *Address at UNAFEIs 60th Anniversary Event: Creating Inclusive Societies: Approaches to Reducing Reoffending*. Tokyo: Ministry of Justice.

Laycock, Gloria. 2016. *Submission to the Senate Legal and Constitutional Affairs Legislation Committee Inquiry into the Australian Crime Commission Amendment (Criminology Research) Bill 2016*, No. 1, 23 October. Canberra: Department of the Senate.

Levi, Michael. 2016. *Submission to the Senate Legal and Constitutional Affairs Legislation Committee Inquiry into the Australian Crime Commission Amendment (Criminology Research) Bill 2016*, No. 25. Canberra: Department of the Senate.

Mayhew, Patricia. 2016. *Submission to the Senate Legal and Constitutional Affairs Legislation Committee Inquiry into the Australian Crime Commission Amendment (Criminology Research) Bill 2016*, No. 13, 27 October 2016. Canberra: Department of the Senate.

Metropolitan Police. 2022. *Update: Two New Metropolitan Police Assistant Commissioners Appointed*. 27 September. https://news.met.police.uk/news/two-new-metropolitan-police-assistant-commissioners-appointed-454472. Accessed 10 November 2022.

National Committee on Violence. 1990. *Violence: Directions for Australia*. Canberra: AIC.

Radzinowicz, Leon. 1973. *Report of Sir Leon Radzinowicz with Respect to the Australian Institute of Criminology*. New York, Canberra: National Library of Australia (6093/72/4182).

Savona, Ernesto. 2016. *Submission to the Senate Legal and Constitutional Affairs Legislation Committee Inquiry into the Australian Crime Commission Amendment (Criminology Research) Bill 2016*, 21 October, No. 25. Canberra: Department of the Senate.

Senate Legal and Constitutional Affairs Committee. 2015. *Australian Crime Commission Amendment (Criminology Research) Bill 2015*. Canberra: Department of the Senate.

Senate Legal and Constitutional Affairs Committee. 2016. *Australian Crime Commission Amendment (Criminology Research) Bill 2016*. Canberra: Department of the Senate.

Smith, Russell G. 2017. Public Sector Criminological Research. In *The Palgrave Handbook of Australian and New Zealand Criminology, Crime and Justice*, ed. Antje Deckert and Rick Sarre, 33–49. London: Palgrave Macmillan.

Smith, Russell G., Peter N. Grabosky, and Gregor F. Urbas. 2004. *Cyber Criminals on Trial*. Cambridge: Cambridge University Press.

Walker, John. 1992. Estimates of the Costs of Crime in Australia. In *Trends & Issues in Crime and Criminal Justice*, No. 39. Canberra: Australian Institute of Criminology.

Zimring, Franklin E. 1984. Preface. In *The Pursuit of Criminal Justice: Essays from the Chicago Centre*, ed. Gordon Hawkins and Franklin E. Zimring. Chicago: The University of Chicago Press.

16

Timelines

Introduction

The chapter includes two tables that present information on the holders of various offices relevant to the Institute's governance, management, staffing and premises each year between 1971 and 2022. Individuals are named without their associated titles and exact dates are given where these were available. The periods of employment of senior research staff are estimates and show periods of employment to the nearest calendar year. Information was drawn from the AIC and CRCs Annual Reports, Minutes and other archived records, supplemented by official government publications. Abbreviations are indicated below and in the introductory pages. Financial details were recorded from the AICs financial statements for financial years. The total number of AIC staff is based on staff lists in Annual Reports and AIC archival lists as at 30 June each year. These numbers relate to individuals employed at that date (headcounts) rather than Full Time Equivalent positions. Numbers were estimated to the nearest year of commencement and cessation of employment.

R. G. Smith, *Public Sector Criminological Research*, https://doi.org/10.1007/978-3-031-28356-7_16

Abbreviations (Tables 16.1, 16.2)

A-G	Attorney-General
ALP	Australian Labor Party
EA	Executive Assistant
H-A	Home Affairs Ministry
Justice	Justice Ministry
J&C	Justice and Customs Ministry
Lib/Country	Liberal Party/Country Party Coalition
Lib/Nat	Liberal Party/National Party Coalition

Table 16.1 Governance, finances and premises timeline

Year	Government in office *Prime Minister*	AICs Minister *in office*	CRC/CRAC Chair	Board Chair	Surplus/(Deficit)	Premises	Notes
1970–1971	**Lib/Country** from 19-12-49 *John Gorton 10-1-68 to 15-3-71 William McMahon to 5-12-72*	Tom Hughes, A-G *12-11-69 to 22-3-71* Nigel Bowen, A-G *to 2-8-71* Ivor Greenwood, A-G *to 5-12-72*					Bill introduced 24-2-71 Act assented to 6-4-71
1971–1972							
1972–1973	**ALP [3]** from 5-12-72 *Gough Whitlam to 11-11-75*	Gough Whitlam, A-G *to Dec 19-12-72*	Frank J. Mahony *(Chair CRC) to 19-7-79* Peter R. Loof *(Deputy Chair CRC) to 20-7-79*	Frank J. Mahony *to 19-7-79* Peter R. Loof *(Deputy) to 20-7-79*	$17,682	Ethos House, 28–36 Ainslie Place, Civic	6-11-72 Act proclaimed/commenced 1-2-73—Muirhead started 18-4-73—1st Board meeting
1973–1974		Lionel Murphy, A-G *to 10-2-75 (died 21-10-86)*			$140,582	10–16 Colbee Court, Philip From September 1973	Official opening 16-10-73 by A-G 1st Residential conference, 16–19th October 1973 Library opening 12-2-74
1974–1975		Kep Enderby, A-G *to 11-11-75*			$190,993	From April 1975, added 18–20 Colbee Court	
1975–1976	**Lib/Nat [7]** from 11-11-75 *Malcolm Fraser to 11-3-83*	Ivor Greenwood, A-G *to 22-12-75*			$87,647		
1976–1977		to Bob Ellicott, A-G *to 6-9-77*			$19,299		
1977–1978		Peter Durack, A-G *to 1-3-83*			$24,060		
1978–1979			Peter R. Loof *20-7-79 to 11-3-82 [3]*	Peter R. Loof *20-7-79 to 11-3-82 [3]*	$6,116		Loof AIC Establishment Review 6-7-1979
1979–1980					$29,765		
1980–1981					$19,346		
1981–1982					$11,336		'Razor Gang' Review 30-4-1981

(continued)

Table 16.1 (continued)

	ALP [13] from 11-3-83 *Bob Hawke*	Gareth Evans, A-G *to 13-12-84*	Andrew C. C. Menzies *21-3-82 to 24-1-84 [2]*	Andrew C. C. Menzies *21-3-82 to 24-1-84 [2]*			Gosling Library Review 16-8-1982
1982–1983	*to 20-12-91*	Lionel Bowen, A-G *to 4-4-90*			$43,159		
1983–1984	*Paul Keating*		Peter R. Loof *25-1-84 to 30-6-91 [7]*	Peter R. Loof *25-1-84 to 30-6-91 [7]*	($58,548)		
1984–1985	*to 11-3-96*				$73,681		
1985–1986					($19,973)		T&I series commences
1986–1987					$231,381		Biles CRC Review Jan 1987
1987–1988					$6570		
1988–1989					$103,243		
1989–1990					$440,848		CPMC Review of Corporate Plan
1990–1991		Michael Duffy, A-G *to 24-3-93*	Herman F. Woltring *1-7-91 to 9-7-92 [1]*	Herman F. Woltring *1-7-91 to 9-7-92 [1]*	$159,794	**4 Marcus Clarke Street, Canberra City** From 25-7-90	Official opening 25-7-90
1991–1992					($268,464)		1991 *Fightback* economic policy of the Liberal Party led by John Hewson
1992–1993					($392,051)		
1993–1994		Duncan Kerr, A-G/Justice *to 27-4-93*	Laurie Glanfield *10-7-92 to 30-6-11 [19]*	Sally Brown *(Chair Board) 10-7-92 to 11-4-97 [5]*	($49,413)		AIC HREC commenced November 1992
1994–1995					($67,267)		Coad and Tanzer Reviews 1994
1995–1996	**Lib/Nat [11]** from 11-3-96	Daryl Williams, A-G/Justice *to 9-10-97*			$540,496	**74 Leichhardt Street, Griffith** From Dec 1995	Official opening Griffith 24-7-96
1996–1997	*John Howard*				$12,396		
1997–1998	*to 3-12-07*			Norman Reaburn *(ActingChair) 28-7-97 to 29-4-98 [9m]*	($62,043)		
1998–1999					($208,589)		
1999–2000		Amanda Vanstone, Justice *to 21-10-98*		Richard Fox *(Chair Board) 29-4-98 to 1-7-11 [13]*	($257,456)		
2000–2001					$41,496		
2001–2002		Justice & Customs (J&C) *to 30-1-2001*			$310,688		9/11/2001 attacks in USA
2002–2003		Chris Ellison, J&C *to 9-3-07*			$149,194		

Year						
2003–2004					$11,437		
2004–2005					$518,493		Uhrig Review of Statutory Authorities 2005
2005–2006					$1,443,228		
2006–2007		David Johnston, J&C *to 3-12-07*			$33,375		Quay Comms Review May 2006
2007–2008	**ALP [6]** from 3-12-07 *Kevin Rudd to 24-6-10*	Bob Debus, Home Affairs (H-A) *to 9-6-09*			($340,714)		Barry Library Review March 2008
2008–2009					($599,607)		Highest number of staff
2009–2010		Brendan O'Connor, H-A *to 14-12-11*			$6439		
2010–2011	*Julia Gillard to 27-6-13*		Penny Armytage *(Chair CRAC)* *1-7-11 to 19-7-13 [2]*		$133,149		1-7-11 FMA Agency starts
2011–2012		Jason Clare, Justice *to 18-12-13*			($193,110)		
2012–2013	*Kevin Rudd to 18-9-13*				($300,662)		13-11-12 AIC 40th anniversary
2013–2014	**Lib/Nat [9]** from 18-9-13 *Tony Abbott to 15-9-15 Malcolm Turnbull to 24-8-18*	Michael Keenan, Justice *to 20-12-17*	Cheryl Gwilliam *(Chair CRAC)* *20-7-13 to 30-6-16 [3])*		($294,777)		12-2-2014 Library 40th
2014–2015					($330,697)		Shepherd Audit Comm. 2014
2015–2016					($956,884)		Dawson Interim Director from 13-7-2015; Staff transfer from 8-10-15 Move to 4NC 10-12-15 Corporate services transferred to ACC under MoG process
2016–2017		Peter Dutton, H-A *to 29-3-21*	Pauline Bagdonavicius *(Chair CRAC)* *1-7-16 to 30-6-17 [1]*		($521,141)	4 National Circuit, Barton (3rd Floor) from 10-12-2015	ACIC commences 1-7-16
2017–2018			Julia Griffith *(Chair CRAC)* *1-7-17 to 30-6-19 [3]*		$418,020	4 National Circuit, Barton (Ground floor)	Rose Acting CEO from August to November 2017 Independent Intelligence Review June 2017
2018–2019					$466,719		
2019–2020	Scott Morrison *to 23-5-22*	Karen Andrews, H-A *29-3-21 to 23-5-22*			$73,078		CRG grants on AusTender for 2019–2020 January 2020 Pandemic

(continued)

Table 16.1 (continued)

Year						
2020–2021		[Scott Morrison, Co H-A *6-5-21 to 23-5-22*]	Adam Tomison *(Chair CRAC)* *1-7-19 to current [2]*	$224,009		Remote working due to COVID
2021–2022				$626,437		Partial remote working; DUMA ceases 31-12-21
2022–2023	**ALP** Anthony Albanese to current	Mark Dreyfus, A-G to current				1-7-22 AIC moves to AGD portfolio 6-11-22 Commencement 50th
2023–2024	current					16-10-23 Official opening 50th

Table 16.2 Staffing timeline

Financial year	Director/CEO (Acting - shaded)	Deputy Director	Assist Secretary Corporate/Finance/CFO	Assist Director (Director) Research	Assist Director Information and Training/Communications	Library Manager	Staff at 30 June	Senior Research Staff (62 with PhD on cessation at AIC in bold) (n = 154) 96 female	
1970–1971									
1971–1972									
1972–1973		None appointed				Diana Solman from 1973–1974 [1]	7	Harold Weir (1973–1976) [3]	
1973–1974	(James Muirhead) 1-2-73 to 27-4-74 [1] (Evan Davies) 22-11-74 to 17-1-75 EA- Joan Swann (1973–1974)		William Miller 1974–September 1987 [13]	David Biles 1974–1984 [10]	Harold Weir 1974–1975 [2]		34	David Biles (1974–1994) [20] Mary Daunton-Fear (1974–1976) [2] Michael Cass (RO) (1974–1975) [1] Cedric Bullard (1974–1978) [4] Selwyn Hausman (1974) [1]	
1974–1975	William Clifford *Appointed Acting Director 4-10-74 Commenced 20-1-75 Permanent Director 5-6-75 Retired 31-8-83[9] Died 6 June 1986* EA-Barbara Harris (1974–1981) EA- Diana Pickering (1982–1984)					Sylvia Blomfield 1974–1979 [5]		Anatole Koneonewsky (1975–1978) [3]	Andrew Hopkins (1977–1978) [2]
1975–1976								Ivan Potas (1975–1994) [19]	John Braithwaite (1978–1983) [5]
1976–1977					Col Bevan 1975–1986 [10]		55	John Newton (1975–1978) [3]	Jeff Marjoram (1979–1980) [1]
1977–1978							44	Bruce Swanton (1975–1995) [20]	Maureen Kingshott (1979–1981) [2]
1978–1979							46	Bill Fitzgerald (1977–1979) [2]	John Walker (1980–1995) [15]
1979–1980						Mary Gosling 1979–1984 [5]	43	Arie Frieberg (1974–1976) [2]	
1980–1981							38	John Seymour (1976–1978) [2]	
1981–1982							34	Grant Wardlaw (1976–1991) [15]	
1982–1983						Gael Parr (Acting May-Aug 1984)	34	Jocelynne Scutt (1976–1981) [5] Satyanshu Mukherjee (1977–2000) [23]	
1983–1984	Richard Harding 30-1-84 to 29-1-87 [3] EA Sylvia Flaxman (1984–1987)	David Biles 1984–1992 [8]				Nikki Riszko Aug 1984–1986 [2]	37	Peter Grabosky (1983–1992; 1995–2002) [17]	Jane Mugford (1984–1998) [14]
1984–1985							39	Kayleen Hazlehurst (1984–1993) [9]	Anita Scandia (1985–1994) [9]
1985–1986						John Myrtle 1986–2003 [17]	45	Suzanne Hatty (1984–1987) [3]	Paul Wilson (1986–1991) [5]
1986–1987	(David Biles *from 30-1-87 to 20-7-87*)			Paul Wilson 1986–1991 [5]	Dennis Challinger 1986–1989 [3]		44		
1987–1988			Joseph Millar *September 1987–1995 [8]*				45	Heather Strang (1988–1994) [6]	
1988–1989	Duncan Chappell 20-7-87 to 30-6-94 [7] EA Sylvia Flaxman						45	Marina Farnan (1989) [1]	
1989–1990							47	Patricia Easteal (1991–1995) [4]	

(continued)

Table 16.2 (continued)

Period							No.		
	(1987–1994)	None appointed			Julia Vernon Conferences 1990–1995 [5]			Jennifer Norberry (1991–1994) [3] Boronia Halstead (1991–1995) [4]	
1990–1991							52	David McDonald (1992–1997) [5]	Jo Herlihy (1992–1995) [3]
1991–1992				Peter Grabosky 1991–1992 [1]			59	Diana Nelson (1992–2008) [16] Lynn Atkinson (1992–1996) [4] Christine Howlett (1992–1993) [2]	Leanne Craze (1993–1996) [3] Nicola Main (1993–1994) [1] Ingrid Wilson (1993) [1] Shona Morrison (1994–1995) [1]
1992–1993							60	Marianne James (1992–2007) [15]	Judith Robinson (1993–1994) [1]
1993–1994	(Grant Wardlaw 7-4-94 to 7-11-94)						58	Vicki Dalton (1992–2002) [10] Paul Omaji (1992) [1]	Nova Inkpen (1994) [1]
1994–1995	Adam Graycar *Director* *7-11-94 to 10-9-03* *[9]* *EA-Sylvia Flaxman (1994–1997)* *EA-Sylvia MacKellar (1997–2003)*			Peter Grabosky 1995–2001 [6]	Garry Raffaele Public Affairs 1995–1998 [3]		39		
1995–1996			Michael Brown 1996–1997 [1]				44	**Russell Smith** (1996–2020) [24]	**Emma Ogilvie** (2000–2002) [2]
1996–1997							35	Carlos Carcach (1996–2002) [6]	Rebecca Tailby (2000–2002) [2]
1997–1998							32	**Judy Putt** (1996–1997)(2003–2010) [8]	**Gregor Urbas** (2000–2006) [6]
1998–1999			Geoff Chapman 1998–2005 [7]		None appointed		38	Melanie Brown (1996–1997) [1]	Frances Gant (2001–2002) [1]
1999–2000							41	Karl Higgins (1996–1998) [2]	**Jerry Radcliffe** (2001–2003) [2] Pat Mayhew (2002) [1]
2000–2001							41	**Toni Makkai** (1997–2008) [11] Bree Cook (1998–2000) [2]	**Maria Borzycki** (2001–2014) [13]
2001–2002		Peter Grabosky 2001–2002 [1]		Toni Makkai 2001–2003 [2]	Stephen Bond 2002–2005 [3] Learning & Knowledge Development		45	Anna Grant (1998–2000) [2]	**Denise Lievore** (2001–2005) [4] **Gregg Smith** (2001) [1]
2002–2003							45	**Pamela Kinnear** (1998–2000) [2] John Chisholm (1999–2000) [1] **Jenny Mouzos** (1999–2008) [9] Santina Perrone (1999–2001) [2] Kiah McGregor/Rollings (2002–2010) [8] **Claire Mayhew** (2000–2002) [2] Paul Williams (2000–2002) [2] **Margaret Cameron** (2000–2002) [2]	**Natalie Taylor** (2001–2010) [9] **Katie Willis** (2001–2012) [11] **Samantha Jeffries** (2001–2002) [1] **Zhigang Wei** (2001–2004) [3] **Jason Payne** (2001–2015) [14] Catherine Rushforth (2001–2004) [3] **Marie Segrave** (2002–2003) [1] **Debra Rickwood** (2002–2003) [1]
2003–2004	(Toni Makkai *from 11-9-03 to 31-7-04*)	None appointed				Janet Smith June 2003–2010 [7] (died Jan 2011)	48	**Yuka Sakurai** (2002–2005) [3] **Katherine Anderson** (2003–2005) [2] Jamie Walvisch (2003–2004) [1]	**Colleen Bryant** (2004–2011) [7] **Holly Johnson** (2004–2007) [3] **Jeremy Prichard** (2004–2005) [1]
2004–2005	Toni Makkai *from 1-8-04 to 2-5-08* *[5]* *EA-Sylvia MacKellar (2003–2008)*		Tony Marks 2005–November 2011 [6]	Judy Putt Manager Research Services 2005–2010 [5]			49	**Tony Krone** (2003–2007) [4] Rob McCusker (2003–2007) [4]	Matthew Willis (2003–2020) [17]
2005–2006					Barbara Walsh 2007–2008 [1] Comms & Information		56	Peter Homel (2004–2015) [11]	Jacqueline Joudo-Larsen (2005–2014)[9]
2006–2007							55	**Pat Jobes** (2003–2005) [2] Jo Sallybanks (2003) [1]	**Julia Tresidder** (2004–2009) [5] Jessica Anderson/Smith (2004–2015) [10]

2007–2008	(Tony Marks *from 3-5-08 to 2-5-09*)				Scott Kelleher *2008–2011 [3]* Communications		60	**Raymond Choo** (2006–2011) [5]	**Damon Muller** (2005–2007) [2] Lance Smith (2004–2012) [8]
2008–2009							64	Rachel Irving (2006–2008) [2] Tabor Akman (2006–2010) [4]	Matthew Lyneham (2007–2013) [6] **Jade Lindley** (2007–2011) [4] David Rees (2007–2011) [4]
							56	Anthony Morgan (2006–current) [16] **Samantha Bricknell** (2006–2020) (2021–current) [15] Fiona David (2007–2010) [3]	Kerryn Adams (2007–2008) [1] **Lorana Bartels** (2007–2012) [5] Julie Walters (2007–2011) [4] Carolyn Budd (2007–2012) [5] **Brent Davis** (2008–2011) [3]
2009–2010									
2010–2011	Adam Tomison *Director 24-6-09; CEO 1-7-11 to 12-7-15 [6] EA-Sylvia MacKellar (2009–2015)*		Brian Russell *2011–2015 [4]*	Rick Brown Deputy Director (Research) *1-7-11 to 2015 [4]*	Colin Campbell *2011–2015 [4]* Communications	Janine Chandler *2010–2013 [3]*	56	**Kelly Richards** (2008–2014) [6]	Tracey Cussen (2010–2012) [2] Penelope Jorna (2010–2019) [9]
2011–2012								51	Josh Sweeney (2008–2012) [4]
2012–2013								42	Lauren Renshaw (2008–2013) [5]	Hayley Boxall (2010–current) [12]
2013–2014							Jane Shelling *from 26 May 2014 to 9 July 2021 [7]*	50	Warwick Jones (2008–2011) [3] Laura Beacroft (2009–2014) [5] Antonette Gaffney (2009–2012) [3] **Evan Smith** (2009–2011) [2]	Andy Chan (2010–2013) [3] **Willow Bryant** (2010–2016) [5] Alexandra Gannoni (2011–current) [10]
								49	Samantha Gray-Barry/Lyneham (2010–current) [12] Georgina Fuller (2010–2015) [5] Amanda McAtamney (2010–2012) [2]	**Alice Hutchings** (2011–2013) [2] Sarah Macgregor/Napier (2010–current) [12] **Susan Goldsmid** (2011–2017) [6] Bo Hedwards (2012–2013) [2]
2014–2015										
2015–2016	(Chris Dawson *14-7-15 to 15-8-17*) [2] *ACIC EA used*	Rick Brown *2016–current [7]*	Yvette Whittaker (CFO) *2015–current [7]*	None appointed	Communications managed by ACIC		39	Shandon Harris-Hogan (2014–2015) [1] **Marcus Smith** (2014–2015) [2] Catherine Emami (2014–2017) [3]	Isabella Voce (2015–current) [7]
2016–2017	(*Nicole Rose 16-8-17 to 13-11-17*) [3m] *ACIC EA used*						22	Tom Sullivan (2016–current) [6] **Christopher Dowling** (2016–current) [6] Rebecca Savage (2016–2017) [2] Andrew Ticehurst (2018–2019) [1]	
2017–2018	Michael Phelan *13-11-17 to 13-11-22* [5] *ACIC EA used*						20	Laura Doherty (2019–current) [3]	**Ben Serpell** (2021) [1] Merran McAlister (2021–current) [1]
2018–2019							23	**Alexandra Voce** (2019–current) [3]	**Dana Thomsen** (2022–2023) [1]
2019–2020							26		Michael Cahill (2022–current) [1]
2020–2021							25	Coen Teunissen (2019–2023) [3]	
2021–2022							26		

(continued)

Table 16.2 (continued)

						Samantha Jackson *from 29 November 2021 to current* [1]	26	Kamarah Pooley (2020–2021) [1] Christie Franks (2019–2021) [2] Timothy Cubitt (2019–current) [3] Amelia Hickman (2019–2021) [2] Alicia Schmidt (2020–2021)[1] Siobhan Lawler (2021–current) [1] Heather Wolbers (2021–current) [1]	Hannah Miles (2022–current) [1] Emily Faulconbridge (2022–current) [1]
2022–2023	(Matthew Rippon 13-11-22 to current)								

Index

Printed in the USA
CPSIA information can be obtained
at www.ICGtesting.com
LVHW020855020923
757044LV00001B/1